Managing Delinquency Programs That Work

Barry Glick and
Arnold P. Goldstein, Editors

American Correctional Association
8025 Laurel Lakes Court
Laurel, Maryland 20707-5075

This publication may be ordered from:
  American Correctional Association
  8025 Laurel Lakes Court
  Laurel, MD 20707-5075
  1-800-825-BOOK

Library of Congress Cataloging-in-Publication Data

Managing delinquency programs that work / editors, Barry Glick and
   Arnold P. Goldstein.
        p. cm.
   Includes bibliographical references and index.
   ISBN 1-56991-011-1 (pbk.)
   1. Juvenile justice, Administration of—United States.
2. Juvenile delinquency—United States—Prevention. 3. Juvenile corrections—United States. 4. Juvenile delinquents—Rehabilitation—United
States. I. Glick, Barry. II. Goldstein, Arnold P.
HV9104.M257 1995
364.3′6′0973—dc20   94-45851
                                                                  CIP

Contents

Part I: Policy Formulation and Direction

Part II: Managing Program Development

Part III: Managing Program Administration

Continued on next page

Contents continued

Part IV: **Managing Program Training And Evaluation**

Part V: **Managing System Issues**

Contributors

Vicki MacIntyre Agee, Ph.D., is a clinical psychologist in Salt Lake City, Utah, with over twenty years of experience with residential treatment programs for juvenile delinquents. She is a founding member of the National Adolescent Perpetrator Network, a member of the American Correctional Association Victims of Crime Committee, and a past member of the American Correctional Association Board of Governors.

Linda Albrecht is a juvenile justice consultant specializing in programs and services for girls. She directed a nationally recognized girls' training school for thirteen years. Ms. Albrecht is a consultant/trainer for the National Institute of Corrections Academy. She frequently designs and delivers programs for juvenile offenders and offers training in correctional leadership.

David M. Altschuler, Ph.D., is principal research scientist at the Johns Hopkins University Institute for Policy Studies in Baltimore, Maryland, and holds a joint appointment in the sociology department. His work focuses on juvenile justice sanctioning and aftercare; community-based delinquency program design, implementation, and assessment; privatization in corrections; and drug involvement and crime among inner-city youth.

Troy L. Armstrong, Ph.D., is a professor in the Department of Anthropology at California State University, Sacramento, and is co-principal investigator on the Office of Juvenile Justice and Delinquency Prevention-funded Intensive Community-Based Aftercare Program. Over the past decade, he has served as a consultant on a variety of juvenile justice-related projects at the national, state, and local levels.

William J. Bradley has served as director of administration, director of residential care, and director of delinquency prevention in the New York State Division for Youth. Currently a management consultant in Oviedo, Florida, he specializes in assisting programs with management and fiscal control problems.

Jimmy Calloway, Ph.D., is vice president for governmental affairs and fund development for the Atlanta Paralympic Organizing Committee in Atlanta, Georgia.

Henry R. Cellini, Ph.D., specializes in the management and treatment of violent juvenile offenders. His work also focuses on drug abuse treatment, juvenile street gangs, mental health, and violence prevention issues. Dr. Cellini, of Albuquerque, New Mexico, serves as a part-time instructor for the University of New Mexico, Division of Continuing Education in the Rural Educator's Project, which is part of the Alcohol and Drug Abuse Studies Program.

William S. Davidson II, Ph.D., is a professor of psychology and chair of the Ecological/Community Psychology Graduate Program at Michigan State University in East Lansing, Michigan. His research interests are in juvenile delinquency, violence prevention, and research methodology. He is the author of the book *Alternative Treatments for Troubled Youth.*

Barry Glick, Ph.D., is associate deputy director for local services, New York State Division for Youth in Rensselaer, New York. Dr. Glick has over twenty-five years of experience administering and managing programs for juvenile delinquents, aggressive and violent adolescents, and emotionally disturbed youth. He has served as a facility director both in the public and private sector, and has managed large systems for youth development and delinquency prevention.

Arnold P. Goldstein, Ph.D., is a professor of special education at Syracuse University, director of the Center for Research on Aggression, and a member of the American Psychological Association's Commission on Youth Violence. Dr. Goldstein collaborated with Dr. Glick to develop Aggression Replacement Training, a multimodal skills intervention that teaches prosocial skills to aggressive and violent juveniles, both those incarcerated and those in the community.

James A. Gondles, Jr., is the executive director of the American Correctional Association in Laurel, Maryland. Previously, Mr. Gondles served as sheriff of Arlington County, Virginia. He is a graduate of Oklahoma City University and has taught, lectured, and conducted training for the Northern Virginia Criminal Justice Academy, the Virginia Sheriffs' Association, the American Jail Association, and various other groups.

Susan Guarino-Ghezzi, Ph.D., is an assistant professor of criminal justice at Northeastern University in Boston, Massachusetts. She also is the former director of research at the Massachusetts Department of Youth Services. Dr. Guarino-Ghezzi is conducting comparative research on deinstitutionalization in juvenile corrections for the Robert F. Kennedy Memorial and is also studying juvenile sex offender treatment and reintegrative programming for juvenile offenders in the Massachusetts Department of Youth Services.

James C. Howell, Ph.D., is director of research and program development at the Office of Juvenile Justice and Delinquency Prevention in the U.S. Department of Justice in Washington, D.C. He has held several federal juvenile justice positions since helping to found the Office of Juvenile Justice and Delinquency Prevention in 1975. Dr. Howell has authored publications on juvenile delinquency research and juvenile justice issues.

Bruce Janes is executive director of Reflections Treatment Agency, Youth Services International of Tennessee, Inc. in Knoxville, Tennessee. He is a trainer and consultant in the field of residential and secure treatment for adolescent sexual aggressors. Mr. Janes has developed and directed treatment programs in a variety of settings from short-term acute care to comprehensive and intensive-care residential programs.

Leticia M. Lleva has a bachelor of arts degree in psychology from Stanford University. She has conducted research in the areas of cognitive dissonance, gangs and violence, juvenile delinquency prevention and intervention, and health psychology. She is currently pursuing a graduate degree at Stanford.

Edward J. Loughran is the director of the Robert F. Kennedy National Juvenile Justice Project in Boston, Massachusetts. He served as commissioner of the Massachusetts Department of Youth Services from 1985 to 1993. Prior to that, Mr. Loughran served for more than five years as the department's deputy commissioner. Before coming to Massachusetts in 1980, he spent ten years with the New York Division for Youth, where he conducted programs for juvenile offenders.

Maurice S. Satin, Ph.D., has been engaged in human services basic research, program evaluation, and policy analysis for over twenty-five years. He has worked at the federal, state, and local levels of government in the areas of chronic disease, mental disorder, social welfare, and juvenile justice. Dr. Satin currently is a research scientist at the New York State Division for Youth in Rensselaer, New York.

Melody G. Scofield is a doctoral candidate in the Ecological/Community Psychology Program at Michigan State University in East Lansing, Michigan, and the assistant director of the Michigan chapter of the National Organization for Women. Her research interests are in female delinquency, youth rights to reproductive health care, and policy analysis.

Fernando I. Soriano, Ph.D., is a professor in the Department of Behavioral Science at the University of Missouri–Kansas City. He had been a research associate at the Stanford Center for Chicano Research. Dr. Soriano is an applied researcher and academician who has generated publications focusing on such social problems as gangs, school violence, substance abuse, AIDS, and mental health outcomes of discrimination—particularly as they affect Latino populations.

John P. Treahy is vice president of Hillside Children's Center in Rochester, New York, and current president of the Juvenile Detention Association of New York State. Mr. Treahy assisted with the development of a national training program for line staff in detention centers. He has been a consultant in the area of program development and evaluation and currently serves on an advisory panel for attorneys who represent juveniles in family court.

Kevin C. Walsh has worked in the field of juvenile delinquency for the past twenty years in both direct service and administrative roles. Presently, he is the associate director for the Berkshire Farm Center and Services for Youth in Canaan, New York.

Dedications

To my wife Joan Ellen, who has deferred her own career and education in order to manage our home and raise our four children ensuring their positive growth and development; and to our children, Brian Hart, Alyson Leigh, Daniel Evan, and Joseph Seth, who have managed to survive their own adolescent environment. —B.G.

To my wife, Susan Striepling—special partner and enabler.—A.P.G.

Acknowledgments

There are many individuals to whom we owe our gratitude and thanks. First and foremost, to our colleagues and those who have contributed to this effort, we wish to express our deepest appreciation and esteem. All have given unselfishly of their knowledge, experience, and background. Together we have provided the field with a compendium of ideas, tools, and techniques with which to better manage a complex system.

Second, there are certain individuals who we hold very dear, both personally and professionally. We single them out because they have been instrumental to the success of this project and to most projects with which we have collaborated:

Leonard G. Dunston, director of the New York State Division for Youth, has been a friend. He also represents the kind of chief executive officer who exudes many of the administrative principles that make for quality youth services and programs.

G. Rosaline Preudhomme, deputy director for the Office of Local Services in the New York State Division for Youth, is both a professional colleague and mentor. She is passionate in her pursuit to do what is right for both the young people in the juvenile justice system and those she vows to keep out of it. She also has taught us to take the high road and always choose what is in the best interests of all for whom we have administrative responsibility.

Sandra Ruiz has provided us the spirit to know that for every problem there is a solution, and for every dark cloud, there is a silver lining. Her pleasant smile and ability to get along with all directs our energy to be positive in a system that often emphasizes the negative.

Finally, there are those hundreds and thousands of young people who have touched our lives by their own individual situations. They are the ones who gave us the motivation to conceive and write this book.

Foreword

Managing a successful delinquency program is a complicated issue that often causes administrators and students of the field to get lost in the twists and turns caused by conflicting demands and philosophies. Dr. Barry Glick and Dr. Arnold P. Goldstein have sought to offer a way out of the maze through *Managing Delinquency Programs That Work*, which not only sets today's juvenile justice concerns into their historical context, but also explores other issues, such as multicultural training and cross-cultural counseling, recreation management, Anger Control Training, aftercare services, budgeting concerns, public relations, staffing treatment programs, and the role of professional associations—issues with which today's juvenile justice professionals must grapple. One of the most important messages this publication heralds is the reassurance that people in the field are meeting head on the many challenges—and succeeding at what they do.

The sixteen chapters—written by the leading thinkers and doers in the profession—focus on issues relevant to both juvenile justice students and practitioners looking for new approaches to old and continuing concerns. Those concerned with the rising tide of delinquency will find this book a valuable resource in deciphering the complexities of the subject.

What all juvenile justice professionals must recognize, and what this book emphasizes by its very comprehensiveness, is that each aspect of the juvenile diversion, treatment, and aftercare process has a role to play in solving our nation's juvenile delinquency problems. Together, we can make a positive contribution.

James A. Gondles, Jr.
Executive Director
American Correctional Association

Introduction

Barry Glick, Ph.D., NCC

Managing programs and services for juvenile delinquents and aggressive adolescents is complex and demanding. Although this is partly due to the nature of the population itself, a great deal of the administrative challenge is due to the complexity of the juvenile justice system in the United States. The juvenile justice system has grown to enormous proportions during the last two decades and now represents a multibillion dollar industry. It is a vast system, fueled by myriad statutes, regulations, court decisions, and advocacy groups—all of which provide challenges and opportunities to juvenile justice administrators, practitioners, and students.

The organization and administration of juvenile delinquency programs has evolved into its own technological discipline. The juvenile justice administrator (whether institutional or community-based, private, or government) may be trained in a variety of academic backgrounds, such as public administration, counseling, psychology, social work, or education.

Administrators must be able to integrate a wealth of information available within the childcare industry to successfully manage rehabilitation programs for juvenile delinquents. This body of knowledge includes the development of childcare services and the history of how the juvenile justice system evolved. It also embodies various administrative models that seemed to have worked in both institutional and community-based settings, whether it be a community-based seven-bed group home, a juvenile camp in the rural countryside, or a large secure center for juvenile felons.

The juvenile justice system in North America is organized at the state or provincial levels of government. A governmental agency, which oversees the system within its jurisdiction, is usually mandated by law to set standards and establish regulations, policies, and procedures. Most systems are comprised of both publicly and privately administered facilities.

The state or provincial agency, whether it be an office whose administrator is a supervisor, a division whose head is a director, or a department whose executive is a commissioner, is responsible for functions such as budget planning, fiscal control, personnel, program design and development, quality-of-care issues, and internal control systems. The overriding

---

Dr. Barry Glick is associate deputy director for local services at the New York State Division for Youth in Rensselaer, New York.

principle is for the agency to provide its public with communities that are safe and a system of programs and services for juveniles who are placed in custody.

A Historical Perspective

The earliest events that involve incorrigible children are first cited in the Old Testament. Parents were provided a mechanism to bring their delinquent children to the elders of the city for judgment and punishment:

> If a man have a stubborn and rebellious son, that will not hearken to the voice of his father, or the voice of his mother, and though they chasten him, will not hearken unto them; then shall his father and his mother lay hold on him, and bring him out unto the elders of his city, and unto the gate of his place; and they shall say unto the elders of his city: 'This our son is stubborn and rebellious, he doth not hearken to our voice; he is a glutton and a drunkard.' And all the men of his city shall stone him with stones, that he die; so shalt thou put away the evil from the midst of thee; and all Israel shall hear and fear (Deut. 21:18-21).

Although this scripture was never implemented as far as historical annals recount, it was clear that the intent of this passage was to serve as a deterrent to juvenile delinquent behaviors.

The modern day juvenile justice system evolved from the childcare institutions of the late nineteenth and early twentieth centuries. Society, as early as 1825, had a growing concern for the undisciplined behaviors of boys, especially those who were neglected by their families. By 1877, the Charity Organization Society, the Associations for Improving Conditions of the Poor, the Society for the Prevention of Pauperism, and other church-affiliated groups maintained large refuge houses and institutions to care for those children who were without family support or were in trouble in their communities. All of these organizations were voluntary—none were empowered to send children to institutions. It was not until 1899, when the first juvenile court was established in Chicago, that a formal system for rehabilitation or control of delinquency was empowered to send children to institutions.

Once juvenile courts were established and empowered to protect the health and welfare of children, a system of voluntary childcare agencies flourished throughout the United States. These agencies were dedicated to dealing with the delinquents who were incapable of living at home. By 1925, the training school, a self-sufficient, large institution that housed delinquent juveniles between the ages of seven and twenty-one, was prominent throughout the South and Northeast. These facilities relied on rigid regimentation and corporal punishment to control acting-out and aggressive adolescent behaviors, and quickly developed into repositories for juveniles who could not be maintained in their homes and communities.

By 1940, the training school movement had developed a reputation for warehousing children. Many advocacy groups developed, including the American Law Institute, to monitor the growing failures of institutional placements for juveniles. During the early 1940s, child advocacy groups recommended that youth correction authorities be established throughout the United States. California, Massachusetts, Minnesota, Texas, and Wisconsin were the first states to heed the recommendation and form some sort of youth authority. By 1945, states such as New York had formalized their youth commissions into state agencies responsible for juvenile services and programs to prevent delinquency and promote positive youth development.

In summary, the juvenile justice system evolved from an informal structure supported by church people who provided services to the unwanted and destitute children of the country, to a multibillion dollar industry that employs thousands of people to provide services and implement programs for juvenile delinquents, some of whom have committed the most heinous of crimes.

The modern juvenile justice system relies upon the public and private sectors to provide services to juveniles. These juvenile programs and services comprise community- and noncommunity-based residential facilities as well as aftercare services available to local family courts needing to dispose of juvenile cases. These programs and services, in turn, are challenged to rehabilitate juveniles placed in their care. The goal is for these programs to return juveniles to their home communities as productive and contributing citizens. The administrators of these programs and services are challenged to manage these institutions and community-based organizations effectively and efficiently to meet the requirements of the twenty-first century.

Administrative Models

The management and administration of juvenile delinquents, whether they are incarcerated and placed in residential facilities, or maintained in their communities in community-based programs and services, requires individuals who are well-trained and experienced. The organizational principles on which the administration of the public or private programs are based date back to ancient China, where in 165 B.C., officials were chosen by examination. Indeed, the modern civil service system with its appointment process is based on aspects of the ancient Chinese model.

However, it was not until Max Weber first described the ideal organization in 1789 and coined the term "bureaucracy," that organizational processes were actually formalized. Weber identified the following five principles that are integral to any bureaucracy:

- division of tasks
- hierarchical structures
- formal sets of rules
- impersonality between superiors, subordinates, and their clients
- employment for life with promotion by merit.

Once Weber's principles were accepted and implemented within the public human services sector, Gullick (1943), Fayol (1949), Urwick (1955, 1961), and Taylor (1975), among other renowned students of organizational and management theory, added significantly to the literature. As a result of these contributions, juvenile justice services evolved a variety of organizational structures, which fall within three theoretical clusters: chain-of-command theories, parent-child management theories, or developmental-community theories.

The chain-of-command theories structure the juvenile justice services systems in a hierarchical fashion. The formal authority and communication flows from the top of the administrative structure to the bottom. Decision making is accomplished by a few at the top of the organization, while those at the bottom are expected to implement whatever decisions are made, usually without question.

The parent-child management theories invest authority in a chief executive officer who is perceived as and behaves like a parent. The organizational structure is flat, with all individuals interacting with the chief administrator. The dynamics under the parent-child administrative structure maintain staff in a dependent, rather immature organizational role. They tend to rely on the chief executive officer to make most, if not all, decisions, and they defer action until they receive instructions and direction.

The developmental-community theories assume that social interaction is an integral part of the administration of the juvenile justice system. These theories advocate that an environment that supports personal and professional growth must be established in order for rehabilitation to occur within the client. As such, the organizational structure is a human-support system that is capable of responding to the individuals within it so that the mission, goals, and objectives of the system may be accomplished.

While each of these administrative theoretical clusters provide a framework under which juvenile justice systems may operate, their success depends upon the administrator being well trained in a particular model. Only then will the organization operate efficiently and effectively. Like many of the program interventions, administrative models must be applied prescriptively, depending upon the needs of the system and the individuals in it. However, it is important to understand some of the conditions that need to be considered to manage a juvenile delinquency system.

To fully comprehend the challenges faced by juvenile justice administrators, one must understand that since the mid-1970s, the juvenile justice system has been asked to program more with less money. The principle of "doing more with less" was first posited by President Nixon and continued throughout every federal administration, including that of President Clinton.

The federal budgets for juvenile programs have been reduced by almost half since President Nixon's first budget proposals. Inflation, recession, and national economic disasters exacerbated an already deleterious economic situation. In addition, the Child Welfare Reform Act transferred the burden for youth programs, including juvenile delinquency, from the federal to the state governments. It is no wonder that during the last two decades, childcare institutions have closed, limiting the number of beds for serious violent offenders; state budgets for certain services have been capped; and delinquency prevention program dollars have been slashed (some up to 65 percent). All of this increases the need for juvenile justice administrators to be more effective, innovative, and efficient.

To respond to the economic conditions that affect managing juvenile justice systems, administrators of these systems must bring certain knowledge and skills to their position. Successful juvenile justice administrators have both training and experience to deal with the myriad of management issues that arise. At the very least, administrators must be knowledgeable in budget and finance, personnel, program development, management of information systems, advocacy, public and community relations, planning, staff development, and politics.

What to Expect

Managing Delinquency Programs That Work is designed to explore these and other issues. We have organized this work so that experts who have both theoretical and practical application in their subject matter address an array of administrative and management concerns. In each subject area, we have included an overview of the situation that currently exists in the field, and then, we identified management issues that are important to consider when administering delinquency programs and services. This book offers solutions to those issues whenever possible.

Finally, we have asked the contributors to share their own assessments and experiences. In that way, we hope to achieve a work that is comprehensive, direct, and practical. Our goal is to provide a resource that systematically and coherently compiles the vast knowledge of the profession.

We hope this work is useful to a broad range of individuals. Administrators may use it for a historical reference and as a practical manual. This book deals with the major themes necessary to be a successful administrator. It has five parts:

Part I "Policy Formulation and Direction," includes managing delinquency systems from a national, state, and community perspective. Dr. James C. "Buddy" Howell draws from his vast experience with the Office of Juvenile Justice and Delinquency Prevention. He offers insights into primary prevention and the direction national policy must take. Edward "Ned" Loughran and Dr. Susan Guarino-Ghezzi focus on what states do to manage delinquency programs and services as they share their experiences of almost a decade of administering Massachusetts' juvenile justice system. This first section concludes with a chapter by Melody Scofield and Dr. William "Bill" Davidson of Michigan State University, who provide concrete examples of how community programs and diversion services affect the juvenile justice system.

Part II is titled "Managing Program Development." In this section, experienced managers deal with topical areas in almost every aspect of the juvenile justice system. John Treahy shares his long experience as a juvenile detention administrator and draws on his experiences as president of an association of large state detention center administrators as he examines the complexities of managing such a system.

Linda Albrecht has changed the very core of facility operations for female offenders and offers us her wealth of information and acumen in the chapter about managing female juvenile institutions. Sex offenders is one example of special populations within the juvenile justice system that require special administrative attention. Bruce Janes provides an overview of the administrative details necessary for managing quality programs and services for this population.

A chapter by Dr. David Altschuler and Dr. Troy Armstrong, who share their experiences over the past seven years as co-principal investigators of the Intensive Community Based Aftercare Programs (sponsored by the Office of Juvenile Justice and Delinquency Prevention), concludes this section. This chapter is filled with management principles and administrative techniques in an area that concerns all who deal with juvenile offenders who must be returned to their communities.

Part III, "Managing Program Administration," is devoted to the special areas of programs and services for juvenile delinquents and at-risk youths. Dr. Vicki Agee has devoted her career to developing, implementing, and managing clinical programs both in the public and private sectors. In "Managing Clinical Programs for Juvenile Delinquents," she shares her abundant experiences and deals with many topics, such as the right to treatment and issues of resources.

We conclude this section with a chapter by Dr. Jimmy Calloway, who has devoted most of his career to managing leisure time activities for inner-city at-risk youth. Some of his management techniques and administrative direction that include, rather than exclude, juvenile delinquents in community programs is refreshing.

Part IV, "Managing Program Training and Evaluation," focuses on training issues for those in the juvenile justice system and those doing research and evaluation. Dr. Henry "Hank" Cellini, president of the Training and Research Institute in Albuquerque, New Mexico, has provided skills training to juvenile justice administrators, especially in the areas of drug abuse and gangs, for more than twenty years. He draws from this experience as he reviews the area of staff development. The training model and administrative techniques he suggests give the juvenile justice manager ideas and strategies to better administer this part of the system. Dr. Maurice Satin combines the idealism of a research scientist who has worked his entire career in the area of human services with the pragmatism that comes from working within systems and bureaucracies. In "Research: A Macro View of Statewide Issues," he provides a candid look into the realities of research and evaluation. His suggestions challenge juvenile justice administrators to aim toward greater horizons and opportunities.

Finally, Dr. Arnold P. Goldstein and I complete this section with "Artful Research Management: Problems, Process, and Products," in which we share our own ideas about evaluating and assessing facility programs, based on two decades of hands-on experience within the juvenile justice system.

Part V of the book deals with "Managing System Issues." Dr. Fernando I. Soriano and Leticia Lleva share their organizational and management insights into multicultural considerations. In "Cultural Sensitivity in Delinquency Prevention and Intervention Programs," they raise some of the more poignant issues that involve cultural diversity and awareness. Kevin Walsh, a seasoned administrator in the private sector, offers his views of how to network and build partnerships to benefit the juvenile delinquent population. William "Bill" Bradley, a private financial consultant, spent an entire career as chief fiscal officer in a large juvenile justice public system. He provides a look into the budget and financing of juvenile programs. We end this section and the book with a statement from James A. Gondles, Jr., executive director of the American Correctional Association and a former sheriff in Arlington, Virginia. He provides administrators with information about the pivotal role professional associations have in managing the juvenile justice system.

It is our desire that this book serve as the foundation upon which other work can be accomplished. Managing juvenile justice systems and serving the juveniles who are part of these systems, as well as those who are at risk of entering into them, is a difficult and often thankless job. The tools necessary to be successful need to be further codified. Each of the areas delineated in this book can be expanded in its own right to monographs for the field to explore. It is our hope that others will build upon this effort and continue to enhance the profession.

References

Fayol, H. 1949. *General and industrial management.* New York: Pitman.

Gullick, L. F. 1943. *The elements of administration.* New York: Harper & Bros.

Taylor, B. 1975. *Management development and training.* London: McGraw-Hill.

Urwick, L. F. 1955. The purpose of business. *Dun's review and modern industry* 52:103-5.

———. 1961. Management and human relations. In *Leadership and organization: A behavior science approach,* ed. R. Tannenbaum, 118-31. New York: McGraw-Hill.

Part I

Policy Formulation and Direction

1   A National Perspective

James C. Howell, Ph.D.*

America's juvenile justice system is at a crossroads. Although its survival is not the issue, a debate focuses on its future role in our society's crime-control apparatus. Despite the fact that some observers have called for abolishing the juvenile justice system, this is unlikely to happen. However, the juvenile justice system is undergoing significant changes brought about by increasing juvenile violence.

Recent Juvenile Justice Trends

Serious and violent juvenile crime has increased during the latter part of the 1980s and the early 1990s. Adult crime has increased at the same time. During the same period the shift from an emphasis on rehabilitation to punishment in political, criminal, and juvenile justice system policies has resulted in a tremendous strain on the juvenile and criminal justice systems.

These developments are presenting a challenge to the juvenile justice system. Violent juvenile crime has been increasing. Juvenile arrests for violent crimes increased 47 percent from 1988 to 1992. In 1991, the juvenile arrest rate for violent offenses reached its highest level in history. Between 1988 and 1992, juvenile arrests for murder increased by 51 percent, compared with 9 percent for those aged eighteen and older (Snyder 1994).

The national scope and seriousness of the gang problem have increased sharply since the early 1980s. Gang violence has risen drastically in many large cities. Gangs are becoming more violent, and gangs, increasingly, serve as a way for members to engage in illegal money-making activity, including street-level drug trafficking (Spergel et al. 1991).

Evidence continues to mount that a small proportion of offenders commit most of the serious and violent juvenile crimes. About 15 percent of

Dr. James C. Howell is director of research and program development in the Office of Juvenile Justice and Delinquency Prevention, U.S. Department of Justice, Washington, D.C.
*The points of view expressed in this chapter are those of the author and do not necessarily represent the official policies or positions of the United States Department of Justice.

high-risk youth commit about 75 percent of all violent offenses (Huizinga, Loeber, and Thornberry 1994). Juveniles with four or more court referrals make up 16 percent of offenders but are responsible for 51 percent of all juvenile court cases—61 percent of the murders, 64 percent of the rapes, 67 percent of the robberies, 61 percent of aggravated assaults, and 66 percent of burglary cases (Snyder 1988).

There will not be an abatement of increasingly violent behavior among juveniles unless effective measures are taken.

Juvenile court caseloads are increasing, largely as a result of the increase in violent delinquency. From 1986 through 1990, the number of delinquency cases disposed of by juvenile courts increased 10 percent. During the same period, juvenile courts disposed of 31 percent more violent cases, including 64 percent more homicide and 48 percent more aggravated assault cases (Snyder et al. 1993).

Admissions to juvenile detention and corrections facilities are increasing. A nationwide study of conditions of confinement in juvenile detention and correctional facilities found crowding to be associated with higher rates of institutional violence, suicidal behavior, and greater reliance on the use of short-term isolation (Parent et al. 1993). Admissions to juvenile facilities rose after 1984, reaching an all-time high in 1990, with the largest increase in detention (Krisberg et al. 1992).

Juvenile cases handled in adult criminal courts have increased, resulting in increasing numbers of juveniles placed in crowded adult prisons. The number of juvenile cases handled in criminal courts is unknown, but it is estimated to be as many as 200,000 in 1990 (Wilson and Howell 1993). Judicial waivers to criminal court increased 65 percent between 1986 and 1990 (Snyder et al. 1993). Between 1984 and 1990, annual admissions of juveniles to adult prisons increased 30 percent (Office of Juvenile Justice and Delinquency Prevention 1991a; 1993).

The volume of juvenile delinquency can be expected to continue increasing toward the end of the 1990s because of the "baby boom echo." Children of "baby boomers" are now entering the crime-prone years. There will not be an abatement of increasingly violent behavior among juveniles unless effective measures are taken. Both juvenile justice and criminal justice system resources are strained to their human and fiscal limits. Innovative solutions must be found to address what can only be described as a crisis in America's management of the juvenile delinquency problem.

Office of Juvenile Justice and Delinquency Prevention's Comprehensive Strategy

The Office of Juvenile Justice and Delinquency Prevention has developed a "Comprehensive Strategy for Serious, Violent, and Chronic Juvenile Offenders" (Wilson and Howell 1993) that is designed to prevent and reduce juvenile crime and provide a systemwide approach for managing juvenile delinquency more effectively. This strategy can be implemented at the state, county, or local levels.

The Office of Juvenile Justice and Delinquency Prevention's Comprehensive Strategy is based on the following principles to prevent and reduce at-risk behavior and serious, violent, and chronic juvenile delinquency (Wilson and Howell 1993):

1. We must strengthen families in their role to provide guidance and discipline and instill sound values as their children's first and primary teachers.

2. We must support core social institutions, including schools, churches, and other community-based organizations, to alleviate risk factors and help children develop to their maximum potential.

3. We must promote prevention strategies that reduce the impact of risk factors and enhance the influence of protective factors in the lives of juveniles at greatest risk for delinquency.

4. We must intervene with juveniles immediately when delinquent behavior first occurs.

5. We must establish a broad spectrum of graduated sanctions that provide accountability and a continuum of services to respond appropriately to the needs of each juvenile offender.

6. We must identify and control the small segment of serious, violent, and chronic juvenile offenders.

The Comprehensive Strategy consists of two components: prevention and intervention. Prevention is the most cost-effective means to deal with delinquency. The prevention component is based on a risk-focused approach that calls on communities to systematically assess their delinquency problem in relation to known risk factors and to implement programs to counteract them. This planning strategy involves community leaders, representatives of local government agencies, other professionals, and citizens in the assessment and planning process. The community then selects programs it wishes to put in place as protective buffers to balance against delinquency risk factors.

The Comprehensive Strategy's intervention component is based on the recognition that an effective model for the treatment and rehabilitation of delinquent juveniles must combine accountability and sanctions with increasingly intensive treatment and rehabilitation. Thus, the intervention component comprises a range of graduated sanctions, extending from sources of referral to the juvenile justice system through system handling, and includes immediate interventions and intermediate sanctions. The intervention component calls for extensive use of nonresidential community-based programs, including referral to prevention programs for most first offenders. Intermediate sanctions use both residential and nonresidential placements, including intensive supervision programs for more serious offenders.

The criminal behavior of some serious, violent, and chronic offenders clearly requires the use of secure corrections to protect the community and provide a structured treatment environment. Because large congregate care facilities, such as training schools, have proven to be ineffective, greater use of small, community-based facilities offers the best hope for successful treatment of juveniles who require a structured setting.

This comprehensive strategy suggests a number of policy and program implications for the juvenile justice system.

Needed Juvenile Justice System Improvements

The following are major areas in which juvenile justice administration and management improvements are needed:

1. The costs of juvenile corrections must be reduced.

2. Conditions of confinement must be improved.

3. Detention and training school populations must be decreased.

4. More widespread use should be made of risk assessments.

5. Identification of treatment needs should be improved.

6. Innovative management techniques must be used to vitalize detention as a treatment opportunity.

7. A continuum of program options must be established and made available to meet the needs of each individual in the system.

8. Use of alternatives to incarceration for nonviolent juvenile delinquents must be increased.

9. Inequality in the administration of juvenile justice must be eliminated.

10. Provision of due process and quality legal representation for juveniles must be increased.

11. Community involvement must be increased.

12. Effective programs for rehabilitating violent juvenile offenders must be developed.

13. Delinquency prevention must be the top priority.

14. Effective aftercare programs must be developed.

The costs of juvenile corrections must be reduced. The Office of Juvenile Justice and Delinquency Prevention has estimated that the annual cost of juvenile confinement in public facilities alone exceeds $2 billion each year (Office of Juvenile Justice and Delinquency Prevention 1991b). Some states, particularly Utah and Massachusetts, have demonstrated significantly lower costs by substituting community-based programs for training schools. This management decision, coupled with the use of sophisticated risk assessments (discussed later) to identify juveniles requiring long-term detention can result in substantial savings nationwide. In some states, the bulk of currently confined juvenile offenders can be successfully managed, with comparably low recidivism rates, in less expensive community-based programs.

Conditions of confinement must be improved. The Office of Juvenile Justice and Delinquency Prevention's recent nationwide study of conditions of confinement revealed serious deficiencies in the management of juvenile detention and correction facilities, many of which could be ameliorated by more effective management, without significant fiscal outlays. Three major themes were summarized by the research team (Parent et al. 1993). First, there are several areas in which problems in juvenile facilities are substantial and widespread. These include: living space, health care, security, and control of suicidal behavior. Second, high levels of conformity to nationally recognized standards do not necessarily mean improved conditions of confinement. Performance standards are needed. Third, deficiencies are distributed widely across facilities. Thus, widespread improvements are needed.

Detention and training school populations must be decreased. The Conditions of Confinement Study (Parent et al. 1993) found that more than 75 percent of the confined juveniles were housed in facilities that violated one or more standards related to living space. Furthermore, crowding was found to be associated with higher rates of institutional violence, suicidal behavior, and greater reliance on the use of short-term isolation. The crowding issue must be addressed. The tools are available to correct the problem. To date, the National Council on Crime and Delinquency has helped correctional administrators in fourteen states to determine the proportions of their training school population requiring long-term secure confinement and those who could be better served in community-based programs (Krisberg et al. 1993). The National Council on Crime and Delinquency used an advanced management technique—a "risk assessment" tool—to determine that at least one-third of the training school residents in these fourteen states did not require secure, long-term confinement and helped each jurisdiction develop its own risk assessment instrument, modeled after those used in other states. The procedure sorted juveniles into groups with differing probabilities of reoffending. Thus, the one-third estimate was based solely on public safety considerations.

More widespread use should be made of risk assessments. Effective risk assessments at intake, for example, can identify subgroups who require the use of detention as well as those who can be released to parental custody or diverted to nonsecure community-based programs.

All too often, detention is viewed as a "dead time" holding period because the juvenile is awaiting a hearing or placement. On the other hand, this is an important opportunity for the system to address the juvenile's needs and problems.

Objective measures will reduce the use of detention to punish juveniles for their offenses even before they have been adjudicated. These instruments should be based on clearly defined objective criteria that focus on the seriousness of the delinquent act, the potential risk for reoffending based on the presence of risk factors, and the risk to the public safety.

Identification of treatment needs must be improved. Advanced techniques are also available to help juvenile justice system professionals assess their clients' treatment needs (needs assessment). This technology has improved greatly over the past few years and uses objective criteria to determine the presence and severity of problems that need to be addressed in major areas of a juvenile's life, including family, school, medical, mental health, and education. Use of these instruments helps ensure that the full range of problems is taken into account when formulating a case plan. A baseline to monitor a juvenile's progress is established, periodic assessments of treatment effectiveness are conducted, and a systemwide data base of treatment needs is used to plan and evaluate programs, policies, and procedures. Use of needs assessments also will help allocate scarce resources more effectively.

The Michigan Department of Social Services is instituting a comprehensive case management approach developed as a result of the department's diminishing ability to manage the increasing numbers of abuse and neglect cases. Major components of the case-management process include actuarial risk assessment instruments, based on original research in Michigan, which estimate the risk of future abuse or neglect; family needs assessment instruments to identify problems and establish a service intervention plan; comprehensive case planning and management procedures which emphasize periodic case monitoring and case reassessment; clear standards for case worker intervention based on risk assessment; an agency budgeting and resource allocation system based on workload; and a management information system (Baird, Wagner, and Neuenfeldt 1992).

Innovative management techniques must be used to vitalize detention as a treatment opportunity. All too often, detention is viewed as a "dead time" holding period because the juvenile is awaiting a hearing or placement. On the other hand, this is an important opportunity for the system to address the juvenile's needs and problems. For many years, New York City's Spofford Detention Center was known as a brutal and inhumane facility. Successful efforts by the city's new Department of Juvenile Justice reduced delays in holding hearings and making placements. The Department of Juvenile Justice used nonsecure options to reduce the detention population by almost one-half and then developed a new management approach. Detention was viewed as an opportunity to identify and begin responding to medical, educational, dental, mental health, and other social service needs, on a twenty-four-hour basis. A computerized case management system helped service delivery. Since instituting this system, the Department of Juvenile Justice has received national recognition for excellence in public sector management.

A continuum of program options must be established and made available to meet the needs of each individual in the system. Because the juvenile justice system has the responsibility to provide treatment and rehabilitation services to minimize each juvenile's likelihood of reoffending, juvenile justice professionals must have available to them a range of treatment options that addresses the entire array of problems that have been identified through comprehensive needs assessments.

Beginning in 1989, Missouri completely restructured its correctional service delivery system. With assistance provided by the American Correctional Association, state officials visited Massachusetts and Utah—states that have successfully implemented a community-based model—and Kentucky, which had developed day treatment services for juveniles. Ideas for change emerged. The Missouri Division of Children and Youth Services developed and implemented a risk and needs assessment procedure to evaluate committed juveniles, and they developed a case management system to provide the assessment, treatment plans, coordination of services, and monitoring and evaluation of the services provided.

Today, Missouri has a comprehensive continuum of care that no longer relies on training schools, but, instead, consists of intensive case monitoring, day treatment, proctor care, family therapy, a short-term treatment program, a ninety-day residential program, group homes, residential facilities in a moderately structured environment, four highly structured secure care programs, a community learning center, a special mental treatment unit, and intensive aftercare. In addition, the state legislature has provided for an innovative system that allows statewide pooling of various treatment funds, so that treatment resources follow the juvenile, rather than vice versa (Missouri Division of Children and Youth Services 1993).

The extensive use of a network of flexible services that calls on all service systems to provide coordinated resources requires innovative ways to integrate and coordinate service management. Massachusetts pioneered a team system, pairing a caseworker and a tracker, who together advocate for the 65 percent of committed juveniles now residing at home under their supervision, helping them with family, school, and employment issues (Lerner 1990). Missouri creatively uses college students as trackers and mentors for juveniles in its statewide continuum of care (Onek 1993). Utah has developed a "proctor program" for older juveniles, now in group homes, who have served time in more secure facilities. Proctors (often college students) live with clients in a semi-independent apartment setting and act as a combined roommate and role model.

Formal monitoring of these clients, in their performance in school or work and while receiving treatment services, is performed by a "tracker," on call twenty-four hours a day. Proctors and trackers are supervised by "case managers" (Lerner 1990).

Use of alternatives to incarceration for nonviolent juvenile delinquents must be increased. Most nonviolent offenders can be successfully rehabilitated and controlled without the necessity of confinement in secure facilities. These include first-time serious offenders, repeat property offenders, and drug offenders. Intermediate sanctions are appropriate for many of these juveniles. A combination of nonresidential and residential sanctions should be made available. One new program model, developed by the National Council on Crime and Delinquency for the Office of Juvenile Justice and Delinquency Prevention, is the Intensive Supervision of Probationers program. It is a highly structured, continuously monitored, individualized plan that consists of five phases with decreasing levels of restrictiveness: short-term placement in community confinement, day treatment, outreach and tracking, routine supervision, and discharge and followup (Krisberg et al. 1991).

Inequality in the administration of juvenile justice must be eliminated. Disproportionate representation of minority youths in the juvenile justice system must be erased. Excessive detention of minority juveniles represents the most egregious situation. Between 1985 and 1991, the proportion of confined juveniles who were minorities increased from 47 percent to 65 percent.

Most of this increase was accounted for by increased detention of minority youths for drug-related offenses (DeComo et al. 1993). The Office of Juvenile Justice and Delinquency Prevention has undertaken a five-state pilot program in Arizona, Florida, Iowa, North Carolina, and Oregon in which techniques for reducing the inequitable detention or confinement of minority juveniles at each step of juvenile justice system processing are being tested. Congress amended the Juvenile Justice and Delinquency Prevention Act in 1992 to require states participating in the Office of Juvenile Justice and Delinquency Prevention formula grant program to address the disproportionate representation of minority youth or face the loss of 25 percent of their formula grants fund allocation.

Juvenile justice system effectiveness can be increased greatly by establishing community-planning teams as part of the overall efforts to improve the operations of the system.

Provision of due process and quality legal representation for juveniles must be increased. Ensuring due process and competent counsel for juveniles in the juvenile justice system is a goal that is consistent with the best interests of the juvenile. Juvenile justice system management of its caseloads will improve as a result of more widespread provision of due process protection. First, third-party advocacy on behalf of the best interests of the juvenile will increase the likelihood that the treatment needs of juvenile delinquents are addressed. Second, due process procedures provide a tool juvenile court judges and corrections officials may use to hold service providers accountable. And third, juveniles and their families will perceive the system as being fair.

Community involvement must be increased. Juvenile justice system effectiveness can be increased greatly by establishing community-planning teams as part of the overall efforts to improve the operations of the system. Successful teams include a broad base of participants drawn from local government and the community, including community-based youth development organizations, schools, law enforcement, social service agencies, civic organizations, religious groups, parents, and teens. Helping to create consensus on priorities and services to be provided as well as building support for a comprehensive program approach is the mission of these teams.

Oregon and New York are excellent examples. Oregon's teams in each county originally were established to develop community-based alternatives to incarceration. They now address youth development, as well (English 1993). New York established statewide youth bureaus in 1945. In 1979, the bureaus began developing comprehensive youth development plans that are incorporated into county plans and then into a comprehensive state plan (Herrick 1993).

Effective programs for rehabilitating violent juvenile offenders must be developed. If its role in handling serious juvenile offenders in America's crime control apparatus is to be maintained, the juvenile justice system must demonstrate its ability to manage violent juvenile crime more effectively. Thus, long-term treatment approaches must be developed.

There are several examples of successful rehabilitation of violent juvenile offenders. Florida's Environmental Institute demonstrated the effectiveness of an intensive treatment program for violent juveniles who had been certified for transfer to adult criminal court and likely incarceration in adult prison. The Office of Juvenile Justice and Delinquency Prevention's Violent Juvenile Offender Program (VJO) combined short-term confinement in secure care with extensive efforts to reintegrate juvenile delinquents into community living. It was somewhat successful (Fagan 1990).

Delinquency prevention must be the top priority. This goal remains elusive, largely because a certain amount of deviance is part of the social development process. Although juveniles will continue to test the system of social controls in the quest for their emancipation, the prospects for success are much greater than ever before for two reasons. First, new approaches are positive in their orientation. They encourage healthy social development rather than attempt to stop juveniles from deviance. Second, advanced prevention technology is patterned after successful efforts in the health arena. It is a risk-factor approach that provides protective buffers against known risk factors. David Hawkins and Richard Catalano have pioneered a strategy called "Communities That Care" (1992).

This program actively involves community leaders in assessing the range of possible local risk factors, identifying those most prevalent in the community, and selecting specific program models from a wide range of options to act as protective buffers against the identified risk factors. Parents, schools, community agencies, police, and juvenile court officials would then refer status offenders, first offenders, and repeat minor offenders to delinquency prevention programs that address underlying risk factors. The programs themselves would provide an outreach to juveniles identified as at-risk of delinquency. Juvenile justice system officials, including those in the detention and corrections fields, must be actively involved in these community-wide efforts.

Effective aftercare programs must be developed. Currently, aftercare may be the weakest juvenile justice system program in the continuum of care. The Office of Juvenile Justice and Delinquency Prevention has funded the development of an Intensive Aftercare Program (IAP) model that will guide jurisdictions in building an effective aftercare system. It incorporates the following five principles:

- prepares juveniles for progressive responsibility and freedom in the community
- facilitates juvenile-community interaction and involvement
- works with both the juvenile offender and targeted community support systems, including families, peers, schools, and employers, to facilitate constructive interaction and gradual community adjustment
- develops resources and community support
- monitors and ensures the juvenile's successful reintegration into the community

Conclusion

America's juvenile justice system faces a formidable challenge at this time from the rising tide of violent juvenile crime. However, the tools are available in new technology and advanced management techniques to effectively prevent and control serious, violent, and chronic juvenile crime. It is a matter of collectively responding to the challenge, beginning at the community level. The Office of Juvenile Justice and Delinquency Prevention is developing a blueprint to help communities assess their present juvenile justice system and plan new programs that respond to community-identified needs.

References

Baird, C., D. Wagner, and D. Neuenfeldt. 1992. Protecting children: The Michigan model. San Francisco: National Council on Crime and Delinquency.

Bureau of Justice Statistics. 1993. Special analysis.

DeComo, R., et al. 1993. *Juveniles taken into custody 1992.* Washington, D.C.: Office of Juvenile Justice and Delinquency Prevention.

English, T. 1993. Senate Report. No. J-102-62. 102nd Congress, Second Session. Hearing on Juvenile Justice: A New Focus on Prevention.

Fagan, J. 1990. *Social and legal policy dimensions of violent juvenile crime.* Criminal Justice and Behavior. 17:93-133.

Hawkins, D., and R. Catalano, Jr. 1992. *Communities that care.* San Francisco: Jossey-Bass Inc.

Herrick, S. 1993. Senate Report. No. J-102-62. 102nd Congress., Second Session. Hearing on Juvenile Justice: A New Focus on Prevention.

Huizinga, D., R. Loeber, and T. Thornberry. 1994. *Urban delinquency and substance abuse: Initial findings.* Washington, D.C.: Office of Juvenile Justice and Delinquency Prevention.

Krisberg, B., et al. 1991. *Juvenile intensive supervision program model, operations manual and guide.* San Francisco: National Council on Crime and Delinquency.

——. 1992. *National juvenile custody trends 1978-1989.* Washington, D.C.: Office of Juvenile Justice and Delinquency Prevention.

——. 1993. *Juveniles in state custody: Prospects for community based care of troubled adolescents* NCCD Focus. San Francisco: National Council on Crime and Delinquency.

Lerner, S. 1990. *The good news about juvenile justice.* Bolinas, Calif.: Common Knowledge Press.

Missouri Division of Children and Youth Services. 1993. Historical overview and program description.

Office of Juvenile Justice and Delinquency Prevention. 1991a. *Juveniles taken into custody: Fiscal Year 1990 report.* Washington, D.C.

——. 1991b. *Children in custody 1987—a comparison of public and private juvenile custody facilities.* Washington, D.C.

——. 1993. *Juveniles taken into custody: Fiscal Year 1992 report.* Washington, D.C.

Onek, D. 1993. *Pairing college students with delinquents: The Missouri intensive case monitoring program.* San Francisco: National Council on Crime and Delinquency.

Parent, D., et al. 1993. Conditions of confinement: A study to evaluate conditions in juvenile detention and corrections facilities. Final report submitted to the Office of Juvenile Justice and Delinquency Prevention.

Snyder, H. 1988. *Court careers of juvenile offenders.* Washington, D.C.: Office of Juvenile Justice and Delinquency Prevention.

——. 1994. *Arrests of juveniles 1992.* Washington, D.C.: Office of Juvenile Justice and Delinquency Prevention.

Snyder, H., et al. 1993. *Juvenile court statistics: 1990.* Washington, D.C.: Office of Juvenile Justice and Delinquency Prevention.

Spergel, I., et al. 1991. *Youth gangs: Problem and response* Final report submitted to the Office of Juvenile Justice and Delinquency Prevention. See the *Executive Summary,* Stage I: Assessment.

Wilson, J. J., and J. C. Howell. 1993. *A comprehensive strategy for serious, violent, and chronic juvenile offenders.* Washington, D.C.: Office of Juvenile Justice and Delinquency Prevention.

2

A State Perspective

Edward J. Loughran and
Susan Guarino-Ghezzi, Ph.D.

The mission statements of most state juvenile correctional agencies express a dual purpose: to protect the community and to provide rehabilitative treatment to juveniles. The ultimate dilemma of juvenile justice agencies is how to devise balanced policies that fulfill both halves of the dual mission. To uninformed observers, the twin missions comprise a contradiction: Placing emphasis on treatment automatically shortchanges public safety, and vice versa, so the mission is unachievable.

Indeed, when citizens grow concerned that public protection is lacking, detention rates increase. Repeatedly, however, institutions have been unable to guarantee the safety of juveniles in confinement, and they have failed to provide adequate rehabilitative services (Parent 1993a). In many states, legal advocates for juveniles have challenged institutional practices, including crowding, lack of medical services, poor sanitation, and physical and/or sexual abuse of juveniles. Institutions have been downsized, dismantled, and replaced by community-based programs—until the next wave of fear tips the balance toward public security, as in Utah and Colorado. These two states were models of community-based reforms during the 1980s. By the early 1990s, however, these states had returned to an emphasis on secure detention.

How does a state create a system of juvenile corrections that balances seemingly competing goals, so that the system does not contain the seeds of its own destruction? It is relatively simple to provide treatment in the community when public safety is not a concern. It is also relatively simple to control juvenile delinquents' probability of reoffending by placing them in detention—as long as rehabilitative treatment and juvenile safety are not concerns. Unfortunately, neither objective is realistic, because all factors must be included in any model that would stand the test of time.

Agencies must embrace policies that allow them to take measured, defensible risks with juveniles in the community, permitting juveniles to "test

---

Edward J. Loughran is the former commissioner of the Massachusetts Department of Youth Services and is now the director of the Robert F. Kennedy National Juvenile Justice Project in Boston; Dr. Susan Guarino-Ghezzi is assistant professor of criminal justice, Northeastern University, Boston, and former director of research, Massachusetts Department of Youth Services.

reality" while remaining within reach of vigilant supervision and counseling to help them maintain resiliency. Simultaneously, agencies must have programs in place that ensure safety and provide an array of services to juveniles who are confined. Finally, agencies must work vigorously to dispel simplistic "panacea" promises offered by opportunistic politicians, which undermine the complex models needed to carry out the juvenile justice mission. As Palmer (1984) pointed out in his definition of "socially centered treatment," rehabilitative services not only complement public safety, but are necessary components to achieve public safety.

The Massachusetts Department of Youth Services, which is the state correctional agency responsible for committed and detained juveniles, has been regarded nationally as a model for juvenile correctional agencies. More than two decades ago, the reputation of the Department of Youth Services was established as a pioneer of deinstitutionalization when it closed its large institutions and gradually replaced them with private, community-based programs. Several years ago, the Department of Youth Services reaffirmed its commitment to rehabilitation by revising its mission statement to emphasize the connection between rehabilitation and public safety. The new mission statement suggests that rehabilitative services need not be dangerous to the public in the short-term and are essential for long-term adolescent development:

> We are the Massachusetts Department of Youth Services, a juvenile justice agency dedicated to helping youths choose productive, crime-free lives, while keeping the public safe. We strive to provide the relationships and environment that enable youths to develop respect for family, community and themselves.

Measured, Defensible Risks in the Community

Experts and practitioners alike now recognize that the community is the most effective location for providing reintegrative treatment. The following are among the advantages of community settings over institutions:

1. They are natural and avoid the "prisonization" effect of institutions that prevents successful reintegration.

2. They are flexible and can provide a wider range of services and experiences for juveniles.

3. They allow correctional staff to conduct "reality testing," for example, by sending juveniles home on frequent passes while continuing to closely monitor their adjustment.

A juvenile placed in Alpha Omega, a Department of Youth Services-contracted group home in Acton, Massachusetts, recently went home on a pass and committed a violation by visiting other relatives without permission—a subtle violation that would have been undiscovered or overlooked in systems lacking intensive community supervision. After returning to the program, the juvenile admitted his violation and asked for help to determine why he had not followed the rules. In group therapy, the program clinicians and residents confronted the juvenile, where he tearfully admitted the sense of satisfaction he received from breaking rules, but also acknowledged the pain he felt about letting down the program and his family. The staff's capacity to elicit such information from the juvenile, and his expectations of their strong, yet understanding, reaction to his tentative limit-testing behavior, activated the juvenile's internal abilities to control his own behavior at a critical stage of his reintegration.

The task for state agencies is to provide offenders with access to the community while neutralizing public safety risks as much as possible.

Despite their important advantages, community-based residential programs create a number of management challenges. The primary disadvantage of community programs for juvenile offenders is the short-term increased risk to public safety, which is probably far more a perception than a reality. Access to the community, which creates opportunities for offending, also seems to significantly reduce long-term recidivism to produce an overwhelming gain in public safety (LeClair and Guarino-Ghezzi 1991). The task for state agencies is to provide offenders with access to the community while neutralizing public safety risks as much as possible. The goal of neutralizing risk must be incorporated in all phases of programming, including managing resources, developing resources, responding to juveniles' behavior, and educating the public about juvenile corrections.

Managing Resources

Resource management is the cornerstone of any organization and is a particularly visible component of juvenile correctional agencies. Suppose a juvenile offender, named Matthew, has been adjudicated delinquent for dealing cocaine in his neighborhood. He is known to the police as a drug dealer and gang member, and he has a court record of previous adjudications for offenses such as assault and battery and attempted breaking and entering. In most states, this case would be handled within the juvenile system, rather than the adult court.

Following an adjudication of delinquency, what should happen to Matthew? Who should have the power to decide? What criteria should they use in making their decision? The answers to these questions vary state-by-state.

In some states, the juvenile court judge has wide discretion to simply "file" or "continue" the case for disposition, which means that for the indefinite future, Matthew would receive probation without anything further happening to him.

The most important question concerns how decisions are made for determining what program is suitable for each individual offender.

Judges in some states might be obligated by statute to place Matthew into a specific institution. In certain states, the judge must follow dispositional guidelines set by the legislature, unless valid reasons not to do so can be found (judges often fail to adhere to such guidelines). In other states, the judge can sentence Matthew to a juvenile correctional agency, but the agency has the authority to decide where juveniles are placed and for how long. Under some administrative models, the juvenile correctional agency decides where to place juveniles, but the aftercare board determines the actual length of stay.

Numerous questions can be asked to determine how cases are decided within a juvenile court or correctional agency. The most important question concerns how decisions are made for determining what program is suitable for each individual offender. Three organizational models are used for making placement decisions. The first is the legislative model, in which guidelines are established by the legislature and merely followed by the court; the second is the judicial model, in which the court determines placement; and the third is the administrative model, in which placement decisions are made by the juvenile correctional agency without direct interference from the legislature or court. Which of these three entities wields the most power in a state's juvenile justice system? The answer depends on whichever one has control of placement decisions. In effect, each entity has been empowered by the state to calculate the severity of punishment. Each has the authority to decide how much weight should be given to treatment concerns, how much emphasis should be placed on retribution, and whether to concern itself with incapacitating high-risk offenders—in short, to determine the purpose, or purposes, of punishment.

Legislative Management

The state of Washington illustrates the legislative model for meting out juvenile dispositions. The Washington State Juvenile Justice Act of 1977 overhauled the system of sentencing and placing juvenile offenders in that state (Schneider and Schram 1980). Among other significant changes was the introduction of "presumptive sentencing" in Washington's juvenile code.

Presumptive sentencing means that each particular offense has an expected or normal sentence, usually with only a very small amount of deviation. In Washington, the sentence is based on the juvenile's current offense, age, and time and nature of prior offenses. Each offense is assigned a certain number of points proportionate to its calculated seriousness. A multiplication factor is derived from the other criteria and assigned. The total point score is then matched against a sentencing grid. The sentencing schedule specifies the level and length of confinement and other sanctions, but does not determine placement in particular institutions. That decision is made by the juvenile courts. The courts also may go outside of the presumptive range to avoid a "manifest injustice," although this finding must be supported by clear and convincing evidence. Although a federal push for other states to adopt the Washington model took place in the late 1980s, the code did not become a national model.

The specific point system used to determine sentencing ranges in Washington is not a part of the text of the code. Instead, the points and corresponding sentencing ranges are established by a Juvenile Dispositions Standards Commission, a body composed of juvenile justice professionals appointed by the governor, which meets at least twice a year. This approach leaves some flexibility in the system by allowing the sentencing calculus to be amended by the commission, rather than requiring it to be put to a legislative vote. The code provides that in setting the actual disposition from the range of available alternatives (which includes going outside of the standard range to avoid instances of manifest injustice), the court should consider several types of aggravating and mitigating factors, such as infliction of bodily injury.

Judicial Management

Unlike Washington, Pennsylvania represents a judicial model of placement authority because no presumptive guidelines are set by the legislature. Pennsylvania's code gives the authority to make specific placements to the juvenile courts. The code states that the courts may commit juvenile offenders to institutions, youth development centers, camps, or other facilities operated under the direction of the courts or another public agency, most likely the state's Division for Youth and Families, and approved by the Department of Public Welfare.

Thus, Pennsylvania's juvenile court has total sentencing and placement power over all types of offenders, except juveniles charged with murder.

Those juveniles are excluded from juvenile court jurisdiction and automatically tried as adults. Pennsylvania judges can contract directly with private vendors to provide a specific placement or service. This is possible because Pennsylvania's judicial management model requires all juvenile court judges to thoroughly understand the programs and services available for adjudicated juveniles in their jurisdiction.

Pennsylvania's code states that dispositional decisions must be made to best suit a juvenile's treatment, supervision, rehabilitation, and welfare. The courts' array of dispositional options includes: probation and restitution; and commitment to an institution, youth development center, camp, or other facility operated under the supervision of the court or another public authority.

As far as sentence lengths, the code sets only the maximum sentence, which is three years or as long as the juvenile could have been sentenced if he or she were an adult. Again, the code provides the courts with considerable discretion for ordering the length of stay in individual programs. The code also provides for modifications or extensions if the court finds after a hearing that the extension or modification will "effectuate the original purpose for which the order was entered." The committing courts review each commitment every six months and hold a disposition review hearing at least once every nine months. This model maximizes the role of the court vis-à-vis the legislature, as well as the juvenile correctional agency that oversees most of the programs, which is the Division for Youth and Families. Although the Division for Youth and Families has responsibility for juveniles sent to them by the court, it is not authorized to decide which juveniles are appropriate for which programs or how much time they should serve.

Administrative Management

Unlike Washington and Pennsylvania, Massachusetts represents the prototypical administrative management model. In Massachusetts, the juvenile code bestows placement authority with the Department of Youth Services, and the courts have no statutory authority to make specific placements. Whereas Pennsylvania's judges and Washington's legislators need to be familiar with the range and quality of available placements, in Massachusetts the judges make only the decision to commit to the Department of Youth Services, and the legislators have even less involvement than that. Commitment to the Department of Youth Services is one of essentially three options available to the court—the case also may be placed on file, or the juvenile may be placed on probation. The code is vague as to the Department of Youth Services' responsibilities to the court subsequent to commitment. It states that, as a means of correcting socially harmful tendencies, the Department of Youth Services may require that the juvenile participate in vocational training, physical education, and correctional training and activities; require that the juvenile's mode of life and conduct when free do not pose a danger to the public; and provide medical or psychiatric treatment, as necessary.

The code states that the purpose of rules, regulations, and by-laws established by the Massachusetts Commissioner of Youth Services and of all education, employment, discipline, recreation, and other activities carried on in the facilities shall be to restore and build up the self-respect and self-reliance of the juveniles lodged in the facilities and to qualify them for good citizenship and honorable employment. Clearly, this kind of language gives the Department of Youth Services a great deal of latitude to decide among programs ranging from home placement to secure treatment facilities.

Of the three types of management models—legislative, judicial, and administrative—the administrative model is most consistent with a well-managed correctional system. This is true for several reasons. First, in administrative models, procedures can be adapted to changes in the characteristics of juvenile offenders and correctional resources far more easily than in other models, since administrative policy changes do not require legislative approval.

Second, administrative models can directly manage available resources in a more rational manner because they do not rigorously mandate that certain offenders be placed in certain programs for designated periods based on offense criteria, which may be an oversimplification of circumstances.

Third, administrative management is particularly important in a system that includes an array of different private providers, because the centralized authority of the juvenile service agency should increase the quality of program monitoring and ensure the enforcement of program standards, rather than employ the "justice by geography" that characterizes so many states' systems.

Finally, administrative models encourage program improvements because the same staff who design and operate programs interact frequently with the same decision makers who place juveniles and allocate resources. In other words, maintaining placement authority within the organization that is directly responsible for carrying out punishment and treatment reduces the randomness and inconsistency that often characterize the juvenile court system and improves the system's resiliency to adapt to changing societal needs.

Developing Resources

The development of juvenile correctional programs in a state system is greatly enhanced by emphasizing two goals: providing a continuum of programs ranging from secure confinement to home placement and involving the private sector in program development and management. In Massachusetts, more than 60 percent of the total Department of Youth Services' budget is allocated to purchasing services from private vendors in the community. Forty-five private, nonprofit companies account for approximately ninety individual contracts. The Department of Youth Services also purchases services from approximately fifty noncontracted providers on an as-needed basis.

Although private vendors predominate, the state is not excluded from operating programs, which provides another level of competition for the vendors. Approximately 85 percent of the Department of Youth Services' commitments are placed into a nonsecure setting. The continuum of programs and services includes: secure treatment; secure detention; shelter care; transitional management programs; group homes; the Homeward Bound program; foster care/mentor model; outreach and tracking; "Tracking Plus," the family continuity program; health; and other services.

Secure Treatment

Secure treatment involves long-term residential programs for juveniles committed on serious charges that warrant placement in a physically secure facility. There are nine such programs in Massachusetts. Seven programs are operated by private vendors. Each program provides five hours of academic instruction each day, group and individual counseling, vocational training, and medical and recreational services, in addition to many other specialized programs that have been developed to meet the changing needs of juveniles involved in serious offenses.

Secure Detention

Secure detention involves short-term residential programs in a physically secure facility for juveniles awaiting trial on serious charges. There are eight such programs in the state, two of which are operated by private vendors. Each program includes five hours of academic instruction per day, interim group counseling, vocational training, and medical and recreational services.

Shelter Care

Shelter care involves placing juveniles awaiting trial on charges that do not warrant secure confinement into short-term residential programs under twenty-four-hour staff supervision. There are eight such programs in the state (all run by private vendors). Each provides five hours of academic instruction daily, interim group counseling, vocational training, and medical and recreational services.

Transitional Management Programs

Transitional management programs are short-term evaluation programs for juveniles awaiting presentation to the classification panel for serious crimes or for juveniles awaiting placement in community-based programs for nonviolent crimes. There are seventy secure transitional beds for serious offenders and forty-six secure transitional beds for juveniles awaiting community placement. All but one of these programs are operated by private vendors.

Group Homes

Group homes are community-based residential homes for juveniles who are committed to the Department of Youth Services for nonviolent offenses and can be placed in a community setting without risk to the public. Juveniles receive academic and vocational instruction in-house or at community schools. The programs provide group and individual counseling and medical and recreational services. There are twelve private, contracted group homes, in addition to more than twenty private, noncontracted group homes that accept the Department of Youth Services' juveniles on an as-needed basis.

Because of the small number of girls in the Department of Youth Services (fewer than seventy new commitments per year), the flexibility of non-contracted programs is particularly helpful in placing girls into community-based residential programs that are shared by other agencies, such as the Department of Social Services.

The Homeward Bound Program

The Homeward Bound program is a short-term, state-run program for forty-five juveniles designed to build self-esteem through rigorous physical challenges in an outdoor setting. The program, based on the Outward Bound model, also serves as a transitional program for juveniles leaving long-term secure treatment and preparing to re-enter the community.

Foster Care/Mentor Model

Foster care involves community-based residential care in private homes for first-time or low-risk offenders who would benefit from a supportive family environment, but cannot return to their own home for reasons such as abuse or lack of supervision. The Department of Youth Services places an average of sixty-five juveniles in foster care on a given day. Approximately half of these receive more intensive services under the mentor model where juveniles live in foster homes and caseworkers from a vendor agency provide additional intensive support and supervision for both the juvenile and the foster parents. The increased supervision expands foster care into a more controlled setting, which may be appropriate as a reintegration program or as an alternative to residential group care.

Outreach and Tracking

Outreach and tracking, pioneered in 1972, is designed to provide intensive supervision of newly committed or low-risk offenders in the community, or it is used for juveniles who are gradually being reintegrated into the community from long-term secure programs. Juveniles must report to their tracking worker daily: three times a week in person and four times by telephone. The program requires that juveniles strictly comply with the conditions of aftercare. Tracking workers help in family counseling and monitor school attendance, employment, counseling, and attendance at Alcoholics Anonymous or Narcotics Anonymous. The Department of Youth Services contracts for more than 250 outreach and tracking slots per year.

"Tracking Plus"

"Tracking Plus" is a tracking program with a residential component that provides supervision to sixteen juveniles. Juveniles are first placed in a four-bed group home for an initial four- to six-week residential phase. In the second phase, juveniles are intensively supervised by a tracker after they return home. If the juveniles violate rules set for them at home or elsewhere in the community, the tracker has the option to return them to the residential program.

Family Continuity Program

Borrowing from the Homebuilder's program that originated in Washington state to provide intensive services to families of troubled juveniles, the Family Continuity Program provides in-home family therapy in the Department of Youth Services' central region. The program provides two therapists, one assigned to the family and one to the juvenile, who work as a team with the juvenile's caseworker.

The cyclical rebidding of contracts maintains a competitive spirit that ensures the development of new and varied approaches to combating juvenile crime.

Families of the Department of Youth Services' juveniles have traditionally resisted going out to attend family therapy sessions, but in this program, a master's level family therapist and a bachelor's level counselor go into the home and provide family therapy on, at least, a weekly basis. They deal with such issues as disciplinary techniques, communications patterns, and reintegration of juveniles returning home from residential programs. Twelve families receive these services.

Health and Other Services

The Department of Youth Services offers a wide range of medical, clinical, and educational services that are made available through private providers and other state agencies. In some cases, for example, juvenile sex offender treatment is supplemented by the Department of Mental Health, while substance abuse treatment is supplemented by the Department of Public Health.

In addition, the Department of Youth Services is affiliated with several hospitals that provide mental health, diagnostic, and medical services. Other Department of Youth Services' provisions include: dental care, AIDS-related education, employment training, special education (cost-shared with local school districts), federally subsidized Chapter One supplemental education, art therapy, Alcoholics Anonymous and Narcotics Anonymous meetings, and religious services.

Several states recently have deinstitutionalized or are contemplating such reforms. In states where deinstitutionalization is occurring, the private sector is an important agent for shifting the programmatic emphasis toward community-based programming. As a result, an increasing number of states are purchasing private services and the state's role in monitoring privately contracted services is becoming progressively more important.

Many strategic methods are available for state agencies to enhance their position in relation to the private sector. The Massachusetts Department of Youth Services has been cited as a national model for program monitoring (Hackett et al. 1987). Within a few years of pioneering deinstitutionalization in 1972, a contract unit was established within the Department of Youth Services' central administrative office to execute each contract under general purchasing guidelines established by the state. Needs assessments of the juveniles to be served are conducted annually and help determine both the retention of existing programs and the development of new ones.

The Department of Youth Services routinely disseminates Requests for Proposals (RFPs), inviting responses from interested vendors. A contract review committee, composed of a contract officer and field staff, is assembled for each review. Their task is to evaluate written proposals, hear oral presentations, negotiate mutual obligations and cost agreements, and make a final recommendation to the commissioner. Contracts are rebid on a five-year basis, subject to the Department of Youth Services' annual budget allocation. The cyclical rebidding of contracts maintains a competitive spirit that ensures the development of new and varied approaches to combating juvenile crime. Forty-five private agencies account for seventy individual contracts, including ones for secure treatment facilities, group homes, alternative schools, outreach and tracking programs, psychological assessments, and health services (Loughran 1988).

Per diem pricing arrangements (per juvenile, per day) offer two significant advantages to state governments. The first and most important is protection against cost overruns. If the contractor underestimates the costs, as recently occurred in Tennessee's Mountain View Youth Development Center, the government is under no legal obligation to increase its reimbursement rate to cover the unanticipated expenses and can thereby force the program to close, as the Department of Youth Development did in Tennessee.

Contractors' inability to automatically pass on excess costs means that they must avoid overly optimistic cost projections when establishing their fee schedules. It also forces them to operate their facilities as efficiently as possible. The government's protection against cost overruns is not absolute, however. Jurisdictions that refuse to pay major cost overruns risk placing contractors in an untenable position, thereby forcing them to cease operations throughout the state (Commonwealth of Massachusetts Legislative Research Council 1986).

Per diem reimbursement provisions offer a second major advantage—the government pays only for space and services it actually uses. Operationally, contracts allow providers to receive full compensation as long as the provider achieves an 85 percent utilization rate. This allows providers some flexibility in scheduling departures and replacement admissions on optimal days, processes that sometimes result in two- to three-day bed vacancies.

One of the principal advantages of privatization is the added flexibility governments gain in adjusting service levels to changing needs. As commitment populations rise, the state can contract for additional space with its private providers; as the number of commitments declines, the government can reduce its reliance on private-sector facilities. In either case, the state avoids the cumbersome, potentially expensive process of adjusting personnel levels and program capacity in response to hard-to-predict fluctuations in offender-population levels.

The down side of per diem payments is that to keep their programs full, private operators might affect the type or length of punishment that an offender may receive. For example, private facilities may feel pressure to maintain high occupancy levels, which has been referred to as the "Hilton Inn mentality." This may lead private correctional administrators to extend sentences by recommending against aftercare or prerelease (Commonwealth of Massachusetts Legislative Research Council 1986). The problem can be neutralized by careful case management conducted by the state, which tracks the progress of juveniles in a private program and determines release dates based on an assessment of the juvenile's behavior and needs. In Massachusetts, lengths of stay in secure treatment programs are established by minimum and maximum time periods set by the Secure Classification Panel, and extensions or reductions must be approved by two assistant commissioners.

Program monitoring includes several informal reviews at the regional and central office levels. The Department of Youth Services staff from the commissioner to caseworkers frequently visit programs during business and nonbusiness hours, which prevents the Department of Youth Services from becoming an isolated and autonomous operation. Fiscal oversight, monthly and quarterly reports, and in-depth program reviews are essential to ensuring mutual satisfaction. The state auditor conducts periodic audits of private agencies. If a provider does not meet acceptable standards, the state can serve notice and rebid the contract. The provider also can end the contract for any reason, with appropriate notification.

These provisions address two concerns: first, that the state can be protected from programs that are performing inadequately, and second, that providers will not be discouraged from responding to Request for Proposals (RFPs) out of anxiety about being obligated to honor an unacceptable contract.

State agencies should carefully consider what types of offenders to place in what types of private programs. Important questions must be answered about security levels of programs, the size and number of programs, and whether special categories of juveniles (e.g., sexually dangerous, psychiatric cases, violent offenders, AIDS-infected) should be referred to privately operated facilities.

Just as important as determining what types of programs are needed is the process for selecting individual program operators. For example, should contractors be selected primarily on the basis of cost or should experience, financial stability, innovative programs, or other qualifications be given greater weight? It is important that procedures not be too restrictive and shrink the pool of eligible bidders; the resulting lack of active competition will reduce a state agency's choice among contractors and contribute to higher costs.

Contract renegotiations should include evaluations of program performance by state monitors. In Massachusetts, an automated program monitoring system that was set up by the Department of Youth Services research unit revealed that a private program, which was seeking to expand its contract, terminated a relatively high rate of juveniles shortly after placement. Based largely on that data, their expansion request was denied.

Program monitoring should include a variety of process and outcome measures because, particularly in a continuum-of-care model in which juveniles obtain multiple services, recidivism alone is an incomplete measure of any one program's effectiveness. Pre- and post-tests can link incremental changes in juveniles to the efforts of individual programs in such areas as academic performance, attitudinal changes, and employment rates. Process variables, such as juvenile participation in program components (e.g., substance abuse counseling or job skills training), in addition to overall rates of program completion, staff turnover, and violent incidents, are essential indicators of program management.

Responding to Juveniles' Behavior

Inconsistent messages that parents send to juveniles, including erratic discipline, weak limit-setting, and failure to establish rules of conduct, is a pervasive theme in the literature on juvenile delinquency. Consistency is critical to teach juveniles they are accountable for their behavior. Studies have demonstrated that certainty of official response is more influential than severity in dealing with adolescents (Paternoster 1989; Schneider and Ervin 1990). According to Altschuler and Armstrong (1991), a key component of juvenile offender reintegration is providing "consistent, clear, swift and graduated sanctions for misconduct," along with developing new resources and supports, working with existing supports, providing opportunities for juveniles to achieve, and preparing juveniles for gradually increased responsibility and freedom in the community.

Clear and consistent responses to juveniles' misbehaviors in the community can be accomplished by a strong system of case management.

Similarly, Gendreau and Ross (1991) identified the need for authority, including clearly spelled out rules or legal sanctions, to be an essential component of community corrections, along with anticriminal modeling and reinforcement, problem solving, use of community resources, and quality of interpersonal relationships.

The Office of Juvenile Justice and Delinquency Prevention's recommendations for serious offenders (Parent 1993a) emphasize the importance of an immediate response to misbehavior, gradational sanctions, and coordination among police, courts, and corrections.

Clear and consistent responses to juveniles' misbehaviors in the community can be accomplished by a strong system of case management. Case management requires sufficient casework staff to track juveniles in the community and enforce rules immediately and consistently. Ideally, caseloads should be limited to fewer than ten juveniles per caseworker. This is the standard in Massachusetts, but only for a small handful of the most serious offenders. Because of limited resources, the maximum caseload is set at twenty-one juveniles, so behavior monitoring must include others in the community who help the caseworker by providing surveillance and support to the juvenile.

Family cooperation is encouraged from the time of commitment, and some programs provide family therapy to heal old wounds and reestablish relationships. In many cases, family members eventually become important players in supervising juveniles in the community.

In other cases, where family support is weak or nonexistent, additional support and surveillance may be provided by purchasing outreach and tracking, employing mentors, or by using foster family placements.

State agencies might also look toward developing cooperative ties with local police departments to assist with a "reintegrative surveillance" approach (Guarino-Ghezzi 1994).

Because successful reintegration often requires caseworkers' intimate knowledge of local community resources and institutions such as schools, jobs, and community centers, case management should be decentralized. That is, resources, services, and programming should be procured and developed on a regional level, and caseworkers hired for regional offices should have a strong familiarity with local areas.

Unlike states such as California, which separates the California Youth Authority and the parole board into two separate agencies, the Massachusetts Department of Youth Services has aftercare authority and can return juveniles to custody following a due process revocation hearing. The conditions of aftercare are established by contract between each juvenile and his or her caseworker.

For example, if a juvenile returns to drug use or violates curfew regulations by staying out all night, he or she would be placed in detention (as space allows). The revocation hearing officer would conduct a hearing to establish the facts of the case and then set a penalty ranging from several days in detention to escalation to the Dispositional Review Panel. The panel may then determine that a long-term residential placement is required, although the ideal for most juveniles is a short-term placement. Massachusetts uses a Transitional Management Program, which is designed to stabilize the juvenile, send a message that contract violations will not be tolerated, and help the caseworker to identify the issues impeding reintegration.

Public Education

From the perspective of a state juvenile correctional agency that relies heavily on community-based programming, public sophistication in understanding correctional issues is essential. Several related issues are a priority for public education. First is the need for gradual reintegration of juvenile offenders back into the community. Related to this is the issue of locating programs in the community and the "NIMBY"—not in my backyard—problem. A related educational priority is defending "good" placement risks that go bad.

There is a fairly strong consensus in the field of juvenile justice that community-based characteristics are relatively effective in the long run (Altschuler 1984; Greenwood 1986; Krisberg, Austin, and Steele 1989), and short-term client management risks engendered by early reintegration can be controlled through effective classification systems (Guarino-Ghezzi and Byrne 1989). However, although reintegrative programs receive theoretical and empirical support, they are easily manipulated for political gain.

Political support for reintegrative programs is difficult to achieve and maintain. Funding for secure facilities in Massachusetts and New York, as in many other states, has been far easier to obtain since the "get tough" movement of the 1980s than any other type or phase of juvenile correctional programming (Guarino-Ghezzi and Kimball 1986; Guarino-Ghezzi 1988; McGarrell 1988). This has translated into a loss of funding for community-based programs and reintegration or aftercare services that are provided from the time of program release to the age of majority.

Agency directors in the field of juvenile justice often are made vulnerable by their own local political colleagues, who seize on juvenile crime issues as a way to secure votes. The juvenile justice system is portrayed as soft and naive, providing expensive services without structure or accountability to undeserving, predatory juveniles, compared to a mythically potent adult system.

Directors of youth service agencies must be proactive in providing information to the media that will reduce the likelihood of unfair or inaccurate reporting. Agency heads should make themselves available to television, radio, and print journalists by scheduling yearly meetings with members of editorial boards at local newspapers and television and radio stations. At these meetings, agency directors can explain their organization's mission and operations, the needs of the agency, population trends, and strategies for managing internal and external forces.

Before leaving the meetings, directors would be well-advised to leave a public information packet for the editor and to request editorial support for their agency. The information furnished to the media often will be included in articles and editorials. Agency directors can also invite members of the media to do stories on the inner workings of programs. After ground rules are set vis-à-vis client confidentiality and other legal issues, the publicity can be beneficial for all parties.

In addition, strict administrative policies that hold agencies accountable for their decisions, such as classification systems and strong case management models, lend credibility to state correctional agencies and help them define realistic responsibilities.

Helping local media to understand the agency regulations and procedures that guide placement and other decisions will provide the necessary background and context for reporters' stories about incidents in which juveniles commit crimes in the community while under agency supervision.

Potential Holes in the System

Problems exist within any system. State juvenile correctional agencies should be particularly concerned about the limits of their authority and jurisdiction. For example, in most community-based correctional models, relying on private vendors to accept offenders allows providers to refuse the toughest juveniles.

Privately operated community-based programs, such as group homes and specialized schools, historically have used their own admission criteria to determine which juvenile offenders to accept. This is both good and bad. The good side is that community-based program operators assume risks with offenders, and they are in the best position to evaluate the juveniles with whom they can work. Particularly with small programs, private operators fear that one "inappropriate" juvenile (such as an arsonist) could be forced into the program without their consent and could seriously disrupt operations. The majority of providers would refuse a contract that did not allow them to have final approval on admissions. However, that should not stop state agencies from requiring clear admission criteria and selection procedures that are not arbitrary. Also, state agencies can monitor the admissions by keeping statistics on characteristics of offenders who are accepted, rejected, terminated early, and so on, to keep providers true to their objectives.

Unfortunately, private selection procedures can cause delays and leave behind a layer of undesirable juveniles. For example, Joe, who has run away from a group home in the past, attempted to assault a program staff person. The state placed Joe in a locked facility for a "cooling off" period and is now reattempting to place him in the community. He is not a violent offender, but he does have a problem with his temper. For months, he spends time in a locked detention facility as staff escort him from one private program to the next for referral interviews. It is a difficult period because Joe had presumed that the detention was temporary. It is also very expensive for the state to hold him there, and it absorbs considerable state employee time and effort to try to place him elsewhere.

Ultimately, if no program accepts Joe, he is sent home from detention. Therefore, in all probability, he will go from one unstable environment to another, without benefit of treatment in a structured community residence. To reduce this problem, vendor programs must be carefully monitored to ensure their admission decisions fulfill their contractual obligations. A potential long-term solution to placing difficult cases in the community might involve a centralized process of classifying low- and moderate-risk youths and then creating a moderate-risk pool of youths who are equitably divided among the various providers. This is similar to the way that automobile insurance is handled. Providers could favorably renegotiate their contracts in exchange for participation in the pool. This method would control against the development of placements of last resort, which are expected to be, and generally are, unsuccessful. It also would save considerable time for caseworkers who spend disproportionate energy attempting to place difficult cases in a privatized community-based system.

Safety and Treatment in Confined Settings

Confined settings are beneficial for correctional program providers for most of the reasons that community-based programs are not. Primarily, confined settings are guaranteed to protect the public in the short term—unless, of course, there is an escape, which may signal a clarion call to re-evaluate just how valuable such programs are. For example, in Alabama, community-based program advocates were helped in their efforts to curtail institutional expansion by a notorious offense in late 1989 in which a juvenile escaped from an institution and committed murder in the community (Special Education Bureau, Alabama Department of Education). That incident seemed to send a message that large institutions were not necessarily the best defenders of public safety.

Another way in which confined settings fail to protect the public is when they become crowded and release decisions are made based on logistical imperatives rather than public safety

---

Another way in which confined settings fail to protect the public is when they become crowded and release decisions are made based on logistical imperatives rather than public safety. The overincarceration of nonviolent committed juveniles has been demonstrated in a series of studies by the University of Michigan's Center for the Study of Youth Policy, including Alabama (DeMuro and Butts 1989), New Hampshire (Butts and DeMuro 1989), and Nebraska (Van Vleet and Butts 1990). Massachusetts does not overincarcerate committed juveniles because placement decisions are made according to the Department of Youth Services' classification guidelines, rather than by courts. However, Massachusetts' pretrial detention programs do suffer from crowding, as do many county systems, because they are under statutory obligation to accept all court-ordered juveniles.

Detention space is critical for short-term sanctions to teach juveniles that their behaviors in the community will produce consequences for them. Previously, in Massachusetts, detention space for administrative purposes, such as revocation of conditional liberty, competed with the demand for pretrial detention slots by the courts. This occurred because the Department of Youth Services operated pretrial detention programs on a statewide basis.

Typical scenarios included sending newly committed juveniles home, even before staff had an opportunity to conduct evaluations and develop treatment plans, to make room for juveniles on pretrial status. This problem was addressed by separating the two functions—pretrial detention and postcommitment detention—into different facilities. Today, however, the pretrial detention facilities are dangerously crowded for a variety of reasons, including statutory changes that have produced lengthier pretrial periods.

A study conducted by the Massachusetts Department of Youth Services (1987) identified patterns showing that the courts were inappropriately exercising their authority to detain juveniles on pretrial status. Although no status offenders were officially ordered into pretrial detention, half of the juveniles in pretrial detention were previously involved with the Department of Social Services, the agency that provides services for status offenders. Along with anecdotal information from caseworkers and court personnel, this suggested that Massachusetts' judges used pretrial detention as a way to control children who needed help that other social agencies, such as the Department of Social Services, could not or would not provide. Not coincidentally, this very group of indigent, nonserious offenders is the target group that pushed the court into its original existence (Bernard 1992). Indeed, a report by the Massachusetts Advocacy Center (1980) made it clear that a disproportionate number of girls, runaways, and generally needy children were being detained because the courts had no better alternatives.

Unfortunately, the existence of institutions often suppresses the development of creative alternatives, such as house arrest, which has been found to be a very effective substitute in Massachusetts and Florida. For example, in 1988, Florida's Broward County Juvenile Detention Center was unacceptably crowded and was the target of a class action lawsuit alleging crowded and unsafe conditions (Schwartz, Barton, and Orlando 1991).

One of the keys to reducing crowding was the knowledge that more than two-thirds of the detained juveniles were charged with nonviolent offenses, which suggested that many placements were needlessly incapacitating. A day center consisting of educational and recreational services was established with the Boys Clubs of Broward to supervise juveniles in the home detention program, and the Lutheran Ministries was recruited to manage a six-bed residential program for low-risk juveniles. As a result of those efforts, yearly admissions to secure detention declined by roughly 800 juveniles, or 22 percent, while admissions to home detention increased by roughly the same number of juveniles (Schwartz, Barton, and Orlando 1991).

Although these experiences highlight limitations of institutions in their primary role of incapacitating offenders, of even greater consequence is the failure of institutions to protect juveniles from one another, from abusive staff, as well as the failure to provide rehabilitative treatment.

Juvenile correctional agencies in the states of Alabama, Arizona, Delaware, Florida, and Oregon have been the subjects of litigation over the past fifteen years.

Florida, for example, was cited in a class action lawsuit for conditions including crowded and substandard living conditions, lack of security and discipline, inadequate medical and psychological care, cruel use of isolation, inadequacies in education and other programming, and inappropriate placements (*Bobby M.* v. *Martinez* 1983). A consent decree was signed by the plaintiffs and the Department of Health and Rehabilitative Services, which is responsible for all committed juvenile offenders. Elements of the negotiated settlement included the following mandates for the department:

- develop effective programs for violent juvenile offenders, specifically small intensive treatment and supervision programs
- develop specialized treatment programs for special needs juveniles, including sex offenders and mentally ill offenders
- generally, improve the quality of care for all committed juveniles
- establish an assessment, classification, and placement process to guide decision makers; develop a case management system
- end crowding in juvenile institutions
- develop community alternatives

An effective approach that anticipates the intrinsic limitations of confined settings is to design programs in ways that will prevent subcultures of violence or abuse from forming. Safety, program size, control of crowding, staff-to-juvenile ratio, program structure, rules and consequences, program components, staff training and supervision, and release decisions all apply.

Safety. Residents should have single rooms that are locked at night. Staff must be vigilant in observing behavior during the day and evening and be particularly attentive to residents who are especially vulnerable.

Program size. In Massachusetts, the working principle has been to limit secure facilities to an average of sixteen juveniles per program. While this increases the expense of the program, the Department of Youth Services tries to combine three programs into a "youth service center" so that economies of scale can be realized by combining food services and recreational facilities. Other than those specific common areas, the programs comprising the youth service centers are distinct and have their own directors, staff, special emphases, and program components.

Control of crowding. The Massachusetts Department of Youth Services runs both public and privately contracted secure facilities. An advantage of the private secure programs is that their contracts protect them from crowding. At the same time, the Massachusetts Department of Youth Services has an unusual arrangement with its privately contracted secure treatment programs in the sense that their contracts prevent the private programs from rejecting juveniles. The decisions are made by the Department of Youth Services' Secure Classification Panel and are guided by the programs' geographical location, its programming emphases, and waiting-list considerations.

It is always a concern that privately run programs might "cream" the best offenders and leave the most difficult offenders for the state. However, it is indicative of these private programs' desire to work with difficult juveniles that there are no differences in seriousness of offenses between private and public programs. In fact, a private program in Massachusetts made the decision to specialize in the treatment of violent sex offenders (Urban Institute 1989).

Staff-to-juvenile ratio. An obvious impediment to treatment and safety in secure facilities is lack of sufficient staff to provide educational, psychological, and other needed services, as well as to provide surveillance and enforce rules. In Massachusetts' secure treatment programs, the staff-to-juvenile ratio, on average, is two-to-one.

Program structure. Highly structured, active days with productive use of time is an essential aspect of good secure programs. Education programs should be approved by the special education bureau of the state's department of education and then by local school departments. They should have a certified teaching staff, so that juveniles can improve their grade level should they decide to return to high school. Programs also should provide opportunities for long-term residents to accumulate enough credits to graduate from high school. Evening and weekend shifts, traditionally the most difficult periods to manage, need to develop creative and challenging outlets for juveniles, perhaps by using community volunteers.

In Massachusetts' Worcester Secure Treatment Program, for example, an extensive volunteer program began with local clergy leading Bible study classes and slowly expanded by encouraging full-time staff to be creative in suggesting ideas. Staff brought in friends and associates to teach model car building and chess. The program also placed letters in student newspapers and recruited dozens of college students who provided tutoring and recreational services. Carlo Morrisey, the former program director and now director of treatment in the Department of Youth Services, cites the importance of bringing a wide variety of people to enhance—not replace—existing staff and services to increase residents' knowledge of opportunities and their access to them (Morrisey, personal communication, May 1994).

Rules and consequences. It is well known that juvenile offenders typically have unstable backgrounds as well as experience with authority figures who have been inconsistent in their use of discipline. A great deal of program effort is often needed to teach juveniles that behaviors have consequences and to monitor staff so that rule violations are quickly and consistently addressed.

Massachusetts' secure programs rely on a rewards-based level system, by which most violations result in the removal of a privilege rather than the application of a punishment. Expectations are spelled out clearly for residents based on program activities, and privileges are increased (or reduced) as juveniles advance (or regress) through program levels. For example, if a juvenile fails to wake up in the morning after two wake-up calls, points are deducted from his or her weekly score. This affects the juvenile's eligibility for privileges, such as extra phone calls, an allowance, a later bedtime, or the choice of a room.

Program components. Programs need to develop a range of services that will allow them to provide individualized treatment and anticipate the need for new treatment models as offender populations and their external environments change. Education must range from special education and Chapter One, education for the disadvantaged, programs to regular high school curricula and college extension courses.

Counseling must include specialized treatment for sex offenders and substance abusers. Group and individual therapy must be provided. Skills training must be periodically evaluated to be sure it targets marketable fields. A critical component for secure programs is reintegration planning, including family visits, family therapy, selection of aftercare programming, and discussions with juveniles about their lives after they leave the secure program to help them develop realistic expectations. A full range of medical services also must be available to residents.

Staff training and supervision. Inconsistent messages within programs are a potential problem, particularly because different staff levels—such as line staff versus counselors—have different backgrounds and perspectives. Line staff must be trained and carefully supervised to ensure that they do not unintentionally undermine the efforts of the counseling staff, for instance, by shaming or humiliating a sex offender who needs to build self-confidence. Local colleges can assist in developing and operating a preservice training program for the youth service staff to supplement the existing in-service training that agencies should regularly provide in such areas as AIDS, mental health needs of juveniles, sex offender treatment, and suicide prevention.

Release decisions. Prison expert John Irwin (1980) has found that indeterminate sentences lead to manipulation of offenders by staff, as well as to frustration, anger, and hostility among offenders (American Friends Service Committee 1971). In the case of offenders who have serious psychological problems, indeterminate sentences may be a necessary evil. However, the norm should be that offenders be given some fairly reliable estimation of their period of confinement, perhaps within a short range, assuming that their participation in the program is acceptable.

Fighting the Panacea Phenomenon

To add confusion to the delicate balancing act in states' juvenile justice systems, several types of programs have been shown empirically to have little effect, or even negative effects, on juvenile offenders, despite a certain panacea mystique. The first is the assortment of so-called "Scared Straight" programs, which are still popular, despite data showing that the programs have no positive effect on juveniles and may, indeed, have an adverse effect (Finckenauer 1982).

Boot Camps. The second is the "boot camp" approach, which is supported by those who believe that discipline is the answer to juvenile delinquency, and the military model is the most effective way of imposing discipline. However, research on boot camps reveals the following (MacKenzie 1991; MacKenzie, Shaw, and Souryal 1992; Parent 1993b): First, there is no evidence that existing boot camps significantly affect graduates' recidivism rates. Second, boot camps do nothing to alleviate crowding in residential facilities and will actually increase incarcerations (unless more than 80 percent of those admitted to boot camps would have served prison terms if boot camps did not exist, a standard which is not being applied). Third, boot camps are least effective with juveniles.

One appeal of correctional boot camps is that they sidestep the difficult task of combining diverse goals. With few exceptions, boot camps offer no claims of treatment, no protection of juveniles from negative environmental influences, no opportunities for offenders to take risks, and no intensive follow-up supervision.

Their philosophy is to instill discipline during a brief period of time, in a setting that incapacitates offenders apart from the community—a relatively unambitious objective. Another appeal of correctional boot camps is that they capitalize on the historical affinity between the military and control of offenders.

Policies created during the Vietnam War permitted juvenile offenders who were confined to substitute real boot camp for their institutional sentence. Offering themselves as human capital in wartime provided offenders with instant value that they could not easily have gained otherwise, given their limited opportunities.

Do correctional boot camps accomplish the goal of turning offenders' lives around? Although they may be effective in instilling compliance in the short term, if boot camps fail to provide programs to address services and needs, such as education and employment, and if they do not provide intensive follow-up supervision, their value in reducing recidivism clearly seems to be limited. The problems of using correctional boot camps for juvenile offenders arise from juveniles' general distrust of authority, which is often accompanied by backgrounds of parental abuse and a need for diverse services to match their individual educational and skill levels. Offenders who need self-discipline resist such a blatant model of control. Discipline can be instilled far more effectively by using more subtle, informal controls that do not risk rebellion or further alienation of the juvenile, and that fit in with other needed services, such as educational and counseling programs.

Like stable families, effective juvenile justice systems can achieve complex goals by developing multidimensional programs and policies that adhere to basic, unwavering principles. While juvenile offenders should be held accountable for their crimes, it is equally urgent that their development not be derailed by parents, politicians, juvenile justice officials, and other overseeing adults. Improvements to the juvenile justice system must come from working not only with juveniles but with adults. For the existing pool of at-risk youths, if adult actions—including neglect, abuse, the rescinding of resources, and the sending of inconsistent and stigmatizing messages—do not change, the youth will become adult offenders and not develop as healthy young adults.

References

Altschuler, D. M. 1984. Community reintegration in juvenile offender programming. In *Violent juvenile offenders,* ed. R. A. Mathias. San Francisco: National Council on Crime and Delinquency.

Altschuler, D. M., and T. L. Armstrong. 1991. Intensive aftercare for the high-risk juvenile parolee: Issues and approaches in reintegration and community supervision. In *Intensive interventions with high-risk youths: Promising approaches in juvenile probation and parole,* ed. T. Armstrong. Monsey, N.Y.: Criminal Justice Press.

American Friends Service Committee. 1971. *Struggle for justice.* New York: Hill and Wang.

Bernard, T. J. 1992. *The cycle of juvenile justice.* New York: Oxford University Press.

Boston Globe. State prison officials say furloughs have decreased over the past year, 11 June 1989, p. 51.

Burkholder, S. 1989. The Lawrence Eagle-Tribune and the Willie Horton story. *Washington Journalism Review* (July/August): 14-9.

Butts, J. A., and P. DeMuro. 1989. *Risk assessment of adjudicated delinquents.* Ann Arbor, Mich.: Center for the Study of Youth Policy (December).

Commonwealth of Massachusetts Legislative Research Council. 1986. *Report relative to prisons for profit.* House Report No. 6225, July 31.

DeMuro, P., and J. A. Butts. 1989. *At the crossroads: A population profile of youths committed to the Alabama Department of Youth Services.* Prepared for the Alabama Department of Youth Services.

Finckenauer, J. O. 1982. *Scared straight! and the panacea phenomenon.* Englewood Cliffs, N.J.: Prentice-Hall.

Gendreau, P., and R. R. Ross. 1991. Correctional treatment: Some recommendations for effective intervention. In *The dilemmas of corrections*, ed. K. Haas and G. Alpert. Prospect Heights, Ill.: Waveland Press.

Greenwood, P. 1986. Promising approaches for the rehabilitation or prevention of chronic juvenile offenders. In *Intervention strategies for chronic juvenile offenders*, ed. P. Greenwood. New York: Greenwood Press.

Guarino-Ghezzi, S. 1988. Initiating change in Massachusetts' juvenile correctional system: A retrospective analysis. *Criminal Justice Review* 13(1): 1-12.

——. 1994. Reintegrative police surveillance of juvenile offenders: Forging an urban model. *Crime and Delinquency* 40(2): 131-53.

Guarino-Ghezzi, S., and L. Kimball. 1986. Reforming justice by geography: organizational responses to the problem of juvenile crime. *Law and Policy* 8(4): 419-36.

Guarino-Ghezzi, S., and J. M. Byrne. 1989. Developing a model of structured decision making in juvenile corrections: The Massachusetts experience. *Crime and Delinquency* 35(2): 270-302.

Hackett, J. C., et al. 1987. *Issues in contracting for the private operation of prisons and jails.* Washington, D.C.: Council for State Governments and the Urban Institute.

Irwin, J. 1980. *Prisons in turmoil.* Boston: Little, Brown and Co., Inc.

Krisberg, B., J. Austin, and P. A. Steele. 1989. *Unlocking juvenile corrections: Evaluating the Massachusetts Department of Youth Services.* San Francisco: National Council on Crime and Delinquency.

LeClair, D. P., and S. Guarino-Ghezzi. 1991. Does incapacitation guarantee public safety? Lessons from the Massachusetts furlough and prerelease programs. *Justice Quarterly* 8(1): 8–36.

Leaf, G. 1988. A history of the internal organization of the state reform school for boys at Westborough, Massachusetts (1846–1974). Unpublished Doctoral Thesis, Harvard University.

Loughran, E. J. 1988. Privatization in juvenile services. *Corrections Today* 50(6): 6.

MacKenzie, D. L. 1991. The parole performance of offenders released from shock incarceration (boot camp prisons): a survival time analysis. *Journal of Quantitative Criminology* 7(3): 213–36.

MacKenzie, D. L., J. W. Shaw, and C. Souryal. 1992. Characteristics associated with successful adjustment to supervision: a comparison of parolees, probationers, shock participants, and shock dropouts. *Criminal Justice and Behavior* 19(14): 437-54.

Massachusetts Advocacy Center. 1980. *Delinquent justice: Juvenile detention practice in Massachusetts.* Boston: Massachusetts Advocacy Center.

Massachusetts Department of Youth Services. 1987. Interim report: Pretrial detention; a comparative study. July 31. Boston: Massachusetts Department of Youth Services.

McGarrell, E. F. 1988. *Juvenile correctional reform.* Albany, N.Y.: State University of New York Press.

Morrisey, C. Personal communication to authors, May 1994.

New York Times. 1989, August 27. Administration moves to curb prison furloughs, p. 20.

Palmer, T. 1984. Treatment and the role of classification: A review of the basics. *Crime and Delinquency* 30(2): 256–68.

Parent, D. 1993a. Conditions of confinement. *Juvenile Justice* 1: 2-23.

——. 1993b. Boot camps failing to achieve goals. *Overcrowded Times* 4 (4): 1-15.

Paternoster, R. 1989. Decisions to participate in and desist from four types of common delinquency: Deterrence and the rational choice perspective. *Law and Society Review* 23(1): 7–40.

Schneider, A. L., and L. Ervin. 1990. Specific deterrence, rational choice, and decision heuristics: Applications in juvenile justice. *Social Science Quarterly* 71(3): 585–601.

Schneider, A. L., and D. D. Schram. 1980. A proposal to assess the implementation and impact of Washington's juvenile justice legislation. Seattle, WA.

Schwartz, I. M., W. H. Barton, and F. Orlando. 1991. Keeping kids out of secure detention. *Public Welfare* 46(Spring): 20–6.

Snyder, H. N., et al. 1990. *Juvenile court statistics 1988.* Pittsburgh: National Center for Juvenile Justice.

Urban Institute. 1989. *Comparison of privately and publicly operated corrections facilities in Kentucky and Massachusetts.* Washington, D.C.: The Urban Institute.

Van Vleet, R., and J. A. Butts. 1990. *Risk assessment of committed delinquents; Nebraska Youth Development Center.* Ann Arbor, Mich.: University of Michigan, Center for the Study of Youth Policy.

3   A Community Perspective: Organizational and Management Implications to Creating Alternatives to Juvenile Court

Melody G. Scofield and
William S. Davidson II, Ph.D.

In the mid-eighteenth century, the concept of "adolescence" as a discrete period of life was emerging (Santrock 1990). This historical transformation developed as a result of changes in family functioning with the Industrial Revolution. Gradually, work became centered outside the home and emphasis on educating the young increased. Previously, children's work had been essential to family well-being, education was secondary. Young people spent relatively little time with their peers, and juvenile crime was not a meaningful social issue (Empey 1982).

With this change, adolescence became an extension of childhood, and young people, who formerly had been part of the family survival unit, now had to be supported and retained within the family structure for an extended time. Inevitably, according to Empey (1982), some families were not up to the task, and young people began to come to public attention as a threat to the established order of society.

Prior to this time, criminal activities were not divided into adult and juvenile categories. Delinquent juveniles were either handled in the adult court system or informally processed and placed in houses of refuge (Krisberg and Austin 1978; Trojanowicz and Morash 1987). Houses of refuge took on the dual tasks of caring for and reforming problem juveniles:

> First, they were designed to house, not merely juvenile criminals, but all problem children: the runaway, disobedient, or vagrant children who were in danger of falling prey to loose women, taverns, gambling halls, or theaters. Given what they considered to be

Melody G. Scofield is a doctoral candidate in the Ecological/Community Psychology Program at Michigan State University in East Lansing; Dr. William S. Davidson II is a professor of psychology and chair of the Ecological/Community Psychology Graduate Program at Michigan State University, in East Lansing.

laudatory goals, reformers were not bothered by any thought that they might be infringing on the rights or wishes of these children. A good dose of institutionalization could only work to the child's benefit.

Second, the people who sponsored and managed the first houses of refuge took the public school, not the family, as the model to be emulated. Children would be saved through education, hard work, and stringent discipline rather than through the loving care of parental surrogates.

The whole community is deeply interested in its accomplishments. It has for its object employment of the idle;—instruction of the ignorant;—reformation of the depraved;—relief of the wretched;—a general diffusion of good morals;—enlargement of virtuous society;—and the universal protection of property and life. (Empey 1982)

Houses of refuge were meant to serve as alternatives to prison for wayward juveniles. Unfortunately, they became convenient holding pens for greater numbers of marginal juveniles (Morash and Trojanowicz 1986). Further, many juveniles were still being sent to prison (Krisberg and Austin 1978). Changes were clearly needed.

Ultimately, a separate juvenile justice system was created, beginning in Illinois in 1899. Because it was distinct from the adult system, it could function as a concerned parent, as well as a rehabilitation and deterrence agency (Mennel 1972; Schultz 1973). Under this system, juveniles' misbehaviors were perceived as youthful wrongdoing rather than criminal activity.

Consequently, the court acted as a caretaker, providing direction and looking out for juveniles' best interests. In return for this protected treatment, minors' constitutional rights were nonexistent (Empey 1982).

During a decade of great changes in constitutional law, juveniles' treatment within the juvenile justice system was challenged. In 1967, the Supreme Court ruled in *In re Gault* that juveniles, like adults, were entitled to due process protection. The result was an increased procedural formality when addressing crimes committed by juveniles (Empey 1982).

Concomitantly, treatment effectiveness was being challenged. Reviews of traditional approaches, such as incarceration and psychotherapy, for handling juvenile delinquents concluded that such approaches were not especially effective (Grey and Dermody 1972; Kahn 1965; Levitt 1971; Lipton, Martinson, and Wilks 1975; Romig 1978). Recidivism rates for juvenile institutions ranged from 50 to 80 percent (Stephenson and Scarpitti 1969).

Specifically, in the late 1960s and early 1970s, Lipton, Martinson, and Wilks (1975) argued that punishment had failed, and new treatments had to be developed and implemented (President's Commission on Law Enforcement and the Administration of Justice 1967).

Advocates of symbolic interactionism questioned the assumptions about the causes of delinquency and challenged research that purported to explain delinquent behavior of all adolescents. This work was viewed as too narrow in focus because data had been drawn only from juveniles who came into contact with the police and courts. This had resulted in the inaccurate conclusions that delinquency was a rare phenomena that existed only within the lower social classes. Studies of juveniles' self-reported delinquent activities found that such behaviors were actually widespread, and not necessarily related to social class (Williams and Gold 1972).

Historically, the 1960s saw social commentators turn away from individual characteristics to explain many social problems, including juvenile delinquency. Instead, environmental and societal circumstances, such as poverty and segregation by race, and the general failure of social institutions like schools to deliver the services they were created to provide, were called on to explain the source of problem behavior (Empey 1982). Within this framework, exceptionalistic explanations of delinquency (i.e., those focusing on individual differences) were inadequate (Ryan 1971).

Still, the problem of juvenile crime was not abating, and it was (and still is) common wisdom that juvenile antisocial behavior tends to produce antisocial behavior in adulthood. Intervention with juveniles, therefore, held at least theoretical promise of preventing crime during adulthood (Fareta 1981; Loeber and Stouthamer-Loeber 1987; Patterson 1986; Robins 1981). Further, because of their young age, juveniles were considered amenable to positive change. Hence, favorable attention was given to a focus on alternative interventions with troubled juveniles. Such programs, if successful, had the potential to address an important social issue.

The Adolescent Diversion Project

Within this social and historical setting, the Adolescent Diversion Project was born. The Adolescent Diversion Project is a community-based prevention project that uses paraprofessionals and volunteers to divert juvenile law-breakers from the traditional juvenile justice system. The Adolescent Diversion Project began in Champaign-Urbana, Illinois, in 1972.

Theoretical Foundations

The Adolescent Diversion Project grew out of three theoretical positions: environmental differences theory, social control/social learning theory, and social labeling theory. The overwhelming majority of juvenile delinquents were (and continue to be) male; these theories were meant only to explain the behavior of male juveniles. There was little consideration of their application to female juveniles. Similarly, from its inception, the Adolescent Diversion Project has worked almost exclusively with males. These theoretical foundations are appropriate for the majority of the juveniles that the Adolescent Diversion Project serves.

Environmental Differences Theories

Environmental differences theories emerged from observations that aggressive behavior is not equally present in all societies, suggesting that cultural factors play a role in creating antisocial behavior. Focusing on macro-level social variables, some researchers suggested that anomie, or normlessness, occurs in complex, capitalistic societies where the expectation of acquiring materialistic possessions is present for everyone, but opportunities to obtain such goods are not equal (Cloward and Ohlin 1960; Merton 1957). Unequal access to the trappings of middle- or upper-class status pressures people to act in deviant ways because legitimate modes of access are differentially unattainable.

Social Learning and Social Control Theories

Social control theories (Hirschi 1969) attempt to explain the ways in which environmental factors, at the interpersonal level of analysis, may lead to illegal behavior by juveniles. Hirschi speculated that juveniles' "bondedness" to society prevents antisocial behavior.

Rather than attempt to explain delinquency per se, Hirschi undertook to explain the mechanisms that prevent criminal acts. In other words, he asked why people *are not* criminals. According to Hirschi, four components comprise juveniles' bond: attachment to others, commitment to traditional goals, involvement in legitimate social activities, and belief in the validity of social norms. When these bonds are severed or nonexistent, the stage is set for the occurrence of delinquent behavior.

A related set of propositions also attempts to explain delinquent behavior at the micro-environmental level. Social learning theory holds that delinquent juveniles have been differentially reinforced for illegal activity (Akers 1977; Patterson 1986). Specifically, they have been differentially exposed to illegal behavior, differentially reinforced for engaging in delinquent behavior, and have failed to be exposed to or reinforced for prosocial behavior. Therefore, such illegal activity is likely to be repeated. To the extent that juveniles believe illegal activity is associated with reward rather than punishment, they are more likely to engage in criminal behavior (Chesney-Lind 1989).

Although some proponents of social control and social learning theory, such as Hirschi (1969) and Matsueda (1982), argue that their theoretical positions are irreconcilable, it is plausible to view them as explanations of perspectives on the same phenomena which apparently lead to the process of becoming delinquent. Within this framework, Hirschi's control theory focuses on the attitudes, beliefs, and values that comprise "bondedness," and social learning theory focuses on the processes (differential association) by which "bondedness" develops (Davidson et al. 1990).

Social Labeling Theory

Finally, social labeling theory holds that delinquency can only be understood as an interaction between individuals and society's response to their behavior. As such, society defines deviants and actually creates deviants through labeling (Becker 1963). Certain behaviors were "designated as crimes when they were repugnant to persons with sufficient political power to have the law impose their standards of conduct on others" (Glaser 1975).

Labeling has at least two consequences for juvenile delinquents. First, juvenile court has created "crimes" that are the result of juveniles' minor status, such as truancy and running away (Schur 1973). Status offenses—crimes for which one can be charged only if one is a minor—lead labeling theorists to point out that this is a clear example of those in power using their authority to criminalize unwanted behavior.

Since there is no single cause of delinquency, there can be no single panacea.

Second, a comparison of self-reported measures of delinquent behavior and court statistics (Elliot, Huizinga, and Ageton 1985; Gold 1970) reveals that becoming delinquent has as much to do with individual circumstances of the alleged perpetrator and the complainant or observer as it does with the actual illegal behavior. Low socio-economic class and minority juveniles continue to be overrepresented in official court records (Bynum, Wordes, and Corley 1993), despite evidence that illegal behavior is common among all juveniles.

The Adolescent Diversion Project in Action

The Adolescent Diversion Project was born out of these three theoretical traditions. In practice, the Adolescent Diversion Project diverts juveniles in legal jeopardy from the court system (thus avoiding labeling) and works to provide resources and behavioral change in the juvenile's natural environment. Once diverted, individualized intense interventions focus on positive environmental changes. The Adolescent Diversion Project's goals are to work for positive change, to involve others in the juvenile's environment to achieve that change, and to respond to the juvenile's specific needs.

Since there is no single cause of delinquency, there can be no single panacea (Shinn 1990). To be successful, interventions must address multiple levels of change. Through efforts that include multiple environmental components, juveniles who previously may have "slipped through the cracks" can be helped to pursue prosocial community interactions, such as employment and education.

Davidson and others (1990) outlined the key components of the Adolescent Diversion Project that follow from its theoretical framework: community-based intervention, the use of volunteers, an alternative to more traditional approaches to juvenile services, diversion from juvenile detention, and an emphasis on the juvenile's strengths.

First, an intervention that took place within the community in which the juvenile lived was expected to yield the most lasting positive effects. Second, use of volunteers rather than professionals was seen as an economical choice, as well as had the potential to provide juveniles with a more concentrated, positive interaction. This approach was less likely to include the labeling effects often resulting from criminal justice system intervention. Third, diversion from the traditional system for addressing juvenile crime had significant policy implications, suggesting that assistance to many troubled juveniles might best be provided outside the juvenile court system. Further, diverting juvenile offenders from environments, such as jails and juvenile detention centers, where they could learn additional undesirable behavior, was a fourth consideration. Finally, the project was designed to avoid a "blaming-the-victim" (Ryan 1971) approach to juveniles. Instead, its purpose was to find a means to identify and build upon juveniles' strengths (Rappaport et al. 1975).

Advocacy is a way for juveniles and their families to become involved in prosocial communities and find avenues through which to attain goals.

The project uses a two-pronged approach to helping juveniles avoid involvement with the juvenile justice system: advocacy for the juvenile and his or her family and behavioral contracting. The focus on advocacy efforts for the juvenile and his or her family rests on the assumption that resources necessary to negotiate successfully throughout life, although often available, are not always easily accessible. For example, volunteers may help their juveniles by working within the school system if it is a source of conflict. Advocates can provide help in getting a job, such as helping with completion of applications, giving advice about what to wear to an interview, and conducting role plays in which they practice questions one might expect to be asked by a potential employer. Volunteers also may be advocating on behalf of parents, perhaps helping them locate resources for completing their General Education Diploma, assisting with housing needs, or providing alternatives to physical punishment as a means of discipline. Throughout advocacy efforts, volunteers involve the juveniles and their families in the process so that they can learn to successfully advocate for themselves in the future. Advocacy is a way for juveniles and their families to become involved in prosocial communities and find avenues through which to attain goals. The specific advocacy model employed was originally detailed in Davidson and Rapp (1976) and Davidson and Rappaport (1978).

The other essential component to the project is behavioral contracting. The contracts are interpersonal agreements between the juvenile and significant others in his or her life and emphasize a balance of reciprocal rights and responsibilities. Through behavioral contracting, juveniles can increase the quantity and quality of their prosocial interactions with others. Behavioral contracting (Stuart 1971) draws heavily on other interpersonal skill-oriented approaches, such as child management skills (Patterson 1975) and Aggression Replacement Training (Goldstein and Glick 1987).

Juveniles are referred to the Adolescent Diversion Project by the intake division of the local juvenile court. During intake, the Adolescent Diversion Project staff explain the program and seek cooperation from the juveniles and their families. Those who agree to participate commit to an eighteen-week intervention. (More than 95 percent agree to participate.) Eighteen weeks allows sufficient time to make changes, yet is short enough to avoid dependency. It also provides a benchmark for holding all parties accountable within a specific time frame. Juveniles who have been charged with all but the most violent crimes, such as rape or attempted murder, may be referred to the Adolescent Diversion Project.

The project currently uses undergraduate students, who receive course credit, as change agents. The Adolescent Diversion Project also has used community college students and community volunteers. Research indicates that each of these different groups can be as effective, but community college students and community volunteers are more expensive to recruit and supervise than students at major universities (Davidson et al. 1990).

Undergraduate students who work as advocates for the juvenile commit two consecutive semesters to the intervention. During the first ten weeks, undergraduates receive instruction in the philosophy and implementation of the intervention, the specific skills of child advocacy and behavioral contracting, and an orientation to juveniles. The learning format is a combination of readings, written and oral quizzes, and role plays. To ensure adequate understanding of the material, a mastery model of training is used. Students' performance must be greater than 80 percent on each assignment before proceeding to the next unit.

Following the initial instruction, each undergraduate is assigned a juvenile with whom to work. Juveniles range in age from nine to seventeen years. The program accepts both male and female juveniles, although approximately 80 percent of the juveniles are males. Male undergraduates work only with male juveniles, and although female undergraduates may be assigned a male juvenile, every attempt is made to match race and gender of juvenile and undergraduate.

The public is less and less willing to accept a deterrence model for working with juvenile delinquents. Instead, punishment has become the treatment of choice.

For the next eighteen weeks the juvenile and undergraduate spend between six and eight hours together weekly, spanning at least two days per week. The undergraduate and juvenile identify areas to work on in the juvenile's life. The most common areas of intervention are school, employment, free-time activities, and relationships with parents and peers. Both advocacy and contracting are undertaken to help the juvenile achieve his or her goals. During the intervention, undergraduates receive weekly supervision and support from two supervisors in a group setting that includes three-to-six other undergraduate advocates. Groups of undergraduates proceed together through the intervention sequence, thus enhancing the degree of cohesion and level of support each undergraduate receives.

At the intervention's end, the advocate prepares a "termination packet" for the juvenile. The packet consists of tips, reminders, and information regarding the areas in which the juvenile and the undergraduate have worked. Undergraduates are also urged to anticipate the juvenile's upcoming needs and to include information for those needs, as well. During the last official meeting between the juvenile and the undergraduate, they review the contents of the packet. This process serves as a reminder of how far the juvenile has come during the intervention, and it also provides the juveniles with a prompt to take advantage of the information contained in the packet when they need help.

The Adolescent Diversion Project has made a positive impact upon a variety of areas. Research shows that the project reduces crime by approximately 50 percent (Davidson et al. 1990; Davidson and Johnson 1992; Davidson and Redner 1988). In addition, it appears that the project keeps many juveniles more involved with their families or school. (Although the Adolescent Diversion Project volunteers work with both male and female juveniles, project efficacy has been empirically tested only on male juveniles. Therefore, conclusions about program success with female juveniles are unavailable.)

The project has other beneficial effects. The undergraduates show signifi-cant attitude change. Over time, they are more likely to display positive at-titudes toward the juveniles and less positive attitudes toward the criminal justice system. This finding suggests a greater understanding and toler-ance of individuals, combined with increased concerns regarding the effec-tiveness of the overall system. Further, undergraduates are more likely to go on to graduate school and remain in the human service field. These ef-fects have been replicated in several studies in multiple settings (Davidson et al. 1990; Davidson and Redner 1988).

Current Situation

The social and political situation in which the Adolescent Diversion Proj-ect finds itself today is considerably different from its origin. The United States has become an increasingly violent place in which to live, making people afraid in their homes and in their neighborhoods. A politically con-servative, get-tough-on-crime attitude extends to juvenile offenders. Al-though total numbers are still relatively low, the number of young people who are victims, as well as perpetrators of violent crime, has increased. The public is less and less willing to accept a deterrence model for working with juvenile delinquents. Instead, punishment has become the treatment of choice.

Although violent juvenile crime receives considerable media attention, leading to a strong perception that juveniles are likely to be violent, the ac-tual crime profile of juvenile offenders has not changed dramatically dur-ing the past twenty years. The majority of juvenile crimes, then and now, are property offenses, such as theft and vandalism. Juveniles committed 51.7 percent of crimes against property in 1970 (Federal Bureau of Investi-gation 1970). That number declined to 31.9 percent by 1990 (Federal Bu-reau of Investigation 1990). Similarly, the Federal Bureau of Investigation reported that juveniles committed 16.2 percent of violent crimes in 1990, down from 22.6 percent in 1970.

Within this context, the Adolescent Diversion Project, with its social learning, environmental resources, and antilabeling focus, survives under markedly different circumstances than were present at its inception. Al-though the Adolescent Diversion Project has progressed from a research project to a service provided by a county government, statistics comparing juveniles who go through the court compared to the Adolescent Diversion Project continue to show that the Adolescent Diversion Project produces a lower recidivism rate than does the court system.

Clash of Values

Placing the Adolescent Diversion Project in contrast to the juvenile jus-tice system, as well as recognizing it as a supplement to that system, results in a clash of values at many levels (Davidson and Saul 1982). Beyond treatment style, another issue is that of responsibility. The Adolescent Diversion Project is based on the belief that troubled juveniles lack access to important resources, but such resources must be mobilized on behalf of the juvenile. However, there is no governmental entity responsible for ensuring that such resources are available.

The Adolescent Diversion Project acts as a liaison between agencies and social institutions that were established to benefit juveniles (both delinquent and nondelinquent) and the juveniles in their program. As liaison, the Adolescent Diversion Project helps these service agencies make greater efforts to serve the juveniles. For example, schools are an important aspect of a juvenile's life. Juveniles who do well in school are less likely to be involved with the juvenile court system (Bowman 1959; Chesney-Lind 1989; Gold and Petronio 1980). This finding suggests that positive interactions with teachers, along with motivation and ability to achieve, helps deter juvenile crime.

Unfortunately, many juveniles who find themselves involved with the court and with the Adolescent Diversion Project are not successful at school. To increase opportunities for success, teachers and other school staff members must be willing to work on the juvenile's behalf. Gaining the cooperation of school staff for a delinquent juvenile is difficult. School staff are not rewarded for fulfilling a change-agent role for troubled juveniles and are reluctant to get involved in the way such juveniles need.

Further, even though some forward-looking schools have created reinforcement incentives for students who succeed, juveniles most in need of reinforcement for small steps in the right direction are often excluded from these incentive systems. This oversight is because their gains, while large compared to their past performance, are not enough to meet standards set for nontroubled students. Advocates must enter into such situations and negotiate for what may well be seen as "special" treatment for a young person who school staff believe is a problem and a bad example for other students.

... juveniles who have an involved, caring parent are less likely to come into contact with the juvenile court ....

In one case, with the encouragement of his advocate, "Phillip," a high school sophomore, improved from typically attending classes unprepared to regularly carrying a pencil, paper, and textbook to class. As a result of his increased preparedness, Phillip's grades soon moved from failing to average. The advocate was unsuccessful at getting official school recognition of Phillip's significant accomplishments, because only "superior" performance was reinforced. It is clear, however, that this student's performance was indeed superior compared to his previous efforts. The happy ending to this story is that the advocate persuaded individual teachers to recognize and praise the student's efforts and, in turn, the student continued to improve. This example illustrates the backdoor approach that advocates must often take to enlist the help of significant adults to gain resources for their juveniles. It also demonstrates that use of official power, such as the authority of the courts, is not the only way to accomplish change.

Similar to students whose efforts are recognized and appreciated by their teachers, juveniles who have an involved, caring parent are less likely to come into contact with the juvenile court (Chesney-Lind 1989; Offord and Boyle 1988). However, involving parents and persuading them to alter their parenting style is often met with resistance. Of course, some parents respond wholeheartedly to suggestions and guidance about spending more time with their child, praising his or her accomplishments, monitoring homework, or being consistent with discipline. Others, however, are anxious for a solution to their juvenile's problem behavior, but are reluctant to make personal changes that have the potential to benefit the juvenile. If the advocate cannot gain full family cooperation, the advocate will seek alternatives.

In one intervention, the advocate, Maureen, quickly pinpointed responses ranging from indifferent to hostile from Ms. Brown toward her daughter, Tonya. At the same time, the advocate observed the daughter making occasional efforts to please her mother.

The advocate's case notes revealed that Ms. Brown was quick to criticize her sixteen-year-old daughter for being lazy. Her complaints were that Tonya did not do enough around the house, refused to care for her younger siblings, and was never around when her mother needed her. Maureen mentally noted that Tonya was washing dishes on several consecutive days when she arrived for their meetings. She also noticed that Tonya's siblings often went to her with requests for assistance before approaching their mother, and that their mother sent them to Tonya when they did ask her first. Tonya, though often impatient with her brothers and sister, tied shoelaces, sounded out reading words, and resolved disagreements for them. Further, Tonya worked part-time at a candy store at a local mall, and maintained a C average at school.

At first Maureen simply voiced her observations to Ms. Brown. Ms. Brown agreed with Maureen's comments, but responded that Tonya had to be told to do her chores, and that as a child, she (Ms. Brown) had worked without being asked. Maureen then began a campaign to praise Tonya, within her mother's hearing, whenever she did a household task or helped a sibling. Usually, Ms. Brown appeared not to notice. Maureen and Tonya also studied together, and as Tonya's grades began to improve, Maureen showed Ms. Brown her daughter's graded papers and tests and invited her praise for Tonya's accomplishments. Ms. Brown begrudgingly complimented Tonya and then indifferently set the papers aside.

Tonya liked her job and in the six months she had been working there had received a raise and increased responsibility to close the store at night. Maureen congratulated Tonya, who, in turn, glowed with pride and revealed that her boss had said Tonya was the most dependable teen worker she had ever employed.

Unfortunately, Tonya's mother was not impressed. Maureen also visited Tonya's teachers to let them know that she was working hard and to ask them to notice and acknowledge her efforts. The teachers responded positively and verified that they had recently noticed a more dedicated effort from Tonya. Although it was not possible to influence her mother's attitude toward Tonya, Maureen was able to increase positive interactions between Tonya and significant adults in her life at school and to help Tonya recognize her value to her employer. Consequently, her grades improved and she came to see herself as a responsible, hardworking young woman.

No Official Role

By its nature, the Adolescent Diversion Project is an alternative service delivery program, operating with paraprofessional volunteers to accomplish its goals. Lack of standing as an "official agency" puts the Adolescent Diversion Project in a tenuous position with regard to the settings in which it operates. Working in such settings is a sensitive endeavor. The Adolescent Diversion Project administrators and advocates must seek and carefully maintain cooperation. For example, the Adolescent Diversion Project's interactions with school officials range from exceptionally positive, expressed by comments such as "How do kids get into your program? I know some others who would benefit from your work," to inordinately negative, expressed by comments such as "You come in here, raise the juvenile's expectations, and then eighteen weeks later you're gone. How can that be helpful?" Many factors influence such interactions. Personality styles of the advocate and school staff, prior perceptions of the juvenile, the advocate's approach, and questions about the advocate's purpose in involving school staff may play a part in making the relationship that forms, or fails to form, between the juvenile, school staff, and the advocate.

Although advocates receive formal consent to discuss the juvenile, ultimately the decision to work with the advocate to aid a juvenile lies with individual school staff members. Staff who disagree with the Adolescent Diversion Project philosophy or who choose not to be helpful cannot be compelled to do so. In such situations, the Adolescent Diversion Project's success will depend on the advocate finding another way to help the juvenile, as demonstrated by the following example from an advocate's case notes:

Julian's standardized test scores revealed that he was far above average intelligence. Similarly, until tenth grade, his A and B grades reflected his superior performance. But, in tenth grade, Julian began to skip classes, and when he did attend, he did not participate.

Consequently, he fell farther behind and eventually failed the first semester of tenth grade. Then he was apprehended with a small amount of marijuana, went to court, and was referred to Diversion. Julian's advocate, Dantaya, quickly began working to get Julian back up to speed in school.

Unfortunately, most of his teachers believed he was a lost cause. They had taught his older brother before him, and although the brother was also bright, he had been a "failure." They had no reason to expect more from Julian. Unable to enlist the cooperation of Julian's teachers, Dantaya and Julian began doing homework together. She encouraged him to attend school, take his books and supplies to class, and turn in his work on time. She talked with him by phone or in-person daily, checking to see how school had been that day, praising his accomplishments, and prodding him to continue to improve.

As he progressed, Dantaya began to draw Julian's father in as a resource to encourage success. She made her pride about Julian's improvements clear, and had Julian show his father graded work. The father responded positively and, with Dantaya's motivation and guidance, began to follow Julian's school progress more closely. Finally, Dantaya arranged for Julian to become part of an after-school program as a tutor for younger students. Julian's sense of humor and mellow attitude drew young people to him. He, in turn, found that he enjoyed helping them. Under the watchful, encouraging eyes of his father and Dantaya, Julian's grades and attendance improved. Further, he realized a sense of accomplishment in being able to use his skills to help younger students. Dantaya had succeeded in activating resources outside of the school system that helped Julian to recognize and value his abilities. Consequently, he had no further contact with the court.

Just as the Adolescent Diversion Project has no authority to involve schools in its efforts to work with young people, it also has no means to keep youth and parents involved with the program. Often, juveniles and their families welcome the help and willingly cooperate. Sometimes, though, juveniles or parents avoid contact with the advocate. In those cases, much of the energy that could be spent helping instead goes toward merely keeping in contact with the juvenile and parents.

Unfortunately, when juveniles refuse to meet with their advocates, little positive work can be accomplished. In such instances, a mechanism that facilitates the Adolescent Diversion Project's success—its voluntary, noncoercive structure—can become a barrier beyond which the advocate and juvenile cannot move to work together. As long as the juvenile gets in no further legal trouble, failure to complete the intervention is simply a missed opportunity. If, however, the juvenile faces more charges, court personnel look uncharitably upon the juvenile's failure to take advantage of the "opportunity" to participate in a nonpunitive program. As a result, they may be less lenient about punishment for subsequent charges.

Organizational Issues

With this understanding of the issues community-based alternative programs face, it is possible to turn to a discussion of concrete concerns. With regard to the Adolescent Diversion Project, three organizational issues present themselves: competing for clients, competing for funding, and making others aware of the program and its success. In addition, there are some administrative concerns with which managers of community-based volunteer programs must grapple.

Clients and Funding

Initially, neither competition for clients nor funding was a problem. The court system was overloaded and welcomed a helping hand, and the Adolescent Diversion Project was funded through federal research grants. Essentially, the court was not willing to "look a gift horse in the mouth." However, as the Adolescent Diversion Project moved from a research to a service provision project, inevitably research funds had to be replaced. State and local funds have been an excellent source of funding. Governmental fiscal agencies that struggle to provide many services with limited budgets are especially drawn to low-cost programs with proven effectiveness.

Ironically, its effectiveness creates a dilemma for the Adolescent Diversion Project, because the program is an effective alternative to the very system from which it receives its referrals—juvenile court. Juvenile court and the Adolescent Diversion Project also are funded from the same source—county funds. Finding one's program in a position of competition with the agency that is the gatekeeper to the population at issue is difficult. Because the Adolescent Diversion Project and juvenile court serve the same client base and compete for funding from a shared, finite source, the Adolescent Diversion Project's better success rate puts it in a tenuous position. When the Adolescent Diversion Project initially applied for local funds (after federal research funding was scheduled to end), court staff offered lukewarm support, even though they had been very involved in the birth and early life of the Adolescent Diversion Project. Their position was to support the Adolescent Diversion Project without sacrificing any of their own funding. This presented a major challenge to the Adolescent Diversion Project staff as they attempted to avoid the political pitfall of asking county commissioners to "appear" to fund the Adolescent Diversion Project out of the same "pot" of money that funds the local juvenile court system.

Despite the Adolescent Diversion Project's real and well-publicized success, the Adolescent Diversion Project constantly battles for referrals. Partly because of philosophical disagreements and partly because of competition for scarce resources, each intake staff member at the court must be newly convinced of the value of the Adolescent Diversion Project. A variety of tactics have been successful. First, the Adolescent Diversion Project continues to take an active approach to seeking referrals. Staff spend two full afternoons, selected by court personnel as the most useful times to be present at the court. During this time the Adolescent Diversion Project staff members are available to conduct intake interviews. Probably more importantly, this is a time when the staff of the Adolescent Diversion Project and court can interact with each other. There is little doubt that if staff stayed in their offices and "waited" for referrals, they would wait a long time, indeed. Second, enhancing interactions between the court and the Adolescent Diversion Project is encouraged through inviting court staff to observe and participate in the Adolescent Diversion Project's training sessions about referral procedures, legal changes, and other important topics. This fosters an open dialogue between the Adolescent Diversion Project staff and court personnel, which ensures that each understands and respects the other's position. Accommodations are made by both staffs to maintain a positive relationship.

Spreading the News

In the beginning, encouraging use of the program was not an issue because the Adolescent Diversion Project had yet to prove itself. Many new service providers work to demonstrate the effectiveness of their program with the goal of having it adopted as the treatment of choice by more traditional service providers. Once the Adolescent Diversion Project's effectiveness was established, it could have become part of juvenile court or social services programs for juveniles. Unfortunately, research has shown that professional service providers were more difficult to train to use the Adolescent Diversion Project model (Davidson et al. 1990).

The Adolescent Diversion Project also requires an advocate to be actively committed to reaching out to and being involved with the juveniles in their environment. This approach is quite different from the more common approach of establishing a site and waiting for clients to come forward with their needs. Assimilation of the Adolescent Diversion Project into the court, or even into the mental health system, could decrease its effectiveness.

The Adolescent Diversion Project presents a challenge for those who seek organizational change. Those interested in true organizational alternatives and innovations need to be aware of the special challenges involved when new roles are required. The change agent role prescribed by the Adolescent Diversion Project model indicates a very different method of operation. It is active, takes place in the natural setting, follows a prescribed model, and is time-limited. Each of these strategies represents challenges for traditional human service systems, and care will have to be taken to ensure they are maintained in replication efforts. There will be organizational pressure to drift from each of these principles. Only through strong leadership, that succeeds in creating an organizational climate supportive of such innovation, can success be anticipated.

Legal Changes

Prior to 1988, the Adolescent Diversion Project operated under the state juvenile code of 1939. It was basically silent on the issue of diversion. In the early 1980s several groups were working within the state to give diversion legal standing within the juvenile code, and several "diversion laws" were drafted and introduced. Due to political disinterest and the fact that diversion programs seemed to be operating well under the old legislation, the diversion law was never passed.

In the fall of 1988, in its closing session, the state legislature passed more than sixty laws governing the criminal and juvenile justice system in a broad attempt to "do something about crime." A "diversion law" was among those passed. However, several compromises had significantly affected the law's impact. Ironically, the law that institutionalized diversion programs in the state and sought to protect young people who were diverted actually may have worked to decrease the likelihood that a juvenile will get a second chance to remain outside the legal system. Theory, supported by data from the Adolescent Diversion Project, holds that juveniles who are diverted have a real opportunity to avoid further legal involvement (Davidson et al. 1990). The expectation that diverting a juvenile from the justice system may result in no further contact with the court is inherent in the law. In effect, the legislation says that young people who are diverted get a second chance to avoid a criminal record. That is, the file in which information about the crime and the diversion order are kept may not be reopened, even if the juvenile commits another crime. It is possible, then, that a young person who was originally diverted may commit another crime, be processed formally for the subsequent crime, and the judge or referee could dismiss the subsequent charges because these charges incorrectly appear to be a first offense.

When intake workers believe that diversion will work, closing an offense in a diversion file is not problematic. If, however, workers do not trust diversion to keep juveniles from the legal system, then concern with punishing habitual offenders becomes paramount. As a result, some workers may be reluctant to refer juvenile offenders who they believe may again break the law, since court officers want to be able to bring the full force of the law upon such offenders. In short, those working on alternative methods of affecting the justice system will have to anticipate the effect of legal changes on their practices.

Networking

Relationships with Community Resource Providers

Juvenile offenders and their families may require many different types of resources. The Adolescent Diversion Project has developed and maintains relationships with some of those resource providers. The Adolescent Diversion Project staff continue to make contact with and establish affiliations with additional providers. Commonly accessed resources include: public schools, free and low-cost health care providers, parks and recreation departments, the YMCA, the Boys and Girls Clubs, and local African-American and Latino-focused agencies. Services provided by housing agencies, food banks, and legal advocates are sometimes relied upon for assistance.

In addition to requesting help from these agencies, their staff members are invited to speak to students about the services they provide. Further, supervisors are careful to create positive interactions between agency staff and the Adolescent Diversion Project by cautioning advocates to acknowledge the overworked, underappreciated work done at such agencies and to treat workers respectfully when requesting help. As a courtesy to new organizations or to new staff at previously accessed agencies, the Adolescent Diversion Project staff make a contact by telephone or by letter. By doing so, potential resource persons can become acquainted with the Adolescent Diversion Project and vice versa. The outcome of such interactions is almost universally a positive working relationship and thus, provides additional assistance for juveniles and families.

Recruiting Advocates

Programs will be most successful when characteristics of the advocate and the juvenile are similar. Issues of race and gender emerge immediately. The Adolescent Diversion Project policy is to pair female juveniles with female advocates. This is easy to do because most volunteers are female. It is preferable to match male advocates with male juveniles. However, because about 80 percent of the volunteers are female, this match is not always possible. The Adolescent Diversion Project focuses on pairing male advocates to older male juveniles and to juveniles who specifically request a male advocate. It is optimal to match juveniles and advocates by race. Not doing so merely enhances real or perceived race and class differences between the college students and the juveniles and families with whom they work.

For example, a young, white male college student, Keith, was assigned to work with a sixteen-year-old African-American juvenile, Damian. Problems soon arose between them surrounding their unequal financial status. Keith drove a new car that his parents had purchased for him. Because he had not been able to afford the car on his own, he perceived himself to be similarly situated to Damian, who also could not afford a car. Keith saw himself as a "poor" student. Damian was jealous of Keith's social standing, which showed in his failure to cooperate and in vague threats toward him. Keith failed to grasp the subtlety of the situation. He sincerely believed that not paying for his own car placed the two of them on a similar plane, not understanding that while he and Damian might be similar at that point in time, there remained fundamental differences in their circumstances. The advocate's situation was temporary; the juvenile's was probably permanent. The situation was resolved by assigning another advocate to the juvenile.

While not downplaying the existence of class, as well as racial barriers, an African-American advocate, even from a middle-class background, probably would have been more sensitive to Damian's feelings due to a shared cultural and historical heritage. Greater comfort and familiarity stemming from interacting with a person of the same race also might have made Damian less likely to confront his advocate.

Matching advocates and juveniles requires targeted recruitment of advocates. Seeking out diverse volunteers requires scheduling time to meet with them, explain the program, and invite their participation. The Adolescent Diversion Project staff have approached African-American sororities and fraternities, as well as black and Latino student unions to recruit advocates from minority groups. Including people from minority groups as staff members and supervisors, preserving contacts with minority community leaders, and conveying a persistent concern for the well-being of juveniles from minority groups increases the Adolescent Diversion Project's ability to recruit minority advocates.

Developing and Maintaining a Commitment

Project staff have the responsibility for nurturing the advocates' commitment and determination. Individuals who agree to work with a juvenile are making a huge time and energy commitment. Faced with the reality of their juvenile's life, such commitment can be difficult to maintain. Some juveniles face overwhelming obstacles, including families whose fondest desire is to be rid of him or her, neighborhoods where drug dealing and prostitution are part of the social fabric, as are homelessness and relentless poverty. Opportunities to create change may be few, and the changes made may be small. Still, for most troubled juveniles, any movement toward positive life goals is preferable to their present situation. Supervisors become part sympathetic listener and part cheerleader as they guide advocates in their work to positively affect the juveniles' lives. Working with juveniles and their families is sometimes a stressful, emotionally draining endeavor.

As such, ongoing support for staff and advocates must be built into the system. Confidentiality limitations preclude discussing interventions with family and friends, making systemic support even more crucial. Within the Adolescent Diversion Project, advocates get support from supervisors and each other during weekly meetings. Additional support comes from telephone conversations between supervisors and advocates, or among the advocates themselves. Supervisors support each other through a weekly staff meeting, during which they solicit suggestions and advice. Of course, there are also high points in this work. Pausing to celebrate successes serves as a reminder of how valuable the work is.

Conclusion

Creating and maintaining a community-based prevention program to help juvenile delinquents requires considerable expertise. Developing and employing interpersonal skill to successfully interact with diverse individuals, such as juveniles, families, court and school staff, and recreational workers is basic. Patience to wait for change to occur, along with a strong belief in one's ability to affect change is crucial. Finally, the ability to be pleased with "small wins" (Weick 1984) is essential. For the dedicated change agent, such programs represent a tremendous responsibility. At the same time, the effort is incredibly rewarding.

By concentrating on juveniles, it is possible to decrease the number of individuals who currently commit crimes (15.6 percent of all arrests and 16 percent of all arrests for violent crimes are juveniles [Federal Bureau of Investigation 1990]) and to affect future crime by reducing the number of people who continue to commit deviant acts. By approaching crime prevention from a multilevel, community-based, empowerment perspective instead of seeking a single solution, success is more likely. Sarason (1978) reminds us that some problems are intractable—they simply cannot be eradicated. Crime is probably one such problem. The philosophy and strategies outlined here, however, hold promise of bringing society closer to its goal than ever before.

References

Akers, R. L. 1977. *Deviant behavior: A social learning approach.* Belmont, Calif.: Wadsworth.

Becker, H. S. 1963. *Outsiders: Studies in the sociology of deviance.* New York: Free Press of Glencoe.

Bowman, P. H. 1959. Effects of a revised school program on potential delinquents. *Annals* 322(1): 53-62.

Bynum, T. S., M. Wordes, and C. J. Corley. 1993. *Disproportionate representation in juvenile justice in Michigan: Examining the influence of race and gender* (Technical Report). East Lansing, Mich.: Michigan State University, School of Criminal Justice and Institute for Public Policy and Social Research.

Chesney-Lind, M. 1989. Girls' crime and woman's place: Toward a feminist model of female delinquency. *Crime and Delinquency* 35(1): 5-30.

Cloward, R., and L. Ohlin. 1960. *Delinquency and opportunity. Glencoe, Ill.: The Free Press.*

Davidson, W. S. II, and C. J. Johnson. 1992. Diversion programs for juvenile offenders. In *Advances in law and child development,* ed. S. M. Fulero and L. Olsen-Fulero. Greenwich, Conn.: JAI Press.

Davidson, W. S. II, and C. A. Rapp. 1976. Child advocacy in the justice system. *Social Work* 21(2): 225-32.

Davidson, W. S. II, and J. Rappaport. 1978. Towards a model of advocacy. In *Advocacy and the disciplines,* ed. G. Weber and G. McCall. New York: Sage.

Davidson, W. S. II, and R. Redner. 1988. Diversion from the justice system. In *Fourteen ounces of prevention,* ed. R. Price et al. Washington, D.C.: American Psychological Association.

Davidson, W. S. II, et al. 1990. *Alternative treatments for troubled youth: The case of diversion from the justice system.* New York: Plenum.

Davidson, W. S. II, and J. S. Saul. 1982. Child advocacy in the juvenile justice system: A clash of paradigms. In *Child advocacy,* ed. G. Melton. New York: Plenum.

Elliot, D. S., D. Huizinga, and S. S. Ageton. 1985. *Explaining delinquency and drug abuse.* Beverly Hills, Calif.: Sage.

Empey, L. T. 1982. *American delinquency: Its meaning and construction.* Homewood, Ill.: Dorsey.

Fareta, G. A. 1981. A profile of aggression from adolescence to adulthood. *American Journal of Orthopsychiatry*, 51(4): 439-53.

Federal Bureau of Investigation. 1970. *Uniform crime reports for the United States*. Washington, D.C.: U.S. Government Printing Office.

——. 1990. *Uniform crime reports for the United States*. Washington, D.C.: U.S. Government Printing Office.

In re Gault, U.S. 1, 1967.

Glaser, D. 1975. *Strategic criminal justice planning*. Washington, D.C.: U.S. Government Printing Office.

Gold, M. 1970. *Delinquent behavior in an American city*. Belmont, Calif.: Brooks/Cole.

Gold, M., and R. J. Petronio. 1980. Delinquent behavior in adolescence. In *Handbook of adolescent psychology*, ed. J. Adelson. New York: Wiley.

Goldstein, A., and B. Glick. 1987. *Aggression replacement training: A comprehensive intervention for delinquent youth*. Champaign, Ill.: Research Press.

Grey, A. L., and H. E. Dermody. 1972. Reports of casework failure. *Social Casework* 16(2): 207-12.

Hirschi, T. 1969. *Causes of delinquency*. Los Angeles: University of California Press.

Kahn, A. J. 1965. A case of premature claims. *Crime and Delinquency* 20(2): 233-40.

Krisberg, B., and J. Austin. 1978. *The children of Ishmael*. Palo Alto, Calif.: Mayfield Press.

Levitt, E. L. 1971. Research on psychotherapy with children. In *Handbook of psychotherapy and behavior change*, ed. A. Bergin and S. L. Garfield. New York: Wiley.

Lipton, D., R. Martinson, and J. Wilks. 1975. *The effectiveness of correctional treatment*. New York: Praeger.

Loeber, R., and M. Stouthamer-Loeber. 1987. Prediction. In *Handbook of juvenile delinquency*, ed. H. C. Quay. New York: John Wiley and Sons.

Matsueda, R. L. 1982. Testing control theory and differential association: A causal modeling approach. *American Sociological Review* 47(5): 489-504.

Mennel, R. M. 1972. Origins of the juvenile court: Changing perspectives on the legal rights of juvenile delinquents. *Crime and Delinquency* 18(1): 68-78.

Merton, R. K. 1957. *Social theory and social structure.* 2d ed. New York: Free Press.

Morash, M. and R. Trojanowicz. 1986. *Juvenile delinquency.* New York: Plenum.

Offord, D. R., and M. H. Boyle. 1988. The epidemiology of antisocial behavior in early adolescents, aged 12 to 14. In *Early adolescent transitions,* ed. M. D. Levine and E. R. McAnarney. Lexington, Mass.: Lexington Books.

Patterson, G. R. 1975. *Families.* Champaign, Ill. Research Press.

——. 1986. *Performance models for antisocial boys.* Paper presented at the annual meeting of the American Psychological Association, Los Angeles.

Polier, J. W. 1989. *Juvenile justice in double jeopardy.* Hillsdale, N.J.: Erlbaum.

President's Commission on Law Enforcement and the Administration of Justice. 1967. *Task force report: Juvenile delinquency and youth crime. Washington, D.C.: U.S. Government Printing Office.*

Rappaport, J., et al. 1975. Alternatives to blaming the victim or the environment: Our places to stand have not moved the earth. American Psychologist 30(5): 525-28.

Robins, P. 1981. Epidemiological approaches to natural history research. *Journal of the American Academy of Child Psychiatry* 20(5): 566-80.

Romig, D. A. 1978. *Justice for our children.* Lexington, Mass.: Lexington Books.

Ryan, W. 1971. *Blaming the victim.* New York: Vintage Books.

Santrock, J. W. 1990. *Adolescence.* New York: Wm. C. Brown.

Sarason, S. B. 1978. The nature of problem solving in social action. *American Psychologist* 33(3): 370-80.

Schultz, J. L. 1973. The cycle of juvenile court history. *Crime and Delinquency* 19(5): 457-76.

Schur, E. 1973. *Radical nonintervention.* Englewood Cliffs, N.J.: Prentice Hall.

Shinn, M. 1990. Mixing and matching: Levels of conceptualization, measurement, and statistical analysis in community research. In *Researching community psychology: Issues of theory and methods,* ed. P. Tolan et al. Washington, D.C.: American Psychological Association.

Stephenson, R. M., and F. R. Scarpitti. 1969. Essexfields: A non-residential experiment in group centered rehabilitation of delinquents. *American Journal of Corrections* 12(1): 12-31.

Stuart, R. B. 1971. Behavioral contracting with the families of delinquents. *Journal of Behavior Therapy and Experimental Psychiatry* 2(1): 1-11.

Trojanowicz, R. C., and M. Morash. 1987. *Juvenile delinquency: Concepts and control* (4th ed). Englewood Cliffs, N.J.: Prentice-Hall.

Weick, K. E. 1984. Small wins: Redefining the scale of social problems. *American Psychologist* 39(1): 40-49.

Williams, J. R., and M. Gold. 1972. From delinquent behavior to official delinquency. *Social Problems* 20(2): 209-22.

Part II

Managing Program Development

4　Detention Services for Juveniles

John P. Treahy

The role of juvenile detention often confuses even those professionals who have worked many years in the field. This confusion is caused by many factors. Juvenile detention programs, historically, have lacked a common definition of what they do, who they do it to, and for how long. As is the case in the criminal justice system, juvenile justice programs, including juvenile detention, vary from state-to-state and even from locality-to-locality.

For years, juvenile detention has provided the juvenile justice system with a place to punish juveniles and a place to put a juvenile offender when other options did not seem feasible. Juvenile detention acts as a surrogate parent, an educational program, or a provider of diagnostic services. Even professional staff who have worked for years in juvenile detention often are confused as to what service they provide to the system: Is their role to punish, to assess, or to rehabilitate?

It has only been in the last ten years that juvenile detention professionals have taken control of their environments. These professionals have begun to define what they are mandated to do, what they are equipped to do, and what resources they need to be effective.

Defining Juvenile Detention

Since 1971, the National Juvenile Detention Association (NJDA) has coordinated the efforts of all state affiliates to establish a common definition for juvenile detention. This association also has acted as the clearinghouse for innovations and problem solving within the field. The National Juvenile Detention Association defines juvenile detention as:

> The temporary and safe custody of juveniles who are accused of conduct subject to the jurisdiction of the court who require a restricted environment for their own and the community's protection while pending legal action and provides a wide range of helpful ser-

John P. Treahy is vice president of Hillside Childrens' Center in Rochester, New York, and is current president of the Juvenile Detention Association of New York State.

vices which support the juveniles' physical, emotional and social development (NJDA 1992).

It should be clear from this definition that juvenile detention is a process and not a place.

Historically, juvenile detention has provided custodial levels of care to juveniles who were awaiting disposition of their cases in the juvenile or family courts. More recently, juvenile detention programs have provided not only custodial care, but also diagnostic services and long-term treatment programs. This change in role has been the result of the growing sophistication of detention programs, the changing profile of the juveniles entering the juvenile detention system, and the ineffectiveness of other services and systems to adequately provide for this population.

The detention process incorporates services that provide an environment that is safe for the detainee, as well as security that ensures the community is equally safe. *All* juveniles who reside in a juvenile detention facility fall under the jurisdiction of the court. Services provided by facilities range from those that constitute an emergency (often medical or mental health) to those that are routine services for all juveniles in residential care. As juveniles' needs have become more complex, so have the services provided within a detention facility. Expectations of the system have changed from providing a *place* for juveniles to stay to providing a safe environment that can help provide the system with information and recommendations as to juveniles' needs.

Juvenile Detention: The Program

The profile and characteristics of juvenile detention programs vary greatly from state to state. Juvenile detention programs vary in size, services and programs offered, and the level of security provided. The difference in security levels often is reflected by reliance on restrictive or secure physical plants or on high-intensity staff supervision.

Regardless of the level of security of a facility, most programs provide services in several general areas. These include: education, medical, recreational, and short-term counseling services. Due to the short-term nature of detention, most programs are designed to meet a juvenile's immediate or emergent needs, and most counseling falls within the purview of crisis intervention.

Secure Juvenile Detention

The most common and traditional form of juvenile detention is secure juvenile detention. Secure juvenile detention facilities are characterized by physically restricting construction, hardware, and procedures. Most of these physical plants closely resemble those constructed for adults and are comparable to adult jails. These facilities generally will use exterior perimeter fences (at times bordered by razor ribbon), automatically locking doors, and mechanical restraints (including wrist and/or leg shackles). Secure facilities generally provide individual sleeping rooms that are locked at night as well as isolation rooms for residents who need to be removed from the general population.

Secure detention facilities vary widely in size and the types of programs that are offered. The population tends to be predominately male children of color. However, female admissions have significantly increased ....

Most secure detention facilities are operated by a state department or a local government. This includes the department of probation or social services, the courts, or a state department for youth services. Generally, secure detention programs are responsible for the custodial care of juvenile delinquents and juveniles who, because of the severity of their crime, have been charged as adults. Some states continue to use secure facilities for status offenders, but this practice continues to diminish.

Secure detention facilities vary widely in size and the types of programs that are offered. The population tends to be predominately male children of color. However, female admissions have significantly increased since the late 1980s (Office of Juvenile Justice and Delinquency Prevention 1993).

Limited-secure Detention

Since the late 1970s and early 1980s, many states have searched for effective alternatives to secure detention, since it can be very costly. Although a high percentage of juveniles need a structured environment, they do not necessarily need the level of security present in most secure juvenile detention facilities. As a result, there has been a significant increase in what has become known as nonsecure, limited-secure, or staff-secure detention. These programs have the same basic mission as a secure facility: to provide a safe environment for its residents, to ensure availability of the detainee for future legal proceedings, and to keep the community safe from additional juvenile crime.

Staff-secure or nonsecure detention provides similar types of programs as secure detention; however, security is attained through the use of enhanced staffing patterns rather than hardware and procedures. As is the case with secure detention, nonsecure detention programs also vary in size, services offered, and levels of security. Some states have used community-based group homes (generally twelve residents or less) as nonsecure detention programs, while others have designed large institutional types of programs.

Some localities have even found success in detaining juveniles in foster family care. Most staff secure or nonsecure detention programs are operated by private agencies that contract with a local government to provide the service for them. Juveniles detained in this level of detention usually have been charged as status offenders or with a relatively minor act of delinquency, such as shoplifting, unauthorized use of a motor vehicle, burglary, or forgery.

Most localities have found that the use of limited or nonsecure detention provides them with a cost-effective alternative to secure detention for a specific offender population. In addition to being cost effective, most of these programs have achieved a high level of success in detaining juveniles pending the implementation of the court's dispositional plan.

Juvenile Detention: The Client

In most states, the juvenile court has jurisdiction over a variety of family-related problems and offenses. These often include: juvenile delinquency proceedings, status offenses, determination of paternity and support, and various family or domestic offenses.

One of the major differences of the juvenile system is that there is no consistency within states as to what age qualifies a young person for juvenile status. In most states, the minimum age for which a child can be brought before the juvenile court is seven. However, upper age limits present the most variation. A few states, such as New York, transfer criminal liability from juvenile to adult court at the age of sixteen. Other states, including Indiana, transfer young people from juvenile to adult courts at age eighteen. Despite the age variation, however, demographics and characteristics of the juvenile detention system remain fairly constant around the country. A high percentage of the detained juveniles in this country are male, children of color, aged thirteen-to-fifteen, products of single parent households, and functioning several years behind their age groups academically. The presenting charge category also has escalated with more criminal charges that involve the use of physical aggression and the use of weapons.

Juvenile detention programs provide custodial care for juveniles who are the respondents in the court proceedings. All of the juveniles have committed some act, which has brought them before the court. Detention will generally occur immediately following an offense and the juvenile's apprehension by a law enforcement agency, or it occurs following a court appearance where a judge has determined that the juvenile needs to be held in custody.

Usually, the ordering of detention by a judge or the seeking of a detention bed by a law enforcement officer is preventive in nature. Preventive detention is ordered when a judge or law enforcement official believes that the juvenile will commit further criminal acts if released into the community. A juvenile court judge also may order the detention of a juvenile if he or she believes that the juvenile may abscond and fail to appear for future proceedings. While these are generally the legally accepted criteria to detain a juvenile, there are times when other reasons are used by the detaining official. These include: protecting a juvenile who has been a witness to the commission of a crime, holding a runaway from another jurisdiction while arrangements are made for the return of the juvenile to the home jurisdiction, holding juveniles whose parents refuse to take them home, and holding juveniles who refuse to return home with their parents or guardians.

Detained juveniles fall into one of three legal categories:

- juvenile delinquent
- status offender
- violent juvenile offender

Juvenile Delinquents

While the age of juvenile delinquents varies by state, the offense usually involves an act, which if committed by an adult, would constitute a crime. Some common offenses that fall into this category include: burglary, unauthorized use of a motor vehicle, and drug possession.

Status Offenders

Status offenders are juveniles who have not been charged with a criminal act, but are before the court for problematic and disruptive types of behaviors, such as running away from home, truancy, failure to adhere to parental curfews, alcohol use, and association with peers who have been forbidden by a parent. The level of detention-intervention for status offenders ranges from secure detention, to nonsecure detention, to respite or emergency-shelter programs.

Violent Juvenile Offenders

Violent juvenile offenders often are charged as adults for violent crimes. Since the early 1980s, many states have legislated new laws that respond to the increase in violent juvenile crime. This response has removed various crime categories from the jurisdiction of the juvenile or family court and placed them in the adult or criminal court system. In these cases, juveniles are arrested, charged, tried, and (if convicted) sentenced in a similar manner to adults convicted of the same crime. For example, New York State's Juvenile Offender Act of 1978 made it possible for New York to try juveniles as young as age thirteen as adults. Crime categories within this legislation include: murder, rape, sodomy, arson, and kidnapping.

Not surprisingly, the number of juvenile cases being processed in the adult or criminal court system has dramatically increased.

One of the more significant changes in the field of juvenile detention over the past ten years has been in the profile of the juvenile who enters care. There has been a significant increase in the number of mentally ill juveniles entering detention programs across the country. These mental illnesses are most often demonstrated by a higher degree of self-destructive and suicidal behaviors, physical aggression, acting out against others, and a lack of connection to the real world around them.

Current Status of Juvenile Detention

Juvenile justice professionals have increasingly accepted the impossible role of "being all things to all people." They accept the fact that they must provide services to all juveniles who arrive at their programs accompanied by a court order. Juveniles must be admitted regardless of their medical, emotional, and psychiatric needs. Many juveniles have been neglected or mismanaged by other human service and educational systems for years. Juvenile justice professionals have accepted the fact that, while the legal basis for detaining a juvenile is to prevent further criminal activity and/or to ensure that the juvenile will appear for future court proceedings, there are many other reasons for detaining a juvenile. These reasons include the following:

- to punish juveniles and to teach them a lesson
- to scare juveniles into not committing other criminal acts
- to take care of juveniles because other systems are unwilling or unable to manage juveniles
- to procure needed medical and psychiatric services that otherwise would not be available
- to provide respite care while juveniles and their families resolve family difficulties

In addition to the confusion about who should be detained, there is intense debate as to what services should be provided to juveniles while they are in detention. Should juvenile detention programs provide purely a "maintenance" function within the juvenile justice system? If so, the services needed are fairly simple and straightforward: three meals daily, adequate clothing and a clean bed in which to sleep. If, as many believe, juvenile detention programs are to be of value to the juvenile justice system, then the service requirements become more obscure.

The lack of a clear definition about the population to be served and the services to be provided has led to the current problems within the juvenile detention system. The biggest dilemma that the juvenile detention system faces across the country is crowding. While the entire juvenile justice system has experienced a significant increase in population since 1984, statistics show that juvenile detention programs have experienced the most dramatic overall increase in admissions. Admissions in 1984 totaled approximately 400,000 juveniles, while in 1990 the figure had risen to 570,000. Preliminary reports show that the figures continued to rise during each of the first three years of the 1990s (Office of Juvenile Justice and Delinquency Prevention 1993).

The staggering increase in admissions, compounded by the severity of the behaviors exhibited by detained juveniles, has resulted in a sharp increase in untoward incidents within detention facilities.

A recently released study by Abt Associates, under the auspices of the Office of Juvenile Justice and Delinquency Prevention reports that 47 percent of detained juveniles are in facilities that are beyond their designed capacity (Office of Juvenile Justice and Delinquency Prevention 1993). The crowding phenomena is caused not only by the significant increase in juveniles entering the juvenile justice system, but also by an overreliance on and misuse of the juvenile detention system by the judiciary, the police, and the community at large. (However, this misuse of juvenile detention programs does not occur because of "bad" judges or police officers, but because of a lack of other appropriate effective alternatives to the detention system.) The crowding problem is compounded by a significant shift in the presenting problems of juveniles who enter the system. Practitioners within the field report that they encounter juveniles with significant unmet mental health needs. These mental health problems have produced juveniles who are much less willing to respond to authority figures. Furthermore, these juveniles are much more willing to use violence as a response to stress.

Detention administrators have relatively little control over admissions, either to maintain the facility within the designed capacity or to reject juveniles whose acting out behaviors are beyond the capabilities of a particular facility.

The staggering increase in admissions, compounded by the severity of the behaviors exhibited by detained juveniles, has resulted in a sharp increase in untoward incidents within detention facilities. These behavior characteristics have led to increases in the areas of suicide attempts within facilities and injuries to detained residents and staff members. The Conditions of Confinement Study (Office of Juvenile Justice and Delinquency Prevention 1993) revealed 18,000 incidents of suicidal gestures (with ten juveniles successfully completing the act), 24,000 client injuries, and 7,700 injuries to staff.

Anyone who closely studies juvenile detention programs across the country would discover a system that is woefully lacking in mental health and medical services that can effectively respond to the needs of these juveniles. Many facilities rely upon casework or direct-care staff to provide counseling and mental health services. While in most cases these are the staff who are most familiar with the residents, they are not adequately trained to respond appropriately to the needs of the juveniles in care. As is the case in the entire juvenile justice system, staff are often inadequately trained in even the most routine aspects of child care and counseling skills. Personnel who are trained in assessing the mental health status of juveniles can work with detention staff to develop effective management and treatment strategies.

In addition to mental health issues, detained juveniles present a plethora of medical problems upon admission, including the following:

- insufficient immunizations
- sexually transmitted diseases
- tooth decay
- lack of prenatal care prior to admissions for pregnant girls
- a wide variety of substance abuse issues

While juvenile detention programs should not be responsible for providing nonemergency medical care, programs need to identify and treat emergency problems and contagious medical problems.

Despite the significant risk that the detained population presents, the 1992 Conditions of Confinement Study found that only 43 percent get a health screening within an hour of admission. Almost 20 percent of juveniles who are detained wait more than a week for the assessment to be completed. The study also found that almost one-third of detained juveniles receive a health assessment from staff who are untrained to provide such care (Office of Juvenile Justice and Delinquency Prevention 1993).

The juvenile detention system is characterized by a high volume of admissions, high turnover of staff, and chronic crisis conditions. Detention administrators and program staff usually spend the day in crisis management. These conditions are primarily responsible for precluding practitioners from taking time to assess where the system is and what steps must be taken to make the system more efficient and effective.

Vision

All staff who work in the field of juvenile detention should be committed to providing comprehensive and quality care to each and every juvenile who enters their facility.

In 1992, under the auspices of the Office of Juvenile Justice and Delinquency Prevention, twenty-two national leaders gathered and developed this vision statement for juvenile justice:

> Our vision is that every child experience success in caring families and nurturing communities that cherish children and teach them to value family and community. Our vision is guided by the fact that our decisions and actions affecting children today determine the quality of life tomorrow (Office of Juvenile Justice and Delinquency Prevention 1993).

Parallels to the Adult System

The juvenile justice system is beginning to show similar parallels to the adult correctional system of the 1970s and 1980s. There is a growing sentiment that those working in juvenile justice have not done a good job and have not effectively solved the problem of juvenile crime. Federal, state, and local politicians seem to believe the system is broken and must be fixed.

Many states have begun to treat certain juveniles charged with specific crime categories as adults. Despite a lack of concrete evidence that this is an effective solution to juvenile crime, states have expanded the categories of offenses that will be waived to the adult system. State and federal legislators seem to be ignoring the fact that the adult system has proven to be far more ineffective, inefficient, and expensive than the juvenile system. Forcing large numbers of juveniles into the adult system will only further cripple an already backlogged and crowded system and will do nothing to remedy the problems of the juveniles who are before adult courts. While, politically this may send the message that "we are doing something to get tough on violent and unresponsive teens," the future will show this strategy has not solved the problem.

Conclusion

The solutions to the problems of the juvenile detention system are both simple and complex. Some solutions will require financial resources; many will require creativity and a change in attitude both within and outside the juvenile detention system.

Juvenile detention practitioners need to define what their role is in the juvenile justice system. While it is important for input from outside of the field of detention, it is equally important for this decision to be made by those individuals who spend every day working within the walls of juvenile detention facilities. It must be clear that juvenile detention centers can no longer be all things to all people.

The most effective and efficient use of juvenile detention is to transform this service from dead time to diagnostic time. Time and resources spent on juvenile detention should be productive for the juvenile as well as the courts. Time spent in detention should be used to develop productive, relevant, and useful data for the courts so they can make more effective dispositions of cases. Currently, data usually is collected by staff who work outside of detention facilities. This information tends to be compilations of historical data rather than a current profile of the juvenile under care in a detention facility.

Often, the resulting picture of the juvenile is somewhat different than what is seen within a structured, nurturing environment of a juvenile detention setting. Collected information needs to focus less on history and more on the current functioning of juveniles who are before the court. Assessments need to be conducted in a variety of areas, including: psychiatric, medical, educational, employment and training, recreation, and environment. The role of juvenile detention staff in the system should be twofold: to develop an effective short-term treatment and management program for each detained juvenile, and to provide the court with the most meaningful and current information possible.

To ensure a system that works both for juveniles and the court system, there must be a commitment of financial resources. Given the scarce resources today, this infusion of funds should not be additional resources, but a shift from postdispositional to predispositional.

Financial resources should provide for the construction and rehabilitation of current juvenile detention centers. The detention centers should provide an environment that ensures the safety of each resident in care, reduces the potential for injury and suicide, and provides accurate assessments of juveniles.

These facilities should be limited in capacity but sufficient enough so that they will not be forced to go over their design capacity, yet be located within a reasonable distance of a juvenile's family and home community.

There must be a commitment of financial resources to hire and train individuals who are committed to providing the highest care possible to juveniles. It would make sense that individuals employed in direct-care positions should be paid on a comparable basis to other professionals who work in the field of human services, education, and law enforcement. Staff should certainly be compensated on the same scale as those who work in direct care in the adult correctional system.

There is a wealth of talent and expertise from within the field. Detention managers must be willing to find these resources and make them available to staff. The mentality that staff training is the first line item to be cut in a budget crunch must change. There must be a commitment to develop and fund staff-to-client ratios that guarantee quality care. There must be a financial commitment to hire individuals necessary to implement a thorough assessment of detained juveniles. These staff will include: on-site doctors and nurses, psychiatrists, psychologists, education specialists, vocational counselors, and clergy.

In addition, attitudes must change from both within and outside of the detention system. Staff who work within juvenile detention need to think of themselves as more than "jailers." To maximize the effectiveness of the juvenile detention system, it will take the cooperation of the entire juvenile justice system. Judges, prosecutors, police officers, and planning agents must acknowledge the role of the detention program and cease to use juvenile detention as a "warehouse" for juveniles. Juvenile detention can provide more than maintenance care and should be used as a valuable resource in a newly constructed system.

References

National Juvenile Detention Association. 1992. NJDA information brochure. Washington, D.C.

Office of Juvenile Justice and Delinquency Prevention. 1993. *Recommendations for juvenile corrections and detention in response to conditions of confinement: A study to evaluate the conditions of juvenile correctional and detention facilities.* Washington, D.C.: Office of Juvenile Justice and Delinquency Prevention.

5 Facility Programming for Female Delinquents

Linda Albrecht

In the 1990s, the issues related to girls in the juvenile justice system have taken a number of tracks. Public concern centers on the increasing number and severity of violent crimes committed by teenage girls, the growing numbers of gangs of girls, and the roles played by girls in creating or adding to violence in schools and communities. Within the system, it is generally recognized that the needs of girls who enter the system and require care and treatment are not adequately met. Girls were barely mentioned in the 1992 Conditions of Confinement Study (Office of Juvenile Justice and Delinquency Prevention 1993). It is safe to assume that if conditions for boys are less than satisfactory, then conditions for girls are much worse.

A few states are taking steps to systematically examine their programs and services in sincere efforts to improve them. The 1993 reauthorization bill for the Office of Juvenile Justice and Delinquency Prevention includes an amendment that requires states to examine gender bias in state systems and services to correct it.

Parallel to the concerns within the system, the body of literature related to girls and women and the problems they experience in the culture is growing. National movements and organizations are forming to focus specifically on the issues related to girls in the juvenile justice system. An example of such a group is the National Girls' Caucus spearheaded by the P.A.C.E. Center for Girls. Other groups that deal with girls' programs in general include the Valentine Foundation's "A Conversation About Girls."

Also relevant to the discussion about girls and delinquency is research about gender as it relates to child and adolescent development (Gilligan 1982; Brown and Gilligan 1992; Gilligan, Lyons, and Hanmer 1990). The themes of this research relate to both the causes of delinquency and the responses to it. Gender bias in the classroom (Sadker and Sadker 1982) significantly affects girls' ability to achieve success in the academic and related realms. Gender differences seen on the playground (Thorne 1993) have implications for understanding some of the problems girls have in so-

---

Linda Albrecht is a private consultant with over thirteen years of experience managing girls' programs.

ciety. Feminist literature points out gender difference in ways of knowing (Belenky et al. 1986) and in communicating (Tannen 1986, 1990). Awareness of these differences is essential in planning and developing programs and services for girls.

Many issues gaining attention in the media are also relevant to discussions of girls in the juvenile justice system. These include issues of physical and sexual abuse of girls and women, the oppressive nature of social and institutional sexism, the exploitation of women in the media and entertainment, and the sexualization of advertising for everything from jeans to cars. Health care, birth control, sex education, abortion rights, child care, access to educational and vocational training, drug and alcohol abuse, HIV, and AIDS are all girls', as well as women's, issues. Findings from women's studies and feminism should also be considered in any discussion about girls in the juvenile justice system. New literature about women in management and women-defined organizations provides important insights that suggest alternative ways of designing, operating and evaluating facilities for girls (Peters 1990, Helgesen 1990).

Daily, people in the institutions and on the lines face the complications presented by troubled girls in a system that was designed primarily for boys.

Reading the literature covering this broad field of issues related to girls is essential for anyone hoping to truly affect the lives of girls. To make a change in the lives of girls in the correctional system, one should be motivated by a vision of excellence and a belief that things can be made better.

If the individuals who design and direct the juvenile justice system intend to address the real issues related to girls within its purview, it must be open to the discussion and debate of any and all of the concerns that matter to girls in the system and in society. The policy makers and staff must be open to looking at itself as part of the problems of girls. Indeed, Meda Chesney-Lind (1989) suggests that "the official actions of the juvenile justice system should be understood as major forces in women's oppression as they have historically served to reinforce the obedience of all young women to the demands of patriarchal authority no matter how abusive or arbitrary."

While all of the debate and discussion is interesting, it is rhetorical. The reality is that there are girls in the system right now. Daily, people in the institutions and on the lines face the complications presented by troubled girls in a system that was designed primarily for boys. It is difficult to deal with the politics of the system, outrage over the social and economic causes of delinquency, even empathy for individual girls when you are face-to-face with the management problems girls present to the system. The people on the lines cannot wait until the debate is resolved, nor can the planners and designers of the system wait for that resolution.

Facility programming for delinquent girls must respond to the current realities that anything done today is likely to need to change almost as soon as it is developed. This process must be ongoing, and its participants must engage in a continuous examination of the most current critical thinking about girls' development and the role of women in society.

Who Are the Girls in Juvenile Justice Facilities?

Girls in juvenile justice facilities are a diverse group. Many, if not most, of the girls in the juvenile justice system are victims of sexual abuse and physical abuse. All of them are directly affected by the inherent sexism in our society, as well as by the politics and economics of racism and "classism." Many girls in the system have significant histories with the mental health system. Some suggest that out of a misguided paternalistic protectiveness, the justice system views girls' delinquency as a sickness. "Upon examination of prevailing social attitudes, we discover that young women who exhibit behavior problems are defined as 'wayward girls' and labeled 'immoral, bad, lacking in religious upbringing, and mentally deficient'" (National Girls' Caucus (flier), c/o P.A.C.E. Center for Girls, Inc., Jacksonville, Fla.). A review of the case records in any girls' institution will show a much higher percentage of girls' cases (as compared to boys') who were referred to the mental health system or psychiatric centers, as the first or as an early intervention. True or not, involvement with the mental health system adds another dynamic that has an effect on girls as they arrive in a facility. This factor needs to be considered in planning the facility and the program for girls.

Many of the girls who arrive in a facility started out in foster care as infants or young children. They "earned" their way to the facility by increasingly deviant, bizarre, or acting-out behaviors. The frequent absence of release options for such girls is a problem. They cannot go back to their own homes; there are fewer group homes or step-down programs for girls. Transition programs are mostly for boys. Because the service network for girls is so limited, girls who come to a facility have long associations with the other girls in the program. These associations are usually not positive. Often they have been based on conflict or collusion to fight or escape from the systems. These associations and relationships present another important factor in dealing with girls in a facility setting.

Given the small number of girls in any system, and the small percentage of the total population they represent, any girls' facility program will present a wider range of service needs than a given boys' facility population. Program developers typically spend a lot of time and energy trying to identify the particular population that they can or should handle. This process inevitably circles back to a discussion of the girls who should not come to a facility and the limited options for them. The developers of programs and facility planners often get bogged down or sidetracked in this discussion. The energy then goes into the system while the specific services provided by a given facility remain unchanged. An attempt to improve the quality of programs for girls within the system (when in an institution or specific program) gets diverted into dealing with the gender bias in the larger system, or at least into diversion, while the quality of life for the girls within the system remains unchanged.

One realistic path out of the cycle is to assume what our experience knows to be true: Any facility for girls is going to have a hodge-podge of types of girls who need a range of services. Because many of the girls in the system have multiple problems, it is almost impossible to separate out the types of services they need. For example, it is impossible to run a drug treatment program for girls without dealing with sexual abuse or victimization. Similarly, it is almost impossible to run a mental health program for girls without dealing with alcohol and substance abuse. Then, no health care program can ignore the mental health issues. Likewise, few treatment interventions are useful without attention to the girls' educational and vocational needs. And, none are helpful without serious attention to issues of self-esteem and relationships. Girls' self-esteem cannot be separated from sexism, racism, and classism in the world and in the system. In short, any facility program for girls must be a holistic program that is designed to deal with the needs of a varying group of girls.

Philosophical Issues
Myths, Assumptions, and Viewpoints

Before examining management issues related to programming for delinquent girls, it is important to look at some of the underlying assumptions, myths, and viewpoints that dominate current discussions about such programs. The ideas presented here are based on thirteen years of experience managing girls' programs, plus critical examination of that experience in the context of the theory and research on girls' development, gender differences, and feminist literature. The ideas here are open to debate and may, at first, be viewed as controversial. However, to many who have worked with girls, the views presented confirm their daily experiences.

View of a Facility

An interesting dynamic among juvenile justice practitioners is the seeming contradiction that permeates our thinking. We tend to be social reformers in thinking that society should eliminate the causes that lead to delinquency because locking juveniles up in institutions is an undesirable thing to do. At the same time, we usually believe that what we do is mean-ingful and valuable.

The view of a facility as a necessary evil may have an adverse effect on the way all view it. This view can undermine organizational effectiveness if it is not counterbalanced with a conscious awareness of the importance of what a facility does for the juveniles in its care. The dichotomy is more in-tense surrounding girls' facilities because of the paternalistic and sexist tendency of the system to overplace girls. Girls are placed in a facility at a higher level of security and are kept longer than boys for the same or simi-lar crimes. People tend to be less comfortable locking up girls than they are boys.

Although that discomfort is never completely eased, a close examination of the individual histories of the girls themselves offers a different view. Most of the girls have been subjected to physical and sexual abuse, as well as psychological abuse. Most have also been victims of exploitation, vio-lence, and neglect.

Our experience has done little to increase the hope that making a differ-ence in individual lives can affect the circumstances to which girls return. The best a facility can do is to offer the girls a haven for a while and hope to strengthen the girls' ability to cope and survive in the world from which they come.

The idea that a girls' facility can be a temporary haven from a cruel world is supported in current women's literature, and in Virginia Woolf's classic, *A Room of One's Own*. The recognition that women need a place of their own, a place to retreat, a place in which women's ways are honored and celebrated is a theme of contemporary women. Arguments supporting all-women colleges, all-women masters of business administration pro-grams, and workshops and training programs for women and girls support the notion that girls need a place to go. They need time away from an ex-ploitative world and a patriarchal society.

These arguments offer a sound rationale for correctional facilities for girls. Such facilities offer girls an effective program experience.

Women who work in such a program often recognize the absence of such an experience in their own lives and wish that their daughters could have such an opportunity to learn about women's roles and experience a supportive environment.

Author Judith Durek, in *Circle of Stones* (1989), began each chapter in her book about women's experiences with questions:

> How might your life have been different if there had been a place for you? A place for you to go...a place of women, to help you learn the ways of women....
> How might your life have been different if there had been a place for you...a place of women, where you were received and affirmed? A place where other women, perhaps somewhat older, had been af-

firmed before you, each in her own time, affirmed, as she struggled
to become truly herself.
How might your life have been different?

Support for a positive view of facility placement was developed by a
group of leaders from the national field of juvenile corrections institutions
and detention (National Institute of Corrections/Office of Juvenile Justice
and Delinquency Prevention 1992). This group described a vision of the juvenile justice field as offering a legitimate, alternative pathway to success
for the select group of juveniles in its care. Their view of a facility program
as a legitimate alternative pathway to education and success in the community provides an option somewhere between the views of necessary evil
and haven.

In any case, a more positive view of a facility program is more likely to
help the girls see the experience as meaningful. Such a view also enhances
staff effectiveness and job satisfaction. When viewed in a positive light,
work has a higher meaning for staff. For girls, there is a tendency to seek
the meaning of experience as a primary method of learning and knowing
(Belenky et al. 1986). Boys accept knowledge based on authority. The girls
themselves must see their placement as meaningful if it is going to make a
difference in their lives. If they do not experience a program placement as
meaningful, the skills, knowledge, and abilities they acquire there are less
likely to become part of their repertoire.

Myth: Girls Are Harder To Work With

A fairly common viewpoint is that girls are more difficult to work with
than boys. This viewpoint is shared equally by men and women, who voice
similar reasons. The anecdotal stories say that girls are more petty, more
prone to hold grudges, more likely to gossip about each other, and more
manipulative and sneaky. No one would argue that working with girls is
more intense and more emotionally demanding than working with boys.
The root of these perceived differences, and this view of girls' attributes results from a misunderstanding and devaluing of attributes that are characteristically female. Reclassifying these attributes from a feminist perspective may make a difference in both public education and for programing
for special populations, including girls in the juvenile justice system.

From feminist theory and research, we now understand that what has
been described as pettiness can be viewed as attention to detail. The details of behavior, emotions, and the dynamics of relationship are of particular interest to females, which is why females gossip and talk about what
other people do and say.

Holding grudges is related to the importance females attach to expectations and values about relationships and how they believe they should operate. Manipulativeness and sneakiness are attributes that describe

techniques of oppressed peoples without legitimate power. Because men do not often behave in these ways and are not socialized in these behaviors, men are more prone to have difficulty dealing with an all-female population. Even the current literature is filled with discussion about the difficulty men and women have communicating and understanding each other (Tannen 1986, 1990; Gray 1992).

In reality, girls may be far more amenable to treatment than boys.

Men who have worked with girls learn to become cautious because they are often the targets of manipulative behavior, especially false accusations. Often, however, men in girls' facilities may, in fact, have allowed themselves to be seduced by girls, if not sexually then emotionally. Women have their own difficulties working with girls because a woman meets herself and her own life experiences every day as she faces the problems girls bring to the facility. This can be a difficult proposition for some women.

Research suggests that women and girls in such a relationship are therapeutic for each other (Brown and Gilligan 1992). This means that women (and men) working with girls must be able and willing to process the development of girls and women in a male-dominated world. This can be a painful but rewarding experience for anyone involved in it. It explains the intensity of the experience of working with girls and the reasons that many may find it difficult, if not impossible.

In reality, girls may be far more amenable to treatment than boys. If treatment is seen as a reflective, growing process about people, behavior, relationships, and change for the sake of relationships, then girls are more likely to willingly participate in it. That is not surprising when we consider that women are the largest audience for the current self-help movement. Women represent the largest percentage of clients in the voluntary mental health system. More women and girls "get into" treatment. The logical conclusion is that if women are more open to and more amenable to treatment, then they are not more difficult to work with. However, working with them may be different and should be understood as different and planned for differently. The result is that working with girls can be effective and rewarding and, when done right, can be easier than working with boys.

The "Coed Is Better" Myth

The myth that coed programs are preferable is an oft repeated one in the juvenile justice field. It is one of the major principles to come out of the juvenile advocacy and the standards movement of the 1970s. There are usually two explanations for this view. The first is that because many, if not all, of girls' problems have to do with their relationships with boys, then they are best treated in a coeducational environment. The other argument is that you have fewer behavioral problems with the boys when there are girls in the program. Of course, there are lots of stories about the behavior of girls in such environments.

The Valentine Foundation (1990) strongly states that programs for girls need to remove girls from the attentions of teenage boys and from those for whom they fill care-giving roles. Traditionally, girls are taught to put their relationships with others, particularly males, before their own needs. They are taught that it is their own need that calls them to do this. Girls in trouble need to focus on themselves for a while. Girls (and boys) need to be okay with themselves before they can be okay in a relationship.

No place that is just right for girls is going to look like the rest of the system. Although there is often a price to pay for that difference, the challenge remains to create an environment that is best for girls.

Much of the public education system is designed around research and theory based on models of male development. Certainly, juvenile justice systems are based on and driven by the needs, interests, and value of males. It is even more of a male institution than the public education system. Both represent a society that is based on and driven by values that are defined and articulated by a predominantly male viewpoint.

Uniquely Female-Oriented Environment

It is possible, given the isolation and size of a typical girls' facility, to create an environment that is uniquely female oriented. This environment is going to be very different from the outside world. The tone, the content, and the process are going to be quite different. No place that is just right for girls is going to look like the rest of the system. Although there is often a price to pay for that difference, the challenge remains to create an environment that is best for girls.

Shared-service Compromise

The shared-service compromise, in which girls' programs are essentially separate, but share certain program or administrative services with boys' programs, is almost as unacceptable as coed programs. The differences that girls present, and the frequent perceptions that those differences represent less desirable attributes, predispose the system to be disadvantageous to girls. Side by side, in systems and programs that are designed for boys, girls will appear to be more problematic. Even the most dedicated staff inevitably start preferring the "easier road," working with boys. Girls intuitively know this and sense the implicit rejection. Hope of a truly therapeutic intervention with them is lost. They get the real but unjust message about their place, their role. This message can come from unequal services that range from academic to maintenance, from medical to business office, from food service to inventory management.

The use of activities or denial of activities between boys and girls as a reward for good behavior or consequence of bad behavior on the part of either perpetuates exploitative relationships between males and females. It is, in itself, exploitative and has no place in a therapeutic environment for girls who have poor self-esteem and a history of destructive relationships with males; nor is it appropriate for young males who may be in the system for exploiting or abusing others.

Although the therapeutic process clearly must prepare girls to deal with the realities of their disadvantaged roles in society, it should not reflect or reinforce those realities. Men and women do not play equal roles in society. They do not have the same experiences or the same opportunities. Juvenile justice facilities are not going to change those realities. They can only hope to prepare the young women who come into their care to return to society stronger and more able to cope.

The argument that a facility that is not like society cannot prepare girls for society is invalidated by research from the Women's College Coalition showing that all-female schools have produced one-third of the female board members of Fortune 1000 companies (Tifft 1990). Women who attend all-female colleges are not taught by experience that certain positions go to boys and certain others go to girls. They get to fill *all* the positions.

There is strong evidence in research to support the notion that same-gender educational environments are more conducive to learning than heterosexual ones. The new schools for African-American boys that are springing up in the nation's cities reflect a similar notion. If all-female colleges are good for upper and upper-middle class girls, why are gender-specific programs for poor delinquent girls not preferable? The whole rites of passage movement is essentially gender based. Girls in placement need a place to which they can come to reflect on who and what they are and to make decisions about what they can be, individually and separately from the world in which they have experienced difficulty.

Leaving this separate, female-oriented environment will, of course, require a transition or reentry phase during which girls are assisted in bridging the strength-building experience of a female environment with the reality of the world. Any effective program for girls will need a definite program for this stage of the process. This stage must be as uniquely female as any other in the process. It should be recognized that the assumptions and procedures of psychological separation—the letting go of relationships at predesignated stages in adolescence—that are required of the system may be contrary to the needs, interests, and values of girls and effective girls' programs.

Program Design and Philosophy

Program philosophy is often something that fills in the blank spaces in a policy and procedure manual. Few people take the time to go through the process of examining their personal philosophy and articulating their values and beliefs about children, staff, and programs. Very often, a program philosophy is a position for or against some other philosophy or perceived philosophy.

A philosophy includes the assumptions that are made about the people and the business of the system. It is by nature value laden. The development of a program philosophy should include a values-clarification process. Given the current debate and tension around women's issues, this could be a very intense process. It certainly should consider the myths and assumptions about girls, women, and girls' programs discussed earlier in this chapter. Development of a philosophy statement should be grounded in the theoretical model or system from which the treatment intervention approaches will be derived. The idea of an eclectic approach is too often a mask for the absence of a clearly identified and articulated philosophy. This absence can result in dysfunctional internal contradictions as models and techniques are identified and implemented.

A philosophy for a girls' facility is likely to be stated in opposition to perceived systematic oppression, sexism, or devaluation of the role of females in society. Before a philosophy for a girls' facility is drafted, those writing it should make a thorough review of the research and literature related to the gender bias in the traditional mental health field. Traditionally, the characteristics of a mentally healthy female often reflect societal expectations related to a submissive role in society. The Stone Center for Developmental Services and Studies at Wellesley College offers a feminist critique of the mental health field. Many of the articles and journals of the Stone Center should be required reading for anyone involved with girls in the juvenile justice system. *Women in Connection: Writings from the Stone Center* is a good place to start. The Stone center publishes a catalog of "writings"— published and unpublished—from which one can order.

Internal philosophical consistency is important if all members of the organization are to clearly understand the programs' philosophy and mission. This is especially true in a girls' facility.

Understanding of the whys, hows, and wherefores, and the need to see connections is important to women's ways of understanding (Belenky et al.

1986). It is also related to the circular thinking characteristic of girls' learning styles (Gilligan, Lyons, and Hanmer 1990). Because girls and women tend to think in circular or connected patterns, they are likely to pick up philosophical inconsistencies. The connections and consistencies tend to reinforce or enhance the credibility of the program in the girls' eyes.

Logistics

"Logistics" as used here includes unit size, unit staffing, physical plant design, and population movement patterns. These are areas that need to be considered separately from any formula or pattern for boys' programs.

Girls' living units should never house more than twelve girls. Units of thirteen or fourteen could be an exception for an occasional surge capacity. The level of emotionality and emotional disturbance among the girls' populations in juvenile justice is a primary justification for smaller unit sizes. The girls' preoccupation with the dynamics of relationship is another factor that recommends limiting the number of interpersonal variables that each student must face. Twelve is an ideal size for groups and for academic programs, even special education classes. With twelve girls per unit, staff teams of eight direct-care staff are ideal. Eight staff give forty shifts per week to cover twenty-one posts. Single coverage at night supports double and sometimes even triple coverage at peak program times, even accounting for leave time and some other absences. A unit team of eight with a unit manager and perhaps some part-time administrative oversight offers optimal conditions for effective programming and treatment. This staffing also accounts for the amount and intensity of the relationship needs girls seem to have.

The physical plant environment is critical in a girls' program. In the same way that girls use clothing to communicate all types of messages about themselves, they read messages from the condition of the environment. Girls' facilities are often far neater and tidier than boys' or they are far dirtier. Color is very important as are simple things such as the number and location of fixtures in bathrooms. Because of girls' attention to the environment and the dynamics of relationship, as well as their connections and their empathy, contamination is a major issue in girls' programs. Units need some distance or physical barriers so that one unit will not be easily set off by others. In most juvenile justice facilities for girls, movement needs to be planned with great attention to security and separation issues.

Program Structure

Most of the psychological evaluations of the girls who come to juvenile justice facilities include statements about their need for a structured residential program. "Structured" is a rather nebulous term that means different things to different people. It could refer to clarity of rules and norms or a highly regulated environment. It often refers to the use of time and the amount of program activity and whether participation in the activities is mandatory or voluntary. "Structured" is often assumed to mean a high degree of physical or mechanical security. It can also mean that every detail of the program design is carefully thought out as it relates to the needs of the girls and the philosophy of the program. In this case, it could be a very unstructured program by the other definitions of the term.

David Hunt (1971), who developed the Conceptual Level Classification system, described the creation of varied degrees of structure in the different learning environments for each of three conceptual levels of learners. He suggested that high-level conceptual learners need less structure than low- or medium-level conceptual learners. His research indicated that high-level conceptual learners will learn more and develop more rapidly in less structure while low-level conceptual learners will develop more effectively in highly structured learning environments. An important caution is that although high-level learners learn more effectively in less structure, they do also learn in high structure. However, low-level conceptual learners do not function well at all in low structure. The implication is to err on the side of structure.

Part of the structure that Hunt proposed is the interpersonal environment "radiated" by the change agent, teacher, or staff. The variable he considered was the directiveness and control of the change agent over the learning activity. Other systems allow a more detailed description of the factors and behaviors that comprise an interpersonal environment. The Jesness Treatment Classification system is one such model (Jesness and Wedge 1974). Both the Hunt and Jesness models are systems by which a facility program can provide individualized differential treatment. Situational Leadership (Hersey and Blanchard 1978) offers yet another model for defining and describing differential treatment. It has been used as a behavior management levels system in institutions, camps, group homes, and even in public schools.

The Jesness System is particularly useful in a girls' facility. The Jesness system is based on a developmental model derived from a theory of interpersonal maturity (Sullivan, Grant, and Grant 1957). A developmental model considering interpersonal relationship is more consistent with what we now understand about girls' development (Jordan et al. 1991). The use of different interpersonal styles, known and recognized by the girls, fits the girls' focus on the dynamics of relationships as expressed by their interest in and dialogue on the details of conversation and interpersonal exchanges—sometimes referred to as gossip—or "he said, she said" context. The care-giving aspect of gender socialization accommodates the notion that different treatment for different people is fair and justified. This notion is different than the traditionally male view of justice in which equal or the same means fair (Gilligan 1982).

In a structured environment, girls can experience the environment as predictable. For girls with chaotic backgrounds and long histories of institutionalism, predictability is a critical component of feeling safe. Girls, especially given their histories of abuse, must feel completely safe from physical harm in the environment before learning and growth can occur. Understanding that the girls in a particular program often know the other girls and their potential for violence, a facility program may need to design and implement a fairly intense structured environment that the girls perceive and experience as safe. Using such a highly structured approach requires a shared philosophy and clear rationale by all the members of the organization.

Other research indicates women express a need for structure in their educational experiences (Belenky et al. 1986). A facility program for girls is an educational experience. Research in human relations laboratory training (Egan 1976) also suggests structure helps channel energies toward learning. Egan reported that structured-learning groups result in greater ego-involvement and more self-perceived personality change than unstructured learning groups.

The amount of acting-out behavior in personal and institutional histories is of greater importance in deciding the degree of structure than criminal charges. Sometimes a facility for status offenders may call for more structure than one for serious offenders. A high degree of structure calls for a theoretically sound rationale that is shared by all the members of the organization. The effectiveness of a structured program sometimes masks the need for the structure, particularly from an outside viewpoint. Yet the girls themselves do not usually seek out structure on their own. For example, program structure (as opposed to security practices) may be less important for older adolescents with very serious criminal charges than for younger, more immature delinquents with "lighter" crimes.

Program Environment

Program environment is another aspect of program design that can be intentionally planned. Unless intentionally designed to be otherwise, a program culture will automatically reflect some version of the general culture, which may not be the most advantageous for the girls in the juvenile justice system. If not planned and facilitated by the models and systems that flow from the program's philosophy, the program environment can evolve from the delinquent subculture brought by the girls or by the dominant, local culture of the staff.

Program environment can be experienced as a feeling or an impression created by a special setting within the facility. Historically, facilities have attempted to create a home- or family-like environment. This is a difficult illusion to create in the face of facility placement. Egan (1976) suggests that a group, or institutional living environment, *must be* different from a day-to-day experience if it is to make a difference in day-to-day life. He goes on to suggest that this difference offers a type of "cultural permission" to engage in or try on new behaviors that would not be allowed in the real world.

The primary criterion for an effective intervention with girls is involvement.

Program environment can also be seen in the informal norms and the perceived characteristics shown by the behaviors and interactions of all its members. Many of these characteristics in a girls' program are or should be those attributes that are described as uniquely female. In a girls' facility, the personal and interpersonal dynamics of relationship are much more pronounced and open than in other facilities. One reason girls seem to exhibit more acting-out behavior is that they constantly test commitment by acting out. Such acting out must be understood as a function of relationship. The primary criterion for an effective intervention with girls is involvement. The use of isolation, medication, or reward/sanction systems does not promote meaningful change in girls' lives. What works is involvement, connection, touch, and passing the "test" when it is time.

Often, uniquely female characteristics can be seen in a girls' program culture. Emotionality can be understood and celebrated, not just tolerated. Relationships among girls on all levels tend to be nonhierarchical. In developing a positive environment, there is no room for superstars; team is more important than individuals. There tends to be a lack of rigidity in roles, responsibilities, and duties.

Women must be in the major decision-making roles in a girls' facility. Girls are used to seeing men in charge. They expect men to be in charge. They expect to be taken care of by men. That is one reason they think *any* man is better than no man. That is why they take the first loser who comes along, why they get involved with pimps, and why they end up alone, looking for someone else to take charge of their lives. When exploited and aggressively reactive girls see men in charge, they are further exploited and challenged. They may revert to the coy and manipulative roles that they have learned so well. This is not real empowerment.

If there are men in charge, for all the reasons that those things happen, the decision making needs to be managed in such a way that the girls can see the women as having overt, not covert, power in the facility. Women need to use that power differently than how they have traditionally used it in organizations. It must be in line with all the other norms and forms of a female organization. The real purpose of power, in a woman-centered culture, is to empower others. Even though some women may not always represent the highest values of a woman-centered culture, while some men do, there is still an overarching need to give girls positive role models.

The most appropriate facility climate for a girls' program must be one that identifies, rejects, and has alternatives to the forms and norms of a traditionally male-defined organization. This is in regard to the rules, norms, disciplinary procedures, and institutionalized services such as food and medicine. Each of these aspects of a program must be reviewed in the context of the now well-researched field of women's studies and feminist literature. However, knowledge alone is not enough. It has to be applied. This means that programs for girls may need some basic, often dramatic operational differences from boys' programs.

Obviously counselors who work with girls around issues of sexual abuse should be female. However, since the behavior of sexually abused girls is driven by the fact of their abuse, even behavioral counseling becomes a sexual abuse issue.

Sexual Abuse as a Program Theme

Although most managers will acknowledge that sexual abuse is a critical issue in the lives of delinquent girls, it is often difficult to know what that means when developing or operating a program for sexually abused girls (or boys, for that matter). Current national statistics indicate that one out of every four girls in this country will be sexually abused before her eighteenth birthday. That figure can be as high as nine out of ten among delinquent girls in detention facilities. In the case of incest, the average age of onset for sexual contact is between the ages of eight and eleven. The consequences for the girl are often dire and always far reaching. Victims of abuse will respond in a variety of ways and exhibit various symptoms.

Sexual abuse victims usually lose the ability to trust, either because they were abused by people they were supposed to be able to trust, or because those they trusted were unable to protect them from the abuse. Finding themselves in a threatening situation, sexually abused girls search for ways to protect themselves from a world that they now see as hostile and aggressive. They may adopt a stance of aggression and hostility so as not to be different and to identify with what they now see as the dominant culture.

As girls approach preadolescence, when society's messages about gender are the strongest, the additional weight of an abusive history may lead them to become even more aggressive. Added to that, the social message that "might makes right," may lead abuse victims to choices that society finds unacceptable within gender roles. Such girls often hold tightly to hostility and aggression and will resist all attempts to intervene. After all, they have learned in a very dramatic way not only that people are untrustworthy but that they are also unpredictable and manipulative.

It should come as no surprise when sexually abused girls adopt the behaviors of their predators. The adaptation of the pattern of aggression exhibited by the abusive predator is a frequent characteristic of sexually abused victims. The pattern of aggressive behavior protects them from further abuse and gives them back a sense of control. Although it is currently underresearched and underreported, there are indications that this pattern occurs in females more frequently than previously realized.

With abuse victims, the assurance that they are safe and secure in a world that has not proven to be such in the past is no easy task. Again, program structure is a critical factor in establishing a sense of safety and security.

The introduction of sexual abuse as a guiding theme into a facility's program philosophy and operation demands that program designers and administrators be familiar with the current research and literature in that field. Questions about the reality of the abuse and the severity of its effects need to be addressed before a meaningful approach can be developed. All staff must be sensitized to the issues of sexual abuse. The principles of all interventions will be colored in some way by the existence of the abuse history.

Of central importance is the need for the facility to provide girls with a strong sense of safety and security before other interventions are brought to bear. With abuse victims, the assurance that they are safe and secure in a world that has not proven to be such in the past is no easy task. Again, program structure is a critical factor in establishing a sense of safety and security.

The program philosophy should also address empowerment of the girls—their ability to resolve prior issues of abuse and to take charge of their lives to prevent its reoccurrence. Institutions run the risk of further victimization of girls by continuing to cast them in the role of a victim, from which they can never emerge. Only by facilitating real and significant growth and development and by challenging gender-role stereotypes will girls begin to experience and develop their innate power to resist victimization. This can, however, be an uncomfortable process for the staff, the girls, and the administration.

An understanding of the process the girls take from being a victim to being a survivor is critical in developing the systems for managing the process itself. As victims move past the culturally imposed phases of guilt and shame, as they come to realize the injustice of the acts to which they were exposed, and as they experience the system's ineptitude for dealing with the problem, anger becomes a focal point. This anger may be seen by others, who have not experienced the victim's loss, as disproportionate. Their internal anger that has been silenced can be extreme.

The total facility environment must be able to predict and facilitate the stages of growth that abused girls go through as they change. At the same time, it must provide systems for managing the concurrent behaviors. Although anger can be one of the most difficult to manage, the subsequent stages can also present unique facility management issues. The implications of this approach pertain not only to the program philosophy and design but to staff training and development. Every worker in a girls' facility, including those not traditionally seen as being involved in treatment, must become treatment agents. They must be conversant in the theory of adolescent female growth and development. They should be knowledgeable about the occurrence and consequences of sexual abuse. They must also be willing and able to challenge the traditional victim's role for girls (in spite of the fact that the girls have truly been victims).

With such staff training and awareness, a facility program has the potential to offer a unique opportunity for girls' growth and to provide an environment that helps break the cycle of abuse in girls' lives. In recommending single-gender therapeutic intervention groups and female-focused curricula, Darcy Miller (1993) suggests the following issues be recognized in programming for sexually abused girls:

- discussing and helping adolescent females overcome crippling dependency issues related to the abuse;
- facilitating positive self-concepts and assisting the females in recognizing their self-worth beyond a sexual standard;
- improving the adolescent females' perception of themselves as women and their prospects for the future;
- helping the adolescent females develop strategies that will prevent them from becoming future victims of sexual and physical abuse.

Program Content and Activities

There is often a tendency toward competition and turf behavior among the various program areas of a facility. Yet, intentional program design can reduce, even eliminate, such tendencies. Cross-departmental decision-making and program-planning activities can help. Each area can, and should, identify ways to support the other areas. Social skills taught by unit or cottage staff can be reinforced by recreation staff and teachers. Unit staff can act as tutors in the classroom, help with homework, and run learning centers for skill development on the unit. During unit activities, girls can practice the skills taught in recreation. This interconnectedness will be appreciated by the girls because it "fits" for them. They also look for contradictions and will find them.

One critical connection occurs among recreation, medical, and food service. Physical wellness is, by definition, tied to these three areas. Each needs a clear, connected philosophy that is derived from the overall program philosophy. These are not ancillary or incidental services. Their functions are as critical as those of counseling or education programs and should be planned, valued, and evaluated, as such.

Medical staff should be involved in the planning and monitoring of the food service or nutrition program. Medical and recreational staff need to work together on issues related to participation in recreation programs. Medical staff can mediate and facilitate an ongoing dialogue between the recreation staff and food service staff on the relationship of meal planning, food intake, and physical activity. The girls can and should be aware of and part of the dialogues, because the content is connected to their lifelong wellness.

Inclusive curriculum and relevant content in the academic program are essential in a girls' program. Beyond content, teaching techniques and strategies are not different from treatment techniques and strategies. All should be driven by what we know about the ways girls learn. Vocational programs should be selected to develop employment, avocational, and entrepreneurial opportunities. There needs to be some compensation for the reality that the girls probably have been exposed to in a traditionally male-oriented educational system.

Program Evaluation

The most important evaluation of facility program effectiveness is outcome. In a residential treatment facility, there are several levels of outcome to consider. The first and most immediate is the quality of life within the program. Are the girls and staff safe? What are the statistics on fights, assaultive behavior, and runaways. In an effectively run girls' program, these can be "zero."

The next level of evaluation is client progress in the program. This can include academic and other measures of achievement. The Jesness Inventory offers a means to measure progress as well as outcome. In the experience of the Lansing program and others who use the Jesness system, it was possible to measure a unit staff team's effectiveness by monitoring the Jesness scores of the unit population. This process can even assess the individual counselor's effectiveness. More important, Jesness scores can be used as a guide for program modifications and staff training.

The standard measure of program effectiveness, recidivism, is not a particularly useful measure of the effectiveness of a girls' program. The official statistics on recidivism show a very low rate for girls, but even this does not demonstrate program effectiveness. The measure of a girl's success or failure usually has little to do with re-arrest, the criterion for measuring recidivism. There is only anecdotal information that comes from the girls themselves as they often maintain contact with staff at the facility long after they leave. The importance of relationship and connectedness in girls' lives inclines the girls to maintain some level of contact with the facility, often at holiday time—as with family and good friends.

In the facility on which the ideas on which this chapter is based, there are some conclusions that can be drawn based on different levels of program development. It is evident that when the length of stay drops to less than a year on average, half of the girls return to the agency. When the length of stay was a full year, with a population of fifty to sixty, no more than one or two girls returned in the course of a year.

The one critical measure of the girls' and the program's effectiveness is successful completion of a high school education. Unfortunately, in the facility referenced, that is the one goal that seems to elude most of the girls. No matter how much they accomplish in the facility, they almost never go on to complete their education. A high school equivalency program for girls that are age-eligible is the only mechanism to offset that fact. However, only about 10 percent of the girls are old enough to take that option.

Unfortunately, long-term evaluation of program effectiveness is difficult to perform because the records of juveniles are closed after they leave the agency. The reality is that we must focus primarily on in-program measures for the type of data needed to evaluate and plan for ongoing program development.

Another option available for program evaluation is the Social Climate Scale measures (Insel and Moos 1974). This process assesses social climate (in a variety of settings), using dimensions that are not typically examined in any structured, meaningful way. The instruments, which survey all members of the organization, consider several dimensions of the environment: relationship, personal development or growth, system maintenance, and change.

The relationship dimension assesses the type and intensity of the relationships that exists in the program: staff to client, juvenile to juvenile, staff to management, staff to staff. Personal development and growth considers the extent to which the climate emphasizes good planning, efficiency, and "getting the job done." Evaluation of the type of systems in place and how well they facilitate or hinder the job to be done is assessed in the system measurement and change dimension.

Using these dimensions, it is possible for program designers or administrators to make some philosophical decisions about the nature of the environment that can be translated into actual behavior interventions. For a new facility, the philosophical ideal can help guide the development of the program. In an operating program, periodic assessment of social climate can provide the facility with a measure of the drift from the ideal and offer avenues for correction of this.

Management Issues

There are management issues and concerns over almost every aspect of this facility model. They are no greater challenges than running a facility that does not fit the differences in girls' needs and characteristics. These needs are, however, familiar. The approaches suggested in this chapter require going beyond the familiar into new territory. They require going back to the theory, learning new things, and applying that learning intentionally.

The management issues and concerns can be divided into four broad areas:

- facility and external environment
- facility within a system
- organizational dynamics within a facility
- working with the girls

Each of these areas contain some practical aspects that can never be separate from the theoretical and philosophical.

Facility and External Environment

As a topic for discussion, women's issues, under any name (feminism, gender bias, gender equity), are guaranteed to be controversial, whether they are raised in a senate hearing, in a board room, on the street, or at the dinner table in a home. Women are as likely as men to challenge, dismiss, or condemn the topic. The debate is not about Gloria Steinam. It is not about the women's movement itself. Debate over the roles of women in society threatens an entire culture that legitimatized the unequal distribution of power, wealth, and choice. The debate gets debated. The debates need to continue. They must happen on an ongoing basis in, around, and about a girls' facility.

The debate is not comfortable. It is stressful. The only thing that is more stressful, for women, is to not have the debate. It is intense and can be hostile. It affects what you do, how you do it, and how you feel about doing things. The perceived backlash against the women's movement (Faludi 1991) is every bit as real as the racism that permeates our culture. Women of color are twice assaulted. It is not racism and then sexism or sexism then racism that must be addressed. It is racism and sexism; sexism and racism.

A girls' facility can be on the leading edge of issues not only in working with a juvenile justice population, but on issues related to girls in the community, women in the agency, and women and girls in society. It is not unusual, looking at the history of the justice system, to find that it has often led the way in innovative programs that later move to the public arena. This is true in education, vocational training, and treatment. Perhaps it can be true also in real gender equity. To avoid or ignore the women's issues as they relate to the girls that are part of the system is to perpetuate the oppression of these young women. Indeed, it has been suggested that "the official actions of the juvenile justice system should be understood as major focuses in women's oppression as they have historically served to reinforce the obedience and the demands of patriarchal authority no matter how abusive or arbitrary" (Chesney-Lind 1989).

A girls' facility developed along the lines recommended in this chapter will most certainly look very different from any component of ordinary society. It can appear very artificial. It is, by nature, a relatively isolated community. The members of that community come together to engage in activities that are of a very personal and very intense nature. These people do not come together naturally and most come against their will. In addition to the program structure, the interactions are prescribed by the learning content: social skills, interpersonal relations, assertiveness, conflict resolution, and problem-solving training.

In all likelihood, the recommended facility environment will appear to be very contrived. This appearance can provoke a very strong reaction from those who do not understand it or who philosophically do not agree with it. Such a facility can expect an almost continuous challenge on this issue.

Facility and the System

As stressful as the philosophical debate can be, it pales to the stress created within the juvenile justice system. Like any other organization, systems, which are really a means to an end, become ends in themselves. The procedures by which girls get in and out of facilities have little to do with their problems and more to do with bed space, cost of care, and advocacy for its own sake. Civil service systems, established to eliminate the manipulation of jobs by politicians, have their own tyrannies. Simply finding sources for the clothing and special products girls need can be challenging. A few areas deserve special comment.

Cost

Girls are going to cost more than boys. Given the mental health histories and experiences of girls, a higher staff-to-student ratio and a higher level of staff training are required.

Sixteen-, eighteen-, and twenty-bed boys' units may operate at a satisfactory level, but this ratio is too high to address the girls' needs. Failure to address these needs can lead to a program operation that is high in overtime, staff burnout, staff injuries, and turnover. Although the cost may be higher than for boys, it is usually a bargain compared to what the same girls have cost in the mental health system and what they will cost in the future if they are not helped in the present.

Medical costs are likely to be higher for at least three reasons: teen pregnancy, the higher percentage of girls showing positive HIV results, and the fact that psychological and physical illness is a large part of the overall case management with girls.

Girls' clothing and personal items are typically not contract items, so purchasing even necessities can cost more. Recent television talk shows have exposed the disproportionate expenses between products for males and those for females. The same products packaged differently for males and females often have higher prices on the female package. The cost of dry cleaning a woman's blouse is always higher than for a man's shirt.

There are hidden costs also. Ordering T-shirts for one hundred boys for a one-year period takes a lot less time than keeping one hundred girls supplied with various-sized bras. Girls, with their long court involvement and history of movement from place to place are more likely to return to court repeatedly. Court trips are expensive. For many reasons, not the least of which are their treatment needs, girls are less likely than boys to participate in the type of facility services that institutions operate.

Because women are the primary care givers of children in our culture, dealing effectively with girls has an impact on the next generation in a way that boys' programs do not.

Treating girls in a relevant program is a pay now or pay later proposition. Because women are the primary care givers of children in our culture, dealing effectively with girls has an impact on the next generation in a way that boys' programs do not. Girls and their babies start the cycle all over again: teen pregnancy; public assistance; and dependent, neglected, abused, abandoned, and delinquent children are all expensive reasons to change the course of girls' lives. Such treatment is the best prevention.

Advocacy for Girls

Because they differ from the "norm," decisions, policies and procedures, practices, and programs are more likely to be scrutinized in a woman-centered girls' facility. The articulation of the details of expectation, processes, and relationship dynamics puts the leaders and staff "out there" for anyone to challenge. Such challenge is, in fact, healthy for a facility. It causes continuous reflection, evaluation, and dialogue that can only enhance quality and commitment.

However, when such challenges result in a significant change in operating procedures, the entire program may be undermined. In a well-designed program in which each component is carefully thought out in the context of a clearly articulated philosophy, any alteration in a part affects the whole. Challenges are often launched at some of the very components selected for the unique nature of girls in a facility. On the other hand, advocacy for girls' and women's issues is an essential element of any program for girls.

Recruitment and Hiring

Public sector juvenile justice is a very male world. Most of the employees are male. Because experience is the qualifying criteria for advancement, males tend to get the jobs and the advancement. Because girls' programming is such a small part of the larger system, there is little experience to be had working with girls, and rarely is working with girls part of the qualifying criteria even for other jobs of working with girls. That is one of the factors that continuously pulls a girls' facility to look and act like a boys' facility.

In the public sector, a balanced, stable workforce selected and trained especially for working with girls can be destroyed by layoffs, cutbacks, and other workforce upheavals. More men have more experience than the women on girls' programs. A girls' facility can be decimated to its core when there is a significant influx of untrained and often unsuited males. Layoffs and bumping are some of the mechanisms by which this can happen. Civil Service tests are another. Promotional tests consider experience as a qualifying item. Most experience in the juvenile justice system is gained by men in male facilities. Thus, a female facility with a civil service list for position candidates will find many more males than females, but few of them will have experience in working with girls.

Performance and Supervision

For all the reasons evident from the discussion so far, the kind and content of supervision in a women-centered girls' program is different from that in most boys' programs. It is generally more intimate, more personal, more likely to cross the boundaries between who one is as a worker and who one is as a person. Most, but not all, women are comfortable with this; few men are. More women than men are likely to see work as part of their identity, or, said differently, women are less likely than men to compartmentalize their lives into work/home categories (Helgesen 1990). Women are not as reluctant to work on their self-identities. Again, women both as staff and as clients tend to pay more attention to nuances and details of behavior and interpersonal dynamics.

All is well with the woman-centered organizational culture until there is a conflict into which the more traditional male system enters, defines the course of action, and attempts to define the content. Formal labor management activities, grievance and appeal procedures, and even certain traditional male definitions of teamwork are often at odds with the norms of a women-centered organization. Such system functions, then, are part of the way that the whole system undermines the ability of an organization to structure itself to be different—to meet the needs of a different population.

Often agency policies and procedures, designed for the larger population (boys), can actually be counterindicated for girls. A suicide policy that considers self-destructive behavior as an extraordinary event calling for extraordinary measures can actually reinforce such behaviors in girls who use these behaviors to call attention to themselves or to manipulate the system.

On the other extreme, a procedure calling for mechanical restraints to be used on all students of a certain adjudication undermines the relationship between staff and students who have made significant progress and diminishes the girl's feeling that she has changed and can change her life. A climate that presses for coed socials between incarcerated girls and boys misses the point about the girls' experiences with such boys. Additionally, it is too often forgotten that girls are typically adjudicated for much less serious crimes than boys at the same level. With such encouragement and such inequities, should we wonder why girls in trouble gravitate toward males who abuse them?

It would be too radical to suggest that every policy and procedure of a larger agency be rewritten for girls. It is not unreasonable, however, to have a process or a forum by which certain policies could be modified to account for gender differences. Such a process might even result in a more careful evaluation of policies and procedures as they relate to boys.

Organization Dynamics Within a Facility

The type of programming recommended for girls in this chapter is a fairly sophisticated proposition. Staff who carry out this suggested programming will get paid the same as those in other facilities who do much less. However, the level of salary has never been a measure of program effectiveness or staff dedication. Still, effective performance in such a program calls for a high level of dedication and commitment.

Staff who are seeking autonomy in their work lives or who have a self-identity that values being different for the sake of difference will have a difficult time adapting to a program such as the one recommended in this chapter.

Part of the intensity that comes from working in girls' programs stems from relationship demands from the girls and from team members. Little issues can become big deals. For some, it is important to be in a place in which that happens. For others, it is stressful. It can be very difficult for staff not comfortable with such intrusions into their private sides, especially for those who often have difficulty separating work-related issues from their personal lives. When it comes to how women act in the roles they have chosen or been given in their lives, the involvement in the facility ways can be threatening and disruptive to their personal lives outside the facility. On the other hand, a facility that lives out the connectedness so important in women's ways can offer tremendous support to those who work there, even in nonwork-related matters.

Given the level of commitment and intensity of the relationships within the facility, conflict can be traumatic. Separation can be difficult, even bitter, not unlike separations in marital and familial situations. In general, both staff and girls who leave express appreciation for even the difficult times, perhaps more than for the pleasant times. The girls view these difficult times as part of the process, part of the growth, part of what mattered.

Staff who are seeking autonomy in their work lives or who have a self-identity that values being different for the sake of difference will have a difficult time adapting to a program such as the one recommended in this chapter. This happens for three reasons. First, in a woman-centered environment team is more important than a star. Second, consistency and predictability is very important, and that means everyone is doing the same thing, the same way. Third, individualized differential treatment means that each staff will follow a script for interaction that is based on the girls' unique characteristics. There is still a lot of room for creativity and personality differences, but staff who are into the superstar mode may not be able to see that far.

Gender-staffing issues also are important. For juveniles, their developmental and treatment needs are as important as their privacy. Role modeling, an absolutely critical part of any effective program, is significantly impacted by gender differences and similarities. With sexually abused girls, most of whom were victimized by males, the gender of the direct care staff and the counselors is of paramount importance. Further, given the social power dynamic of male authority over females, even therapeutic male staff/counselor relationships can be unhealthy for girls. Surely there must be a male presence in the environment, but the roles must be very clearly defined and understood.

Working with the Girls: Miscellaneous Issues

The girls who come to a juvenile justice system present a very complex picture. It can be difficult to remember that they are victims. They often know the system better than staff do and with institutional and psychiatric center histories, they have learned all the games. Although girls may be easier to treat once a program is operating smoothly, getting to that point is another story. Part of that process has to do with establishing the climate. Another part of it is to get the individual girls to focus on themselves and get to the business of their treatment.

The process from external control to autonomy is a very important consideration. The programs experienced by this author have been extremely controlling with new students, while other students have gone to school and worked in the community, on the other end. Yet, experience dictates that safe environments begin with control of behavior. The up-front control often generates resistance from the girls and concern from critics; yet, it eliminates the period of time it would take to wait for that inevitable resistance to emerge. It eliminates all the games, the plots, and the focus on establishing oneself in the social order of the group. It eliminates fear.

Of course, to be truly effective, the control period has to be balanced with an equally strong period of autonomy. This may be hard to do in a program with a short length of stay and a large population turnover.

With the limited number of girls' options and the way girls earn their way to juvenile justice, in the context of their relationship orientation, the prior relationships between the girls must be addressed. There are several ways of doing this depending on the nature and size of the program. In a small facility with a few "light weight" girls, it can be dealt with by bringing the issue out in a group setting. With larger groups of girls who have more serious histories and a strong delinquent-culture background, the strategies have to be more varied and thorough. One way is to significantly restrict free social interaction of new students—to allow them interaction only with staff and those students who have been in the program for a long time and have given up the delinquent values.

Girls who are successful in a program inevitably go through a period of overidentification with the program and the staff. This is a natural part of the change and the transfer of learning process, but this stage should not be perceived as institutionalized behavior, nor should the tendency to share a common language be considered a problem. All facilities have their own culture and their own language. When that language resembles what you hear on the streets, many people are unconcerned. When a group of street delinquents start talking like human relations trainers, words like "brainwashed" and "robot" are used.

The skills and content that girls are expected to acquire must be role modeled by all staff at all times. Credibility is very important to girls. Without credibility there is no such thing as relationship. Girls notice every detail and see everything as connected, even when it is not. They pick up on the gaps and loopholes. Failure of one staff member to put into practice what is said can, with some girls, undermine the credibility of all staff and the program, in general.

The overidentification; the common language; and the results of effective role modeling are both cause and effect of intentional overlearning. This, too, is an important part of the learning and change process and should not be viewed as a negative.

There is some liability to the facility personae that girls take on. If they do not choose the right time and place to exhibit it, they can find themselves rejected by people their own age. Some, on the other hand, find themselves elevated in a group situation. Girls who become very articulate in the human relations treatment language and women's issues can be threatening to the staff in group homes and transition programs because of their verbal skills and jargon. Some may incorporate these skills into their old pattern of aggression and intimidation.

In general, the use of room confinement with girls is counterproductive. It gives them time to brood and feeds their sense of rejection and hostility. It does nothing to build the relationships that are essential to the treatment process. Physical restraints are a far more bonding experience if they are perceived as part of the treatment process. Several hours in a physical, hands-on restraint will demonstrate commitment to a girl and will offer a basis for relationship. Separation or room confinement or isolation will impair relationships. It should be used only when there is not enough staff or time to do a hands-on, involved intervention. The girls themselves say "they would not give up on me."

Hands-on intervention is very important with girls. When girls test, they are testing more than the limits. They test the relationship. They test commitment. They test credibility.

Literature on behavior change recommends that reinforcers for positive behavior should be determined by the particular needs and interest of the learner. The new literature on girls' development suggests that relationship and responsibility are important parts of a girl's identity. These two categories provide a broad field from which to select the reinforcers that will be helpful in promoting significant change and growth in girls.

Relationship can be described as the social interaction with meaningful others in the environment. Those others can be staff, other students, and/or outside parties. Using such interaction as a reward is very different than using it as a means or process by which learning is facilitated. It requires defining and categorizing the interaction in some graduated manner. With staff, the relationship can be seen in the high task/low relationship to low task/high relationship transition of situational leadership (Hersey and Blanchard 1978).

Conclusion

Any program is a result of a unique combination of people, places, times, and program models. Only the program models can be replicated, and they will be altered by the differences in the other variables. It is the selection and implementation of various models that are particularly suited to the population that make a program a model to be considered as a reference for other programs.

In developing programs for girls, planners and administrators can draw on a wealth of new and exciting models and programs. Unfortunately, in juvenile justice, there are not many examples. There is little to take us forward. However, the growing body of research and feminist literature offers an ever-increasing body of knowledge from which to plan, implement, and evaluate programs for girls. It may, in fact, be the best time to engage in a detailed process of facility development for new and old girls' programs.

References

American Association of University Women. 1992. *How schools short-change girls*. A joint publication of the American Association of University Women and the National Education Association.

Belenky, M. F., et al. 1986. *Women's ways of knowing: The development of self, voice and mind*. New York: Basic Books.

Brown, L. M., and C. Gilligan. 1992. *Meeting at the crossroads: Women's psychology and girls' development*. Cambridge, Mass.: Harvard University Press.

Burke, V. B., and L. Ravoira. 1993. *Inspiring change and empowering troubled adolescent girls: National focus on gender issues and the juvenile justice system*. Washington, D.C.: Community Research Associates. Office of Juvenile Justice and Delinquency Prevention.

Chesney-Lind, M. 1989. Girls' crime and women's place: Toward a feminist model of female delinquency. *Crime and Delinquency* 35(1): 5–29.

Durek, J. 1989. *Circle of stones: Woman's journey to herself*. San Diego, Calif.: LuraMedia.

Egan, G. 1976. *Interpersonal living: A skills/contract approach to human relations training in groups*. Monterey, Calif.: Brooks/Cole Publishing Company.

Faludi, S. 1991. *Backlash: The undeclared war against women*. New York: Crown Publishers.

Gilligan, C. 1982. *In a different voice: Psychological theory and women's development*. Cambridge, Mass.: Harvard University Press.

Gilligan, C., N. P. Lyons, and T. J. Hanmer. 1990. *Making connections: The relational worlds of adolescent girls at Emma Willard School.* Cambridge, Mass.: Harvard University Press.

Gray, J. 1992. *Men are from Mars/women are from Venus: a practical guide for improving communication and getting what you want in your relationships.* New York: HarperCollins.

Helgesen, S. 1990. *The female advantage: Woman's ways of leadership.* New York: Doubleday.

Hersey, P., and K. H. Blanchard. 1977. *Management of organizational behavior: Utilizing human resources.* Englewood Cliffs, N.J.: Prentice-Hall.

———. 1978. *The family game: A situational approach to effective parenting.* Reading, Mass.: Addison-Wesley Publishing Company.

Hunt, D. E. 1971. *Matching models in education: The coordination of teaching models with student characteristics.* Toronto: Ontario Institute for Studies in Education.

Insel, P. M., and R. H. Moos. 1974. *Social climate scales.* Palo Alto, Calif.: Consulting Psychologists Press.

Jesness, C. F., and R. F. Wedge. 1974. *Classifying offenders: The Jesness inventory classification system.* Sacramento, Calif.: California Department of Youth Authority.

Jordan, J. V., et al. 1991. *Women's growth in connection: Writings from the Stone Center.* New York: The Guilford Press.

Loevinger, J. 1976. *Ego development.* San Francisco: Jossey-Bass.

Miller, D. 1993. Sexual and physical abuse among adolescent offenders: Gender differences and implications for programming. *Journal of Correctional Education* 44(3): 146–51.

National Girls' Caucus (flier), c/o P.A.C.E. Center for Girls, Inc., Jacksonville, Fla.

National Institute of Corrections. 1992. *Designing training for the National Institute of Corrections Academy: Instructional theory into practice.* Washington, D.C: U.S. Government Printing Office.

Office of Juvenile Justice and Delinquency Prevention. 1993. *Recommendations for juvenile corrections and detention in response to conditions of confinement: A study to evaluate the conditions in juvenile correctional and detention facilities.* Washington, D.C.: Office of Juvenile Justice and Delinquency Prevention.

Peters, T. 1990. The best new managers will listen, motivate, support: Isn't that just like a woman? *Working Woman* (September): 142–43.

Sadker, M. P., and D. M. Sadker. 1982. *Sex equity handbook for schools.* New York: Longman.

Sullivan, C., M. Q. Grant, and J. D. Grant. The Development of Interpersonal Maturity: Application Delinquency. *Psychiatry,* 1957, 20:273-285.

Tannen, D. 1986. *That's not what I meant! How conversation style makes or breaks relationships.* New York: Ballantine Books.

———. 1990. *You just don't understand. Women and men in conversation.* New York: Ballantine Books.

Thorne, B. 1993. *Gender play: Girls and boys in school.* New Brunswick, N.J.: Rutgers University Press.

Tifft, S. 1990. Dollars, scholars, and gender. *Time* 85 (21 May).

Valentine Foundation and Women's Way. 1991. *A conversation about girls.* Philadelphia: Valentine Foundation.

Woolf, V. 1929. *A room of one's own.* New York: Harcourt, Brace and Company.

6 Facility Programming for Sex Offenders

Bruce Janes

In the mid-1970s, most social service agencies saw a rapid influx of referrals where sexual abuse was alleged. Child protective service programs were created to interview and investigate these allegations. At that time, most professionals expected that the allegations would identify an adult perpetrator, but no one expected to find that nearly half of all investigations would reveal that the alleged offender was an adolescent.

None of the agencies was prepared to respond to this phenomenon, and the adolescent sexual aggressor soon became one of the most difficult populations for social service agencies to handle.

Depending on the jurisdiction, the adolescent received a multiplicity of services ranging from complete dismissal of the referral by the investigator to incarceration with no formal intervention designed specifically to alter or change the offending behavior.

In some instances when the adolescent did not fit a preconceived stereotype of a sex offender, there was no effort to provide any intervention. Gradually, however, the adolescent sexual aggressor started to filter into the systems that provide services to juveniles. In most states, this resulted in an increase of referrals to the juvenile courts and mental health agencies. Once again, the response by the juvenile courts varied widely.

Slowly, treatment programs started to develop around the country. Knopp (1982) researched existing programs and identified twenty-six programs specifically designed to deal with the issue of adolescent sexual aggression. More than half of these programs were located in just three states: Colorado, Minnesota, and Washington. These programs varied from short-term community-based programs which offered outpatient services to residential treatment programs with intensive and comprehensive interventions. Most adolescent programs were based on research and findings of adult offender programs. States that had existing adult services for sex offenders were among the first to develop programs for adolescents.

Bruce Janes is executive director of Reflections Treatment Agency, Youth Services International of Tennessee, Inc. in Knoxville. He also is a member of the National Task Force on the Assessment and Treatment of Adolescent Sex Offenders.

When community and residential programs failed to meet the treatment needs of some of the juvenile offenders, juvenile justice agencies began committing the juveniles to secure-custody institutions. Most of these juveniles were simply placed in secure custody without the benefit of any intervention services and were eventually released back to the community with no corrective action taken in regards to their sexually aggressive behaviors.

Ultimately, programs emerged in some of the secure-custody institutions; others grew out of efforts of the mental health institutions to respond to this population. Regardless of the etiology of the treatment programs for these juveniles, programs around the country appeared to evolve similar strategies as key components of their intervention programs.

Currently there are more than six-hundred programs in the United States specifically designed to provide treatment services to the adolescent sex offender. These programs still tend to be clustered in a handful of states, but most states have some intervention programs available. One of the last social service agencies to respond to the issue of adolescent sexual aggression has been the juvenile correctional facilities, but like other agencies, juvenile corrections has had to develop programs as sex-offending juveniles were being committed by the courts in increasing numbers.

Program development for juvenile sex offenders during the past fifteen years has met some resistance from juvenile corrections at the administrative level.

In recent years, juvenile corrections has moved to shorter lengths of stay, and the adoption of treatment programs within juvenile corrections was viewed as contrary to national trends to move towards de-institutionalization and community-based programs. There was a fear that creating an intervention program within juvenile correctional facilities would draw more juveniles into their facilities and, thereby, create administrative problems with population management.

No other event will create a greater public uproar than a sex crime committed by someone who has been released or has escaped from state custody.

Despite these concerns, sexually aggressive juveniles were ending up in secure custody agencies, and frontline staff and administrators recognized the need for structured and intensive treatment for juveniles in their custody.

Many programs were initiated by concerned staff who recognized the need for a formal, systematic, and structured response that provided treatment within their programs. They often started these programs with no re-sources and minimal support from administrators. They faced criticism, doubt, and ridicule in their attempts to provide services to this unpopular clientele.

Development, implementation, and management of juvenile sex offender treatment within juvenile corrections programs presents unique challenges to anyone attempting to start or expand a treatment program. Some of these challenges deal with the stereotypes, attitudes, and belief systems about sexual abusers, in general. Others are more generic, such as how to create new programs in the face of budget reductions and dwindling re-sources; how to select and train staff; how to locate and design the physi-cal setting for optimal treatment; and how to create a positive atmosphere within the program and the agency to enhance the delivery of services to sexually aggressive juveniles.

The first task by anyone attempting to start a treatment program is to define the problem and the population. In some states there are statistics compiled by child protective service agencies, or there are ad hoc groups that have banded together to educate the public about this growing issue. Legislators, judges, and district attorneys have become aware of the prob-lems presented by juvenile sexual aggressors, and they could lend critical support to the implementation of a treatment program within juvenile cor-rections.

Creating a treatment program that has anything to do with sex crimes should be considered high-profile and likely to catch the interest and scru-tiny of the media and the public. No other event will create a greater public uproar than a sex crime committed by someone who has been released or has escaped from state custody. Usually the ensuing tide of hysteria and outrage results in substantial negative impact on the treatment program. During the past two decades, several treatment programs have suffered re-ductions or complete closure as the result of the actions of one offender who committed such an atrocious offense that the quality and efficacy of the entire program was brought into question.

Reoffense can occur in the community during aftercare or while the of-fender is on pass. It can occur after an escape, or an offense can occur within the treatment program if the administrator overlooks the potential for reoffense while in custody or treatment. Programs must be able to en-dure these difficulties, and this can only be done by a recognition that treatment programs must be supported in the face of inevitable failure due to the recidivism of sex offenders.

To initiate a program, therapists may make exaggerated claims of suc-cess to convince others to support their efforts. Caution must be exercised in this regard, or those claims may be used to discredit the therapist and the program.

To gain the interest and support of influential legislative, community, and administrative leaders, a program director must be able to harness support for the program from different and divergent groups. One of the best sources of support has been from programs that work with victims of sexual abuse crimes. These programs frequently recognize the need for effective offender treatment, and representatives from these programs can lend a very powerful voice to support new efforts.

It is critical to network with other professionals, not only to support efforts to provide treatment but also to give emotional and personal support. Isolation from the therapeutic community can lead to programs and staff being overwhelmed or destroyed by the lack of community and official support or by the discontinuation of funding.

In addition to community safety, the safety of the offenders is also a consideration in selecting a location for the treatment program.

Although there has been rapid development of sex-offender treatment programs during the past twenty years, very little has been written about the problems that may be unique to the creation and implementation of sex-offender treatment programs. Most programs were started without extensive planning. Instead, they may have developed as a result of a "knee-jerk" reaction to a public outcry about the problem of sexual abusers. To design a treatment program and set into motion all those aspects that enhance program development, the therapist/administrator must consider and evaluate the following issues:

- securing available facilities
- working in community settings
- staffing
- training
- effective programming

Securing Available Facilities

Once the decision has been made to initiate a treatment program, the director has to consider the available space in which the treatment program will operate. In some cases, this decision has been made simply by assigning a unit or ward to house a sex-offender treatment program. However, some may have the option of housing the program outside of the juvenile correctional institution in a vacant hospital wing or transitional facility.

The primary consideration is community safety. The selection of a facility may also be influenced by community reaction to the program. Most correctional administrators have had the experience of attempting to locate a correctional program in the community. Whether the surrounding community is rural or urban makes no difference; there is almost always unanimous opposition to locating such programs anywhere outside existing correctional facilities. In some cases, the outspoken opposition of a few influential community leaders is all that is needed to put a stop to an excellent program.

In addition to community safety, the safety of the offenders is also a consideration in selecting a location for the treatment program. This consideration is often overlooked, but if the treatment program disregards the issue of the juveniles' safety, the program will not succeed in providing effective treatment. The juveniles will learn to avoid issues relating to their treatment because they fear being harmed. They may undermine the program and support denial in other juveniles. The credibility of administrators and therapists will be questioned, and their efforts to provide treatment may be met with indifference or outright opposition.

The safety of the juveniles involves several considerations. First, there is safety from ridicule, harassment, and physical harm from other juveniles in the correctional facility and in the treatment program. Then, there is the concern about safety from staff whose negative attitudes and beliefs about treatment, in general, and sex offenders, in particular, may result in negative behaviors toward sex abusers and staff in the program. There is also a concern about possible harm from staff within the treatment program who might become burned out, disenchanted, or overwhelmed by the nature of work with sex offenders. All these concerns must be considered if the manager has the option to select a facility. The first two can be dealt with by segregating the program from the remainder of the general correctional population. The other two concerns are handled by carefully selecting and training the staff, and program design.

The director can minimize the contact and interaction between the offenders in treatment and others who might consider sex abusers easy targets for abuse. Some argue that segregating sex abusers furthers the stigmatization of the offender, maintains stereotypes by others, and minimizes the opportunity to mainstream the offender with other programs and juveniles. While this may be true, it is expected that the many benefits of a segregated program outweigh all other considerations.

It may also be desirable to have a separate school program specifically designed to support the treatment program. In most states, juveniles are required to be in school a minimum number of hours per day. This may represent a substantial block of time that the juvenile is away from specially trained staff and the treatment milieu. The juvenile may engage in behaviors that would provide important feedback to the therapist about the juvenile's progress in treatment. Unless the instructor is aware of the specific treatment issues, these behaviors may go undetected and not be reported to the treatment program. In selecting a facility, the director may want to consider the possibility of the school being located within the treatment unit. The other option would be to designate certain classrooms within the school for the treatment program.

The physical layout of the facility must be evaluated to determine whether adequate and effective supervision can occur. "Blind spots" and other barriers to direct visual supervision tend to promote the possibility of abusive behavior towards the residents in the treatment program. Size of rooms, location of staff, bathroom facilities, and showers are all important considerations. Proximity to other nonoffending programs can be an issue, depending on the amount of acceptance the sex-offender treatment program has within the facility. The director will have to consider sleeping arrangements: how many to a room, location of the beds, and whether doors will be closed or kept open.

For example, a model sex offender-specific treatment program was developed within an existing facility. It was placed in a unit that traditionally held two juveniles to a room, with the doors to each room closed at night. The unit had a capacity of twenty-four residents, but there was only one staff member on duty at night. The night staff visually checked each room at regular intervals through the shift by looking through a small window in each door. Before too long, more aggressive offenders were randomly assigned in rooms with less assertive abusers. As a result, several instances of sexual contact occurred.

There are a number of things which could have been avoided with careful planning and research on available facilities. Some of these problems were the result of physical limitations of supervision, some were due to attitudes and beliefs of staff, and other problems occurred as a result of budget considerations, staffing patterns, and lack of staff training.

In selecting a facility, the director must anticipate the problems and be prepared to design the program around the physical limitations of the facility. Even the most modern and carefully designed facilities have potential hazards to resident safety. These issues are often magnified when dealing with a population of sexually aggressive juveniles.

Working In Community Settings

Adolescent sex offender programs can be developed in a variety of different settings. There are states where judges have the option of placing juveniles in short-term outpatient programs, specially trained foster care, community-based residential treatment facilities, secure custody, or hospital programs. No matter what level of treatment an adolescent sex offender is assigned, the major concern is escape or elopement from the treatment program.

Over the years, many model sex-offender treatment programs for juveniles and adults have been closed down as a result of a single offender illegally leaving the program and reoffending in the community. Program directors must consider the risk that escaped offenders pose to the community and the program.

There is some reticence on the part of mental health professionals to deal with the issue of containment. Their training and background experience does not prepare them to respond to hostile and aggressive clients, and some feel that any effort to secure a person in treatment is contrary to the concepts of developing a therapeutic relationship. To avoid the potential of escape or aggressive behavior, they prescreen residents and take only voluntary and willing therapy candidates, and leave the vast majority of offenders to do their "time" and return to the community without any effort to provide services to deal with their sexually aggressive behaviors.

Positive peer pressure is often the catalyst that results in constructive changes.

Every effort must be made to evaluate the security risks inherent within each facility to minimize escapes, but physical and mechanical security is not enough. To establish an atmosphere of safety and confidence for the residents, the director must establish a culture or community within the treatment program that fosters support and pro-social behaviors in a population that historically resists authority.

Different programs label this process differently. The terms most commonly heard are therapeutic community, positive peer culture, and guided group interaction. These programs strive to promote personal growth and accountability through support and confrontation from the peers in treatment. The treatment environment is highly structured, with clearly defined boundaries and expectations. Sanctions are imposed if expectations are not met; privileges are awarded for recovery and personal growth.

Positive peer pressure is often the catalyst that results in constructive changes. Commitment to the process must be high among the residents. If this positive therapeutic environment is not established by the treatment staff, the program is likely to have the opposite effect—a negative peer culture with its usual problems and pitfalls.

The primary practice is to establish a positive treatment environment by selecting a "seed" group of carefully screened offenders who appear to be in the greatest need of treatment and have the best chance to benefit from the program. Depending on the size of the overall treatment program and the content of the population to be screened, this seed group can vary in size from four-to-twelve individuals. Care must be taken not to dilute this seed group by a rapid increase of new residents until this seed group is firmly established. Then, the resident population can gradually increase until it reaches capacity. It sometimes takes six-to-twelve months to establish a therapeutic culture to the point that the residents are taking responsibility for their program. An indication that a positive culture is functioning is a reduction in behaviors that require direct staff intervention.

Staffing

Depending on the circumstances, a director may find that an existing unit has been reclassified as a sex-offender treatment program but inherits the existing staff. Ideally, the director will be able to interview applicants to staff the sex-offender treatment program. In state correctional programs, the issues of seniority and union guidelines enter into the selection process.

Having female staff members in sex-offender treatment programs is an important aspect of the therapeutic process. Many offenders are not skilled or comfortable in relating to women, which may contribute to their offending behaviors.

To avoid potential grievances, care must be taken during the initial planning to carefully define the knowledge, skills, and abilities attached to the various staff positions. The range and number of staff hired will determine the quality of treatment, but staffing is the primary cost in any budget. Limitations set by budget constraints will determine the staffing content of the treatment program.

Selecting staff to work in a sex-offender treatment program should be done with great care and thought. At times, staff will apply for positions based on seniority and the potential to work a more desirable shift, without regard for the actual work to be done in the therapeutic program. When staff vacancies are announced, a comprehensive description of the duties and tasks of the position will tend to discourage those who are not interested in working with this population or those who are antagonistic to this population and carry with them oppositional biases.

There are several factors to consider while interviewing and selecting staff for a sex-offender treatment program. Strong clinical skills are mandatory in a sex-offender treatment program. It is also important to identify potential staff who are strong team members and who will work with the program, not against it. During the interview, attempts should be made to determine knowledge and comfort level in responding to and discussing explicit sexual behaviors. Potential staff should display an appropriate familiarity with human sexual behavior and be able to discuss aspects of sexuality without undue embarrassment or discomfort.

Traditionally, juvenile correctional facilities are staffed by male line staff. Having female staff members in sex-offender treatment programs is an important aspect of the therapeutic process. Many offenders are not skilled or comfortable in relating to women, which may contribute to their offending behaviors. Responding to women in positions of authority and control is a skill that most offenders must learn to handle. Female staff members are invaluable in helping offenders improve their social and interpersonal skills. Directors may encounter some resistance to hiring female staff. Claims of concern for their personal safety are often raised, but there is little evidence to support this position. Anecdotal reports have not disclosed that female staff are at more risk than male staff.

Many programs attempt to use volunteers in the programs. In some programs, female volunteers teach offenders a range of social and dating skills (Knopp 1984). Sex-offender treatment programs are also valuable training for practicum students in graduate schools of social work, psychology, theology, and psychiatry.

Despite careful screening, many employees find themselves in situations for which they are totally unsuited. Because of the nature and intensity of the work, staff may burn out or experience other negative reactions to the work or to the clients. This makes the staff incapable of dealing rationally and fairly with the juveniles.

Many staff members have experienced traumatic sexual abuse or know someone who has. Emotions and memories of this abuse are brought to the surface by the content of their work. Some may choose to seek professional assistance, while others may prefer to discontinue their employment in the program. The program director must be aware that these elements are part of the staff issues, and the director should be prepared to lend support and assistance, when necessary.

There are several debilitating reactions by staff to work in intense treatment programs. Residents develop erotic fantasies toward their care takers, and in some cases, the staff may become romantically or sexually involved with the juveniles.

Prolonged exposure to traumatic events by therapists can lead to a phenomenon called *Vicarious Traumatization* (McCann and Pearlman 1990). Staff begin to show effects similar to those of actual survivors of trauma. Staff will have to listen and respond to graphic depictions of abhorrent sexual behaviors. It must be anticipated that staff will experience personal and philosophical discomfort in relating to certain offenders. Program directors should consider resources that would allow staff to express their feelings regarding their own sexual lives or their feelings toward certain juveniles.

Training

Everyone recognizes that the key to quality staff is quality training. Training new staff to start a new sex offender program can be challenging, depending on the availability of local resources and the amount of time the administrator is allowed to train and develop the new staff. In addition to start-up training, on-going training must be offered to stay abreast of new developments in this rapidly changing field. New findings from research are appearing weekly in journals and are being reported at training conferences around the country. The director can become the expert trainer or the broker for guest trainers who consult with sex-offender treatment programs. Local, state, and national networks can be rich resources for information and training experts.

The content and length of training are decisions that will be influenced by budget limitations and pressures to start the treatment program. More often than not, once a program has been funded, there are continuing demands to get it started because of the offenders who are "waiting in the wings" or who are being inappropriately placed and held in units not designed to meet their treatment needs.

In general, new staff should participate in at least eighty hours of training. Specific topics for training include, but are not limited to, the following:

1. **Offender characteristics**. This module should cover the different typologies of offenders (Groth 1979; O'Brien and Bera 1985; and Lanyon 1986).

2. **Treatment theories**. This module would explore behavioral, psychoeducational, psychodynamic, and addiction theories of offender treatment.

3. **Victim issues**. Every staffer must have a comprehensive and thorough understanding of the effect and dynamics of sexual assault on the victims. In many offender treatment programs, the staff is the only voice for the victim. Empathy and victim awareness are the keystones of effective intervention.

4. **Evaluation and assessment.** All staff should understand the nature and rationale behind typical assessment tools used to evaluate sex offenders.

5. **Legal issues**. Staff must be aware of all pertinent laws that affect delivery of services as well as criminal laws affecting the juveniles in treatment. A comprehensive understanding of the judicial system and its process is also necessary.

6. **Community resources**. To provide comprehensive treatment, staff must be aware of what is available to the juveniles when they return to the community.

7. **Drug and alcohol treatment**. Appropriate referral to substance abuse programs should be emphasized along with training in this area so as to provide a unified program for sex offenders who also have substance abuse issues.

8. **Sexual attitudes, myths, and stereotypes**. Most offenders (and their families) have poor sexual knowledge and need remedial instruction in human sexuality.

9. **Social skills training**. In this module, staff will learn how to teach social skills, such as assertiveness skills, anger management, and dating skills.

It is most desirable to train new staff prior to opening a new program. The director may need to convince supervisors of the need for comprehensive training prior to beginning a new program, but every effort needs to be made to ensure that training is provided to all new staff prior to their involvement with the treatment program. It is essential that comprehensive training be delivered to staff working in a sex offender program. Quality oriented and systematic training coupled with ongoing training and supervision will help ensure consistent, timely, and appropriate treatment (A Systems Approach to Training and Education 1986).

Effective Programming

Nearly half of all correctional programs will fail to meet the program's original objectives (Greenwood 1988). To develop and maintain effective programs, administrators must consider the elements that make programs successful. In the past, most program development has been based on historical factors without regard for what makes a program successful. Reliance on program design is not sufficient. Greenwood and Zimring (1985) researched effective programs and discovered that they shared several common factors. They found that traditional treatment approaches were ineffective because they failed to provide relevant treatment techniques. Gendreau (1981) described it as "who does what to whom, where, when, and for how long."

One of the most striking ingredients that successful programs share is their exceptional staff. Greenwood (1988) listed personality characteristics of exceptional staff members:

- patience
- strong work ethic

- deep commitment to core cultural values
- resourcefulness
- advanced social skills
- personal maturity
- hardiness in handling stress
- commitment to challenge
- rapid adaption to change
- good sense of humor

Staff of this caliber are not easy to find and keep in a system that traditionally has low pay and is often hamstrung by bureaucratic issues.

Ineffective programs also have common characteristics. To avoid the likelihood of program failure, administrators should try to circumvent the following pitfalls:

1. **Understaffing**. The optimal staffing pattern for an effective sex-offender treatment program should approach one staff member for every resident.

2. **Nonprofessional staff.** Line staff should have a minimum of four years of college in the social sciences and/or equivalent experience with adolescent sex offenders.

3. **Poor training.** All staff should receive between 80 to 120 hours of preservice training, with additional training during the first two years.

4. **Poor supervision**. Supervisory staff must work in the program as well as provide other staff with the support necessary to work with this difficult population.

5. **Poor expectations of outcome**. Staff must believe in the ability of the program to produce positive outcomes.

6. **Poor expectations of staff.** Staff must be viewed as competent by the residents and their supervisors.

Leadership is another key element found in Greenwood's (1988) research. He described effective leaders as strong and capable individuals who are charismatic. They often are considered mavericks who are not afraid of taking risks and setting new trends. Effective leaders are idealistic and consider the possibilities and proceed with optimism toward creative and nontraditional solutions. They are able to communicate their goals and infect others with enthusiasm. Finally, they are able to develop and maintain a smoothly functioning team and possess strong interpersonal skills.

Systemic issues impact program effectiveness. Length of stay is generally mandated by judicial, legislative, and financial directives. Most programs are hampered by pressures to move the residents through the program quickly. In these situations, as soon as a resident complies with behavioral expectations, the juvenile is released back to the community. Although there is no clear recommendation from research about the optimum length of stay with sex offenders, it is believed that the longer the time in treatment, the greater the chances of success. Keep in mind that the stay-in-treatment time may be shared between secure programs and community-based programs.

Administrators of effective programs agree that an average of six months in treatment is not enough. What usually occurs with shorter lengths of stay is superficial behavior changes with no significant alteration of underlying belief systems, cognitions, or values. After a short stay the juvenile is released although deep-rooted behavior is unchanged and the juvenile is only pretending to exhibit positive behaviors. The other possibility in this scenario is that the juvenile is released back to the community because the juvenile's behavior is so aversive that the program refuses to deal with the offender any longer.

Ross and Fabiano (1985) described effective programs to be multi-faceted; they used a wide range of treatment interventions and modalities. They found that the main emphasis in treatment and intervention was similar, regardless of treatment approaches. They defined the primary consideration of these programs to be the protection of the community. These programs had a cognitive-behavioral approach to treatment which focused on the thinking errors in the offender's belief systems. There also was a strong emphasis on teaching victim empathy and awareness.

Treatment and intervention for sex offenders is best conducted within a positive peer culture that promotes positive role models and eliminates peer support for negative behavior. Under the best of circumstances, it can take six months to a year to establish a positive peer culture. Without a foundation of a positive peer culture, programs will flounder and ultimately fail at their attempts to provide useful treatment.

Most sexually aggressive juveniles have profound issues around anger control, which is often compounded by poor social skills. Sex offenders use anger as a tool to manipulate staff, but lack more socially adequate skills negotiating to get their needs met without hurting others. Effective programs have designed training and/or educational modules to address these issues throughout their programs. These modules include training in the following:

- basic compliance with tasks
- development of complex reasoning skills
- decision making
- moral development

- being held accountable
- exercising behaviors that are regarded as responsible and valuable

For intervention to be effective, the treatment must be individualized and focus on specific treatment. (Sex-offender programs have led in the use of this approach.) Individual differences must be addressed through performing a comprehensive diagnosis of the problems and setting specific treatment goals through problem-oriented treatment. The following specific areas must be addressed:

- victim empathy
- offense patterns/characteristics
- drug and alcohol use and abuse
- sex education
- social skills

Once the juveniles have completed a highly structured and secure program, they must make a transition back to the community. There are critical elements to effective transition and aftercare. Greenwood (1988) maintains that the following elements are critical to aftercare:

- prerelease assessment planning/relapse prevention
- continuity in programming
- high frequency of contact
- highly motivated and energetic staff
- mobilization of educational, vocational, and family counseling services
- recreational programming

There is a consensus that without an intensive aftercare transition, residential programming is usually ineffective.

Sex offender programs for juveniles are vital and necessary at all levels of treatment. Most states are striving to respond to the treatment needs of juvenile sex offenders. Effective programs can be developed within a wide variety of settings, from short-term community-based programs to long-term secure residential programs. With careful planning and consideration of available resources, administrators can ensure their efforts are effective and the programs will survive the organizational transformations and crisis conditions that often accompany the implementation of treatment for juvenile sex offenders.

References

Gendreau, P. 1981. Treatment in corrections: Martinson was wrong! *Canadian Psychology* 22:232-238.

Greenwood, P. W. 1988. *Correctional programming for chronic juvenile offenders: Characteristics of three exemplary programs.* Santa Monica, Calif.: Rand.

Greenwood, P. W., and F. E. Zimring. 1985. *One more chance: The pursuit of promising intervention strategies for chronic juvenile offenders.* Santa Monica, Calif.: Rand.

Groth, A. N. 1979. *Men who rape.* New York: Plenum Press.

Knopp, F. H. 1982. *Remedial intervention with adolescent sex offenders: Nine program descriptions.* Orwell, Vt.: Safer Society Press.

——. 1984. *Retraining adult sex offenders: Methods and models.* Syracuse, N.Y.: Safer Society Press.

Lanyon, R. I. 1986. Theory and treatment in child molestation. *Journal of Consulting and Clinical Psychology* 54(2): 176-182.

McCann, I. L., and L. A. Pearlman. 1990. Vicarious traumatization: A contextual model for understanding the effects of trauma on helpers. *Journal of Traumatic Stress* 3(1): 131-149.

O'Brien, M., and W. Bera. 1985. *The phase typology.* Minneapolis, Minn.: Program for Healthy Adolescent Expression.

Ross, R.R., and E. A. Fabiano. 1985. *A time to think: A cognitive model of delinquency prevention and offender rehabilitation.* Johnson City, Tenn.: Institute of Social Sciences and Arts.

A Systems Approach to the Development of Treatment Programs for Sex Offenders. 1986. Training presented at the National Institute of Corrections National Academy of Corrections at Boulder, Colo.

7 Managing Aftercare Services for Delinquents

David M. Altschuler, Ph.D. and
Troy L. Armstrong, Ph.D.

Juvenile aftercare continues to be a highly troubled area within the larger juvenile corrections system nationwide. One complaint regularly voiced by professionals in the field is that juvenile corrections, especially at its deeper end, is having to deal with a new type of juvenile offender, one who is entering the system at an earlier age, has been adjudicated delinquent for violent crimes, continues to fail and reoffend regardless of placement and treatment modality, comes from a dysfunctional and chaotic family background, and is plagued by a wide array of personal problems. The argument is frequently made that the system is simply not equipped to work successfully with this type of juvenile.

Given the observation about the inability of the system to control the "new breed" of serious juvenile offenders, a particularly ironic problem is that juvenile aftercare suffers from a lack of funds and support and is plagued by a paucity of new, innovative, and experimental program initiatives. In part, this predicament reflects an opinion widely shared by the public, politicians, and many justice practitioners that serious juvenile offenders at the deep end of the system are already beyond help and will be "graduating" shortly, in many instances, into the adult correctional system. An air of despair and self-fulfilling prophecy appears to hover over most attempts to move forward and actively engage the difficult challenges associated with juvenile aftercare. Fortunately, there is a relatively high degree of consensus about the nature of the problem and the complexity it poses. This consensus helps to provide focus and can guide steps to more effectively manage and promote positive change in the behavior of these chronic, serious, and sometimes violent juvenile offenders.

Research findings indicate that a small number of chronic juvenile offenders are disproportionately responsible for most serious crime being perpetrated by juveniles and that this subpopulation of delinquents is also intensely resistant to interventions and treatment efforts to normalize their

Dr. David M. Altschuler is principal research scientist at the Johns Hopkins University Institute for Policy Studies, Baltimore, Maryland; Dr. Troy L. Armstrong is a professor in the Department of Anthropology, California State University at Sacramento.

behavior (Wolfgang, Figlio, and Sellin 1972; Shannon 1978). Further, these youth appear to be entering the juvenile justice system at younger and younger ages, thereby greatly increasing the possibilities of their having extended delinquent careers and being reprocessed through juvenile corrections, repeatedly, as they experience failure in the community and recidivate back into secure institutional settings.

... any assumptions about or steps toward a single agency or organization taking sole responsibility for designing, funding, and managing programs that comprehensively address the problems and needs of high-risk delinquents is probably short-sighted and impractical.

This chapter will explore and comment on a set of related management and administrative issues that must be taken into consideration if substantial progress is to be made in structuring the institutional and aftercare experience of high-risk juvenile offenders. The observations presented are based on the authors' involvement over the past six years as co-principal investigators on the United States Justice Department's Office of Juvenile Justice and Delinquency Prevention funded research and development project, Intensive Community-based Aftercare Programs (IAP). Work accomplished to date on this project has led the authors to reflect on the range of circumstances, obstacles, and program components, as well as on the facilitating factors, that must be engaged in attempts at designing, implementing, and managing intensive aftercare programs.

Several orienting themes are representative of the major advances in the state of knowledge about community-based programming strategies. These themes establish the framework for the way in which innovative interventions for serious, chronic juvenile offenders will emerge in the foreseeable future. First, there is the growing influence of the intensive supervision movement. Here, the major contributions have been advances in the technology of assessment (both in terms of risk and need) and in supervision (enhanced ability to impose far higher levels of social control through the use of techniques such as electronic monitoring and drug testing). Second, there is a growing consensus that the most thoroughly criminalized delinquents are also among the most troubled juveniles in society, in terms of personal problems, skill deficits, and emotional instability. In fact, the serious, chronic juvenile offender is usually a multiproblem youngster, who requires the simultaneous use of an array of treatment strategies.

Thus, juvenile corrections has reached a point in its history where any assumptions about or steps toward a single agency or organization taking sole responsibility for designing, funding, and managing programs that comprehensively address the problems and needs of high-risk delinquents is probably short-sighted and impractical. It is time to initiate collaborative approaches to delinquency remediation for serious juvenile offenders. Programs will necessarily be more complex and draw on the expertise and resources of multiple disciplines and specialized practices. To effectively administer and manage programs of this type will be an enormous challenge.

The generic Intensive Aftercare Program model provides juvenile corrections professionals an opportunity to adapt this framework, or any of its constituent parts, to their own needs. The model has been developed fundamentally for use as a comprehensive intervention framework to address the problems posed by a particularly difficult, high-risk juvenile offender population. However, many of the techniques and procedures identified as critical to the successful implementation of the model can be readily adopted to the alteration or refinement of existing aftercare systems. Although the stated, primary goal of this ongoing project is to demonstrate the value of the model for reducing rates of recidivism among serious, chronic juvenile offenders being transitioned from secure confinement, the framework offers a much wider application for contributing to emerging efforts across many jurisdictions to reform juvenile aftercare in general.

Background to the Initiative

Growing concerns about crowding in secure juvenile correctional facilities, high rates of recidivism, and escalating costs of confinement have fueled interest in bringing change and innovative programming to juvenile aftercare philosophy and practice. Unfortunately, the juvenile corrections field has compiled a dismal record in its effort to reduce the reoffending rate for a substantial number of juveniles released from secure confinement.

Research indicates that, in general, failure tends to occur disproportionately with a subgroup of released juvenile offenders who have established a long record of misconduct that began at an early age (Wolfgang, Figlio, and Sellin 1972; Hamparian et al. 1978; Shannon 1978; McCord 1979). These "high-risk" juveniles tend to exhibit a persistent pattern of justice-system contact (e.g., arrests, adjudications, and placements). But they also are plagued by a number of other need-related risk factors frequently involving a combination of problems associated with family, negative peer influence, school difficulties, and substance abuse.

In addition to these risk factors, other important ancillary needs and problems, although not generally predictive of reoffending are still problems that some, and at times many, high-risk juveniles have that must be addressed. For example, although there is widespread consensus that learning disabilities and emotional disturbance do not cause delinquency, this is hardly grounds for ignoring these conditions when they are present in identified juveniles.

Responding to these concerns, the Office of Juvenile Justice and Delinquency Prevention issued a request for proposals on "Intensive Community-Based Aftercare Programs" in July 1987. This research and development initiative was designed to assess, test, and disseminate information on intensive juvenile aftercare program prototypes or models for chronic, serious juvenile offenders who initially require secure confinement. The Office of Juvenile Justice and Delinquency Prevention staff view the initiative as one means to assist public and private correctional agencies in developing and implementing promising aftercare approaches:

> Effective aftercare programs focused on serious offenders which provide intensive supervision to ensure public safety and services designed to facilitate the reintegration process may allow some offenders to be released earlier, as well as reduce recidivism among offenders released from residential facilities. This should relieve institutional overcrowding, reduce the cost of supervising juvenile offenders, and ultimately decrease the number of juveniles who develop lengthy delinquent careers and often become the core of the adult criminal population (*Federal Register* 1987).

Design

As originally formulated by the Office of Juvenile Justice and Delinquency Prevention, the intensive aftercare project consisted of the following four stages:

Stage 1—Assessing programs currently in operation or under development and reviewing the relevant research and theoretical literature related to the implementation and operation of community-based aftercare programs for chronic juvenile offenders who are released from residential correctional facilities.

Stage 2—Developing program prototypes (models) and related policies and procedures to guide state and local juvenile correctional agencies and policy makers.

Stage 3—Transferring the prototype design(s), including the policies and procedures, into a training and technical assistance package for use in training.

Stage 4—Implementing and testing the prototype(s) developed in Stage 2 in selected jurisdictions.

The Johns Hopkins University Institute for Policy Studies, in collaboration with the Division of Criminal Justice of the California State University at Sacramento, received funds to conduct this multistage project. The first three stages have now been completed. This included a comprehensive literature review focused on research, theory, and programs; a national mail survey of juvenile corrections officials to identify innovative or promising programs and approaches; telephone interviews with the directors of thirty-six recommended programs; on-site fact finding at twenty-three different programs in six states, including three statewide systems; formulation of a risk-based, theory-driven prototype to guide the development and implementation of intensive community-based aftercare programs; development of an intensive aftercare program training curriculum; and selection and training of action planning teams of senior-level managers from eight states. Currently, the project is providing follow-up technical assistance as the eight states further develop and implement their Intensive Aftercare Program pilots. The eight states are Colorado, Michigan, Nevada, New Jersey, North Carolina, Pennsylvania, Texas, and Virginia. Up to four of the states will be part of a recently announced federal demonstration Intensive Aftercare Program initiative.

Intensive Aftercare Program Model

The project's review of research revealed that risk factors regularly associated with juvenile reoffending behavior, broadly defined, include both justice-system contact factors (such as age of juvenile at first justice-system contact—often referred to as "age of onset,"—and number of prior offenses) and need-related factors (such as family, peers, school, and drug involvement). In addition, this review revealed a variety of other special-need and ancillary factors, which, while not necessarily "predictive" of recidivism, remain relatively common among juvenile recidivists, such as learning problems and low self-esteem. Finally, a small minority of juvenile offenders have other very serious problems, such as diagnosed emotional disturbance.

Given the range and nature of both offense- and need-related risk factors as well as other special need and ancillary factors, the challenge is how to link this array of factors with a sufficiently broad-based, practical strategy that holds promise for combating recidivism. Through the Intensive Aftercare Program model the project has arrived at just such a strategy. Figure 1 shows a schematic of this model.

Central to the Intensive Aftercare Program model is the fact that the guiding principles, program elements, and array of services establish parameters and boundaries that must be specifically tailored to the needs, problems, and circumstances of each jurisdiction trying to reduce the recidivism of its own juvenile aftercare population. Organizational characteristics, the structure of juvenile justice and adolescent-service delivery systems, the size and nature of offender populations, and resource availability differ widely among and even within states.

In addition, managing identified "high-risk" juveniles in aftercare requires pursuing multiple goals, which include maintaining public protection both in the short- and long-term, ensuring individual accountability,

Figure 1
Intervention Model For Juvenile Intensive Aftercare Program

An Integration of Strain Theory, Social Learning Theory, and Social Control Theory

Underlying Principles

- Progressively Increased Responsibility & Freedom
- Facilitating Client-community Interaction & Involvement
- Working With Both Offender & Targeted Community Support Systems
- Developing New Resources, Supports, & Opportunities
- Monitoring & Testing

Program Elements

- Organizational & Structural Characteristics
- Overarching Case Management
  - —Assessment & Classification for Client Selection
  - —Individual Case Planning with a Family and Community Perspective
  - —Surveillance/Service Mix
  - —Incentives & Graduated Consequences
  - —Service Brokerage & Linkage with Social Networks
- Management Information & Program Evaluation

Service Areas

- Special Needs & Special Populations
- Education & School
- Vocational Training, Job Readiness, & Placement
- Living Arrangements
- Social Skills
- Leisure & Recreation
- Client-centered Counseling (individual & group)
- Family Work & Intervention
- Health
- Special Technology

and providing treatment/support services. Exactly how these goals can be achieved may vary from jurisdiction to jurisdiction across the country. Moreover, due to current economic constraints on state governments, in general, and correctional budgets, in particular, all three goals must be achieved with limited resources. The Intensive Aftercare Program offers a challenge to the professional community in that it requires an unequivocal commitment by the major juvenile justice, child-serving, and community agencies and groups to come together to develop a detailed plan on precisely who will assume responsibility for different aspects of the Intensive Aftercare Program, as well as how these will be accomplished and when.

Although some practitioners are apt to wince when they hear about the lack or inadequacy of the conceptual or theoretical underpinnings of their programs, many have more than a passing acquaintance with some of the consequences of this deficiency. If the overall mission or philosophy underlying a program is either ambiguous or absent, it can be difficult if not impossible for staff, program participants, or anyone else to understand clearly what practices, services, and approaches should be used and why; how this can be accomplished and when; and who needs to be involved. However, through a conceptual framework or referent, one can go from identifying risks, problems, and needs that are part of the dynamics of recidivism to developing a coherent, defensible, and assessable program model for reducing recidivism and failure. In short, tackling recidivism requires a knowledge of what can be done to address the multifaceted and complex circumstances that produce or are part of the dynamics of recidivism.

A number of previous efforts to develop just such a framework for intervention with serious, chronic juvenile offenders have recognized the multifaceted nature of the problem, and, accordingly, recommended integrating formerly freestanding theories, notably social control, strain, and social learning theories (Elliott and Voss 1974; Conger 1976; Elliott, Ageton, and Cantor 1979; Elliott, Huizinga, and Ageton 1985; Weis and Hawkins 1981; Fagan and Jones 1984). Consistent with a number of these efforts, the Intensive Aftercare Program model is grounded in a similar integration. Distinctive to this model, however, is the focus on the numerous issues and concerns arising out of the mostly disconnected and fragmented movement of offenders from court disposition to juvenile authority and/or institution, to aftercare supervision and discharge. Further, it is clear that if properly designed and implemented, the Intensive Aftercare Program model directly addresses two of the widely acknowledged deficiencies of the current system of secure correctional commitment: institutional confinement does not adequately prepare juveniles for return to the community, and those lessons and skills learned while in secure confinement are not monitored, much less reinforced, outside the institution.

The Intensive Aftercare Program model employs a theory-driven, empirically based approach that is derived both from integrated theory and risk assessment. It is simply inadequate and irresponsible to approach the "high-risk" juvenile recidivist problem in less than a comprehensive, carefully coordinated, multifaceted fashion that cuts across institutional and professional boundaries.

Given these requirements, five principles of programmatic action are requisite to the Intensive Aftercare Program model. The principles are as follows:

- preparing juveniles for progressively increased responsibility and freedom in the community
- facilitating juvenile-community interaction and involvement
- working with both the offender and targeted community support systems (e.g., families, peers, schools, and employers) on qualities needed for constructive interaction and the juvenile's successful community adjustment
- developing new resources and supports where needed
- monitoring and testing juveniles and the community on their ability to deal with each other productively

---

One of the major reasons why juvenile aftercare has proven so stubbornly resistant to reform or much improvement nationally is its reluctance to tackle seriously the problem of reoffending in the very settings where it originates: in the home, the neighborhood, and the street.

The five principles collectively establish a set of fundamental operational goals and a mission on which the model rests (Altschuler and Armstrong 1991). They allow for a reasonable degree of flexibility in how the goals will be achieved. As formulated, the Intensive Aftercare Program model can be structured and applied in a number of ways as long as it remains consistent with the stated specifications. The overall aim is to transition and reintegrate identified "high-risk" juvenile offenders from secure confinement gradually back into the community and, thereby, lower their high rate of failure and relapse. Although it is essential to give planners, administrators, and staff sufficient latitude to consider a range of features and processes that best suit the needs of both their own communities and confined juveniles, three major elements must be taken into account as planners and practitioners translate the Intensive Aftercare Program theory and principles into actual practice.

These elements are as follows:

- organizational factors and the external environment

- overarching case management, which includes: risk assessment and classification for establishing eligibility; individual case planning incorporating a family and community perspective; a mix of intensive surveillance and services; a balance of incentives and graduated consequences coupled with the imposition of realistic, enforceable conditions; and service brokerage with community resources and linkage with social networks
- management information and program evaluation.

The Management and Operation of Juvenile Aftercare

One of the major reasons why juvenile aftercare has proven so stubbornly resistant to reform or much improvement nationally is its reluctance to tackle seriously the problem of reoffending in the very settings where it originates: in the home, the neighborhood, and the street. At the same time, from an organizational perspective there must be a commitment to putting resources, staffing, and programming in the hands of a team that possesses the legal authority and responsibility to make basic decisions about correctional commitment, placement, length of stay, release, revocation, and service provision. These decisions are generally made by a wide range of officials spread across different branches and levels of government, as well as various departments and divisions.

Consequently, administering and managing juvenile aftercare poses particularly difficult challenges. The division of authority and responsibility among levels of government, conflicting bureaucratic and organizational interests, as well as divergent professional orientations collectively serve to complicate the overall goals of the system. Depending on the state, the cast of stakeholders directly involved with decision making in relation to aftercare may include: judges, aftercare authorities and community review boards, centralized state juvenile correction agencies, institution staff, regionalized state aftercare staff, county government and court service staff, plus other public and private service providers.

The sheer size and organizational complexity of juvenile justice make it exceedingly difficult to achieve basic communication, much less coherence in aftercare. Yet, progress has been evident when the right combination of leadership, commitment from the top, collaboration and cooperation, bottom-up planning and organization, proper staffing, and focused, well-run programming are present (Altschuler and Armstrong 1993), but it is not easy, especially when working with the most difficult and problematic juveniles in the system.

The justice system has to contend with pressures and directives emanating from many different sources, including: the public at large, the judiciary, prosecutors and defense lawyers, legislators and the state executive, appointed public officials, career civil servants, private-sector contractors and service providers, victims' groups, child advocates, and the media.

This represents an almost overwhelming collection of vying interests and countervailing forces, many of which are adversarial.

All segments of the system from the courts through aftercare must be involved in planning and decision making and have a very clear understanding of the larger picture of confinement and reintegration.

Likewise, the justice system is itself somewhat schizophrenic: it is not entirely judicial although both of its front gates (e.g., adjudication and disposition) and its back gate (e.g., revocation) are; it is not entirely an executive function; it is heavily shaped by legislative action and statute; families, schools, businesses, and other community resources tend to become involved; and public opinion can exert an enormous influence. The net effect is an inherent organizational schizophrenia that, if not very consciously, carefully, and properly treated and soothed, can result in chaos, finger-pointing, and scapegoating. In spite of these inherent problems, however, it is managerially and administratively possible to implement and sustain coherent and responsible juvenile aftercare. There are a number of basic issues that must be clearly identified and explicitly addressed.

Competently managing as complex a system as juvenile aftercare requires attention to basic aspects of organization and administration. The term "system" is used advisedly because, as suggested earlier, there is all too frequently little connection and continuity between its constituent parts. Yet, juveniles are processed as if a fully functioning and seamless juvenile justice system, from the point of court contact to community reintegration, were in place. Much greater coherence and continuity can be brought to processing if these basic administrative factors are carefully meshed.

Organizational Structure and Administrative Functions

The juvenile justice system is complex and compartmentalized. Key staff with responsibilities in particular parts of the system are often not familiar with how and why certain basic decisions are made or even who is involved in making them. However, developing and maintaining a coherent system of aftercare requires that this problem be resolved. Particular emphasis should be placed on understanding decision making in the following nine areas:

- commitment to the state corrections system

- choice of institutional placement
- reception and diagnosis
- length of stay
- individual assessment and development of the service plan while confined at the institution
- prerelease and discharge planning while confined
- aftercare social control and supervision
- aftercare service provision and advocacy
- enforcement of aftercare conditions, technical violations, graduated sanctions, and revocation

All segments of the system from the courts through aftercare must be involved in planning and decision making and have a very clear understanding of the larger picture of confinement and reintegration. Considerable program inefficiency, duplication, discontinuity, and incoherence plague juvenile corrections simply because there is limited common knowledge about and collaboration among different parts of the system. Common among the examples of fragmentation and discontinuity is the tendency for individual assessments of the same juvenile to be conducted separately at a number of points in processing without information ever being shared. Although reassessment can be very useful, there is no justifiable reason for multiple assessments if findings from these evaluations are not shared, not tied directly to the development of a master case plan involving all parts of the system, and not used to guide practitioners to provide a service in response to an identified problem or need.

Prerelease or discharge planning not directly involving both institutional and aftercare staff, as well as aftercare service providers, is illogical and shortsighted. Substance abuse treatment and other "special need" services provided during aftercare must be linked to institutional services that previously addressed the same needs. Reinforcement and continuity must characterize the transitional experience if gains made during confinement are to persist. Further, there can be no waiting period for crucial aftercare services following release from confinement.

At the critical point of release from institutional confinement, the individual cannot be left unsupervised and undirected. Decisions to provide aftercare services solely on the basis of available "slots" and rigid rules, rather than on the basis of individual need, are neither sensible nor rational.

Families not involved in preparations for the return of their children are unlikely to be useful in maximizing efforts to achieve successful reintegration. Families, along with aftercare staff, must become deeply involved in these preparations long before the juveniles are released from confinement. Closely monitoring the daily progress and/or setbacks the juveniles are experiencing in aftercare is the only readily available means that workers have to identify what motivates positive performance as well as what triggers misconduct. A number of activities such as placement in an educational setting, enrollment in a training program, or job search, will likely require, at least initially, frequent in-person contact between the juvenile and the worker.

How can all this be best accomplished? Is there a way to structure, target, and manage limited resources? This is possible as long as there is consensus among organizational interests across the entire juvenile justice system about the need to consolidate efforts into a more collaborative, streamlined operation. These reforms must be directed toward seeing that juveniles who pose the highest risk of reoffending receive the greatest concentration of aftercare supervision, support, resources, and service. The most problematic population of juvenile offenders must command the greatest attention and commitment on the part of juvenile corrections.

Complicating the situation further is the fact that the administrative and organizational landscape in juvenile corrections varies among states and has shifted over time as states reorganize. One common variation concerns whether institutions and community-based aftercare are organizationally separate. For example, in North Carolina, juvenile institutions fall under the Division of Youth Services of the Department of Human Resources, while juvenile aftercare falls under the Juvenile Services Division of the Administrative Offices of the Court. In Virginia, both institutions and aftercare come under the Department of Youth and Family Services. In Pennsylvania, juvenile institutions fall under the Bureau of State Children and Youth Programs within the Department of Public Welfare and aftercare is a county probation responsibility.

Another variation concerns whether juvenile corrections is a separate, autonomous agency or part of a larger, combined department of corrections. For example, in Colorado, juvenile institutions and aftercare services are administered by the Department of Institutions' Division of Youth Services. A third variation concerns whether there is an independent juvenile agency, which has (apart from the judiciary) the authority over whom is placed in secure facilities (for example, Massachusetts).

There is nothing especially advantageous about having one agency or department assuming primary responsibility for all or most parts of the juvenile corrections system. In fact, in the administration of human services agencies nationwide, the pendulum has generally swung back and forth between a single, consolidated, centralized authority and smaller, decentralized, specialized authorities. The former approach was thought to be the most effective means to reduce needless duplication, diseconomies of scale, and turf battles, while the latter approach has been viewed by some as an excellent way to make the system more responsive and accountable, less bureaucratic, and, ultimately, less costly.

The consolidated juvenile services agency has in some cases displayed the same divisions and rivalries between its internal units that are experienced by separate agencies. Another problem plaguing some consolidated agencies is the fact that particular functions can lose their visibility and any sense of separate identity in these umbrella settings. A major negative repercussion is that these units are sometimes ill-equipped to wage intra-agency battles in the fight over resources against larger units within the same organization. On the other hand, the greater the number of separate, single-function agencies that are accountable to their own administrative hierarchies and rules, the more difficult it may be to establish cooperative guidelines and procedures when issues of common interest arise.

In short, the debate over separate versus consolidated administration in juvenile corrections is secondary in importance to how well the key units with specialized authority and responsibility for managing juvenile offenders can actually work together, share equitably in the division of labor, and cooperate in the interest of providing supervision and services to this population. To the extent that conflict exists over such issues as who ultimately retains jurisdiction over the management of juveniles at particular junctures, who is accountable when a major problem surfaces, and who is credited for successes and blamed for failures, true collaboration becomes a very difficult and elusive goal.

Aftercare cannot function in isolation either in the arena of program development or program implementation. Developing, implementing, and managing an aftercare system requires the active participation of high-level administrators responsible for policy formulation in the key sectors of the larger juvenile corrections system, mid-level management responsible for interpreting policy and supervising line staff, and staff responsible for daily program operations. The mission and goals must be communicated clearly from the top. The policies and procedures must explicitly recognize how goals and objectives will be accomplished. Job descriptions and staff training must reflect these expectations. Workload, caseload size and composition, and number of staff must be structured to accommodate job responsibilities. Finally, accountability from all levels of staff must be overseen through a management information system.

Eligibility According to Risk and Jurisdictional Boundaries

The strategy of "one-size-fits-all" in the area of community-based interventions is neither practical nor justified in determining who should be targeted for participation in intensive aftercare and what the individualized plan should entail. Research has shown that juveniles are confined in juvenile correctional facilities for a number of very different reasons and under a variety of circumstances (Bureau of Justice Statistics 1989; Champion 1992; Krisberg et al. 1993). Moreover, some confined juveniles are less likely to reoffend than others. Some juveniles who are confined have been involved in a violent crime, but have no prior record of violence; others are confined because of having committed a serious property crime. Still others are confined because they have an "extensive" arrest history and are considered more serious because of the large number of arrests rather than the severity of any individual charge. Consequently, the likelihood of reoffending on release varies enormously across these circumstances.

Evidence increasingly suggests that providing intensive aftercare to lower-risk offenders results in poorer performance, not better (see, for example, Andrews 1987; Baird 1983; Erwin and Bennett 1987; Markley and Eisenberg 1986). One reason frequently cited is that intensive supervision is almost always accompanied by an increase in technical infractions, owing to the increased ability to detect these rule violations. At times, technical infractions, although relatively minor, are not treated as such by aftercare officers and judges. Rather, they can and do order revocations and reconfinement on the basis of these minor infractions. This tendency is more likely if graduated, community-based sanctions are not in place, because officials may feel they have little recourse if the accountability message is to be properly conveyed.

The widespread perception that the juvenile justice system is unable to manage certain types of the most severely delinquent offenders has led to a national trend over the past two decades to expand the jurisdiction of the adult system and, correspondingly, to constrict that of the juvenile system.

Another reason to avoid assigning low-risk offenders to intensive aftercare is related to the human inclination to react negatively to being constantly watched and evaluated. Applying this type of microscope obviously creates pressure, and as a result, some juveniles will challenge it and lash out. Given this set of cautions and considerations, administrators would be well-advised to consider limiting intensive aftercare to juveniles who, based on a validated risk assessment process, are found to be at high-risk of reoffending.

This discussion of offender targeting underscores why it is important for judges and other parties who handle technical violators and minor offenders to take part in the development of a carefully structured system of graduated sanctions and alternatives to revocation. An unfortunate by-product of intensive supervision in a number of jurisdictions across the country has been a marked increase in the number of juveniles being returned to correctional confinement for having committed technical violations or petty offenses. In such cases, intensive supervision is exacerbating the overcrowding problem, not reducing it.

The litany of failures regularly associated with juvenile aftercare likely contributes to the view of some that this deep-end segment of the system is fatally flawed and, therefore, should either be fundamentally changed or abolished. The widespread perception that the juvenile justice system is unable to manage certain types of the most severely delinquent offenders has led to a national trend over the past two decades to expand the jurisdiction of the adult system and, correspondingly, to constrict that of the juvenile system. Yet, the population being transferred in increasing numbers to adult jurisdiction can potentially benefit and be better served through the use of intensive intervention approaches, including intensive aftercare, that operate within the framework of the juvenile justice system. However, to be effective, a broad-gauged reform of juvenile incarceration and aftercare practice is required. These reforms can vary along a number of dimensions. For example, depending on its intensity, the type of monitoring and service delivery, and its duration, aftercare will vary in costs and staffing requirements. It is, therefore, essential that administrative decisions regarding aftercare carefully consider how many staff are available to provide intensive aftercare supervision for those juveniles who pose the greatest risk for reoffending. Once it is known how many staff will be assigned intensive caseloads and how many cases will constitute an intensive caseload, the total number of intensive cases that can be accommodated with existing staff can be determined.

The Structure of Juvenile Aftercare

Both the juvenile justice system, grounded in the concept of protecting and rehabilitating children, and the adult system, long identified with punishment and retribution, have, in practice, functioned quite differently than their ideological roots would suggest. Although juvenile justice has in the view of many not realized its ideals—providing neither community protection nor rehabilitation—it is heresy to others working in the system to suggest that anything remotely resembling punishment be part of juvenile justice. Fortunately, however, a consensus is beginning to emerge among juvenile justice planners, administrators, and practitioners that a "balanced approach," incorporating accountability, public safety, and social competence, should guide juvenile justice theory and practice into the next century. It is precisely this balance of principles on which intensive aftercare is premised.

Simply stated, aftercare, as an extension of steps initiated in an institutional setting, is based on the notion that a continuation of service provision, social control, and support in the community where success or failure will ultimately be measured is essential to maximizing the potential for long-term positive change and normalization. Aftercare must directly build on progress already made in the institution. Fundamental to achieving this continuity across the institution-community boundary is that the aftercare worker be sufficiently involved early on to begin building the bridge. Work on the aftercare foundation must be started while the juvenile is still confined so that the community-based components are prepared for the juvenile's reentry. It must be a team effort involving both institutional and aftercare staffs. The committing authority, the institution, the aftercare agency, as well as all support systems in the community must be enlisted in the effort.

Juveniles who are at highest risk of reoffending will potentially benefit the most from involvement in *intensive* aftercare. The surveillance and monitoring aspects of the program should be structured so that greater restriction on movement is imposed initially, but can be substantially reduced as positive adjustment is noted. If problems arise, there is always the option to increase the degree of structure and the level of social control. In general, however, the longer a restriction or sanction is left in place, the less effective it becomes. The implication is that while sanctioning or punishing misconduct swiftly and with certainty is important, it is equally important to desist in the consequence as soon as possible and to reward or acknowledge all accomplishments and successes. A mix of graduated consequences and positive reinforcement taken together can be a powerful modifier of behavior. There is an important place for punishment and sanction, but it must always be tempered by responding positively to prosocial conduct.

Service delivery speaks exclusively to the issue of need, regardless of risk. Some individuals may well be high-need and have serious problems, but that is quite different than being at high risk for reoffending. For example, one juvenile may have a serious learning disability that may prevent him or her from completing high school and a record indicating two previous arrests for shoplifting, while another juvenile may have a learning disability coupled with a history of child abuse, suspensions from school for fighting, eight prior arrests (some for violence), and close associations with gang members. Both have high need, but on the face of it there is less likelihood that the first juvenile will reoffend. The first juvenile would appear to be an excellent candidate for services, but not enhanced surveillance and monitoring. The second juvenile would appear to be a candidate for the Intensive Aftercare Program, though the referral decision should depend on the results of a validated risk-assessment.

In sum, to the extent there is consensus about the need for cooperation and collaboration among the judiciary, correctional facilities, and aftercare agencies to jointly embrace a balanced multifaceted approach to community reintegration involving a wide range of organizational factors, there should be sufficient common ground to proceed with the development and implementation of intensive aftercare. The remaining five factors discussed in this chapter constitute the major programming dimensions that an implementation plan geared to accomplishing this goal must address.

Confinement, Prerelease, and Transition: Prospects and Impediments

The history of the collaboration between correctional institutions and aftercare agencies to provide effective supervision and appropriate service provisions for juveniles reentering the community has been marked by a multitude of problems. Most notably, this inability to ensure a smooth transitional experience has been driven by poor, insufficiently informed case planning, and inconsistent, often fragmented, case management.

Among the most frequently cited problems has been the repeated failure of the system to adequately prepare the offender for the liberation and disorientation of moving from the closely monitored and highly regimented life in a secure institutional environment to the relatively unstructured and often tempting life in the community. This has been further exacerbated by a failure to support the transitional experience with clear, well-structured administrative guidelines and procedures that ensure close, interagency coordination. The difficulties identified as obstacles in providing continuity of service and supervision across the boundary between institutional confinement and community living are numerous. Lack of communication and coordination among staff in correctional facilities, aftercare agencies, and community social institutions (e.g., schools, local organizations, public mental health agencies, drug and alcohol treatment centers, employment and training programs, churches, business associations, and employers) have been a grave impediment to effective aftercare programming.

Recommendations for improved communications, shared decision making, coordinated planning, and clear lines of authority have been made many times. Unfortunately, however, these recommendations have, with some notable exceptions, met only with a modicum of success. Part of the problem is that because of funding limitations, bureaucratic and professional intransigence and turf battles, understaffing and inefficient deployment of existing staff, community fear and resistance, and inadequate or nonexistent community resources, the juvenile aftercare agencies, correctional facilities, and community-based service providers have been unable and/or unwilling to enter into an actively functioning, working partnership. The Intensive Aftercare Program model was formulated with a sense that the institution-community linkage component of the overall process would, to a considerable extent, determine the success of the proposed approach. The survey of existing juvenile aftercare programs and the identification of gaps indicated a need to address systematically the entire set of principles required to maximize the opportunity to achieve successful reintegration. A number of specific, tangible approaches can readily be identified as the means to ensure the set of principles is being implemented. Among these ideas are the following:

- an increased presence of the aftercare worker in the institution on a regular basis throughout the period of the client's confinement
- adopting a collaborative approach to prerelease planning that involves relevant individuals from both the institution and the community so that information can be more effectively gathered and shared to ensure better decision making
- the use of transitional cottages, or other forms of staged placements, that are located outside the institutional boundary, to facilitate a more gradual step-down into the community
- the inclusion of service providers who can prepare juveniles to access in a more systematic fashion their resources once they have returned to the community
- the gradual testing and probing of the juvenile's readiness for community reentry through the use of weekend passes, furloughs, and day visits to potential educational sites for placements and employment

A geographical and logistical issue regularly complicating efforts to improve the reintegrative process is the distance between the home and the institution. The problems that plague linkage and transition, difficult to resolve under any circumstances, become especially pronounced when great distances exist between the home community and the institutions in which juveniles are being confined. In most instances the suggested approaches are more difficult to set in motion if substantial distances are involved. In working with the Intensive Aftercare Program pilot sites, the distance between the institution and the community varied considerably. For example, the Pennsylvania program that selected the City of Philadelphia as the home community from which Intensive Aftercare Program juveniles will be drawn is located only twenty-seven miles from the correctional facility where the most chronic, serious juvenile offenders from Philadelphia are placed. Here, the implementation of strategies concerning linkage should encounter no major geographical obstacles.

In contrast, the Nevada program chose Las Vegas as its pilot site. In this instance, the juvenile correctional facility in which the vast majority of the more serious, chronic juvenile offenders from this community are placed is the Nevada Youth Training Center, which is located in Elko, approximately four hundred miles from Las Vegas. This circumstance creates enormous logistical impediments for putting into place institution-community linkage strategies that will ease smooth, well-coordinated reentry. However, the planning process in this jurisdiction has resulted in the identification of innovative ways to reduce these obstacles. For example, a second, more conveniently located facility will be used as a transitional point of confinement for the Intensive Aftercare Program population in a step-down arrangement whereby all juveniles targeted for this program will spend the final thirty days of institutional stay in a special reentry cottage. This will allow a far higher level of contact and interaction by these juveniles and institutional staff with community agencies and services, family members, and aftercare staff.

Finally, a major stumbling block in developing an institution-community linkage is the existence of two "organizational cultures." Widespread evidence points to substantial difficulty for collaboration across institutional and aftercare staff. Ideas being advanced to aid the development of a more commonly shared outlook, as well as greater insight and understanding across this boundary, include cross-training of institution and aftercare staff, opportunities for staff in both settings to actually experience the nature and demands of each other's work environment, and joint planning drawing on the best ideas in each arena to design more effective interventions that focus on institution-community linkage.

Advocacy and Service Delivery Capacity-Building in the Community

An increasingly acknowledged challenge of the entire juvenile justice system is the need to open communications and devise collaborative strategies so that there is a larger, jointly defined role for the community in addressing the problems of crime and delinquency. Comprehensive models of intervention, especially those targeting high-risk, multiproblem juveniles, can only be effective if major community resources are given a role. It is through community networks, resources, and supports that informal mechanisms of social control are exerted. The effect and influence of justice agencies are rather minimal. Further, the long-term effect of the entire justice system through formal social control mechanisms is limited because these interventions are externally imposed and relatively short-term. Potentially far more influential and long lasting are supports and opportunities for legitimate, prosocial activity that occur within community settings.

Families, peers, neighbors, as well as a broad range of community social institutions, such as schools, workplaces, and churches, are better equipped to structure and sanction juvenile behavior and to internalize a sense of right and wrong than are police, judges, probation and aftercare officers, or the staff of correctional facilities. A viable and responsive social fabric is a far greater long-run deterrent to crime than any justice technique, such as the squad car, the electronic bracelet, or the prison cell.

The nature of the communities in which serious, chronic, and violent juvenile offenders are found will greatly influence the strategies that juvenile corrections professionals devise for responding to the problem. The convergence of guns, gangs, and drugs has greatly heightened public awareness of and fear about juvenile crime and violence in the major metropolitan centers of this nation. Yet, growing concern does not easily translate into possible solutions, especially given the enormous, complex, and entrenched social, economic, and political problems plaguing these communities. In most instances these areas are economically deprived and politically marginal sectors of large cities. Characterized by decaying and devastated infrastructures, the communities have been rendered largely impotent in terms of their ability to provide resources and services or to promote the well-being of troubled juveniles. The legacy for inner-city America over the past decade and a half has been one of increasing federal neglect and a corresponding decrease in social and economic vitality.

In the face of this level of disarray, the idea of juvenile corrections professionals serving as a catalyst for promoting greater community involvement is formidable. Clearly, the Intensive Aftercare Program approach to reintegrating and normalizing juvenile offenders is dependent to a substantial degree on the availability of locally based, supportive services and resources. For this to occur, the wider community must display some sense of responsibility for the problem and some degree of responsiveness to the need. Juvenile advocacy, capacity-building, and social services development, as well as mobilization of existing but latent resources, are among those areas of community involvement that must be targeted.

Regardless of the circumstances of individual communities, several steps should be initiated to guarantee the systematic delivery of necessary services and resources. First, it is vital to assess the extent and nature of community needs and then take steps to fill them. The Intensive Aftercare Program model identifies a specific array of service areas that should be available when working with high-risk delinquents. Although it is highly unlikely that any one program would or even could provide the necessary range of services, an adequate continuum of interventions are required to address this array of services. Further, although it is doubtful that any one juvenile will require the total set of services, a constellation of services may be required to respond appropriately to the needs of these multiproblem delinquents.

The task of both mobilizing inadequate or fragmented resources and developing entirely new services will likely require considerable collaboration and planning between representatives of juvenile corrections and community organizations. Community resources have a potential for helping to remediate delinquency and can be systematically identified and explicitly incorporated into models of intervention. It is precisely in those environments where a lack of economic opportunity, political marginality, and social disorganization have greatly reduced the ability and motivation of residents to address their own crime problems that there are the greatest concentrations of serious, chronic, and violent juvenile offenders. Consequently, deliberate efforts to mobilize the population in these communities must be initiated so that juvenile offenders released from secure confinement do not return to the same old environment, the same old neighborhood, the same old friends, and the temptation to readopt the same old bad habits. It is unrealistic to think that large numbers of these juveniles can be relocated for any substantial period of time to entirely new community settings—however desirable this step might be—at the point of their institutional release. Consequently, one of the major challenges currently facing juvenile corrections—and, in a sense, the larger society—is to somehow qualitatively alter that same old environment.

Given the profound level of deprivation experienced by many serious and chronic delinquents and the devastation in their home communities, it will likely be necessary for workers to offer help in solving very mundane, day-to-day problems, but that is part of building trust and establishing a new beginning.

A number of different strategies may facilitate the qualitative alterations of the social environment for these juveniles. Capacity building and community development cannot be overlooked. One approach that has, however, been largely overlooked in the past for normalizing delinquents involves identifying circumstances that produce crime avoidance for many juveniles in the same environments. In spite of living in high-crime areas, most juveniles do not engage in serious misconduct or illegal behavior. Apparently, their psychological and social development is aided by the presence of certain supportive or so-called protective factors that can negate the potential or propensity for delinquency.

Among factors that have been identified as playing a positive role are nurturing and supportive families (regardless of how many parents are present); meaningful engagement in education, vocational training, and skill building; religion; the presence of significant others providing mentoring relationships; apprenticeships and employment; and the opportunity to see and experience life beyond the confines of the local neighborhood.

Steps can be taken to assess the extent to which these factors are absent from the lives of high-risk juvenile offenders returning to the community. Once this determination has been made, juveniles should be linked to available supports. Where no such supports exist, workers must seek out alternatives. Given the profound level of deprivation experienced by many serious and chronic delinquents and the devastation in their home communities, it will likely be necessary for workers to offer help in solving very mundane, day-to-day problems, but that is part of building trust and establishing a new beginning.

In some situations, wrapping the requisite supports around the juvenile means drawing on positive supports already present in the community, but ones not previously experienced by particular juveniles. Fostering a qualitative shift in the daily life experiences of juveniles in aftercare should be designed both to help reduce the erosion of positive gains when they are present following institutionalization and to start the juvenile on a different path than that taken previously.

It should be clear that tied to the availability of services and resources in the community is a need for strong, ongoing advocacy on the part of juvenile corrections in that community. Only in this way can it be ensured that juveniles who are labeled as serious, chronic, and violent offenders will be given the opportunity to actually access the appropriate agencies, organizations, and programs. The field of juvenile justice has been plagued throughout its history by the tendency for particular agencies and interests (e.g., public education, mental health, vocational training, and employment) to resist providing services or resources to these juveniles and not to extend equal opportunities to them.

Service Brokerage and Referral

The Intensive Aftercare Program model is risk-driven in terms of identifying and targeting appropriate high-risk juvenile offender populations, but as an approach to intervention it is heavily oriented toward individualized service and support. This reflects basic philosophical and theoretical assumptions that assert long-term behavioral change can only be accomplished in working with serious and chronic delinquents when highly intensified treatment and services are combined with adequate levels of social control and supervision. The need for a more balanced approach in which an intensified mix of surveillance and services is present is further linked to formal assessment procedures for determining the nature of specific problems and needs.

A continuum of services and resources that is required to normalize high-risk delinquents is incorporated in the Intensive Aftercare Program model. No one agency would likely possess the technical expertise or ability to provide such an array. In terms of programming and supervision, it is simply impractical to expect that the primary aftercare caseworker would have sufficient time and expertise to handle case management activities and simultaneously provide many of the needed services. Thus, referral and brokerage become crucial functions. Although the Intensive Aftercare Program caseworker may well be directly involved in counseling and role modeling, the use of referral and brokerage explicitly acknowledges the need to obtain the expertise, talent, and resources of others who have sufficient time, background, and capabilities to provide the range and intensity of required services.

Usually, the provision of services for juvenile aftercare populations in a given jurisdiction will involve a mix of public and private agencies. Approached from the perspective of the model, it does not matter whether a public or private agency is providing the services. Rather, the key concern is that the necessary service is being made available for this population and is being offered with a high degree of quality.

Assessment of existing aftercare systems and programs revealed some interesting examples of how juvenile corrections officials are configuring the array of services they regularly access. One that has moved most in the direction of privatization by developing an aftercare service-delivery framework through a formalized purchase-of-care contracts is the Juvenile Division of the Arizona Department of Corrections (ADC). A separate purchase-of-service unit within the division contracts with a broad spectrum of private agencies to provide a continuum of care for those juveniles requiring aftercare. There are four major areas of responsibility and activity within this unit: (1) contractor identification and selection, (2) service specification, (3) juvenile needs assessment and referral, and (4) for contract compliance and quality assurance monitoring.

The continuum of care extends from part-time supervision offering a minimal level of supervision to residential placement with relatively high levels of intervention and service provisions. The intensity of supervision also varies from day support services where participants are largely unsupervised outside regular program hours to so-called conservation programs, where there is twenty-four-hour-a-day supervision in remote, rural settings.

Accompanying this approach is a formal needs assessment instrument. By checking off specific categories, a juvenile's specific needs within service categories can be established. These include: psychiatric, emotional/behavioral, substance abuse, educational, vocational, and independent living/social skills.

The aftercare program in Delaware County, Ohio, stands in marked contrast to the Arizona purchase-of-care system. There is an almost exclusive reliance on local public agencies and resources, such as the county council on alcoholism, the county mental health, and county public schools, as well as Narcotics Anonymous, and Big Brother and Big Sister organizations. This program focuses considerable attention toward developing and sustaining excellent professional relationships between the juvenile court, which manages the intensive aftercare program, and the network of local public agencies.

These two quite distinct approaches illustrate the wide range of variation that can characterize the formulation of service brokerage strategies and the development of the appropriate network of providers. Regardless of whether the auspice is public or private, two sets of issues are critical in achieving the goals of service brokerage. First is the need to guarantee that an appropriate match is being made between the client and a particular service, which is largely a targeting and assessment matter. Second is the need to devise a procedure to monitor the extent and quality of services provided. This issue is one of system accountability in which steps must be taken to ensure treatment and services are being delivered in an appropriate fashion. Although the juvenile frequently is blamed over failure to make progress, there are certainly instances in which the service providers are not being fully responsible in these contractual arrangements.

Staffing

Qualified and committed staff clearly play a crucial role in the kind of intensive, integrated institution-aftercare program advocated. The various roles assumed by staff must be carefully and thoughtfully delineated. In some instances traditional roles must be redefined. Job descriptions that carefully specify the day-to-day responsibilities and role expectations establish the yardstick on which hiring should be based. The competency and qualifications of a person to serve in a specialized role in the provision of intensive aftercare in a truly integrated institution-aftercare initiative must be based on what good aftercare in such a context requires.

People often make career decisions, at least in part, on the basis of what they are willing and able to do. Potential employers make personnel decisions with an eye toward finding someone who is suitable given what the job demands. Working with troubled juveniles and families in institutional and community-based settings is clearly not a career option for everyone. Such work, therefore, requires a recruitment and screening process whereby employers place emphasis on locating individuals who are qualified and interested in the goals and approach that characterize the program's working environment and culture. While there are some jobs that most people could competently do, this is simply not the case with juvenile corrections where highly complex and stressful situations are regular features of working with troubled juveniles and their families.

Both potential staff and the employer must have a clear sense of the rather extreme demands of this kind of job and the kind of difficulties posed by such a workplace. Someone who in the past has qualified as a "good" worker in a traditional institutional or community-based setting may not make the grade in work environments that are being defined in terms of a highly intensified, integrated institution-aftercare approach.

One problem frequently encountered in selecting qualified and committed staff relates to workplace and staff rules, regulations, and job protection. In some civil service and unionized environments, as well as in procurement and contracting procedures, there may be immutable or excessively rigid rules and policies regarding hiring, job responsibilities, transferring, and firing. However, intensive aftercare, particularly with its implications for highly coordinated teamwork between institutional and aftercare workers, requires flexibility and accommodation. Operational issues that must be addressed include: job classification; line of authority; use of volunteers, paraprofessionals, and contract workers; performance reviews; and privatization. If civil service or union rules are inconsistent with programmatic requirements and if no exceptions, exemptions, or waivers are available, it may not be possible to initiate this kind of intensive aftercare program within the existing system.

Juveniles participating in intensive aftercare programs are likely to require much more contact with aftercare workers and service providers, both in terms of monitoring and service delivery. This situation poses special considerations in establishing appropriate staff roles. Round-the-clock coverage can be achieved in many ways and through a number of different staffing arrangements. Team supervision, designated trackers, electronic monitoring, and short-term residential back-up are examples of techniques and approaches that a number of aftercare programs are using during the community phase.

Whatever approach is used, however, administrative and managerial requirements must be tailored to meet the particular circumstances of the program and its surrounding environment. For example, team approaches are used in some jurisdictions whereby two workers share a caseload. One worker handles the surveillance role while the other is primarily responsible for case management and casework. Other needed services are likely to be delivered through contract or agreement with various agencies or individuals. Under such an arrangement, the division of labor and sharing of authority must be carefully delineated to avoid confusion and discontinuity. Another team approach involved two-to-four workers sharing responsibility in the surveillance and case management of all clients on a combined caseload. This approach guarantees an exceedingly high level of monitoring and attention to needs. One of the Intensive Aftercare Program pilot sites is preparing to have teams in which each member will specialize in a particular need area, such as in-home family work, job development, training and placement, and sex offender treatment.

In all of the team approaches to supervision, a great deal of attention must be focused on the ways in which the members will collectively function, share authority, and provide feedback. The key is to design a structure where each individual is fully aware of the nature of involvement by other team members with these juveniles. Staff qualifications may well vary depending on the role and responsibility of the particular team member. Requirements by way of credentials, training, experience, and aptitude will likely differ by worker. Personnel policy must accommodate such differences. Some team members may, in fact, be paraprofessionals or volunteers.

Entry-level training, regardless of the position being assigned to the worker, cannot be minimized or overlooked. Although on-the-job learning is important and will certainly occur, this is not a substitute for a structured and systematic orientation, as well as ongoing training, that all workers should receive. Structured training compels managers to be resolute that their program has not lost sight of its mission (often referred to as "goal displacement"). Such training also provides an opportunity to revisit how staff responsibilities and roles advance that mission. Regular involvement in training for all workers is well worth the investment of time and re-sources. Workers need support and reinforcement, particularly when engaged in stressful and demanding work. Further, it is vital that staff be updated on advances or innovations in the field, bearing directly on their own work. Giving workers an opportunity to suggest changes, react to ongoing developments, and review program operations can be an important source of information for assessing and fine tuning program operations and staff activities. It is also the means by which staff can develop a greater personal investment and stake in the program.

Good management and well-run programs are generally the result of closely tracking program activities and results.

Caseload size and workload are additional aspects of staffing that require close administrative scrutiny. Allowing insufficient time for workers to perform or complete their responsibilities is indicative of poor personnel management. It does little good to devise elaborate programs if workers are consistently unable to meet their job requirements. Accordingly, job performance expectations and roles must be reflected not only in staff selection and training, but in caseload size and composition. It is only logical that caseload size vary depending on the risk level of the offenders and their accompanying scope and level of need. Workers with responsibility for high-risk juveniles in aftercare exhibiting special needs should have smaller caseloads with correspondingly high minimum supervision (contact) and case management standards.

Management Information and Evaluation

Often overlooked during program planning and start-up, a management information and evaluation capability is one of those elements that administrators and staff will find enormously useful when available. Likewise, the absence of this kind of information can have a debilitating effect on successful program operations. Good management and well-run programs are generally the result of closely tracking program activities and results. Making changes as they are needed and fine-tuning operations is largely what management is about. To do this, however, administrators and staff need accurate and timely information. Unfortunately, information systems and evaluation in the human service arena, in general, and in corrections, in particular, have not received the attention they deserve. This gap is often the result of limited resources, insufficient evaluation or research capability within the organization, and unrelenting crisis management.

Evaluation design should speak to the following questions. What are we trying to achieve—in measurable terms—with program clients, within what time frame, and by what means? Two major sets of issues are involved. The first concerns the overall goals of the program—what outcomes or effects are being pursued in terms of the juveniles and the broader system of which the program is part. In the case of an intensive, integrated institution-aftercare initiative, key participant outcomes would likely include reduced recidivism rates, as well as cognitive, behavioral, and emotional changes. Key system outcomes might include changes in reception and diagnostic processing, lengths of stay, and collaboration between the institution and the aftercare staff.

The second set of issues concerns program implementation and quality. Is the initiative serving the appropriate juveniles, delivering the intended services, reflecting in day-to-day practice the case management components, and employing and deploying staff appropriately? In short, process evaluation primarily addresses issues of start-up and implementation; this represents the systematic collection and analysis of information to answer questions regarding program performance. To obtain accurate answers to such questions, a program needs to routinely collect reliable and relevant information about its clients, staff, and activities. A management information system provides the means to collect this information, both for administrative and evaluation purposes. In turn, this data must then be aggregated, analyzed, and interpreted within the context of the original questions being asked.

Administrators must rely on sound evaluation to assist them in performing five functions.

1. Planning improves when management has information concerning the amount of staff time and other resources needed to ensure optimal program operations. Outcome results linked to program activities and costs can help administrators readjust priorities or modify budgets, if needed.

2. Documenting program activities can be used for general accountability purposes as well as an aid to supervising staff.

3. Evaluation can indicate which aspects of a program are operating as intended and whether various components are producing desirable outcomes at a reasonable cost.

4. Many funders require some evaluation capability to inform future funding decisions.

5. Sound evaluation can assist in marketing and public relations by providing information on program performance and by demonstrating a program's willingness to undergo scrutiny and examination.

Unfortunately, many evaluations can neither answer the kind of questions that need to be asked nor provide information that is reliable and trusted. Thus, developing an appropriate evaluation design can be as important a step as conducting the evaluation process itself. Planning for an evaluation can maximize its value by ensuring the following: input from all interested and relevant individuals, the proper framing of the central questions, and the channeling of resources toward the areas of greatest need. Careful planning for the evaluation is intended to help administrators make decisions about who will conduct the technical evaluation tasks (e.g., should the program hire and manage staff or consultants, or use a local university?), how the data collection can be accomplished without impeding other program operations, and how the results can be used constructively.

Evaluation planning should include a group of people with a major stake in the performance of the program (e.g., staff from the program, staff from other involved agencies, individuals from funding sources and oversight committees, and representatives of client and advocacy groups). Along with the evaluators, this planning group should focus on the following five factors:

- the set of specific questions that will be answered
- the type of research design(s) that will be used for the different kinds of questions (such as random assignment, a nonrandom comparison group of similar clients in other programs, a comparison with outcomes reported in other studies, a comparison with stated program goals, or a comparison with the program's contractual goals)
- the sources and methods of data collection
- the type of analysis that will be conducted
- who will take responsibility for each of the evaluation tasks and when the tasks need to be accomplished

The implementation or process evaluation must provide answers to the set of questions related to the program intervention. Who is doing what for whom, when, where, and how? Process evaluation can use both quantitative information (e.g., frequency, duration, and nature of staff/client contacts; number of clients placed in jobs or training programs; and average length of time it takes clients to complete a program stage) and qualitative information (e.g., line staff and juvenile reports on their expectations, experiences, and frustrations with different aspects of the program).

Having access to reliable information on day-to-day operations and performance is the only way managers ultimately can know whether or not their program's policies and procedures are realistic and are being followed. Timely information is required so that needed adjustments and changes can be made before a program has veered substantially off course from its designed framework. In addition to collecting basic information on who is being served and in what ways, it is important for administrators to monitor staffing patterns and composition, job responsibilities and division of labor, staff turnover, and the results of routine performance reviews.

Five major questions regarding program design should be asked:

1. Is the program serving the population for which it was intended, and how has this been defined?

2. Are program principles, components, and services being implemented as intended?

3. Is the program structured and managed well?

4. How is the program relating to and being perceived by the surrounding community?

5. What is its relationship with the larger system of which it is a part?

As suggested earlier, outcome evaluation focuses on the effects the program or intervention has had on the participants, the juvenile justice system, and the community. One problem in juvenile corrections is that each part of the juvenile justice system understandably tends to judge its effect simply in terms of its own relatively narrow role in the larger system. Institutions and residential programs tend to look at progress or change during the stay, not after. In contrast, aftercare is assessed on what happens following placement in the community, where many more forces are obviously at play. In a truly integrated institution-aftercare initiative targeting high-risk offenders, however, the measure of outcome is how juveniles in such an initiative fare in relation to juveniles who are processed in the traditionally fragmented juvenile corrections system, where the institution and aftercare systems barely communicate, let alone collaborate.

Multiple measures of outcome that include but go beyond recidivism are best to consider. Measures that relate to social activities, emotions, familial relationships, peers, education, work, values, and aspirations should all be assessed because these are important indicators of adjustment and change that apply equally to the placement and aftercare period. In addition, nonrecidivist measures are important because, in combination with recidivism, they provide a comprehensive picture of how juveniles are functioning and the prognosis for the future.

Even when considering recidivism on its own, programs would be well advised to look at multiple measures that take into account the actual complexity of recidivism and its interpretation. For example, comparing the preprogram rate of arrest or conviction with the postprogram rate permits a comparison of a program's effect on the frequency and type of misconduct. The seriousness of recidivism and the distinction between technical violations and new offenses should be carefully analyzed. In addition, using self-reported measures of recidivism as well as record data and including a long enough follow-up period can add extremely important information. It is also critical to account for the effect that "attrition" or loss of subjects (through dropping out where it is possible or inability to locate for follow-up purposes) can have and the problems associated with small sample sizes that can severely limit generalization.

In sum, effectively managing delinquency programs that incorporate aftercare requires close attention to management information and evaluation. If planned and presented properly, management information and evaluation need not be met by suspicion, anxiety, and fear. Concerns that evaluation will disrupt or displace direct service provision, absorb limited program resources, misrepresent reality, and make the program or staff look bad must be confronted head-on and regularly. Implementation and outcome evaluation information is far too important to neglect or ignore. It is the only way to know with confidence what will work, whether it is cost-effective, and if so, with whom the particular intervention strategy is most useful. Valuable information also can be made available about needed changes. Any hope of making progress in the areas of system accountability and program innovation demands sound and reliable evaluation.

Conclusion

After seven years of involvement in the Intensive Aftercare Program research and development initiative, experience suggests a number of crucial lessons and key insights relevant to the design and management of juvenile aftercare. First, the overall organizational complexity of juvenile corrections makes it exceedingly difficult to achieve even basic communication among its constituent parts. This is particularly problematic for aftercare where continuity and coherence in the transitional process across the institution-community boundary are inherently difficult. It is remarkable under the sheer organizational weight and labyrinth-like nature of the system's infrastructure that anything is accomplished. Yet, success does occur on those occasions when the right combination of top-level leadership, true collaborations, appropriate bottom-up input, as well as high quality and energetic staff are present. But, the challenge of designing and operating an effective aftercare system is rendered even more difficult when the targeted offender population is the most serious and chronic group being processed through juvenile corrections.

Second, aftercare for high-risk offenders cannot perform effectively if it is structured to operate in a relatively isolated and self-sufficient fashion. True collaboration, both in terms of planning and implementation, is a vital aspect of innovative programming in the aftercare arena. Lip service about coordination and collaboration is simply not sufficient. Designing, implementing, and managing an aftercare system requires the active participation of senior administrative staff drawn from the key parts of the juvenile corrections system, mid-level managers who translate policy into practice and monitor daily program activities, and line staff who are charged with direct service delivery from all involved agencies and organizations.

Further, the broad mission of aftercare must be clearly communicated from the top. Policies and procedures must explicitly recognize and state how goals and objectives will be accomplished. Job descriptions and staff training must reflect these expectations. Workload, caseload size and composition, as well as the number of required staff, must be accordingly structured to support these responsibilities.

Accountability at all levels of staff involvement and program operations must be maintained. Arguments touting the efficacy of compartmentalized versus consolidated administration are of secondary importance. Regardless of administrative structure, the central issues of management should focus on concerns, such as how can the key units with authority and responsibility work together most effectively and how can they share equitably in the division of labor and expenditure of resources.

Third, clarity on the mission of juvenile aftercare and intensive aftercare must be established at the outset. The agency with primary aftercare responsibility, acting in collaboration with the other parts of juvenile corrections, must champion and act on an approach in which the judiciary, correctional facilities, and community-based support services jointly embrace a programming strategy where maximal benefits can be derived from these diversified inputs. This approach should, in turn, be directly linked to a common understanding about which juveniles are being targeted to participate in which form of supervision. Inappropriate referral to the Intensive Aftercare Program, for example, can be extremely counterproductive. A central component for achieving this kind of collaboration and agreement will be the use of an integrated institution-aftercare implementation plan that specifies the respective roles and responsibilities of this entire network of involved agencies and staff.

Fourth, the implementation plan must address, minimally, the following set of considerations:

- decisions about confinement and length of stay
- steps facilitating prerelease and transition
- advocacy and service delivery capacity-building in the community
- service brokerage and referral
- staffing
- management information and evaluation capability

In designing and planning the Intensive Aftercare Program, it is imperative that all key organizational actors be fully "on board." The goal is to build a sound organizational and professional foundation through which an Intensive Aftercare Program approach to managing high-risk juveniles can be successfully implemented and maintained. In juvenile corrections, the system is simply so complex and so easily plagued by fragmentation, discontinuity, miscommunication, and conflicting goals that innovation and change can only proceed in a positive direction if clear, carefully considered, and appropriate strategies for program planning and development have been devised and initiated.

Fifth, follow-through and prioritization are a must. Strong leadership, quality staff, shared responsibility, and a workable division of labor can counter the all-too-common tendency for collaborative initiative to succumb to crisis management and reactive planning. It is easy to lose momentum in planning when no one individual possesses the leadership skills, competence, and authority within his or her own agency to keep crucial development activities, as well as the scheduling and background work for implementation, on track.

Sixth and finally, any attempt to develop intensive approaches to juvenile aftercare must build on the emerging knowledge base and evolving technology of treatment and social control. Much of this progress can be traced to recent experiments in intensive supervision. Fundamentally important advances have been made in a wide range of programming areas relevant to managing high-risk juveniles in aftercare. In part, this reflects the availability of far more sophisticated techniques to achieve substantially higher levels of surveillance and intrusion into daily activities of these juveniles. Through careful and thoughtful application, these tools can collectively provide an opportunity to develop far more structured and responsive approaches to normalizing the behavior of serious and chronic juvenile offenders in the community.

References

Altschuler, D. M., and T. L. Armstrong. 1991. *Intensive community-based aftercare prototype: Policies and procedures.* Washington, D.C.: Office of Juvenile Justice and Delinquency Prevention, U.S. Department of Justice.

———. 1993. *Intensive aftercare for high-risk juvenile parolees: Strategies for program development and action planning.* Paper presented at 1993 Annual Meeting of the American Society of Criminology, Phoenix.

Andrews, D. 1987. *Implications of classification for treatment of juveniles.* Paper presented to American Probation and Parole Association, Salt Lake City.

Baird, S. C. 1983. *Report on intensive supervision programs in probation and parole.* Washington, D.C.: National Institute of Corrections, U.S. Department of Justice.

Bureau of Justice Statistics. 1989. *Children in custody, 1975–85.* Washington, D.C.: Bureau of Justice Statistics, U.S. Department of Justice.

Champion, D. J. 1992. *The juvenile justice system: Delinquency, processing, and the law.* New York: Macmillan Publishing Company.

Conger, R. D. 1976. Social control and social learning models of delinquent behavior. *Criminology* 14:17–40.

Elliott, D. S., and H. Voss. 1974. *Delinquency and drop-out.* Lexington, MA: D.C. Heath.

Elliott, D. S., S. Ageton, and R. Cantor. 1979. An integrated perspective on delinquent behavior. *Journal of Research in Crime and Delinquency* 16:3–27.

Elliott, D. S., D. Huizinga, and S. Ageton. 1985. *Explaining delinquency and drug use.* Beverly Hills, Calif.: Sage Publications.

Erwin, B. S., and L. Bennett. 1987. New dimensions in probation: Georgia's experience with intensive probation supervision. In *Research in Brief.* Washington, D.C.: National Institute of Justice, U.S. Department of Justice.

Fagan, J., and S. J. Jones. 1984. Toward a theoretical model for intervention with violent juvenile offenders. In *Violent juvenile offenders: An anthology,* ed. Mathias, et al. San Francisco: National Council on Crime and Delinquency.

Hamparian, D., et al. 1978. *A study of the dangerous juvenile offender.* Lexington, Mass.: Lexington Books.

Krisberg, B., et al. 1993. *NCCD focus. Juveniles in state custody: Prospects for community-based care of troubled adolescents.* San Francisco: National Council on Crime and Delinquency.

Markley, G., and M. Eisenberg. 1986. *The Texas Board of Pardons and Paroles case management system.* Austin: Texas Board of Pardons and Paroles.

McCord, J. 1979. Some child-rearing antecedents of criminal behavior in adult men. *Journal of Personality and Social Psychology* 37:1477–86.

Shannon, L. 1978. A longitudinal study of delinquency and crime. In *Quantitative studies in criminology,* ed. C. Wellford. Beverly Hills, Calif.: Sage Publications.

Weis, J. G., and J. D. Hawkins. 1981. *Reports of the national juvenile justice assessment centers: Preventing delinquency.* Washington, D.C.: National Institute for Juvenile Justice and Delinquency Prevention, Office of Juvenile Justice and Delinquency Prevention, U.S. Department of Justice.

Wolfgang, M., R. Figlio, and T. Sellin. 1972. *Delinquency in a birth cohort.* Chicago: University of Chicago Press.

Part III

Managing Program Administration

8 Managing Clinical Programs for Juvenile Delinquents

Vicki MacIntyre Agee, Ph.D.

At every level of the juvenile correctional system there is a subgroup of emotionally disturbed juveniles who need intensive mental health care. Since the mental-health deinstitutionalization movement in the 1960s, there is no long-term secure care in most mental health systems. For juvenile offenders who have a chronic mental disorder that severely affects their ability to adjust in society, this means they spend a considerable amount of time rotating through juvenile correctional programs and often eventually end up in adult corrections.

Juvenile corrections managers are faced with finding ways to handle the most difficult-to-treat juveniles with very few resources. Juveniles may be dealt with on a case-by-case basis or juveniles with mental disorders may be treated as a group. The latter is far less time-consuming and more practical.

Emotionally Disturbed Juveniles

Options for dealing with the problem of what to do with emotionally disturbed juveniles vary and may include the following:

- coordinate with the local mental health system to provide a forensic mental health program either on the site of a juvenile correctional facility or at a mental health residential facility
- hire full-time or part-time mental health clinicians to provide services to emotionally disturbed juveniles on site at juvenile correctional facilities
- develop separate residential treatment program(s) for emotionally disturbed juveniles who are in the juvenile correctional system
- contract with private-sector providers for residential treatment programs

Dr. Vicki MacIntyre Agee is a clinical psychologist in Salt Lake City, Utah, with more than twenty years of experience with residential treatment programs for juvenile delinquents. She is a founding member of the National Adolescent Perpetrator Network and a member of the American Correctional Association's Victims of Crime Committee.

Coordinate with the local mental health system to provide a foren-sic mental health program either on the site of a juvenile correctional facility or at a mental health residential facility. Mental health services will be under the aegis of the mental health system and, therefore, usually more credible in the eyes of the public than the correctional system.

However, there are many drawbacks to this option. Few mental health professionals are trained to deal with aggressive juvenile delinquents. In addition, research has indicated that traditional mental health techniques are ineffective with this population (Andrews 1990).

In this option, admissions and discharges usually are controlled by the people providing the service. This may lead to a program accepting only the easiest to manage of the emotionally disturbed juveniles and rapidly discharging juveniles who act out aggressively. In fact, it is not uncommon for juveniles to be discharged from programs for the very behaviors that were exhibited in the first place. For example, sex offenders may be dis-charged for sexually acting out. Conduct disorder/oppositional-defiant dis-order juveniles may be discharged for being noncompliant. Even depressed juveniles may be discharged for attempting suicide.

Hire full-time or part-time mental health clinicians to provide serv-ices to emotionally disturbed juveniles on site at juvenile correctional facilities. In this option, juvenile correctional managers select and hire their own mental health staff. They have direct responsibility for hiring cli-nicians who are committed to work with this difficult population, who know a lot about their special problems, and who are able to use their edu-cation, training, and skills in creative problem-specific treatment planning.

Unfortunately, juvenile correctional mental health staff are often re-stricted to providing ancillary treatment in a nontherapeutic milieu. That is, the treatment they recommend is done as an aside to the routine pro-gram, rather than as an integral part of it.

In addition, it is difficult to find experienced mental health professionals who want to work in the often unpleasant and stressful juvenile correc-tional environment. As a result, inexperienced clinicians or those new to the field are likely to accept the positions. Those who do not learn quickly and adapt to the special needs of the correctional milieu may develop an elitism which is decidedly unhelpful. This elitism stems from training in traditional treatment approaches and may result in a tendency to project blame for their clients' problems onto others (for example, staff, parents, society).

As a result, it is not unheard of for correctional mental health staff to ex-acerbate the problems by enabling or rescuing. For example, therapy ses-sions may become solely "grievance" meetings, where juveniles complain about being misunderstood and being treated unfairly. The mental health professional conducting the group might even reinforce the juvenile's self-pity and denial of responsibility for his or her own behavior and increase the stress on the juvenile care staff by siding with the juvenile in opposing their authority.

Develop separate residential treatment program(s) for emotionally disturbed juveniles who are in the juvenile correctional system. At its best, this would involve providing a long-term intensive treatment program that uses the most progressive cognitive-behavioral techniques in combination with effective medications, when necessary, in a therapeutic environment. In this option, correctional managers do not have to worry about whether the juvenile will be accepted for or remain in treatment, because the manager controls admissions. The manager can provide more appropriate programming than is usually done in mental health programs, which addresses the specific criminal thinking and other problem areas of each juvenile. In addition, separating out the emotionally disturbed juveniles from the rest of the population allows the other juveniles to get the attention they need and decreases undue stress on staff.

The negative side to this option is that providing mental health programming in a correctional setting opens the program up to criticism from outsiders. Important treatment issues include: the right of the juvenile to refuse treatment, use of restraints, and use of psychotropic medications. As an example, because many clients are severely depressed, it is not uncommon for suicide attempts to occur (and even, on rare occasions, a successful suicide) in mental health residential treatment programs. Although there is naturally concern, there is usually little public criticism. When such incidents occur in a correctional setting, it is cause for immediate official investigation and, often, uproar and criticism in the media.

Contract with private-sector providers for residential treatment programs. The advantage of this option is that the private-sector providers must offer quality service or the contract will be discontinued and will be offered to a competitor. Private providers often have more flexibility in hiring, financial management, program planning, and operations than public agencies.

However, in some localities it is difficult to find and select high-quality private providers and to monitor programs effectively (without "micromanaging" or unduly constricting them). Although promises for high-quality treatment are made to win proposals, not all programs actually deliver all that they propose. It is difficult to design the proposal selection process to ensure that the selection committee is competent to choose programs geared to the special needs of emotionally disturbed juvenile offenders.

Clearly, there are drawbacks to each of these solutions. And, all of them are expensive.

What Does Not Work

No matter who provides the treatment to the emotionally disturbed juvenile, it is important to remember that research has shown that traditional mental health techniques are ineffective with the aggressive juvenile delinquent (Andrews 1990).

Finally, traditional psychodynamic and nondirective client-centered therapies are to be avoided with most offenders. These therapies are designed to free people from personally inhibiting controls of "superego" and "society" while neurotic misery and over-control are not the criminogenic problems for a majority of offenders.

Extrapolating from the treatment effectiveness literature for juvenile delinquents, it appears traditional "medical model" treatment programs are similarly ineffective with emotionally disturbed juvenile delinquents. The following are some of the deficits noted in using traditional methods with this specialized population:

1. Traditional diagnostic assessments do not provide sufficient information. Such information should include: offense histories, victim-impact statements, and risk assessments to allow for relevant placement and intervention decisions.

2. Traditional treatment fails to engage the involuntary, noncompliant juvenile who resists treatment, denies his or her problems, and is engaged in aggressive, ritualized, and addictive behaviors.

3. Traditional psychotherapeutic techniques of insight-oriented therapy have practical and theoretical limitations with juveniles with characteristic deficits in social cognitive skills (such as low empathy, poor means-ends reasoning, and concrete thinking).

4. Traditional techniques, such as "venting" anger, are inappropriate with juveniles who characteristically have difficulty controlling their aggression.

5. Traditional nondirective techniques do not provide the intensive supervision, confrontation, limit-setting, and directive guidance in learning socially acceptable behaviors that is required by a population that is often aggressively noncompliant and victimizes others.

6. The traditional approach of focusing on early childhood experiences allows juveniles to shift the focus from personal accountability in the present. This tends to encourage externalization of blame to dysfunctional families, staff, and society and provides juveniles with more justification to victimize others.

7. The traditional emphasis on one-to-one therapy is contrary to the peer-based group therapy, which is seen as the most effective form of intervention.

8. Traditional approaches tend to direct services toward problems not predictive of recidivism, such as anxiety, depression, fitness, self-esteem, and moral development.

What Works

The following description provides a brief summary of some of the components of effective treatment of juveniles in correctional settings described by researchers (Gendreau 1981, 1993; Gendreau and Ross 1979; Greenwood and Zimring 1985; Greenwood 1986; Andrews et al. 1990; Ross and Fabiano 1985).

Effective Assessment

To begin to cope with the problem of emotionally disturbed juveniles in the juvenile corrections population, it is critical to have assessment staff who can provide a comprehensive evaluation that is relevant to a juvenile correctional population. This assessment should not be the typical psychiatric interview or psychological testing done in a vacuum. Because of the characteristic denial of this population, it is extremely unwise to base any kind of assessment on information garnered from the juvenile alone. It is critical is to know what kinds of harmful thinking and behaviors have occurred in the past and are likely to continue to occur so that the treatment planning can be specific to the problem areas and risks.

According to John Monahan (1993), a leading researcher on prediction of violence, there are generally four sources in which relevant information can be found: in the records of past treatment, in the records of current treatment, from interviewing the patient, and from interviewing significant others. In some criminal contexts, additional records in the form of police and aftercare reports, arrest records, and trial transcripts may also be available and should be consulted.

To do an adequate assessment, the evaluator must secure as much information as possible from both in-house and community-based sources. This is not just social history information and behavior observations, because neither of these give a balanced picture of the problems. The perpetrators of offenses are obviously poor sources of information since it is assumed they felt justified in committing the acts. What is most important with juveniles who have victimized others is to get a clear idea of what the victim experienced. Juveniles themselves feel justified in doing whatever they did or they would not have done it, so their version is very biased. Social history information is often provided by people who have strong bonds with the juvenile (even to the point of having been enablers or rescuers) and who never met the juvenile's victims. Also, there is a strong tendency among parents, staff, and additional significant others to "normalize" their perceptions of the problems of the juvenile. It is difficult to accept the reality of the juvenile being disturbed and dangerous, particularly when he or she is your child or someone you have counseled.

Therefore, accurate assessment should incorporate information from police reports on the offense(s), as well as any available information from the victim(s). Correctional managers may have to help interface with the courts and police to get this information for their assessment staff. Efforts should be made to gather every piece of descriptive information on the offense(s), impact on the victim, and the victim's perception of the offense(s). Then, based on interviews, tests, victim information, social history information, and staff observations, the following information should be obtained:

- degree of disclosure to interviewers of offending behavior
- personal responsibility for offending behavior
- degree of aggression and level of violence
- frequency and duration of offenses
- targets of the offender/victim characteristics
- other abusive, addictive, or compulsive behaviors
- length and progression of history of emotional disturbance
- medical history, with special emphasis on any brain trauma or other neurological problems
- social relationships
- family system functioning
- history of sexual, physical, and emotional victimization
- criminal arrests, convictions, and incarceration history
- school and employment history
- treatment history
- intellectual functioning
- educational achievement

Of course, no matter how intensive the assessment, the evaluation ends up having little value to correctional managers and their staff unless the information is used for effective programming.

Comprehensive Cognitive Behavioral Programming

According to researchers Ross and Fabiano (1985):

> Although a wide variety of treatment modalities have been used in effective correctional programs, research has revealed that one program component is common to almost every treatment effort which has been successful: some technique which would influence the offender's thinking ... teaching offenders how to understand and consider other people's values, behavior and feelings; how to recognize how their behavior affects other people and why others respond to them as they do; and how to develop alternative, pro-social rather than anti-social ways of reacting to interpersonal conflicts.

Cognitive-behavioral programs help juveniles identify and own (become accountable for) their negative thinking and behavior and the consequences for their victims. This provides the motivation and support for change. Cognitive-behavioral techniques also teach juveniles how to intervene in cycles of negative thinking and behavior and teach alternative prosocial behaviors.

Positive Peer Communities

A positive peer culture is considered by researchers to be a critical ingredient of effective juvenile rehabilitation programs. Greenwood and Zimring (1985) state that successful treatment programs "… reduce or eliminate negative role models and peer support for negative attitudes and behaviors." Without a positive peer culture, the antisocial subculture of violence that exists in many urban areas is reproduced in juvenile correctional settings. Emotionally disturbed juveniles who have been in this environment reproduce it rapidly in the treatment setting, with the stronger peers being predatory over the weaker ones.

The most salient premise of positive peer-community approaches is that each juvenile entering the program needs help to learn responsible behaviors and that this cannot be done without the deep involvement of their peers (fellow clients) and staff. Peers are important in this process because juveniles need involvement with others who are like them in order to learn positive, helpful, caring relationships. Adolescents, particularly, are focused on what their peers think and do. The positive peer culture provides juveniles with both a sense of ownership and control over what is going on in their lives and constant input from peers who are similar to them. Emotionally disturbed juvenile offenders can often recognize each other's thinking and behaviors better than staff.

Anger Management

One of the most prevalent traditional techniques used with emotionally disturbed juveniles with severe anger problems has been to encourage them to "vent" their "repressed" anger. More recently, however, it has been found that repressed anger is not the major problem with these juveniles because anger is frequently expressed openly with devastating consequences to their victims.

The research on anger indicates that people who are most prone to vent their rages get angrier, not less angry. Venting rage also tends to freeze the distorted cognition present in all anger by providing social approval. According to McKay, Rogers, and McKay (1989), "Venting anger rarely leads to any real relief or any lasting catharsis. It leads instead to more anger, tension, and arousal."

Rather than encouraging venting, the current emphasis in treatment programs is training in aggression control or anger management (telephone conversation with B. Glick and A. Goldstein). These training modules involve understanding the symptoms (physical and mental) of anger and philosophical issues of responsibility for anger, thoughts that trigger escalation of anger, "hot spots" or situations that escalate anger, the use of relaxation techniques and calming thoughts to control physical and mental symptoms, and responsible prosocial assertive negotiation skills that help to work through conflicts.

Empathy Training

Empathy training (also known as victim awareness) is a pivotal concept in raising and maintaining motivation for treatment in the population of chronically emotionally disturbed juveniles. Their characteristic strong sense of denial, minimalization, and self-justification prevents them from feeling remorse. They have little or no awareness of their victims as human beings; rather, they see their victims as objects. A great deal of the reinforcement they derive from their criminal offending is the feeling of power over their victims.

A critical part of any effective juvenile corrections program is a clear, firm, consistent, and potent discipline system.

Techniques to teach victim empathy vary. They include: individual therapy, group therapy, educational approaches, and combinations of the three. The key is to implement these approaches throughout the positive peer culture so that the concepts permeate the program.

Discipline

A critical part of any effective juvenile corrections program is a clear, firm, consistent, and potent discipline system. Personal growth cannot take place without learning self-discipline and the need to honor responsibilities and obligations. Resistance to complying with even basic requests from others and an inability to express anger appropriately are common problems among a majority of juvenile offenders, particularly those who are emotionally disturbed. This cripples them in their interpersonal relationships because even if their emotional disturbance is under control and their criminal behavior ceases, the inability to function in mainstream society without alienating people prevents them from adapting to the community. Emotionally disturbed juvenile offenders characteristically act in ways that repel the very people they need for survival.

Few programs have an effective system of setting limits. This is particularly the case in mental health facilities where treatment is considered separate from teaching self-discipline. It is not uncommon for mental health evaluations to indicate a client does not need treatment, but needs structure, limits, and controls. Unfortunately, it is not possible to separate the two with this population, because their characteristic aggressive non-compliance mitigates against treatment and against their adjustment to society in general.

An effective treatment program for emotionally disturbed juveniles should not be the nurturing, nonconfronting model found in traditional settings. Yochelson and Samenow (1976) have said that effective change agents must be "unapologetic moralists," and the program must meld treatment and discipline. An effective discipline system makes doing things responsibly rewarding and acting irresponsibly nonrewarding.

An effective discipline program must clearly state the structure of the program, including the group norms that are designed to promote socialization and the offenses that are considered serious and not to be tolerated. The consequences for breaking these major and minor offenses also are clearly specified in the program. This structure needs to be very comprehensive. Juveniles need to know the consequences for unacceptable behavior. Consequences must be prompt, relevant, effective, humane, and *extremely consistent.* Because many juveniles in this population have had success in avoiding consequences by intimidating others or by manipulating others to rescue them, consistency is perhaps the most important component.

Prosocial Skills

Another failing of traditional treatment programs is their neglect to teach juveniles the practical prosocial skills they need to survive in mainstream society. Being able to understand one's problems is important but does not eliminate the need to learn alternative behaviors. Prosocial skills models use creative techniques to teach successful community living skills. Major areas of these models include core and social skills as well as skills in: stress management, listening, problem solving, goal setting, accountability, and values clarification.

Drug and Alcohol Abuse Counseling

Drug and alcohol abuse is a common problem among emotionally disturbed juvenile offenders. In these cases, chemical abuse assessment is necessary along with education about the effects of different types of drug use, the dynamics of chemical abuse, family issues, and the principles of recovery programs.

Transition and Aftercare

The reality is that most programs end prematurely and do not provide effective aftercare. Often the juveniles' behavior problems reappear rapidly without support or follow-up in an aftercare program. The problems are chronic and are not cured by a stint in a residential treatment program. Intensive support and supervision is critical and must be given for extended periods of time. Juveniles must learn how to establish a long-term support system in the community that they are likely to need throughout their lives. The family counseling component of the program is a critical part of the transition process. Again, because traditional techniques do not work well with families of emotionally disturbed juvenile offenders, it is important to provide relevant and appropriate intervention.

Overview of Diagnostic-Specific Programs

Emotionally disturbed juveniles in a correctional program are likely to cluster in the diagnostic categories that are associated with more aggressive and impulsive behavior (because community facilities are less willing to deal with them). Therefore, attention-deficit disorder, conduct disorder/oppositional-defiant disorder, depression, and bipolar disorders predominate while other disorders, such as obsessive-compulsive disorders, panic disorders, and psychoses, are rare. In addition, the possibility of underlying organic brain damage is extremely high in this population, but is very seldom diagnosed or treated appropriately.

Programs for Juveniles with Attention-Deficit-Hyperactivity Disorder

A significant percentage of the population of emotionally disturbed juveniles committed to state departments of juvenile corrections are diagnosed with attention-deficit-hyperactivity disorder (ADHD). Because of underlying organicity, noncompliant and aggressive ADHD juveniles respond poorly to traditional attempts at intervention and often experience repeated failures at all levels of the continuum of care.

Although it is said that misdiagnosis has been a serious problem with ADHD, new measures have been developed that allow for more accurate diagnosis. These include the Connors Rating Scales, Parent Interview, Wender Utah Rating Scales, California Personality Test, and a review of the individuals' histories as early as age three-and-a-half, for such symptoms as the following:

- inability to sustain attention, distractibility, restlessness
- impulsive, poor impulse control
- irrelevant movement, hyperactivity, destructiveness, noisiness
- immature emotional control, not reflective, excitability
- problems in rule-governed behavior, lack of conscience
- poor means-ends reasoning, misbehavior looks purposeful, inability to learn from consequences
- immature self-speech (internal language)
- poor social relations, intrusive behavior
- noncompliance with commands
- unpredictable, variable moods
- immature physical size
- enuresis/encopresis
- short sleep cycles

- high pain tolerance
- poor motor coordination
- learning disabilities and underachievement academically
- frequent allergies, respiratory infections, and otitis media

The specific causes of ADHD are unknown, although there is clearly an underlying genetic link. ADHD parents frequently have ADHD children. Drug/alcohol abuse in both parents is a strong risk factor. Cocaine use is felt to be particularly risky for the development of severe ADHD ("the crack babies syndrome").

At one time it was felt that ADHD was a problem that most children would outgrow, but research is now showing that ADHD is often a chronic, lifelong condition (Sood and Resnick 1992). The ADHD adult has a high possibility of significant impairments in interpersonal relationships. According to Kevin Murphy (1992):

> Most ADHD adults are restless, easily distracted, have trouble focusing, concentrating, and sustaining attention, are impulsive and impatient, have inconsistent work performance, are often unorganized and fail to plan ahead, often fail to finish tasks they have started, have frequent mood swings and a short temper and often have a chronic pattern of underachievement.

It is little wonder that many people with ADHD end up in the correctional or mental health system.

Fortunately, promising research is taking place in the area of ADHD. Research has shown that symptoms can be reduced significantly using both medication (Methylphenidate) and behavior modification (Sood and Resnick 1992).

Programs for Juveniles with Depression or Bipolar Disorder

Another often undiagnosed problem with this juvenile population is severe chronic depression (and/or bipolar disorder). As with the population of ADHD juveniles, there is often an underlying biochemical imbalance contributing to the intensity of the problem and to the lack of effectiveness of counseling alone.

The popular notion of depression includes such symptoms as loss of energy and appetite, low self-esteem, sleeping too much, sadness, and suicide attempts. However, equally common symptoms include: weight gain; insomnia; loud, obnoxious, antisocial behavior; violent outbursts; difficulty concentrating; and trouble with self-control. These symptoms are associated with offending behavior also, and this is why some clinicians feel that depression often goes undiagnosed in the population of delinquents.

Because of the underlying biochemical imbalance in depression, "talk therapy" alone is ineffective. Even though medication helps control depression, it does not cure it. Clients remain vulnerable to periodic bouts of depression throughout their lives. A combination of medication and learned coping behaviors should be used.

Programs for Juveniles with Conduct Disorder/ Oppositional-Defiant Disorder

The diagnosis of conduct disorder/oppositional-defiant disorder describes the behavior, but does not help with understanding the reason for the behavior. It is important to find out whether the juvenile is reacting to a situational conflict (such as a family conflict), is being influenced by a negative subculture, or is responding to an underlying organicity, such as ADHD, depression, substance abuse, or organic brain syndrome. If the behavior is chronic and accompanied by a marked lack of empathy, it could be a sign of a developing antisocial personality disorder.

The treatment plan should emphasize structure and discipline. As in overall cognitive-behavioral programming, cognitive behavioral techniques, such as anger management, victim awareness, and a point and level system, are effective tools.

Programs for Juveniles with Psychoses and Other Disorders

The number of juveniles diagnosed as psychotic is generally quite low in this age group, although the beginning symptoms of adult-onset schizophrenia may be seen. Unfortunately, at this state of research, there is no effective way of stopping the progress of the disorder, although a significant percentage do improve with medication and cognitive-behavioral modification to the point where they can function in society. It is important that the psychotic juvenile not be reinforced for "crazy behavior." For example, one chronic schizophrenic juvenile learned to say, "Check myself for my crazy behavior" whenever he could see that he was behaving inappropriately and could control his bizarre behavior. Unfortunately, when this juvenile was later hospitalized as an adult and was exposed to a population of other psychotics, his behavior control dissipated almost immediately.

Other possible mental health diagnoses are also rare, such as obsessive-compulsive disorders and panic disorders. These two are often treated with a combination of medication and cognitive-behavioral intervention.

Working with the family to provide both information and support is extremely important. Families need to know what resources are available for them and how to access them.

Conclusion

One of the most frustrating challenges for the juvenile correctional managers is to obtain services for the rapidly increasing population of emotionally disturbed juveniles in their systems. The commitment to treatment of juvenile offenders is not only unpopular, unpleasant, unrewarding, and risky, it is felt to be futile by many. Nevertheless, most dedicated correctional managers cannot tolerate to "do nothing, since nothing works," an attitude that is sadly prevalent.

Traditional mental health systems are unresponsive to the need for effective treatment programs for emotionally disturbed juvenile offenders. The reality is that the clients are often in the juvenile correctional system, while the resources needed for effective intervention are usually found in the mental health system. There are effective solutions to this problem, such as having private-sector providers offer the service, but they require definitive action on the part of managers and their funding sources. Emotionally disturbed juvenile offenders can cause untold harm to themselves, their peers, their families, and their crime victims. Left untreated, they will continue to fill the nation's correctional facilities. The cost to society is enormous, and the damage to the quality of life cannot be ignored.

References

Andrews, D. A., et al. 1990. Does correctional treatment work? A clinically relevant and psychologically informed meta-analysis. *Criminology* 28:369–404.

Gendreau, P. 1981. Treatment in corrections: Martinson was wrong. *Canadian Psychology* 22:232–338.

——. 1993. The principles of effective intervention with offenders. Presented at "What works in community corrections: A consensus conference," Philadelphia, Penn., 3–6 November.

Gendreau, P., and R. R. Ross. 1979. Effective correctional treatment: Bibliotherapy and cynics. *Crime and Delinquency* 25:463–89.

Greenwood, P. W. 1986. *Correctional supervision of juvenile offenders: Where do we go from here?* Santa Monica, Calif.: Rand.

Greenwood, P. W., and F. E. Zimring. 1985. *One more chance: The pursuit of promising intervention strategies for chronic juvenile offenders.* Santa Monica, Calif.: Rand.

McKay, M., P. Rogers, and J. McKay. 1989. *When anger hurts: Quieting the storm within.* Oakland, CA: New Harbinger Publications.

Monahan, J. 1993. Limiting therapist exposure to Tarasoff liability: Guidelines for risk containment. *American Psychologist* 48(3): 242–50.

Murphy, K. 1992. Coping strategies for ADHD adults. *CHADDER* (Fall-Winter):10-11.

Ross, R. R., and E. Fabiano. 1985. *Time to think: A cognitive model of delinquency prevention and offender rehabilitation.* Johnson City, Tenn: Institute of Social Sciences and Arts.

Sood, B., and R. L. Resnick. 1992. Attention deficit disorder. *Psychiatric Consultant*, Medical College of Virginia 2(2):1-4.

Yochelson, S., and S. Samenow. 1976. *The criminal personality II, The change process.* New York: Jason Aronson.

9 Managing Recreation and Leisure for Juvenile Delinquents

Jimmy Calloway, Ph.D.

America's juveniles have a great deal of discretionary time, much of it unstructured, unsupervised, and unproductive. Only 60 percent of juveniles' waking hours are committed to essentials such as attending school, doing homework, eating, performing chores, or working at paid employment, while the remaining 40 percent is undirected discretionary time, giving rise to excessive television watching, sex, drug abuse, gang activity, and violence (Carnegie Council on Adolescent Development 1992).

Because they lack sufficient afterschool supervision, the nation's juveniles have become truly at risk. Lacking structured programs and knowledge about constructive activity alternatives (recreation), juveniles are left to engage in negative pathological pursuits. Often, the only rehabilitative alternative is the juvenile detention center.

This chapter focuses on how to manage and implement recreation programs and structured leisure opportunities, both for at-risk juveniles who are in the community and juvenile delinquents detained within juvenile facilities.

Between 1966 and 1975, juvenile arrests increased by nearly 300 percent (Goldstein and Glick 1987). According to the Carnegie Council on Adolescent Development (1992), all Americans have a vital stake in the healthy development of today's juveniles, who will become tomorrow's parents, workers, and citizens. But millions of America's juveniles are not developing into responsible members of society. Many will not lead productive or fulfilling lives. Juveniles aged ten-to-fifteen years do not become mature adults without help. They are profoundly influenced by experiences they have had at home and in school, but they also are affected by experiences in their neighborhoods and communities.

The role of leisure in addressing the juvenile delinquent problem in today's society has received minimal attention by juvenile justice professionals (Rojek 1989). When a juvenile commits a misdeed or offense against

Dr. Jimmy Calloway is vice president for governmental affairs and fund development for the Atlanta Paralympic Organizing Committee in Atlanta, Georgia.

society, he or she is said to be delinquent. Crime and delinquency is behavior which is socially unacceptable, whether the act is committed by a minor or an adult.

Activity, crime and delinquency, and recreation have many similar characteristics. Delinquency, in its early stages, is clearly a pathological form of play. Reimer (1981) believes it is important to acknowledge the "fun" dimension of deviancy to better understand the many forms of deviant behaviors. That is, some deviant behaviors may provide entertainment and challenge to the deviant actor. An obvious and indisputable fact about leisure in modern society is that many of the most popular activities are illegal. Consider the examples of drug abuse, pornographic home videotaping, unlawful sexual activity, and trespassing. These activities are routine free-time pursuits for many people. Perhaps 20 percent of all successful men, when bored, will turn to adultery, adventure seeking, or alcohol or drug abuse (Richards, Berk, and Foster 1979).

Delinquent juveniles characteristically lack recreational skills and interest and have a low motivation toward participation in socially acceptable group activity.

In addition, stealing apples from a fruit stand or driving a stolen car can satisfy some of the basic desires for adventure, achievement, recognition, and response that traditionally have been met by recreational pursuits such as camping, athletics, or creative arts. The issue is further complicated if the delinquency becomes financially profitable.

Children's peer groups are both recipients and bearers of tradition governing rules, regulations, and modes of play of a variety of games and means of entertainment. Similarly, members of delinquent groups are the recipients and bearers of tradition on subjects such as shoplifting and avoiding authorities (Reimer 1981). In spite of these similarities, these group activities are widely different. One is considered constructive, desirable, and recreative; the other is destructive, undesirable, and illegal. Even random play-group activity, which in its beginnings is neither delinquent nor recreational, becomes one or the other depending on whether the culmination of the activity is acceptable to the community.

Delinquent juveniles characteristically lack recreational skills and interest and have a low motivation toward participation in socially acceptable group activity. A lack of knowledge and awareness of socially acceptable recreation activities results in negative pathological pursuits. Many recreation professionals find it sacrilegious to associate leisure with negative pursuits. Yet, every recreation professional is defined by the amount of damage the profession can do if it fails to ethically and morally deliver professional recreation services to juveniles.

The personality patterns of established juvenile delinquents and adult criminals may help to explain why many do not respond to incarceration by permanently giving up their criminal behavior. As a group, they exhibit markedly different personality traits and attitudes about leisure than the population at large. They are socially assertive and defiant toward adult authority, more resentful of others than the general population, and hostile and destructive. They are more impulsive in all behaviors, less cooperative and dependent on others, and less conventional in their ideas and behaviors.

The families of criminals have been observed to behave differently than those of others. It seems that their families rarely engage in constructive forms of recreation. Instead of hobbies or active participation in athletics, the principal form of leisure is usually passive, such as watching television or sleeping more than eight hours a day. Indeed, some authorities have attributed subsequent criminal behavior to faulty patterns of leisure behavior developed in the early years. According to Kraus and Bates (1975):

> . . . it is within leisure and as a form of pathological play, that many adult criminals-to-be begin their careers, carrying on illegal gambling, becoming involved in vice and drug addictions, or engaging in theft or vandalism for sheer excitement.

Garrett Heyns (Kraus 1966), a Michigan reformatory warden, has described the problems faced by many inmates of correctional institutions when dealing with their leisure, including the following:

- no knowledge or skills, such as reading, to enable them to make acceptable use of their leisure time
- a lack of avocational interests (hobbies) of the well adjusted
- a lack of the ability to engage in any cooperative act with their friends
- a lack of self-control or a sense of fair play

Heyns advocates that correctional institutions help offenders to overcome these deficiencies. He believes that these needs must be filled and the missing interests, knowledge, and skills provided if rehabilitation is to occur.

Unfortunately, prisons and jails have not provided creative leisure programming that results in a long-lasting, positive change in inmates' leisure behavior. One reason is the continuing prevalence of the idea that a correctional institution is a place to punish. Offenders within the institutions are denied many of the rights accorded to law-abiding citizens. Taxpayers resent the use of tax money to provide any unnecessary services for offenders, especially services that many regard as contributing to a "country club" atmosphere within the institution.

Most recreational programs are basic (sports programs, such as baseball or handball; cards; checkers and chess; reading; and choral and instrumental groups) but do not tap the potential of recreation and leisure activities that could permanently change the offender's life.

These programs do not provide an opportunity for all offenders to satisfy their leisure needs. They are not designed to encourage offenders to develop leisure pursuits that could easily be continued once offenders return to their communities because of the following reasons:

- lack of professional recreation staff
- administrative authority's resistance to change
- too strong an emphasis on custodial care and security
- lack of proper facilities

Of the four, the attitude of administrators (lack of understanding of the value of recreation in a correctional institution) is probably the one that must be addressed and changed first. The significant role that leisure and recreational experiences can play in the institutional setting must be emphasized to administrators responsible for managing and funding the program. Perhaps then recreation can be recognized as more than a way to relieve juvenile boredom. In addition, recreation should be accepted as a vital step in the process of mainstreaming juveniles back into the community as law-abiding citizens.

The key role of leisure service managers serving juvenile delinquents is understanding how to manage organizational structures that rehabilitate today's juveniles. A secondary challenge is to help facility or program administrators understand the role of correctional recreation in juvenile delinquency programs.

The Role of NCRA and AALR

The National Correctional Recreation Association (NCRA) and the American Association for Leisure and Recreation (AALR) believe that recreation and leisure are valued aspects of the human life experience. The National Correctional Recreational Association and the American Association for Leisure and Recreation promote professional programs and services that help offenders to eliminate barriers to leisure, develop leisure skills and attitudes, and optimize leisure participation.

These organizations are committed to improving the quality of life within the institution as well as preparing offenders for their use of leisure time after release. These two organizations further strive to ensure that the leisure services in correctional institutions meet two objectives: to relieve the daily tensions that are created by incarceration and to develop, through leisure education, leisure skills that personally benefit the offender and carry over value into the community. In addition, recreation and leisure services should continue to be employed as an essential tool for therapy and rehabilitation.

Managing Juvenile Recreation and Leisure Activities

Currently, almost 5,000 correctional facilities and 17,000 afterschool programs offer some form of recreation to adult and juvenile offenders. Correctional recreation services operate under two assumptions. First, their input of raw material is human beings (juveniles) with specific attributes, and their output is persons changed in a predetermined manner. Second, their general mandate is that of service to maintain and improve the general well-being and functioning of the juveniles in their care (Hasenfeld and English 1983).

The primary function of correctional recreation services in the community or the correctional facility is to alter people's behaviors, attributes, and social status to maintain or enhance their well-being. Through mechanisms, such as treatment or therapy, leisure education, and recreation participation, recreation service organizations attempt to prevent social disintegration and reintegrate the juvenile into society (Hasenfeld and English 1983).

Failure to respond to the needs of the population served is indicated by the discrepancy between professed objectives and actual performance. Examples of this failure include:

- poorly designed services and programs
- inconsistencies in service and attitudes
- dehumanizing, degrading, and insensitive methods
- poor management

Poorly Designed Services and Programs

Haphazardly designed programs are sometimes planned within minutes of implementation and generally do not serve the juveniles' needs. Correctional recreation managers should use a systems analysis approach to design recreation services. Peterson and Gunn (1984) identify sequential steps in a systems approach: analyzation, conceptualization, investigation, determination, and program design.

Analyzation. According to Peterson and Gunn (1984), one of the most important aspects of designing a leisure program is understanding the characteristics and leisure needs of the juveniles who will be served. Then, program designers must study the nature of the agency, identify resources, and understand the community.

Conceptualization. Once the data analyzation phase is finished, recreation program designers should develop the correctional recreation services. This begins with writing a purpose statement, usually a one-sentence statement, that concisely indicates the overall direction of the therapeutic service. It is the backbone of the program design process and contains the specific services that will be provided: treatment, leisure education, and/or recreation participation. Service goals describe aspects of the statement of purpose in greater detail. They are not directly measurable; they are statements of intent that correspond with the nature of the specific type of therapeutic recreation service found in the purpose statement.

Investigation. Recreation program designers translate identified correctional recreation service into some aspect of operationalized program components. Investigation also involves brainstorming about potential programs and alternatives.

Determination. This involves the actual selection of program components that will operationalize the intent of the purpose statement and goals. Programs should be directly related to one of the overall service areas identified in the purpose statement and should fulfill at least one overall department goal. The specific service area is implied in the program purpose statement and can be identified as the appropriate intervention.

Developing the Specific Programs

The comprehensive program is made up of a number of different program components or specific programs. Three stages of development for each specific program are necessary:

1. Specific program design. A statement of purpose is written; terminal program objectives are established.

2. Implementation plan. The sequencing of material within each session and the sequencing of the sessions themselves are specified.

3. Evaluation plan. Each specific program is developed, implemented, and evaluated independently of all other specific programs (Peterson and Gunn 1984).

Inconsistent and Poorly Organized Service Techniques

Another major criticism of correctional recreation services is that the service technology may be inconsistent and poorly organized. This results in the failure to demonstrate any effectiveness in the achievement of the desired outcomes. A key structural and administrative issue in these organizations is the implementation of effective change technologies.

The field of correctional recreation has recently become more concerned with closing the gap that exists between the production of research results and the use of research results by practitioners. One current gap within correctional recreation services is using what is known about helping juveniles and what is used by rehabilitation practitioners to actually help those juveniles.

Dehumanizing, Degrading, and Insensitive Methods

Another criticism addresses the mechanisms organizations develop to work with juveniles. These methods often are characterized as dehumanizing, degrading, and being insensitive to juveniles' individual attributes and needs. In contrast with most bureaucracies, the raw material to be worked on in human service organizations is not value neutral. The persons being processed and changed are vested with cultural values and have a social and moral identity. This fundamental fact has profound implications for the organizational and administrative character of human service organizations.

A juvenile's background serves as a critical indicator of the types of processing and changes he or she requires, his or her potential for change, and the desired outcome. Moreover, juveniles' affiliations and their reference social groups exert considerable influence on their motivational and behavior patterns. This influence must be considered by the juvenile justice program if its techniques are to be effective. Thus, the organization is constrained to minimize the potential conflict between the juvenile's ascriptive affiliation and social status and the consequences and implications of its activities on these affiliations and status. It also must develop mechanisms to buffer itself from juveniles' social ties that are detrimental to the attainment of the objectives. Such buffers may include: isolation of juveniles from their social affiliations, the development of boundary roles to mediate between the organization, and social organizations' activities that serve only juveniles having similar social affiliations (Hasenfeld and English 1983).

Poor Management

Human service organizations often are ill managed, wasteful, and inefficient and consume an increasing share of public and private resources. There are many social service agencies in every community to help clients and consumers and their families. These systems include: county welfare agencies, child protection agencies, juvenile courts, juvenile employment programs, mental health programs, childcare and early childhood development agencies, private agencies funded by the United Way and other sources, city recreation and parks departments, and dozens of programs within the public school systems.

Human service organizations face the following problems within their environments that are not shared by other types of organizations:

1. Because the goals of correctional recreation services are value laden and reflect ideological commitments, the sociocultural context within

the organization particularly affects the definition and goals. The value system that prevails in the community will set significant limits on the range of service ideologies that the organization can select. The lesser the congruency between the two, the more precarious will be the legitimation of the organization in the community.

2. Because the raw materials of human service organizations are juveniles, they always present a strong environmental influence on the operations of the organization. Even when the organization controls the input of juveniles, it cannot effectively neutralize the juveniles' ties with their community. Thus, the juveniles' social milieu becomes one of the major sources of environmental control over the organization.

Most human service agencies are nonprofit organizations. Often their product is not salable or negotiable on the market. Consequently, the ability of most human service organizations to produce profit that can then be used to purchase needed resources is nonexistent. As a result, human service organizations are likely to be dependent on external resources. This dependency characterizes many human service organizations and indicates the powerful role that external agencies have in shaping the policies and service patterns of these organizations (Hasenfeld and English 1974).

The Manager's Functions

A manager's functions can be considered a series of action steps in which each component leads to the next. Although the functions can be identified as a separate set of actions, for purposes of analysis, the manager in actual practice carries out these activities in a complex, unified manner within the total process of managing (see Figure 1). Barnard (1938) brought together the significant underlying premises about the role of the manager in his classic work, *The Functions of the Executive*. These functions include: planning, decision making, organizing, staffing, directing or actuating, controlling, and training.

Planning

Strategic planning gives organizations antennae to sense the changing environment. Strategic planning includes establishing goals, selecting objectives, determining the existing situation, and assessing the desired future of the program. Strategic planning allows correctional recreation managers to deal with new factors, such as the changing external environment, competitive conditions, the strengths and weakness of the organization, and opportunities for growth.

Figure 1
The Interrelationship of
Management Functions

Planning
- identifying goals and objectives
- stating premises and assumptions
- developing specific, detailed plans

Organizing
- breaking work down into components
- grouping related work activities and units
- defining authority relationships
- developing organizational chart
- developing position descriptions

Actuating/Motivating
- communicating objectives to members
- leading members to objectives
- training and supervising
- integrating individual into organization

Controlling
- measuring accomplishments against stated goal
- correcting deviations from the goal
- developing feedback mechanisms

Achieving the Objectives

Decision Making

This function is a part of the planning process in that a commitment to one of several alternative decisions must be made. While other staff may help in planning, decision making ultimately is the responsibility of managers. Decision making includes the development of alternatives, conscious choice in selecting an option, and commitment to implementation once a choice decision has been made.

An organization that functions effectively is one that makes good decisions. After a decision is made, it must be implemented. As a manager, the style of decision making affects the performance of the organization. Management functions are interrelated and fluid, as depicted in Figure 2.

Figure 2
Decision-Style Characteristics

	Decisive	Flexible	Hierarchic	Integrative
Values	Action Efficiency Speed Consistency	Action Adaptability Speed Variety	Control Quality Rigorous Method System	Results Information Creativity Variety
Planning	Low Data Short Range Tight Controls for Results	Low Data Base Short Range Intuitive & Reactive	High Data Base Long Range Tight Control of Method	High Data Base Long Range Adaptive Results

Goals	One
	Organization
	  Focus
	External Origin
	Accepted as Given
		Many
		Self-Focus
		External Origin
		Changing
			Few
			Self-Focus
			Internal Origin
				Many
				Self &
				  Organization
				  Focus
				Internal, External
				  Origins

Organization	Short Span of
	  Control
	Rules
	Hierarchical
	  Organization
	High Structure:
	  Orderly
	High Delegation
		Control by
		  Confusion
		Loose
		High Delegation
		  Minor Things
		Flexible Rules &
		  Authority
			Wide Span of
			  Control
			Elaborate
			  Procedures
			Automation
			Low Delegation
			High Structure
				Team Process
				Matrix
				  Organization
				High Delegation
				Flexible Structure

Communication	Short Summaries
	Results Focus
	One Solution
	To and Through
	  Leader
		Short Summaries
		Variety
		Several Solutions
		Everyone Talking
		  to Everyone
			Long, Elaborate
			Problem Solving
			Methods and
			  Data Analysis
			Give "Best
			  Conclusion"
				Long, Elaborate
				Problem Anaylsis
				  from Many
				  Views
				Multiple Solution

Leadership	Based on Position
	Motivation:
	  Reward or
	  Punishment
	Power and Orders
	Unilateral
	  Decisions
		Based on Liking &
		  Charm
		Motivation:
		  Positive
		  Incentives
		Feelings and
		  Needs
		Participation
			Based on
			  Competence
			Motivation with
			  Information
			Logic and
			  Analysis
			Consultative
				Based on Trust,
				  Information
				Motivation:
				  Mutual
				  Understanding,
				  Cooperation
				Feeling & Facts
				Participation

Organizing

The organizing function involves the design of a pattern of roles and relationships that contribute to the goal. Roles are assigned, authority and responsibility are determined, and provision is made to coordinate activities. Organizing typically involves developing an organizational chart and writing job descriptions and statements of workflow. Similarly, organizational and performance characteristics of different management systems yield various results. Figure 3 illustrates organizational and performance characteristics of different management systems.

Figure 3
Interests of People and the Organization
Under Three Orientations

Orientation	Interests of People		
	Security against economic, political, and psychological deprivation	Opportunities for voluntary commitment to worthwhile goals	Opportunities to pursue one's own growth and development independent of organization goals
Power orientation	Low: At the pleasure of the autocrat	Low: Unless one is in a sufficiently high position to determine organizational goals	Low: Unless one is in a sufficiently high position to determine organizational goals
Role orientation	High: Secured by law, custom, and procedure	Low: Even if, at times, one is in a high position	Low: Organizational goals are relatively rigid; activities are closely prescribed
Person orientation	High: The individual's welfare is the major concern	High: But only if the individual is capable of generating his or her own goals	High: Organizational goals are determined by individual needs

Staffing

This function involves determining personnel needs and selecting, orienting, training, and continuing evaluation of the individuals who hold the positions identified in the organizing process. Staffing is always an issue for correctional recreational managers. An often overlooked contributor to the growth of correctional recreation is the paraprofessional.

The employment of paraprofessionals fulfills some needs in the agency as well as the community. While less skilled and/or professionally prepared, they are better able to identify with many of the clients being served by virtue of their personal experiences with crises or barriers.

Developing guidelines to determine staff participation and staff-to-juvenile ratios is another area of concern for correctional recreation managers. Unfortunately, the therapeutic recreation profession has never determined specific staff-to-juvenile ratios or guidelines for juveniles until the National Correctional Recreation Association and the American Association for Leisure and Recreation established their guidelines (American Association for Leisure and Recreation 1990).

Directing or Actuating

Adequate directing provides the guidance and leadership toward goal accomplishment. It involves teaching, coaching, and motivating workers. The essence of leadership is the ability to transform followers into leaders. It involves the ability of the manager to create values and establish ethics while reflecting the needs, values, and goals of those who are served. The leader and follower both grow in this process.

Correctional recreation managers should possess the skills to ascertain when and how effective leadership should be used with their employees. Correctional recreation managers also should seek counseling on an ongoing basis to ensure their own objectivity when dealing with offenders (Zaleznik 1989).

Controlling

This function involves determining what is being accomplished, assessing performance and its relationship to the accomplishments of the organizational goals, and initiating needed corrective action. How organizations manage and resolve conflicts, manage interactions within their structure, and assess superior/subordinate relations is depicted in Figure 4.

Training

Training allows for creative strategies. Most training programs reflect the attitude that the training obligation to the participants ends on the last day of the program. Indeed, the final contact between trainer and participants occurs as the groups disband. The period following the meeting is much more crucial for knowledge retention than either the preplanning period or the actual seminar.

Research indicates that four or five sources of information are necessary before adoption occurs. Traditional training programs tend to be only one source of information and fail to fully reach the vast majority of participants. It is clear that the trainer's contact with the participants should not cease with the end of the program. Seventy-five percent of the participants stated heightened aspiration to innovate once back on the job. After six months, however, their rate of adoption of new ideas into their daily work was exactly the same as the 25 percent who did not have heightened aspirations to innovate. This study also found that after six months, more than 90 percent of the participants were unable to identify the training programs as a source of any new ideas. It is clear from this research that training programs should not be the only source of information.

Correctional recreation professionals are no different from corporate America or any other governmental agencies when it comes to the need to provide training and professional development to their employees. The most frequent excuse for not providing formal training is the potential cost. However, each day that training is delayed is costly to the juvenile justice system.

Figure 4
Diagnosing Organizational Processes

Organizational Process	Identifying Remarks and Explanation	Typical Information Sought	Common Methods of Diagnosis
Communication patterns, styles, and flows	Who talks to whom, for how long, about what? Who initiates the interaction? Is it two-way or one-way? Is it top-down, down-up, lateral?	Is communication directed upward, downward, or both? Are communications filtered? Why? In what way? Do communications patterns "fit" the nature of the jobs to be accomplished? What is the "climate" of communication? What is the place of written communication versus verbal?	Observations, especially in meeting; questionnaires for large-size samples; interviews and discussions with group members—all these methods may be used to collect the desired information.
Goal Setting	Setting task objectives and determining criteria to measure accomplishment of the objectives takes place at all organizational levels.	Do they set goals? How is this done? Who participates in goal setting? Do they possess the necessary skills for effective goal setting? Are they able to set long-range and short-range objectives?	Questionnaires, interviews, and observations all afford ways of assessing goal-setting ability of individuals and groups within the organization.
Decision making, problem solving, and action planning	Evaluating alternatives and choosing a plan of action are integral and central functions for most organizations.	Who makes decisions? Are they effective? Are additional decision-making skills needed?	Observation of problem-solving meetings at various organizational levels is particularly valuable.
Conflict resolution and management	Conflict — interpersonal, intrapersonal, and intergroup — frequently exists in organizations. Does the organization have effective ways of dealing with conflict?	Where does conflict exist? Who are the involved parties? How is it being managed? What are system's norms for dealing with conflict? Does the reward system promote conflict?	Interviews, third parties, and observations of group meetings are common methods for diagnosing these processes.

Continued on next page

Figure 4
(Continued)

Organizational Process	Identifying Remarks and Explanation	Typical Information Sought	Common Methods of Diagnosis
Managing interface relations	Interfaces represents those situations wherein two or more groups (subsystems) face common problems or overlapping responsibility. This is most often seen when members of two separate groups are interdependently related in achieving an objective but have separate accountability.	What is the nature of the relations between the two groups? Are goals clear? Is responsibility clear? What major problems do the two groups face?	Interview, third parties, and observations of group meetings are common methods for diagnosing these processes.
Superior-subordinate relations	Formal hierarchical relations in organizations dictated that some people lead and others follow; these situations are often a source of many organizational problems.	What are the existent leadership styles? What problems arise between superiors and subordinates?	Questionnaires can show overall leadership climate and norms. Interviews and questionnaires reveal the desired leadership behaviors.

Reinventing the System

In the future, drastic changes will challenge the current practices and service delivery within communities and organizations. Thus, developing a vision is important. In an era of constant and rapid change, the onus is on correctional recreation managers to develop the art of being a visionary capable of reflecting the past, mirroring the present, and projecting the future. The following suggestions should be high priorities on any agenda for change and innovation:

1. The concept of lifestyle analysis, founded on a sound and realistic analysis of the potential changes within American culture, must underlie the development of program efforts. With lifestyle analysis as a guiding concept, an operational solution to meet the needs of excluded populations is possible.

2. The equitable distribution of service for excluded populations presents the human service delivery system with a range of difficult choices in the decades ahead. We must carefully review recent court decisions (McKnight 1977).

3. Correctional recreation services call for a nontraditional framework to examine the delivery of human services in the decades ahead. This challenges the majority of existing approaches. The development of service alternatives and equitable distribution of services represents only a few of the nontraditional approaches that must be considered.

4. The correctional recreation population represents the ultimate challenge. If we accept the concept that the juvenile delinquent is the ultimate challenge, we must not only change ourselves but also assume an innovative role to change the human service delivery system, of which we are a part.

The Recreation Manager as a Problem Solver

Recreation managers are problem solvers and must help the process through their own behavior. They must be able to calculate the interest or opposition to their program, stage and time the introduction of controversial issues, and reduce tensions. Throughout this process, managers must be flexible in the use of tactics: negotiating, bargaining, and using rewards, punishments, and other forms of persuasion. Recreation administrators must monitor the organization's environment to anticipate change and bring about the adaptive responses required for the program's survival.

The role of the correctional recreation administrator is reinforced further by various legal, regulatory, and accrediting agencies that often require managers or department heads to be qualified practitioners in their disciplines. The manager's role then becomes a predictable part of the recreation practitioner's tenure in a program.

Managing in Small and Large Systems

Only recently have correctional recreation specialists received the opportunity to manage their own service units. Managing recreation services (from a personnel perspective) may mean managing oneself, if a person is the only therapeutic recreation staff within the service unit. In organizational settings where the therapeutic recreation specialist may not have staff to manage, the focus is on interorganizational relationships with other health care staff within the agency's health-related milieu.

Quite often the therapeutic recreation specialist, in addition to being the only provider of recreation services, is not afforded the same status and recognition as other members of the treatment team. Recreational professionals then need to rely on personal charisma and sound management techniques to effectively administer their unit, since they have no formal authority to exercise over other related therapies within the organization.

In a study of correctional recreation organizational structures, Calloway (1985) reported that professional staff involvement in the participation and delivery of recreational services resulted in cooperation from other related human service providers within the correctional institution. These findings are important to the therapeutic recreation specialist who may be the only deliverer of recreation services among many other providers of therapies within their institutions.

A therapeutic recreation specialist may develop a successful program for offenders. As the practitioner most directly involved in the work, this individual may be given full administrative responsibility for that unit. The role of manager then begins to emerge: budget projections need to be developed, job descriptions must be updated and refined, and staffing patterns need to be reassessed and expanded.

As leisure becomes more significant to society and claims a more central role in people's lives, leisure dysfunction may well appear as a major problem.

The future success of correctional recreation managers will be determined largely by the profession's ability to assess and respond to a changing society as well as introduce new ideas and technologies. Therapeutic recreation managers must develop their visionary skills and adopt new strategies and techniques as demanded.

Crawford (1991) identifies the following economic, social, and political macrotrends that will challenge therapeutic recreation managers in the future:

- reintroduce the service ethic of the correctional recreation profession to public recreation services by advocating for increased budgetary and program resources
- reverse some of the current social conditions such as homelessness, children living in poverty, increased recidivism, and crowded prisons and have the public concentrate on the positive development of juveniles through structured leisure time activities
- examine the delivery of services and challenges that exist within the great majority of our approaches to develop service alternatives and an equitable distribution of recreation programs

The Role of Therapeutic Recreation With At-risk Juveniles

The purpose of therapeutic recreation is to promote positive change in an individual emotionally, socially, cognitively, and/or physically through recreation experiences. Many at-risk juveniles do not have the skills to participate in recreation experiences. At-risk juveniles cannot learn these skills if they are not allowed to participate in recreation programs, if they are not helped to initiate involvement in these programs, if the state does not understand their needs and behaviors, and if they are asked to leave programs for inappropriate behavior. If at-risk juveniles were involved in recreation programs and had the skills to do so, they might not be involved in the variety of high-risk situations they currently are.

It is beneficial to examine the conditions and behaviors of at-risk juveniles relative to the actual limitation their condition and environment imposes on them in terms of their physical, mental, social, and emotional functioning. These limitations then need to be analyzed for their effect on leisure functioning. It is this analysis and assessment that provide the rationale as well as the content for therapeutic recreation service.

Currently, individuals with medical and psychiatric conditions are primary clients involved in therapeutic recreation. However, there appear to be substantial and logical reasons for expansion of populations in the future. As leisure becomes more significant to society and claims a more central role in people's lives, leisure dysfunction may well appear as a major problem. When and if that occurs, any individual with problems or conditions that negatively affect leisure functioning may seek and receive specialized therapeutic recreation services. These services would most likely be delivered through existing recreation and leisure service agencies, community mental health centers, and various public and private counseling practices (Peterson and Gunn 1984).

Perhaps the future is now. Numerous articles in recreation journals have appeared recently, asserting that at-risk juveniles could be aided by the services of the therapeutic recreation professional. Involvement in alternative forms of recreation and leisure have the potential to create changes within individuals, should opportunities be made available.

Therapeutic recreators must be keenly aware of the unique relationship developed between themselves and at-risk juveniles, remembering the responsibility that this role carries with it: the professional provides the opportunity for the juvenile to explore alternative ways of thinking and dealing with life, using a recreation and leisure experience. The role played by the therapeutic recreation specialist is that of a key resource person for the juvenile concerning the diverse areas of his or her life.

Problem juveniles typically lack the necessary and appropriate insight with which to view consequences for action taken. Troubled juveniles may not remember or may negate acceptable forms of behavior, causing them to operate from a different perspective than that of mainstream society.

Munson (1991) indicates that the therapeutic recreator is a change agent who focuses on dysfunctional interactions that maintain problem behaviors while working with significant persons within the system to design strategies for change and providing direct and indirect service. According to Howe-Murphy (1987), ecological therapeutic recreation refers to a "planned process of invention directed toward specific environments and/or individual change."

Conclusion

Although governments around the world recognize the value of leisure in society, American juveniles remain the most neglected in the developed world. The health, education, and welfare opportunities for our juveniles remain low on the government's agenda, while punitive measures against those suffering such neglect continue to rise. Leisure experiences determine the quality of one's life, and the absence of leisure results in the absence of a full life, yet the government takes no responsibility to make appropriate leisure activity available to all juveniles. Although clearly, much deviant behavior results from unmet needs (for survival, security, self-esteem, love, and self-actualization), continued cuts in government spending for education and social services aggravate the problem. Those most disadvantaged and deprived early in life stand the greatest chance of costing society later with the expenses of police, courts, and prisons (Calloway 1981).

All juveniles need recreational group activities, yet juvenile delinquents characteristically lack recreational skills, interest, and motivation toward socially acceptable group activity. Given that juveniles often soundly integrate life-long values into their attitudes and behavior by age twelve, they need exposure to appropriate play options early in life (Calloway 1991). America's prisons contain hundreds of thousands of individuals who lack any sense of recreational alternatives. Few entered the prison system with any knowledge of the healthy recreation alternatives available to them in their communities.

At-risk juveniles are everyone's problem. Religious organizations, police departments, parents, businesses, and politicians must all work together to create a positive environment for our juveniles. We must recognize that society's ills cause the majority of their problems. We must aggressively shepherd our human service resources to ensure that sensitivity, collaboration, and understanding is on the agenda for the future.

References

Adler, J. 1994. Kids growing up scared. *Newsweek* (2): 51.

Aguilar, T. E. 1986. Leisure education program development and evaluation. *Journal of Expanding Horizons in Therapeutic Recreation 1(16): 18-21.*

——. 1987. Effects of a leisure education program on expressed attitudes of delinquent adolescents. *Therapeutic Recreation Journal* 1(4): 43-51.

——. 1991. Social deviancy. In *Therapeutic Recreation: Introduction*, eds. D. A. Austin and M. E. Crawford. Englewood Cliffs, N.J.: Prentice Hall.

American Association for Leisure and Recreation. 1990. National Mission Statement, Policy Statement, Personnel Standards, Fault Standards for Correctional Institutions. St. Paul, Minn.: The Minnesota Department of Corrections.

Austin, D. R., and M. E. Crawford. 1991. *Therapeutic services, looking ahead in a time of transition.* Washington D.C.: ICMA.

Barnard, C. 1938. *The functions of an executive.* Cambridge, Mass.: Harvard University Press.

Benest, F., J. Foley, and G. Welton. 1984. *Organizing leisure and human services.* Dubuque, Iowa: Kendall-Hunt Publishing Co.

Calloway, J. 1981. The courts and correctional recreation. *Journal of Physical Education and Recreation* (April): 40-3.

——. 1981a. Recreation today, a pitiful reflection of our past inadequacy. *Parks and Recreation.* (February): 22-30.

——. 1985. Recreation program services and perceptions toward program change in selected correctional institutions following court mandates. Dissertation. College Park, Md.: University of Maryland.

Carnegie Council on Adolescent Development. 1992. A matter of time: Risk and opportunity in the nonschool hours. *Carnegie Report.* Carnegie Council on Adolescent Development.

Cavallo, D. 1981. *Muscles and morals: Organized playgrounds and urban reform, 1880-1920.* Philadelphia: University of Philadelphia Press.

Cheek, N. H., and W. R. Burch. 1976. *The social organization of leisure in human society.* New York: Harper and Row.

Conrad, P., and J. W. Schneider. 1980. *Deviance and medicalization: From badness to sickness.* St. Louis: C. V. Mosby.

Crawford, M. E. 1991. *Therapeutic recreation: introduction*, eds. D. A. Austin and M. E. Crawford. Englewood Cliffs, N.J.: Prentice Hall.

Edginton, C. R., and J. G. Williams. 1978. *Productive management of leisure service organizations: A behavioral approach.* New York: John Wiley and Sons.

French, W. L., and C. H. Bell. 1973. *Organization development.* Englewood Cliffs, N.J.: Prentice Hall.

Gerhard, G., and F. Rennekamp. 1990. *Barriers to youth at-risk programming.* University of Nebraska and University of Kentucky: Cooperative Extension.

Gibbs, N. 1993. Laying down the law. *Time.* 142(5): 23-33.

Goldstein, A. P., and B. Glick. 1987. *Aggression replacement training.* Champaign, Ill.: Research Press.

Grossman, A., and F. Wallach. 1991. *Options for at-risk youth.* New York: New York State Park and Recreation Society.

Hall, R., et al. 1974. *Human service organizations: A book of readings.* Ann Arbor, Mich.: University of Michigan Press.

Hasenfeld, Y., and R. English. 1983. *Human service organizations: A book of readings.* Ann Arbor, Mich.: University of Michigan Press.

Hersey, P. 1984. *The situational leader.* Escondido, Calif.: Warner Books, Inc.

Howe-Murphy, R., and B. G. Charboneau. 1987. *Therapeutic recreation intervention: An ecological perspective.* Englewood Cliffs, N.J.: Prentice-Hall.

Jacobs, J. 1961. *The death and life of great American cities. New York:* Vintage.

Johnson, D. W., and F. P. Johnson. 1975. *Joining together: Group theory and group skills.* Englewood Cliffs, N.J.: Prentice-Hall.

Kantrowitz, B. 1993. Wild in the streets. *Newsweek* (5): 40-8.

Kaplan, M., and P. Bosserman. 1971. *Technology, human values and leisure.* Nashville, Tenn.: Abingdon Press.

Kaslow, F. W. 1976. *Issues in human services.* San Francisco: Jossey-Bass Inc.

Kennedy, D. W., D. R. Austin, and R. W. Smith. 1987. *Special recreation opportunities for persons with disabilities.* New York: CBS College Publishing.

Kirchbaum, D., and M. A. Alston. 1991. Youth restitution and recreation: A successful mix. *Parks and Recreation* 45(2): 42-5.

Kraus, R. 1966.*Recreation today.* New York: Appleton Century Crafts.

Kraus, R. G., and B. J. Bates. 1975. *Recreation leadership and supervision: guidelines for professional development.* Philadelphia: W.B. Saunders Co.

Leary, P. 1972. The change agent. *Journal of Rehabilitation.*

LeBoeuf, M. 1985. *The greatest management principle in the world.* New York: Berkeley Books.

Liska, A. E. 1981. *Perspectives on deviance.* Englewood Cliffs, N.J.: Prentice-Hall.

McKnight, J. 1977. *Professionalized service and disabling help.* London, England: Marion Boyars Publisher.

Mehr, J. 1980. *Human services concepts and intervention strategies.* Boston: Allyn and Bacon, Inc.

Mintzberg, H. 1979. *The structuring of organizations.* Englewood Cliffs, N.J.: Prentice-Hall, Inc.

Munson, W. W. 1991. Juvenile delinquency as a social problem and social disability: The therapeutic recreator's role as ecological change agent. *Therapeutic Recreation Journal* 25:19-30.

Murphy, J. F., et al. 1991. *Leisure systems: Critical concepts and applications.* Champaign, Ill.: Sagamore Publishing Co. Inc.

O'Brien, K. A. 1992. Effective programming for youth at-risk. *Voice* 25:19-30.

O'Morrow, G. S., and R. P. Reynolds. 1990. *Therapeutic recreation: A helping profession.* Englewood Cliffs, N.J.: Prentice Hall.

Olsen, M. E. 1968. *The process of social organization.* New York: Holt, Rinehart, and Winston.

Parson, T. 1949. *The structure of social action.* Glencoe, Ill.: The Free Press.

Perrow, C. 1967. A framework for the comparative analysis of organizations. *American Sociological Review* 32(April): 194-208.

Peterson, C. A., and S. L. Gunn. 1984. *Therapeutic recreation program design: Principles and procedures.* Englewood Cliffs, N.J.: Prentice Hall.

Pinchot, G. 1985. *Entrepreneuring.* New York: Harper and Row.

Reimer, J. W. 1981. Deviance as fun. *Adolescence* 16:39-43.

Richards, P., R. A. Berk, and B. Foster. 1979. *Crime as play: Delinquency in a middle class suburb.* Cambridge, Mass.: Ballinger Publishers.

Rojek, C. 1989. Leisure and recreation theory. In *Understanding Leisure and Recreation, Mapping the Past, Charting the Future,* eds. E.L. Jackson and T.L. Burton. State College, Penn.: Venture Publishing.

Russel, R. V. 1986. *Leadership in recreation.* St. Louis, Mo.: Times Mirror/Mosby College Publishing.

Ryan, J. J. 1991. Breaking the circle of destruction. *Park and Recreation* 26(12) (October): 46-8.

Scott, W. G. 1967. *Organization theory: A behavioral analysis for management.* Homewood, Ill.: Richard D. Irwin, Inc.

Tice, D. 1992. *National Recreation and Parks Association perspective: A national issue. Parks and Recreation* 26(10) (November).

United Way of America. 1982. *Needs assessment: The state of the art.* Alexandria, Va.: United Way of America.

U.S. Department of Justice. 1992. *National Update.* Washington, D.C.: U.S. Department of Justice.

U.S. Department of Justice. 1992a. *National Update.* Washington, D.C.: U.S. Department of Justice.

Wright, A. N. 1991. Therapeutic potential of the Outward Bound process: An evaluation of a treatment program for juvenile delinquents. *Therapeutic Recreation Journal* 22(2): 33-42.

Zaleznik, A. 1977. Managers and leaders: Are they different? *Harvard Business Review* 22:44-56.

Part IV

Managing Program Training and Evaluation

10 Training Programs and Staff Development

Henry R. Cellini, Ph.D.

Training managers need to understand the key concepts, strategies, and methods necessary to expedite a state-of-the-art training program for administrative and line staff who work with juvenile offenders. Over the last few years, the number of sex offenders, violent offenders, and drug abusers entering juvenile justice systems across the United States has increased dramatically. One common factor in the lives of many juveniles is severe family problems which reflect many of the changing dynamics within society. The challenge to the training manager is to stay current with innovative training technologies and design strategies and to couple this knowledge with the latest information on issues of families, development, psychology, social concerns, security, and other juvenile justice issues.

Managing Training Programs

Empowering employees to work with a changing juvenile justice population requires that criminal justice organizations offer effective training programs. Administrators must assess the level of skills and knowledge their employees possess and provide them with whatever additional information is necessary for them to become successful. Criminal justice agencies need a systematic approach to determine the specific skills needed for each position within the organization. This approach must go beyond preparing a detailed job description and include job-task analyses for all positions within the agency.

Many criminal justice systems have no mechanism to determine whether employees are applying the skills they have learned in training. It is imperative to develop a system where the supervisor's feedback on a specific employee's skill level is given to the training department. This type of system will ensure that the training is transferred from the classroom to

Dr. Henry R. Cellini, president of the Training and Research Institute in Albuquerque, New Mexico, is a part-time instructor for the University of New Mexico, Division of Continuing Education. He specializes in the management and treatment of violent juvenile offenders, drug abuse, and juvenile street gangs.

the job. This measure is the guide to determine whether the training has been successful.

Many criminal justice systems maintain data on a variety of different types of training and educational programming but only a small percentage of that data yields information that can be used to improve the program's quality. To improve the effectiveness of training, the following steps are necessary:

- develop a strategic plan
- identify major dimensions of quality that should be improved by the training
- determine whether the training helps employees develop their knowledge and skills as it relates to managing a program or working directly with the juveniles
- test employees to see if they have mastered the information and skills taught to them in the various orientation or in-service training programs

Training administrators should develop a strategic training plan to manage a successful training program. Exactly what does a strategic training plan do for a criminal justice agency? A strategic training plan is designed to define the training topics needed to achieve the goals of a criminal justice system; it specifies a comprehensive road map to meet those needs (Frantzreb 1993). The strategic training plan provides the method to meet the vision of the juvenile criminal justice system. The plan should answer the following questions:

- What are the challenges that face your criminal justice system?
- What are your strategies and goals to deal with these challenges?
- What skills, knowledge, and competencies does the staff of your agency need to achieve the agency's mission and philosophy?
- As a training manager, how can you ensure that the employees of your system know what to do and how to do it? What is the role of the training department in this process?
- Does the present training system adequately address these needs?
- What kind of training system is needed to effectively train for the goals, mission, and philosophy identified earlier?
- What should the training system look like three-to-five years from now?
- What strategic short- and long-term goals will be established for the training program?
- What training strategies will most effectively and efficiently achieve these goals?
- What is the estimated training workload needed for each staff member to execute these strategies?
- How many resources should be committed, and what is expected in terms of return on investment?

- What organizational management and administrative systems need to be deployed to use the resources effectively and get the job done?
- How will the strategic training plan be implemented?

The Strategic Planning Process

Whatever the size of the criminal justice agency, when developing a strategic training plan for the first time, it is important to divide the training process into phases. The first strategic training plan for an organization can be a complex undertaking. Therefore, the project should be divided into phases with specific benchmarks at the end of each phase that are designed to make the process measurable and less overwhelming to those participating in the planning process. A three-phase process is recommended as a logical way to track the planning process. Within this paradigm, the foundation exists for creative training managers to tailor the plan to the specific needs of their agency (Svenson and Rinderer 1992).

In the project planning and management of training programs, it is important to develop a preplanning checklist. The training manager should follow the phases of the process which include: developing a strategic vision and goals, organizing and managing strategies, and implementing the plan.

Phase One—Developing a Strategic Vision and Goals

The following items are the components necessary to develop a strategic vision and goal statement to guide and direct the planning process:

- examine training implications of current policy and procedures
- assess the existing training system
- write a mission statement that includes the philosophy of training
- ensure that the program meets national training standards

Phase Two—Devising Organizing and Managing Strategies

Management structure is important to successfully implement the strategic vision and goal statements designed in Phase One. The needed management structure includes the following:

- developing an organizational structure
- developing an administrative and supervisory structure
- writing a results-oriented measurement plan
- describing the financing and financial accountability system
- developing the supervisory and management support system to implement the training process

Phase Three—Implementing the Plan

Once the organization's vision and goals have been set and the management structure is in place, it is time to develop the implementation plan. The plan should include:

- clearly identified implementation activities
- guidelines for staff accountability and responsibilities
- timelines
- list of resource needs
- list of training costs
- statement of potential barriers and measures that can be taken to overcome them
- annual updates of the plan for the management team

Having a plan in place is only the first step in effective management of a training program. The next step is setting and maintaining the highest quality standards for the department.

Managing the Quality of a Training Program

Total Quality Management (TQM) provides an easy method to achieve goals that training managers have long pursued, unfortunately with only moderate success. "Total quality" managers can direct, implement, and track the progress and success of training programs with a systematized instructional design, performance-based training, and evaluation.

Training managers should assess the critical events in each stage in the process before, during, and after training, and then measure and track those critical events to detect and improve variations in the training that interfere with the quality. Training managers within juvenile justice systems are increasingly being requested to help their organizations benefit from the quality revolution (Cocheu 1989). However, few trainers are allowed to apply quality principles across the board. Usually, the principles are applied in piecemeal and superficial ways.

However, it is possible to implement total quality management of training programs within juvenile corrections systems. The approach, which is referred to as Total Quality Managed Training (TQMT), is designed to integrate the concepts of leading contributors of the quality movement with the best practices of human resource development. Many managers of training departments find it difficult to apply the Total Quality Managed Training processes across their entire department (Brinkerhoff and Gill 1992).

Typically, training operations are bureaucratically and politically distanced from the day-to-day operation of the criminal justice organization within which they work. Many administrators realize the importance of training, but in many systems training is not given the amount of time, resources, or focus necessary until that system gets involved with the court and training is mandated or training is required to achieve accreditation from professional associations.

Total Quality Management

Some of the key figures in the quality movement offer definitions of quality that can be adapted to training. Deming (1986) defines quality as "meeting the customer's needs." He argues that the way to do this is to continuously improve the processes that produce products and services.

Crosby (1979) defines quality as conformance with requirements, with a high-quality product that consistently meets the specifications set for that particular product. According to Crosby, the ultimate goal of quality improvement is "zero defects." This is achieved by identifying problems early in the process with the emphasis on prevention over detection.

These concepts identify total quality in relation to the business community's production of products and the delivery of services. Total Quality Managed Training is directly related to the strategic plan discussed earlier, and the specific mission and goal statements that provide a framework in which to assess the individual jobs, tasks, and training needs required by the various staff throughout the system. The specific products that each staff is required to produce need to be clearly delineated in the strategic plan. The following example illustrates some positions in a juvenile correctional facility and the work products and services they provide:

Staff	Product
Mental health counselors	Psychological screening and assessments, counseling services
Nurses	Physical examinations
Shift supervisors	Staffing plans and schedules
Correctional officers	Institutional security

The services that various individuals would offer include:

Staff	Services
Mental health counselors	Counseling services
Kitchen employees	Food preparation

Although it is difficult to compare the outcomes in a juvenile justice system to that of a business or private enterprise, training managers should think in terms of the products and services that each staff person working in the system is required to provide to make the system more effective.

Therefore, training managers must incorporate strategies using the following basic principles:

1. Total Quality Managed Training is integrated with other organizational subgroups, such as performance appraisals, promotions, and strategic planning, that add value to individual and organizational performance.

2. The cost of nonconformance with standards is identified and solutions are determined.

3. The goal of Total Quality Managed Training is to ensure that 100 percent of the employees learn 100 percent of what they need to learn to be successful on their job.

4. Continuous efforts are made to identify and eliminate variations in the training process that threaten quality.

5. Quality in training is a product of design. The highest quality training is designed to consistently produce results that add to the value of the organization and its products and services.

6. Quality training is defined by the needs and expectations of society in general *and* the juveniles served. High-quality training is training that provides the greatest value to the correctional staff who work with the juveniles. As such, supervisors, managers, administrators, and other employees who work within the criminal justice system are the customers for whom training managers must develop programs.

A Systems View of Training

Training outcomes must affect the learner, but also affect meaningful changes within the organization. To apply the TQM approach, training must be defined within the context of the criminal justice agency as well as in the desired organizational performance. Training is a complex process that is affected by many organizational, small-group, and individual interactions. Training processes, components, and critical interfaces must be considered, along with other organizational processes and subsystems. This comprehensive systems analysis of training requires a broad view of the training process—a much broader view than is typically taken by training administrators and managers.

Training is intended to add value to the organization by affecting job performance. Although training may add value through sustained changes in the capacity of employees to perform in new ways, training also can add value when learning creates a positive attitudinal change. Often, these attitudinal changes lead to improvements in the individual's overall performance, which, in turn, further enhances organizational performance. Learning must be further transformed through retention, reinforcement, and support activities to maintain the new information and attitudes.

Certain key issues are essential for training managers to consider when attempting to implement a total quality training system within a juvenile criminal justice system. These include enhancing the training system and environment, transforming the learning into added organizational value, and maintaining organizational support for training.

Enhancing the Training System

Enhancing the training experience refers to the activities that produce or reinforce the learning. The process includes whatever is done to ensure that the trainees learn what they are supposed to learn in the most effective and efficient manner possible.

Teaching is the most obvious activity in this process, but managing the learning environment, providing for physical and psychological comfort and individual encouragement to the learners, monitoring learning activities, and providing feedback are also important. Learning activities should be measured and tracked to detect variations in this process. Tracking training ensures the following:

- trainees are learning at effective rates
- individual learning deficits are identified, analyzed, and ameliorated
- trainees master objectives
- learning includes individual clarification of job tasks and duties
- trainees develop a clear understanding of the link between personal training and organizational goals
- learning feedback is accurate and timely

Transforming Learning Into Added Organizational Value

Training goals are not accomplished simply by trainees acquiring new skills, knowledge, and facts. For learning to translate into added value for the organization, training must transcend the individual in the workplace and enhance the individual's and ultimately the organization's performance. The many activities that must occur to support this transfer include: follow-up assessment of job performance, periodic meetings with trainees to encourage use of the training, rewards for the application of new learning, and a feedback network between supervisors and training managers.

When training is not intended for immediate use, such as training staff to manage a crisis situation, activities such as refresher training, written updates, and assessment of skills, represent an important part of the process. Transforming training into day-to-day behaviors is important and must be measured to detect and track the variations in an individual's learning and improved job performance.

Therefore, to improve the quality of training, it is important to develop methods to measure the following:

- how quickly trainees apply learning to on-the-job activities
- supervisors' support of learning on the job
- impediments to the transfer of learning
- learning retention over time
- trainees' receipt of accurate and timely feedback on their use of the learning
- supervisors' receipt of feedback on their coaching and support efforts
- impact of incentives, rewards, and recognition

Finally, feedback is needed on the effect of learning on the organization's progress toward its statutory goals, objectives, and vision statement.

Training managers should remember that certain key activities guide the TQM approach for training, including the following:

1. Expectations for outcomes for each process are discussed, negotiated, clarified, and agreed on with the trainees.

2. Critical interfaces with other organizational subsystems are analyzed and translated into shared goals for training.

3. Specifications for various goals are constructed so that they can be measured.

4. Negative training outcomes are communicated to administrators so that corrective action can be taken.

5. Knowledge created by the activities is clarified and formalized into new procedures and expectations that continuously improve work performance and the quality of training.

Maintaining Organizational Support for Training

The importance of organizational support for training cannot be underestimated. Considering that many of an agency's training topics are guided by standards from the American Correctional Association (ACA), the maintenance of organizational support is not difficult. It is important to remember that American Correctional Association's standards are considered minimum acceptable standards. It is up to the training manager to insist that the training offered meets and exceeds these standards.

Delivery of Training

Recently, criminal justice systems have recognized the worth of the information generated through training needs assessments. The training needs assessment yields information that provides a snapshot of the skills and knowledge levels of the employees who work within their system. This skill and knowledge inventory leads to training focused on the areas where the greatest needs exist.

Some training managers view the training needs assessment as a more generalized survey of the supervisors, administrators, and line practitioners who receive the training. Other training managers believe that a training needs assessment should be a comprehensive and detailed summary of the methodologies and topic areas that staff need to ensure that staff perform the highest quality work. To accomplish this type of training needs assessment, it is necessary to conduct written surveys and random interviews with key individuals.

This systems approach is hierarchical in nature because it is open and each component is not strictly independent of any of the other parts of the system. The following are the seven fundamental steps in using a systems approach to conduct a needs assessment:

1. Determine whether to use internal or external resources.

2. Define the goals of the assessment.

3. Get a commitment from upper management.

4. Select the most appropriate training methodology.

5. Administer and conduct the assessment.

6. Analyze the results.

7. Present the results and make recommendations.

Determine whether to use internal or external resources. When making this decision, training managers should determine the advantages and disadvantages of each choice. Outside experts tend to be neutral about a project because they are less affected by the organizational politics and the institutional culture. They tend to avoid preconceived notions about the results generated by the training needs assessment. However, there are some disadvantages to using an external consultant:

- administration may resist opening their organization to external review

- internal trainers and training managers may feel that they will lose some control of the assessment process if they are not used as the consultant
- an external consultant is likely to cost more than an internal expert

Define the goals of the assessment. After administrators decide who will conduct the training needs assessment, they should define the goals of the assessment. These goals serve as the reference point from which all steps in the process are drawn. The data produced by the assessment should directly reflect the goals outlined at the project's beginning. Having specific and measurable goals is crucial to the development of a quality training needs assessment.

Get a commitment from upper management. Regardless of who ultimately conducts the needs assessment, the entire project is doomed from the start if senior administrators do not offer their support to the project or the individuals conducting the assessment. The chances of gaining this support will be much higher if the goals and objectives of the assessment are specifically defined. Senior administrators must perceive the benefit of this information and its ultimate impact on the goals and mission of the organization.

Select the most appropriate methodology. There are many different assessment techniques and methods that can be used to develop a training needs assessment. It is important for a training manager to select one that complements the culture and structure of the organization. For example, a training manager of a large juvenile correctional system may find it necessary to narrowly define goals so information can be gathered most effectively. This may involve the use of a written survey with occasional random personal interviews. Using this approach will provide the manager with a detailed consensus that will allow him or her to focus on any specific operational areas. On the other hand, in a small organization, a training manager may prefer to use focus groups or individual interviews that specifically address areas of interest. The key factors to consider when determining which assessment method is most appropriate for your system are the following:

- the ability to keep surveys or interviews confidential
- cost factors (for example: whether to use internal or external resources)
- availability of experienced personnel to conduct the assessment
- the time needed to conduct the assessment

Administer and conduct the assessment. The type of assessment method chosen by a specific agency will determine the necessary steps to successfully complete the process. This includes: collecting survey instruments, tabulating the data, scheduling personal interviews, determining costs, obtaining clerical and administrative support, and keeping the project on schedule and within budget. If an agency decides to use an external consultant from the start, it should clearly delineate administrative issues and project expectations. Specifically, it should identify each person's responsibility and the deadlines to meet the objectives. Thorough planning at the beginning of the project will provide the desired results.

Analyze the results. The results of even the most fastidiously defined assessments will contain variables that may be hard to quantify or identify. It is important for the training manager to regularly refer to the initial assessment goals so that the information relates directly to the goals. Information that is peripheral to the goals of the assessment should be considered secondary and reported accordingly.

Present the information and make recommendations. The training manager should be prepared to justify the recommendations and have the data available to substantiate the findings. If any statistics are used to analyze the results, it is wise to quote only the most important statistical information in the presentation. Be sure that all statistical calculations are available, possibly as an appendix in the final report. If actual training programs or formats are part of the recommendation, include a topical outline for each training program, along with a statement of the objectives and projected estimated cost for the delivery of each program.

Instructional Design

After a training needs assessment has been conducted, it is important to develop a training program that has the greatest likelihood of effectively meeting the organization's objectives. Training administrators should remember that the effectiveness of an instructional program is defined by whether the instruction meets well defined objectives that are based on the needs of the audience and organization. The objectives are the backbone of a successful training program. The entire program, including the pre- and posttests, practice exercises, training materials, and amount of time necessary to deliver the training should be driven by the objectives.

Managing effective instructional design is an important function of the training manager. In some agencies, the training manager may have a training staff who will design the actual lesson plans and training materials. In small organizations, the training manager also may be the curriculum designer, trainer, and evaluator. The following points are a road map the training manager may use to design effective training:

1. Emphasize performance analysis. Performance analysis refers to the specific instructional materials and approaches that are necessary to ensure an individual the highest probability of success on the job. Performance analysis ensures that trainees will receive the information necessary to do their job well. Unfortunately, administrators often direct the training managers to take shortcuts to try to get training pro-

grams delivered quickly, ignoring the fact that the shortcuts may cause the training to be ineffective.

2. Conduct your performance analysis as creatively as possible. Training managers should challenge others' assumptions. Remember, a problem-oriented focus will improve the design of training programs that enhance the systems throughout an agency. Productivity can be directly affected by using strategies, such as spreading more work across fewer workers, broadening the responsibility of work groups, or linking groups more closely.

3. Educate managers and administrators about performance analysis. More recently, the training field seems to emphasize work systems enhancement, rather than focus on enhancing performance. However, training managers should still work with their administrators to ensure all staff are aware of the training goals. Administrators may accomplish this by reviewing the training manager's findings, their performance analyses, and by writing and circulating briefing papers describing the philosophy and goals of the program.

4. Consider the long-term consequences. When reviewing how well a specific problem has been solved, determine whether any additional problems were created. If a solution introduces new problems not initially considered, managers may repeat many of the steps. Training managers should consider whether anything will change current conditions, predict the consequences of actions taken in response to contemporary problems, consider whether assumptions will change, and follow-up to ensure that the solution works as expected.

5. Determine changing environmental conditions. To maintain professional confidence, it is important to adapt to changing environmental conditions. Training managers should be willing to revisit the steps in the instructional design process and periodically reassess their own competencies and the competencies of their staff, and compare these to the needs of their organization.

Evaluation Methods and Issues

An increase of federal and state regulations have pressured agencies to properly train staff to meet new workplace standards. In addition, many correctional agencies are under federal consent decrees. Because of increasing federal and state regulations, administrators should be aware that they are accountable to ensure that staff receive adequate safety and compliance training. One internal control to minimize the risk of providing improper, inadequate training is a comprehensive audit of ongoing training programs from their inception. The audit's primary function is to review and identify nonperformance issues within the existing training programs. The auditor evaluates overall training effectiveness and its compliance with policy and procedures, and recommends necessary changes.

Training audits should include several key issues, and be tailored specifically to the agency or site where the evaluation occurs. The general focus should be on training goals, compliance, content, testing procedures, outcomes, and evaluation results.

Training Goals

The training manager is ultimately responsible for determining whether the training plan's goals have been implemented in the actual training. The evaluation or audit should determine whether management has taken an active role in planning and reviewing the training program. The audit also should determine whether management is aware of the areas of liability and risk within their system, and which ones are being addressed by the training program. It is also important to determine whether enough money has been allocated to appropriately deliver the training.

Training Compliance

Unmet goals are of little use to any training manager. The second stage in the evaluation process is to audit the number of training sessions being offered, the amount of time devoted to each of the training topics, basic attendance, and related issues that focus on how agency managers have responded to the requests of the training department and referred appropriate staff for training.

Training Content

Training managers should attend training sessions to confirm that they accomplish their goals and objectives. During these audits, the training manager can measure the use of training strategies, how well the program meets policies and procedures, and the focus of the training.

Training Procedures

Training managers, while monitoring the training session, can determine whether the presentation of the training allows the information to be easily understood and whether the "classroom environment" is conducive to learning. Under teaching techniques, it is important to note that few people can learn from instructors who are not interested in their material or who present information in a manner that is not consistent with adult learning theory. Evaluators should ask the following questions:

1. Are the instructors interested in the material they are teaching?

2. Are the instructors gaining the interest of the attendees?

3. Is the information repeated and reinforced sufficiently so attendees can remember it?

4. Does the instructor review materials?

5. Are written materials handed out to supplement or reinforce the information provided in the training sessions?

Effective training programs should include oral explanations, visual aids (such as overheads), handouts, and hands-on experience with the techniques and skills, which can be taught through the use of role playing and simulations.

Testing Procedures

No training program can guarantee 100 percent retention. Tests need to be developed that can provide a reliable measure of what has been learned during the training. A fair and comprehensive test will give the trainers valuable feedback on the effectiveness of their instruction. The evaluator should determine whether testing is taking place and whether the trainees are demonstrating sufficient retention of the information.

Training Outcomes

Evaluation of the results of the training can be done from either management or the employees' perspective. Both are equally important. Managers must determine if the training has fostered skill acquisition and productivity of the employees who work for them. On the other hand, employees are often concerned about whether the training was interesting and whether they learned new information and skills.

Evaluation Results

Management must be willing to address any problems identified during the audit. Many managers tend to view evaluations as a method for administrators to dispense blame and look for faults. However, the concept of evaluation from the training manager's viewpoint should be a method of providing self-correcting training.

Civil Liability

Since the 1970s, criminal justice agencies have been engulfed in a continuing and rising wave of lawsuits. Many of the cases have been directed against law enforcement officers and correctional specialists (Fay 1988). Two factors appear to be at work in this trend—the increasingly litigious nature of society and an expanding social conscience operating in support of citizens injured by governmental employees.

One common thread runs through the proliferation of lawsuits—negligent training (Fay 1988). Rather than bemoan the situation, it is time to assess the dimensions of the problem and take action. The first step is to understand the major concepts of law pertaining to civil litigation, especially as they relate to training.

Theory of Negligence

Under the negligence theory the argument is not that the injurious conduct was malicious but that the injury and damages resulted from a failure to perform a duty with due care. Title 42, Section 1983 of the Civil Rights Act of 1971 provides the basis for legal liability resulting from the failure of supervisors to fully and properly discharge responsibilities of their office.

Liability results from negligence or failure to give proper attention or care to one's duty and, thus, cause deprivation of rights secured by the Constitution. Within the negligence theory there is a particular vulnerability to the accusation of improper training. Many courts have consistently ruled in favor of plaintiffs who can show injury caused by negligence that resulted from the absence of training or the delivery of faulty training. This is especially true in law enforcement and corrections, where excessive use of force and concerns for offender or staff safety are the issues being litigated.

As a training manager, a strategy to counter civil litigation should eliminate any and all conditions that might contribute to charges of improper instruction. Even the finest training facilities must anticipate that negligent training lawsuits will be filed, and they should be prepared to answer these charges with a positive defense based on accurate and detailed documentation. Training managers' strategies should include the following basic tactics to positively defend actions in court:

- administer training to specifications
- validate the training
- evaluate the trainees both before and after training
- maintain good records
- establish standards for instructors
- evaluate the entire training process

If a training manager ensures that these strategies are fulfilled, the likelihood of successfully defending a case in court greatly increases.

Conclusion

The importance of quality training within juvenile justice agencies cannot be underestimated. The changing needs of new staff and residents require training managers to adapt and modify current programs while simultaneously anticipating future trends and issues. As new regulations and court decisions continue to direct training needs, the training manager's importance will continue to rise within the organization.

References

Brinkerhoff, R., and S. Gill. 1992. Managing the total quality of training. *Human Resource Development Quarterly* (Summer 1992): Jossey-Bass, Inc.

Cocheu, T. 1989. Training for quality improvement. *Training and Development Journal*, 43(1): 56-62.

Crosby, P. 1979. *Quality is free.* New York: McGraw-Hill.

Deming, W. 1986. *Out of the crisis.* Cambridge, Mass.: Massachusetts Institute of Technology Press.

Fay, J. 1988. *Approaches to criminal justice training.* Athens, Ga.: Carl Vinson Institute of Government, The University of Georgia.

Frantzreb, R., (ed.). 1993. *Training and development yearbook, 1993/1994 Edition.* Englewood Cliffs, N.J.: Prentice Hall.

Svenson, R., and M. Rinderer. 1992. The strategic training plan. In *The Training and Development Strategic Plan Workbook.* Englewood Cliffs, N.J.: Prentice Hall.

11 Research: A Macro View of Statewide Issues

Maurice S. Satin, Ph.D.

It should be considered that nothing is more difficult to handle, more doubtful of success, nor more dangerous to manage, than to put oneself at the head of introducing new orders. For the introducer has all those who benefit from the old order as enemies and he has lukewarm defenders in all those who might benefit from the new orders ... This lukewarmness arises partly from ... the incredulity of men, who do not truly believe in new things unless they have come to have a firm experience of them (Machiavelli [1513] 1985).

The context in which delinquency research is conducted at the state level is most often within public and private human service bureaucracies. Although bureaucracy now has a negative connotation, in its ideal form, it emphasizes rationality and would, therefore, seem to be fertile ground for research efforts. Ironically, contemporary human service bureaucracies are not noted for their use of research findings in the development and evaluation of their programs.

To understand why this is so, it is important to examine the explicit and implicit mandates given public and private human service organizations by their various constituencies. Both government agencies and private, nonprofit human service organizations serve three masters: the clients (service recipients), the taxpayers or contributors (service supporters), and the service organization itself. In health, social services, and juvenile justice, as well as in other domains, organizational success is measured differently by each constituency. This results in different and often conflicting agency goals. What is good for the clients may be unacceptably costly to the organization's supporters or be judged not in the organization's interest by top-level administrators. Similarly, organizational interests, such as increased size or extended survival, may lead to program and policy initiatives that neither benefit clients nor make optimal use of available resources.

Conducting scientifically valid research in this context of conflicting priorities is clearly problematic. First, research program designers must de-

Dr. Maurice S. Satin is a research scientist at the New York State Division for Youth in Rensselaer, New York.

cide for which constituency the research is being done. The reality is that while research is nominally funded to promote client and supporter interests through effective and efficient programs, too often it is used to support purely organizational goals—sometimes to the detriment of the other constituencies. The rationale for such goal displacement is often that organizational survival is fundamental to any client or supporter benefits. Although this argument is particularly plausible in government agencies mandated to serve particular constituencies, it depends on the often fallacious assumption that the agency in question is the one best able to meet client needs.

Instead of producing facts on which to base rational policies, researchers engage in "evaluation-by-objective," where "findings" are designed to rationalize policy positions based on political strategy.

The effect of such decisions on research should not be underestimated. They result in "research horses being pulled by the policy cart." Instead of producing facts on which to base rational policies, researchers engage in "evaluation-by-objective," where "findings" are designed to rationalize policy positions based on political strategy. In such environments, researchers cease to provide insights that will produce a better future and, instead, become apologists for the status quo.

One should not assume that placing the interests of the organization above those of an agency's clients or financial supporters is rare and unsupported by institutional policy. For example, human services agencies in New York State have systematically replaced "research scientists" with "program research specialists." These two occupations differ in the explicit purpose of their research efforts. Scientists are expected to develop new knowledge that results in "contributions to the scientific field" (New York State Department of Civil Service 1981). The knowledge developed by research specialists, on the other hand, is expected to be useful for the "effective direction of … agency programs" (New York State Department of Civil Service 1976). Thus, using civil service rules, bureaucracies' research priorities have changed from putting clients' interests first to putting organizational interests first. Other examples hide in the downward infiltration of political appointees in the human service hierarchy and the increasing practice of contracting out research to private firms whose economic viability lies in returning results in line with agencies' organizational interests.

As distasteful as this situation may be, there is an argument to be made for it. The basis for the argument in government-operated human services is that in a democracy, a program's political acceptability is more important than either its effectiveness or efficiency. Thus, since many small geographically distributed facilities for incarcerating juveniles can garner more legislative support than fewer, larger, and more efficient facilities, the former strategy is considered more appropriate. Democratic government demands that people, through their representatives, get what they want, even if it is not necessarily in their best interest.

Given that the context outlined previously is not likely to change soon, what is the function of juvenile delinquency research? The answer depends on an analysis of the functions delinquency research performs for various constituencies as well as the perceived threats such research poses for them.

The Functions of Delinquency Research

Delinquency research fills a variety of functions, including assessing the magnitude and distribution of the problem, understanding the problem's causes, and evaluating intervention efforts.

Assessing the magnitude and distribution of the problem. An organization can use research describing the magnitude of a problem (such as juvenile gangs) to mobilize political support. This is a necessary first step for any new or expanded program. Such research can provide service supporters a justification for resource allocation and benefits program recipients by indicating to program developers where resources should be directed. Service organizations can use the research about the size of a problem to justify a greater share of the resources.

Understanding the problem's causes. All delinquency program development depends on a theory (or combination of theories) of the causes of delinquency. Though fundamental to the types of preventive or remedial services provided, the theory underlying a program is often not explicitly stated. Because of their fundamental organizing function, such theories should be tested before costly programs based on them are implemented. At the state level, such testing usually involves only an analysis of the literature describing other programs based on the theory. For example, most states begin shock-incarceration programs based on information gained from articles about other states' deterrence-based programs.

Basic causal research, though funded in the past on the state level, is currently undertaken mostly in federally funded university settings. Nevertheless, even these literature reviews are often skipped. More often than not, initiatives dependent for their success on causal mechanisms with little more than "common sense" supporting their validity are proposed and implemented at great financial and, sometimes, political cost. It is not surprising how often such programs fail or are quietly discontinued. Thus, research regarding the causes of delinquency is fundamental to the effective and efficient provision of services.

Evaluating intervention efforts. Independent of the examination of the adequacy of a program's theoretical underpinnings, delinquency program evaluation has traditionally examined the effectiveness and efficiency of rehabilitation programs. Efficacy research helps sharpen the focus of the intervention by asking the following questions:

- What problem does the intervention really seek to address?
- For what population is the intervention effective?
- Under what circumstances does the intervention work?

The answers to such questions are essential, unless a program is being provided for reasons other than the clients' benefit.

Research efforts aimed at questions of efficiency have been less popular. Such research addresses issues of the cost effectiveness of intervention. It seeks to answer questions such as "Does the program pay for itself?" and "Is it cheaper than equally effective interventions?" The benefits of efficiency research go beyond the supporter and even the organizational constituencies. Such research benefits clients by enabling more service to be provided with the same amount of funding. Service programs rarely have unlimited funding. Therefore, anything that results in cost reduction in one service has the potential for making more of the remaining resources available for other services that could not have been provided otherwise.

Threats Posed by Delinquency Research

Clients, taxpayers, and agency bureaucrats all perceive research as posing different threats. Some of these perceptions stem from the strongly held values of these various constituencies and some from a perceived loss of control of agency operations. These beliefs concern experimental research and research costs and benefits.

Experimental research. One of the most widely held values among all the constituencies affected by human service research is the disdain for the reality or appearance of experimentation on human subjects. This disdain is based on the fact that some experimental designs may conflict with existing agency policy designed to protect human subjects. In the past, subjects' rights have been violated, and every agency is justified in protecting clients from such excesses. Unfortunately, such policies invariably require action to permit proposed research, thereby making the safest route to take no action. The effect is that either no research takes place or nonexperimental research of diminished value is conducted.

Another reason experimental research often is avoided is the misconception that random assignment of subjects (to new and conventional programs) constitutes "dangerous" experimentation. Those responsible for agency operations will frequently implement a new program in part, or in full for a population with little evidence that it works. However, these same people will balk at the prospect of assigning subjects either to the new program or an existing service on a random basis. There are three arguments usually advanced to support this position.

1. There are logistical difficulties in implementing random assignment. Although random assignment poses special difficulties for ongoing operations, these difficulties are not insurmountable. The added confidence that findings are the result of program effects and not due to differences between experimental and control group subjects may be worth the extra effort.

2. Random assignment denies a part of a population the new service. Unless an organization seeks wholesale implementation of yet another untested program, it is likely to "pilot" or "demonstrate" the program's utility on some segment of its clientele. Such activities likewise deny the new service to potential eligibles, but without the added benefits of valid experimentation. In both cases, the service being "denied" is of unproven benefit; otherwise, research would be unnecessary. Therefore, what is being denied has, as yet, no demonstrable value.

3. Random assignment does not adequately protect some subjects from harmful program effects. This is illogical because if one assumes that conventional services have no harmful effects, the only risk for subjects in an experiment would have to come from the proposed program. And if a new program is believed to have harmful effects, it would not be proposed.

The real danger lies in erroneous findings based on imperfectly matched control groups or on studies with no controls at all. Many factors affect the outcome of delinquency interventions, and invariably, some of them are unknown. It is dangerous to assume that mechanical matching of treatment and control groups on a few variables of unknown relevance creates truly equivalent groups. Even before-and-after studies of the same subjects fail to account for maturation or important changes in the environment over time.

Research costs and benefits. There are two widely held beliefs about research, which underlie most of its perceived costs and benefits. First, research is viewed as an important rhetorical tool that can help bolster program and policy decisions. In other words, research is useful for supporting programmatic and policy decisions, even if these initiatives have no empirical support. Having done "research" per se makes the proposal more credible.

Second, many administrators believe that inadequate research is more useful than sound research because the results of inadequate research are less definitive and more easily shaped to the outcome desired by agency administrators. Furthermore, inadequate research is usually cheaper than sound research, which often has large numbers of subjects and control groups whose importance is not well understood by program administrators.

Beyond these beliefs, it is certainly true that research results may reveal that existing policies or procedures are counterproductive. Studies can uncover shortcomings in the existing prevention-treatment system. They also may demonstrate the ineffectiveness of popular intervention strategies or the effectiveness of unpopular interventions. Even if a politically useful program is largely effective, it may take until after the next election to show it. Any of these potential outcomes alone is managerially unpalatable. For these and other reasons, many administrators prefer to propose and implement programs justified by personal instinct and experience rather than risk systematic evaluation.

Finally, research has real costs and may pose an unacceptable financial or programmatic burden to the agency. A particular research design may entail significant disruption of ongoing programs. For example, the day-to-day care of incarcerated juveniles must go on and cannot be laid aside temporarily for the sake of conducting research. For many "real-time" programs, doing research poses a problem analogous to changing a tire on a moving car. While such disruptions can be avoided or at least mitigated through creative study design, the fact remains that program administrators cannot cease delivering services.

The short-term financial costs of research are undeniable. The inability to see beyond the annual budget horizon impedes decision making that could reduce program costs in the long run. In failing to use research findings, administrators guarantee that the same unproven and wasteful programs used today will continue unimproved or be replaced with efforts that are equally ineffective and inefficient.

Making Research Valued and Acceptable

For research to be beneficial for juvenile justice organizations, both researchers and program administrators should change their approach. Even when administrators have sought research advice, they often receive inconclusive answers or results they perceive to be irrelevant or unrealistic. Thus, researchers must develop study designs that guarantee definitive answers to issues of administrative interest. To assuage fear and enhance credibility, researchers should maintain clarity of purpose and design programs and analyze data that reveal program successes as well as shortcomings.

Clarity of Purpose

Delinquency researchers should maintain clarity of purpose both for themselves and for those with whom they negotiate research projects. Legitimate research must directly benefit delinquent juveniles. Studies with no apparent effect on juveniles should be acknowledged as such. When researchers acquiesce to demands for inappropriate research, they squander their talents and betray public trust. Much of the lack of credibility characteristic of social science research is the result of researchers taking this "hired gun" approach to their craft. Researchers must constantly remind themselves and those for whom they work of the limits to which their talents may be legitimately put. Failure to do so places them in jeopardy of doing a disservice to both those who support an organization and those who are supposed to benefit from it.

Research Reveals Program Successes and Shortcomings

Researchers should design studies and analyze data to reveal program successes as well as shortcomings. Few programs are so good that every participant benefits or so bad that there are no benefits at all. If researchers back away from this all-or-nothing approach to evaluation, they will find their results more managerially acceptable and useful. The most direct method for doing this is to determine which characteristics differentiate program successes from program failures. The best way to do this is to differentiate among variables, such as instructor, gender, ethnicity, program site, and curriculum sequence, to determine which ones made a difference for the subpopulation. Such evaluation results are more useful for program replication and improvement than merely reporting that most clients were, or were not, successful.

Although some administrators might be tempted to suggest that researchers focus on process rather than outcomes and that they engage in formative studies that examine how programs achieve their goals, rather than summative evaluation that assesses how well program goals are achieved, experience suggests that process studies usually entail disproportionate costs for recording "wing flaps" with little attention to whether the program "flew." Changing human beings is a tough proposition and most programs are effective for only limited subpopulations. Thus, it is better to first identify winning programs with relatively cheap studies emphasizing outcomes and then return to identify the processes that account for the success. One need not understand the pathologic processes involved in numerous diseases to prevent them—it is enough to simply separate the drinking water from the sewage.

To achieve the goal of producing relevant and useful delinquency research, researchers must actively negotiate the design and conduct of studies with the organization's management. Researchers must assure themselves that management:

- is willing and able to implement the program to be evaluated
- is committed to the measures of the concepts used
- understands both the costs of the study and the benefits that the findings will produce

Surprisingly, organizations often decide to implement programs without considering important aspects, such as staffing, program development costs, and restructuring needs. When unanticipated problems arise, the response is usually to change the program being implemented. This can result in the implementation and evaluation of a program that bears little resemblance to the original plan. Furthermore, such ad hoc changes usually decrease a program's potential for achieving the desired outcome. Researchers should enumerate the implications of new programs before implementation, to allow administrators to adjust implementation plans or redesign the program entirely. Researchers who fail to do this often find themselves with study designs for programs different from the ones being implemented or for programs that never get implemented at all.

Beyond enumerating program requirements, researchers need to ascertain an administrator's goals and expectations for a proposed program. To develop appropriate outcome indicators, researchers need to understand what administrators believe the program should accomplish. This process is not as easy as it might appear. In practice, one efficient way to do this is to propose various quantitative criteria for program success. Rather than hassle over the semantic nuances of outcomes, such as "improved family functioning" or "reduced recidivism," program providers are asked to choose between specific outcome measures. The choice between "lack of future PINS petitions" and "improved intrafamilial attitudes" as an index of improved family functioning, or between "return to juvenile facility" and "being retaken into custody" as an indicator of recidivism reveals both the explicit goals of the program as well as the implicit expectations administrators have for it.

The closer the negotiated outcome is to tangible client benefit, the closer the explicit goals are to the administrators' expectations for a program. Outcomes, such as "improved intrafamilial attitudes" or "enhanced self-esteem," in the context of an agency's mission, may not be relevant for long-term benefits. They are a sign that the program is being implemented for purposes that do not require empirical research to determine program success.

Even when the goals of a program warrant a study, administrators should approve the actual measures used. Much of the dissatisfaction with past research stems from an up-front failure to agree on the operational criteria for program success. Thus, while researchers and managers may agree on "being retaken into custody" as the outcome criterion for a study, they also need to agree about what events (e.g., PINS petitions, violations, AWOLS) constitute new custody and over what periods of time such occurrences are to be counted. Definitive findings depend on whether a study reaches "inescapable" conclusions based on agreed-upon concepts and measures.

Finally, researchers should keep the financial and administrative burdens of their projects to a minimum and proportionate to both clear, definitive results and the overall importance of the project. Thus, the resolution of an issue involving relatively little expense or affecting a relatively small client subpopulation should not involve herculean efforts more appropriate to research on issues affecting virtually all an agency's clients or involving massive program restructuring.

For research to have maximum benefit on service delivery, administrators should adopt client-oriented goals. This calls for a fundamental shift away from a view of human services as a Machiavellian, zero-sum competition for resources. Instead, we need a public service model aimed at providing the greatest good for the greatest number of clients. One way to reduce this counter-productive competition is to consolidate programs with common goals under a single agency. For example, employment programs currently exist in several agencies. This results in multiple appropriation requests to perform similar functions, with multiple overhead costs and a proliferation of programs competing for the same resources and clients.

Research findings are most effective in a culture willing to periodically and repeatedly redesign programs to better meet its goals.

Therefore, research should obtain information leading to improved service and not simply justify the status quo or support policies aimed at issues beyond an agency's official mandate. Making government work only requires that organizational leaders consistently articulate agency mandates as the first priority for agency activities. Administrators also should have client-centered goals for the interventions they propose. While they cannot be oblivious to the political and fiscal impact of these programs, they must commit themselves to well-conceived programs early-on. Too often, promising programs are abandoned at the first hint of opposition because it is organizationally safer to do nothing. Good research can be an effective shield against an unpopular, though effective, program. However, sound research is impossible without managerial commitment.

Administrators also need to envision program design as an evolutionary process. The current practice of seeking instant success or political gain by jumping from one program model to another accounts for much of the expensive ineffectiveness in juvenile delinquency services. Research findings are most effective in a culture willing to periodically and repeatedly redesign programs to better meet its goals.

One of the natural consequences of these recommendations will be a reallocation of resources away from ineffective programming to program research and development. Only when administrators are convinced that research is a guidepost to the future, instead of merely one of many sources of politically useful rhetoric, will research receive an appropriate share of resources and significantly affect client services.

Conclusion

Because there is little institutional support for changes to the researcher-administrator relationship, it falls to individual researchers and administrators to recognize their interdependence. Obviously, delinquency research, if it is to exist outside collegiate walls, must accommodate itself to the service agency environment. Therefore, an accommodation based on shifting the role of research from rhetorical device to one aimed at improving client-oriented services is necessary.

Progress in preventing and controlling juvenile delinquency ultimately requires the clear understanding and systematic program development that is achievable only through scientific research. Individuals and organizations may come and go, but if juveniles increasingly victimize society and become themselves victims of ineffective social controls, the juvenile justice field has accomplished nothing—no matter how large the organizations we build nor how many resources we control.

References

Machiavelli, N. 1985. *The prince.* Translated by H. C. Mansfield, Jr. Chicago: University of Chicago Press.

New York State Department of Civil Service. 1976. Classification standards, program research specialist series, occupational code 2459201. Albany, N.Y.: State Department of Civil Service.

——. 1981. Classification standards, research scientist series, occupational code 6162000. Albany, N.Y.: State Department of Civil Service.

12 Artful Research Management: Problems, Process, and Products

Arnold P. Goldstein, Ph.D. and Barry Glick, Ph.D., NCC

This chapter examines the management of an extended-research program designed to evaluate what at its inception was a new approach to delinquency intervention—Aggression Replacement Training (ART). We will describe what the program is, the problems we encountered, the solutions we implemented, and the management lessons we learned.

Aggression Replacement Training (ART): Procedures and Curriculum

Counselors, teachers, and others who deal with aggressive juvenile delinquents understand that these juveniles often make use of high levels of acting-out behaviors combined with substandard and deficient alternative prosocial behaviors. Many of these juveniles are skilled in fighting, bullying, intimidating, harassing, and manipulating others. However, they are frequently inadequate in more socially desirable behaviors, such as negotiating differences; dealing appropriately with accusations; and responding effectively to failure, teasing, rejection, or anger. Aggression Replacement Training is our response to this behavior-deficit. It is a multimodal, psychoeducational intervention that consists of skill streaming, anger control training, and moral education.

Skill Streaming

Skill streaming, a fifty-skill intervention curriculum of prosocial behaviors, is systematically taught to chronically aggressive adolescents (Goldstein et al. 1980) and younger children (McGinnis and Goldstein 1984; 1990). The skill-streaming curriculum is implemented with small groups of

---

Dr. Arnold P. Goldstein is professor of special education and director of the Center for Research on Aggression at Syracuse University, Syracuse, New York; Barry Glick is associate deputy director of local services at the New York Division for Youth, Rensselaer, New York.

juveniles (preferably six-to-eight). The following teaching strategies are employed:

- modeling—The groups see several examples of experts using the behaviors and the skills in which they are weak or lacking.
- role playing—Individuals are given several guided opportunities to practice and rehearse competent-interpersonal behaviors.
- performance feedback—Instructors praise and provide feedback on how well the juvenile's role playing of the skill matched the expert model's portrayal of it. Reinstruction is given when necessary.
- generalization training—Juveniles are encouraged to engage in a series of activities that are designed to increase the chances that the skills learned in the training setting will be available for them to use when needed in their real-life environment—the institution, the home, the school, the community, or other real-world settings.

The skills that students learn from these procedures fall into one of the following six categories that comprise the entire curriculum:

- beginning social skills (starting a conversation, introducing yourself, giving a compliment)
- advanced social skills (asking for help, apologizing, giving instructions)
- skills for dealing with feelings (dealing with someone's anger, expressing affection, dealing with fear)
- alternatives to aggression (responding to teasing, negotiating, and helping others)
- skills for dealing with stress (dealing with being left out, dealing with an accusation, preparing for a stressful conversation)
- planning skills (goal setting, decision making, and setting priorities for solving problems)

Anger Control Training (ACT)

Anger Control Training (ACT), first developed by Feindler, Marriott, and Iwata (1984), is partially based on the earlier anger control and stress inoculation research of Novaco (1975) and Meichenbaum (1977). Its goal is to teach juveniles to control their own anger. In Anger Control Training, the participating juveniles must bring to each session one or more descriptions of recent anger-arousing experiences. Usually these experiences are written in their "Hassle Log." During ten sessions, the juveniles are trained to respond to their hassles with a chain of behaviors that include:

- identifying triggers (external events and internal self-statements that provoke an anger response)

- identifying cues (individual kinesthetic or physical experiences, such as tightened muscles, flushed faces, and clenched fists that let the individual know that the emotion he or she is experiencing is anger)
- using reminders (self-statements, such as "stay calm," "chill out," and "cool down," or nonhostile explanations of others' behaviors)
- using reducers (techniques that are designed to lower the individual's level of anger, such as deep breathing, counting backward, imagining a peaceful scene, or imagining the long-term consequences of one's behavior)
- using self-evaluation (reflecting on how well the hassle was responded to by identifying triggers and cues, using reminders, and using reducers and then praising or rewarding oneself for effective performance)

The juvenile trainees, who participate in both skill streaming and Anger Control Training, are knowledgeable about what to do and what not to do in circumstances that instigate aggression. But because aggressive behavior is so consistently, immediately, and richly rewarded in many of the real-world settings in which juveniles live, work, go to school, and interact, they may still consciously choose to behave aggressively. Thus, we believe that it is important to add a values-oriented component to this intervention approach. The final component of Aggression Replacement Training, therefore, is moral education.

Moral Education

Moral education is a set of procedures designed to enhance the juvenile's sense of fairness, justice, and concern with the needs and rights of others. In a pioneering series of investigations, Kohlberg (1969, 1973) demonstrated that exposing juveniles to a series of moral dilemmas (through discussion groups that include juveniles reasoning at differing levels of morality) arouses cognitive conflict. When resolved, this cognitive conflict will frequently advance a juvenile's moral reasoning to that of his or her peers in the group who reason at a higher level. Such advancement of moral reasoning is a reliable finding, but, as with many other single-component interventions, efforts to use it alone as a means of enhancing actual, overt moral behavior have resulted in mixed success (Arbuthnot and Gordon 1983; Zimmerman 1983).

We thus reasoned that Kohlberg's moral education has marked potential for providing constructive direction toward sociability and away from antisocial behavior when juveniles have in their behavioral repertoires the actual skills for acting prosocially or for successfully inhibiting antisocial or more aggressive behaviors. Because a combination of all three components—skill streaming, Anger Control Training, and moral education—is stronger than any one alone, we used all three to effect demonstrable changes in delinquent juveniles.

We have offered the Aggression Replacement Training curriculum in a variety of lengths, but a ten-week sequence has emerged as a "core" curriculum, as detailed in Table 1, on pages 242-243.

Program Evaluation
Annsville Youth Center

We conducted our first evaluation of the effectiveness of Aggression Replacement Training at a New York State Division for Youth facility in central New York State (Goldstein and Glick 1987). Sixty male juveniles at Annsville, a limited-secure detention center, participated in the study; most of the juveniles were in juvenile detention for crimes such as burglary, unarmed robbery, and various drug offenses. Twenty-four juveniles received the ten-week Aggression Replacement Training program outlined in Table 1.

Because of the indifference or hostility of family and peers to newly formed prosocial skills, juvenile delinquents who have been placed in detention often fail to successfully transfer skills learned in the protective and benign training setting to community settings.

This required them to attend three sessions per week, one each of skill streaming, Anger Control Training, and moral education. An additional twenty-four juveniles were assigned to a no-Aggression Replacement Training, brief-instructions control group. This group controlled for the possibility that apparent Aggression Replacement Training-derived gains in skill performance were not due to Aggression Replacement Training but instead to enhanced motivation to display skills the juveniles might already have possessed. A third group, the No-Treatment Control Group, consisted of twelve juveniles not participating in Aggression Replacement Training or the brief instructions procedures.

The evaluation goal of this project was to examine the effectiveness of Aggression Replacement Training for the following purposes:

1. Skill acquisition. Did the juveniles learn the ten prosocial skill streaming skills in the Aggression Replacement Training curriculum?

2. Minimal skill transfer. Can the juveniles perform the skills in response to new situations, similar in format to those on which they were trained?

3. Extended skill transfer. Can the juveniles perform the skills in response to new situations, dissimilar in format and more real-life-like than those on which they were trained?

4. Anger control enhancement. Do the juveniles actually demonstrate fewer altercations or other acting-out behaviors as reflected in weekly behavior-incidents reports that center staff complete on all participating juveniles?

5. Impulsiveness reduction. Are the juveniles rated as less impulsive and more reflective and self-controlled in their interpersonal behavior?

Analyses of study data revealed that juveniles undergoing Aggression Replacement Training, compared to both control groups, significantly acquired and transferred four of the ten skill-streaming skills at both a minimal and extended level. These skills included: expressing a complaint, preparing for a stressful conversation, responding to anger, and dealing with group pressure. Similarly, in the control group there were more and higher intensity in-facility acting-out behaviors (than are measured by behavior-incidents reports), as well as more examples of staff-rated impulsiveness among the control groups.

Control Group Becomes New Project Group

Following completion of the project's posttesting, in week eleven, new Aggression Replacement Training groups were constituted. They were composed of thirty-six juveniles who had been in the three control groups. In these new groups, sessions also were held three times per week for ten weeks. In all major respects (such as curriculum, group size, and materials) these groups replicated the first phase of the Aggression Replacement Training sessions. Our goal in this second phase was an additional test of the efficacy of Aggression Replacement Training, with particular attention to discerning possible reductions in acting-out behaviors by comparing, for these thirty-six juveniles, their incident reports during the eleventh-through-twentieth weeks (while in Aggression Replacement Training) with their incident reports from the period (weeks one through ten) when they had served as control group members. Both of the statistical comparisons—on number and severity of acting-out incidents—conducted to test for replication effects yielded positive (p.01) results.

Because of the indifference or hostility of family and peers to newly formed prosocial skills, juvenile delinquents who have been placed in detention often fail to successfully transfer skills learned in the protective and benign training setting to community settings. Family and peers frequently serve as reinforcers of antisocial behaviors. They ignore or even punish constructive alternative actions. To test for such possible transfer

Table 1
Aggression Replacement Training Core Curriculum

Week	Skill Streaming	Moral Reasoning	Anger Control
1.	**Expressing a complaint** 1. Define what the problem is, and who's responsible for it. 2. Decide how the problem might be solved. 3. Tell that person what the problem is and how it might be solved. 4. Ask for a response. 5. Show that you understand his or her feelings. 6. Come to an agreement on the steps to be taken by each of you.	1. The used car 2. The dope pusher 3. Riots in public places	**Introduction** 1. Rationale: presentation and discussion 2. Rules: presentation and discussion 3. Training procedures: presentation and discussion 4. Contract for anger control training, initial history taking 5. Antecedent provocations-behavioral response-consequences (A-B-C)
2.	**Responding to the feelings of others (empathy)** 1. Observe the other person's words and actions. 2. Decide what the other person might be feeling, and how strong the feelings are. 3. Decide whether it would be helpful to let the other person know you understand his or her feelings. 4. Tell the other person, in a warm and sincere manner, how you think he or she is feeling.	1. The passenger ship 2. The case of Charles Manson 3. LSD	**Assessment** 1. Hassle log: purpose and mechanics 2. Anger self-assessment: physiological cues 3. Anger reducers: Reducer 1: deep breathing training; Reducer 2: refocusing, backward counting; Reducer 3: peaceful imagery
3.	**Preparing for a stressful conversation** 1. Imagine yourself in the stressful situation. 2. Think about how you will feel and why you will feel that way. 3. Imagine that other person in the stressful situation. Think about how that person will feel and why. 4. Imagine yourself telling the other person what you want to say. 5. Imagine what he or she will say. 6. Repeat the above steps using as many approaches as you can think of. 7. Choose the best approach.	1. Shoplifting 2. Booby trap 3. Plagiarism	**Triggers** 1. Identification of provoking stimuli: a. Direct triggers (from others); b. Indirect triggers (from self) 2. Role play: triggers + cues + anger reducer 3. Review of hassle logs
4.	**Responding to anger** 1. Listen openly to what the other person has to say. 2. Show that you understand what the other person is feeling. 3. Ask the other person to explain anything you don't understand. 4. Show that you understand why the other person feels angry. 5. If it is appropriate, express your thoughts and feelings about the situation.	1. Toy revolver 2. Robin Hood case 3. Drugs	**Reminders (Anger reducer 4)** 1. Introduction to self-instruction training 2. Modeling use of reminders under pressure 3. Role play: triggers + cues + reminders + anger reducer 4. Homework assignments and review of hassle log

5. Keeping out of fights
1. Stop and think about why you want to fight.
2. Decide what you want to happen in the long run.
3. Think about other ways to handle the situation besides fighting.
4. Decide the best way to handle the situation and do it.

1. Private country road
2. New York versus Gerald Young
3. Saving a life

Self-evaluation
1. Review of reminder homework assignment
2. Self-evaluation of postconflict reminders: a. Self-reinforcement techniques; b. Self-coaching techniques
3. Review of hassle log postconflict reminders
4. Role play: triggers + cues + reminders + anger reducers + self-evaluation

6. Helping Others
1. Decide if the other person might need and want your help.
2. Think of the ways you could be helpful.
3. Ask the other person if he or she needs and wants your help.
4. Help the other person.

1. The kidney transplant
2. Bomb shelter
3. Misrepresentation

Thinking ahead (anger reducer 5)
1. Estimating future negative consequences for current acting out
2. Short-term versus long-term consequences
3. Worst to least consequences
4. Role play: "If...then" thinking ahead
5. Role play: triggers + cues + reminders + anger reducers + self-evaluation + skill-streaming skill

7. Dealing with an accusation
1. Think about what the other person has accused you of.
2. Think about why the person might have accused you.
3. Think about ways to answer the person's accusations.
4. Choose the best way and do it.

1. Lt. Berg
2. Perjury
3. Doctor's responsibility

The angry behavior cycle
1. Review of hassle logs
2. Identification of own anger-provoking behavior
3. Modification of own anger-provoking behavior
4. Role play: triggers + cues + reminders + anger reducers + self-evaluation + skill-streaming skill

8. Dealing with group pressure
1. Think about what the other people want to do and why.
2. Decide what you want to do.
3. Decide how to tell the other people what you want to do.
4. Tell the group what you have decided.

1. Noisy child
2. The stolen car
3. Discrimination

Full sequence rehearsal
1. Review of hassle logs
2. Role play: triggers + cues + reminders + anger reducers + self-evaluation + skill-streaming skill

9. Expressing affection
1. Decide if you have good feelings about the other person.
2. Decide whether the other person would like to know about your feelings.
3. Decide how you might best express your feelings.
4. Choose the right time and place to express your feelings.
5. Express affection in a warm and caring manner.

1. Defense of other persons
2. Lying in order to help someone
3. Rockefeller's suggestion

Full sequence rehearsal
1. Review of hassle logs
2. Role play: triggers + cues + reminders + anger reducers + self-evaluation + skill-streaming skill

10. Responding to failure
1. Decide if you have failed.
2. Think about both the personal reasons and the circumstances that have caused you to fail.
3. Decide how you might do things differently if you tried again.
4. Decide if you want to try again.
5. If it is appropriate, try again, using your revised approach.

1. The desert
2. The threat
3. Drunken driving

Full sequence rehearsal
1. Review of hassle logs
2. Role play: triggers + cues + reminders + anger reducers + self-evaluation + skill-streaming skill

effects, we constructed a global-rating measure of community functioning. During the year following Aggression Replacement Training's initiation at Annsville, fifty-four juveniles were released; seventeen had received Aggression Replacement Training—thirty-seven had not. We contacted the Division for Youth Service team members (analogous to parole officers) around New York State to whom the fifty-four released juveniles reported regularly.

Without informing the worker whether the juvenile had or had not received Aggression Replacement Training, we asked the worker to complete the global-rating measure on each of the youths discharged from Annsville. In four of the six areas rated—home and family, peer, legal, and overall, but not school or work—Aggression Replacement Training juveniles were rated significantly superior in community functioning than were juveniles who had not received Aggression Replacement Training.

MacCormick Youth Center

We conducted the second evaluation of the efficacy of Aggression Replacement Training at the MacCormick Youth Center, a New York State Division for Youth, maximum-security facility for male juvenile delinquents who are between thirteen and twenty-one years of age (Goldstein and Glick 1986). This second evaluation project sought to both replicate the exact procedures and findings of the Annsville project, as well as extend them to juveniles in detention for more serious felonies. At the time of the evaluation, fifty-one juveniles were detained at MacCormick for crimes such as murder, manslaughter, rape, sodomy, attempted murder, assault, and robbery.

In all its procedural and experimental particulars, the MacCormick evaluation project replicated the effort at Annsville. It employed the same preparatory activities, materials, Aggression Replacement Training curriculum, testing, staff training, resident training, supervision, and data analysis procedures.

... Aggression Replacement Training appears to be a multimodal, rehabilitation intervention with considerable potency with juvenile delinquents in detention.

On five of the ten skill-streaming skills, significant acquisition and/or transfer results emerged. These findings, as well as others on which particular skills did not hold, essentially replicated the Annsville skill-streaming results. In contrast to the Annsville results, however, the MacCormick data also yielded a significant result on the Sociomoral Reflections Measure. At MacCormick, but not at Annsville, juveniles participating in moral education sessions grew significantly in moral reasoning stages over the ten-week intervention period.

Juveniles receiving Aggression Replacement Training significantly increased the facility base-rate levels of their constructive, prosocial behaviors. This included offering or accepting criticism appropriately and employing self-control when provoked. The level of their impulsiveness decreased significantly.

In contrast to the Annsville findings, however, MacCormick juveniles receiving Aggression Replacement Training did not differ from controls in either the number or intensity of their acting-out behaviors. These findings may be explained by the substantial difference in potential for such behaviors between the two facilities. Annsville is not a locked facility. Its sixty juveniles live in one dormitory, in contrast to the locked, single-room arrangement at MacCormick. MacCormick's staff is twice the size of Annsville's. MacCormick operates under a considerably tighter system of sanctions and control than does Annsville. Thus, the opportunity for acting-out behaviors are lower across all conditions at MacCormick, and thus a "floor effect" seems to be operating. This makes the possibility of decreases in acting-out as a result of Aggression Replacement Training participation at MacCormick more difficult to judge than at Annsville. At Annsville, such behaviors were more possible and thus could (and did) decrease over the intervention period. At MacCormick, all juveniles started low and, probably for these same contextual reasons (e.g., sanctions, controls and rich staffing), they remained low. The MacCormick groups' use of prosocial behaviors (in regard to which no floor or ceiling effect influences were relevant) did increase differentially as a function of the Aggression Replacement Training intervention.

Community-based Evaluation

Based on these two investigations Aggression Replacement Training appears to be a multimodal, rehabilitation intervention with considerable potency with juvenile delinquents in detention. It enhanced prosocial skill competency and overt prosocial behavior. It reduced the level of rated impulsiveness, and, in one of the two samples studied, both decreased the frequency and intensity of acting-out behaviors and enhanced the participants' levels of moral reasoning. Furthermore, juveniles released from the Annsville Center during the project period and in the six months following were independently rated by their Division for Youth aftercare workers for the quality of their postdetention community functioning. These raters were not aware of whether the juveniles had received Aggression Replacement Training. On three of the community-functioning areas that were rated (home and family, peer relations, and the legal system), the juveniles who had received Aggression Replacement Training significantly surpassed those who had not. Yet, no such positive findings were found for either school or work adjustment.

The possibility that Aggression Replacement Training can lead to enhanced community functioning—combined with the general movement in the juvenile justice field away from residential and toward community-based programming for delinquent juveniles—led to our third evaluation of Aggression Replacement Training. We sought to determine its value to eighty-four juveniles previously released from juvenile detention (Goldstein, et al. 1989). We were aware of the potent contribution to functioning in the community which parents and others may make in the lives of delinquent juveniles. This belief led to our attempt to determine not only how Aggression Replacement Training affects juveniles, but also to determine how training parents and other family members to reinforce the juveniles' new skills affects the juveniles. Our experimental design is depicted in Table 2.

Table 2
Evaluation Design for Aggression Replacement Training In the Community

	Trainee	Evaluation	Condition
	I	II	III
A.R.T. for Delinquent Youths	X	X	--
A.R.T. for Parents and Family	X	--	--

As Table 2 depicts, the community-based project provided a three-way comparison of Aggression Replacement Training. In Condition I, Aggression Replacement Training was provided directly to juveniles and to the parents and other family members of juveniles. In Condition II, Aggression Replacement Training was provided to juveniles only. In Condition III, a control group, participants received no Aggression Replacement Training.

For the most part, participating juveniles were assigned to project conditions on a random basis. Departures from randomization become necessary on occasion as a function of the multisite, time-extended nature of the project, largely as a result of how long the New York State Division for Youth has aftercare responsibility for juveniles discharged from their facilities. The Aggression Replacement Training program offered to project participants was designed to last three months. It met twice per week, for a total of twenty-five sessions. Each session was one and one-half to two-hours long. Sessions were spent in brief discussions of current life events and difficulties, training in skill-streaming skills (relevant to the life events/difficulties discussed), and, on an alternating basis, Anger Control Training or moral education. Once a week, an Aggression Replacement Training session was held for the parents and other family members of a sample of participating juveniles. Those parents selected to participate, but who did not appear, were provided Aggression Replacement Training in modified form via a weekly home visit or telephone call.

Since the different Aggression Replacement Training groups that constituted the project's two treatment conditions each chose, in collaboration with their respective trainers, which of the fifty skills that comprise the full skill-streaming curriculum that they wished to learn, different groups learned different, although overlapping, sets of skills. We did not, therefore, examine change in individual skills. Instead, analyses focused on total skill change for the juveniles participating in Aggression Replacement Training (Conditions I and II) versus both each other and the no-Aggression Replacement Training control group juveniles (Condition III).

Results indicated that while they did not differ significantly from one another, the two Aggression Replacement Training condition groups each increased significantly in their overall interpersonal skill competence compared with the no-Aggression Replacement Training juveniles (Condition III). A similarly significant outcome emerged (both Aggression Replacement Training versus no-Aggression Replacement Training groups) with a decrease in self-reported anger levels in response to mild (e.g., seeing others abused, minor nuisance, unfair treatment) but not severe anger-provoking situations, (e.g., betrayal of trust, control/coercion, physical abuse).

Recidivism

A particularly important evaluation criterion in delinquency intervention work is recidivism. The large majority of previously detained juveniles who recidivate do so within the first six months following release (Maltz 1984). Thus, the recidivism criterion employed in the current project—to be retaken into custody—was tracked for that time period. For Condition I and II juveniles, the six-month tracking period consisted of the first three months during which they received Aggression Replacement Training, and three months during which they received no Aggression Replacement Training. Condition III juveniles, of course, received no Aggression Replacement Training during the entire tracking period. Analyses examining the frequency of being retaken into custody by condition showed a significant effect for Aggression Replacement Training participation. Both Condition I and Condition II juveniles were retaken into custody significantly less frequently than were juveniles not receiving Aggression Replacement Training.

Comparison of the percent of the retaken-into-custody rate for the two Aggression Replacement Training conditions revealed a substantial decrease in that rate when the juveniles' parents and siblings also participated simultaneously in their own Aggression Replacement Training groups. These latter groups focused on teaching interpersonal skills that were reciprocal to what the delinquent juveniles were learning, as well as anger control techniques. This training of adults may have provided the juveniles a more responsive and prosocially reinforcing real-world environment.

Gang Intervention Project

Our research group's final Aggression Replacement Training evaluation, in which trainees were all gang members with substantial histories of involvement in illegal and aggressive behavior, as well as with the juvenile justice system, grew from precisely the same spirit. We sought to discover whether it was possible to use Aggression Replacement Training to teach juveniles not only to be more prosocial but to enable fellow gang members to accept, support, and even praise prosocial behavior.

... our primary rationale for working with intact gangs in this project was the opportunity afforded by such a strategy to attempt to "capture" a major feature of the juveniles' environment and "turn it" in prosocial directions.

This project was conducted in collaboration with two Brooklyn, New York, juvenile care agencies—the Brownsville Neighborhood Community Youth Action Center and Youth DARES (Dynamic Alternative for Rehabilitation through Educational Services) of Coney Island. Each agency conducted three four-month sequences of Aggression Replacement Training for trainees who were all members of the same gang. We also established a control group, whose members were also from the same gang as one another—though from a different gang than the Aggression Replacement Training trainees, for each sequence. Thus, across both agencies, twelve different gangs participated in the program. Six received Aggression Replacement Training and six served as no-Aggression Replacement Training controls. All the juveniles, Aggression Replacement Training and controls, also received the diverse educational, vocational, and recreational services offered by the two participating agencies.

Study Findings

Repeated measures of analysis of variance crossing project condition (Aggression Replacement Training versus control) with time of measurement (pre versus post) revealed a significant interaction effect favoring Aggression Replacement Training participants for each of the following skill categories:

- beginning social skills
- advanced social skills
- feelings-relevant skills
- aggression-management skills
- stress-management skills
- planning skills
- total skills score

None of the analysis of variance comparisons of Aggression Replacement Training with control group scores for anger control yielded significant differences. Of the five community domains, only work adjustment yielded a significant difference favoring those youth who had received Aggression Replacement Training. This result accords well (and no doubt largely reflects) the real-world employment pattern for project participants. For example, in the months immediately following their Aggression Replacement Training sequence, the majority of the participating Lo-Lives gang members left their gang and took jobs in local retail businesses. At an analogous point in time, following their own Aggression Replacement Training participation, a substantial minority of the participating Baby Wolfpack gang members obtained employment in construction trades.

Custody data were available for the juveniles participating in our first two Aggression Replacement Training sequences and their respective control groups. Five of the thirty-eight Aggression Replacement Training participants (13 percent) and fourteen of the twenty-seven control group members (52 percent) were retaken into custody during the eight-month tracking period—a significant difference. It will be recalled that our primary rationale for working with intact gangs in this project was the opportunity afforded by such a strategy to attempt to "capture" a major feature of the juveniles' environment and "turn it" in prosocial directions.

We wondered whether once they learned certain prosocial behaviors, their transfer and maintenance of these skills would be increased or be discouraged by the persons with whom the juvenile interacted regularly in the real-world environment. Our favorable outcome vis à vis being retaken into custody implies the possibility that such a more harmonious and prosocially promotive post-Aggression Replacement Training peer environment may have been created. While it is important that future research examine this possibility more directly, it is interesting that similar outcomes were obtained in our earlier attempt to create a prosocially reinforcing post-

Aggression Replacement Training environment for juvenile delinquents by employing this intervention with both them and their families. For juveniles who received Aggression Replacement Training for themselves and their family, the retaken-into-custody rate was 15 percent. For the control group of juveniles, the comparable figure was 43 percent. Both outcomes parallel closely that found here (13 percent and 52 percent) for the presence or absence of a rather different type of "family"—the juveniles' fellow gang members.

The efficacy evaluations suggest that Aggression Replacement Training is an effective intervention. It appears to promote the acquisition and performance of skills, improve anger control, decrease the frequency of acting-out behaviors, and increase the frequency of prosocial behaviors. Beyond facility walls, its effects persist—less fully perhaps than when the juvenile is in a controlled environment, but the effects persist nonetheless. In general, the potency of the results appears to be sufficiently adequate that its continued implementation and evaluation with chronically aggressive juveniles is clearly warranted. This encouraging conclusion is supported by four additional investigations evaluating the efficacy of Aggression Replacement Training with delinquent and aggressive juveniles that were conducted by other investigators in widely dispersed research sites: Texas (Coleman, Pfeiffer, and Oakland 1991), Washington State (Curulla 1990), Brisbane, Australia (Jones 1990), and Ohio (Leeman, et al. 1991).

Program Management

Management of a four-study, multisite delinquency intervention evaluation program lasting seven years and involving dozens of facility and agency staff as well as hundreds of delinquent juvenile trainees required diverse planning, training, supervision, data collection, data analysis, budget management, and resource coordination efforts.

Program Planning

These investigations were supported by research grants from the New York State Division of Criminal Justice Services, a state agency concerned with the creation, evaluation, and dissemination of effective interventions for juvenile delinquents. Three of the four studies described (Annsville, MacCormick, and the community) were conducted at New York State Division for Youth locations with juvenile delinquents in that agency's charge. The final (gang) program investigation was conducted at two, private, non-profit, community-based agencies: the Brownsville Neighborhood Youth Action Center and Youth DARES, both located in Brooklyn, New York.

Our experiences with this project provide valuable information for both those who seek to replicate this project as well as those who are managing other programs. Starting from the beginning of project planning, project managers must seek to plan not only good science (design, measurement, analysis), but also to conduct skilled consultations and negotiations among the many interested parties. Open, honest, and frequent communication among several agencies and facilities maximized our opportunity to reflect their thinking in program planning and meet their needs as they defined them in such plans.

Just as in skill streaming itself, in which trainee motivation is enhanced when the skill curriculum is negotiated with the trainee, staff motivation to participate in program procedures and carry them out is enhanced when major aspects of the program are negotiated. Such a planning strategy need not negate research requirements such as standardization of intervention procedures nor disturb randomness of assignment to a particular condition. However, it does provide all interested parties with a genuine sense of participation in program planning and a shared ownership of program outcomes.

A crucial planning consideration, relevant to both the participatory process just described and the ultimate design of the research to be conducted, is the notion of rigor-relevance balance. Good intervention evaluation research, in both our view and that of the several agency and staff collaborators with whom we worked, is both experimentally rigorous and highly relevant to the real lives of its recipients. O.R. Lindsley (1964) spoke of three orientations to experimentation on intervention effectiveness. The "Rigorless Magician" orientation is reflected in the "shoot from the hip," "impressions-count-for-everything" stance held by the individual who eschews objective measurement of effect and relies totally on his or her "clinical judgment." At the opposite extreme is the "Rigor Mortician," so fixated on objective measurement that he or she sacrifices the richness, the uniqueness, and the individuality of the phenomena being studied in the effort to obtain standardized measurement information. At an intermediate position, and to be recommended, is the "Rigorous Clinician." Here, a fruitful balance of the rigor of experimental design and measurement, and relevance to the real world of those being studied, is striven for. Perhaps aided by the fact that our participatory planning team consisted of both principal investigator researchers and agency-staff clinicians, our program-evaluation goal clearly became that of the rigorous clinician.

Training, Monitoring, and Supervision

Program integrity, defined as the degree to which program implementation is faithful to, consistent with, or corresponds to the program plan, is primarily a function of three related management activities—training, monitoring, and supervision. In each of the studies described, we initiated these functions by distributing to the staff at the participating agencies copies of the training process manual, *Aggression Replacement Training* (Goldstein and Glick 1987). This manual describes all Aggression Replacement Training procedures and their implementation in a highly comprehensive, step-wise, concrete manner. We urged the staff to read and reread this manual prior to the next step in the training process, the trainer's workshop. Here, all staff of the participating agencies underwent an intensive, participatory, experiential series of lessons in the actual conduct of Aggression Replacement Training groups. These workshops also gave the project manager the opportunity, based on overt displays of Aggression Replacement Training-relevant competence and incompetence, to select from among the workshop participants those staff members who would actually serve as project trainers. The workshops also enabled the project managers to determine which of the three components of the Aggression Replacement Training staff members were most able and willing to lead.

Once each project's Aggression Replacement Training sessions with participating juveniles actually began, we initiated an ongoing process of regular monitoring and supervision. This process took several forms, depending partly on the physical distance of the facility or agency from where the project managers were located, but also on the competence levels of particular trainers. We accomplished such monitoring and supervision by regular visits to the training sites where we observed Aggression Replacement Training sessions in progress and met with the trainers afterwards to offer feedback. We supplemented this on site by requiring trainers to keep weekly session notes, which they mailed to the managers for feedback. We held twice weekly (and often lengthy) telephone conversations. Most of the latter were regularly scheduled, but some occurred on an as-needed basis as issues or crises arose.

Perhaps the most valuable feature of this multipronged training, monitoring, and supervision process was the opportunities it provided not only to point out and correct intervention delivery "errors" (trainer behaviors departing from Aggression Replacement Training manual procedures), but also the chances it offered to "catch trainers being good." Trainers, as the participating juveniles themselves, are often especially deserving of recognition and praise for skilled enactment of training procedures. Unfortunately, trainers often do not receive this recognition, although it helps to maintain and improve performance.

Each of the two evaluations of Aggression Replacement Training in residential settings lasted a year. Each of the community and gang Aggression Replacement Training evaluations lasted two years. How do research managers keep staff trainers interested, involved, and true to intervention procedures as planned during such extended periods? The Aggression Replacement Training programs offered to participating juveniles within these respective programs were twenty to thirty-two sessions long, conducted on a twice-a-week basis. How do trainers keep juveniles with short attention spans, most of whom have found antisocial behavior to be consistently rewarding, interested and motivated to attend, participate in, and use the lessons of an intervention designed to teach prosocial alternative behaviors?

Our first answer to these often daunting questions is "it ain't easy!" It was our clear sense in the management of this and other research programs that satisfactory program initiation was conducted much more easily than was satisfactory program maintenance. At launch time, all are often excited and eager to "travel" several miles down the road. However, when implementation feels routine, novelty has long since departed, and problems—both anticipated and unexpected—have arisen, continuing to be eagerly involved and rigorous in our application of intervention procedures can and does become problematic.

Maintaining Motivation

We used two classes of motivators—extrinsic and intrinsic. Extrinsic motivators are tangibles provided in advance of or following competent performance. For staff trainers—in the community and gang studies, but not the institutional studies in which it was not permitted—project grant monies were used to pay for participation. Juveniles were "paid" also, in all four studies, but in the institutional case, they were not paid with money. Although we had wanted to offer them money for participation, the funding agency disallowed this request. Instead, we provided them with food; we also provided movie privileges when deserved, and we gave each juvenile a specially designed "Angerbuster" T-shirt, as well as other material reinforcers.

As the program developed, for many staff the primary intrinsic motivators became their enhanced sense of professional competence and their enhanced belief that they were significantly intervening for the better in the lives of some very troubled juveniles.

Intrinsic motivators—reinforcers inherent in the intervention itself, or intangibles associated with it—began early in each program's implementation. In the two residential studies, before the program began, we placed a series of posters throughout each facility proclaiming in one or another way to both juveniles and staff that Aggression Replacement Training was coming and that it would provide the juveniles a special opportunity if they participated. For staff, as noted earlier, program participation also was preceded by motivation-enhancing involvement in program planning and decision making. This provided them with a sense of program ownership. As the program developed, for many staff the primary intrinsic motivators became their enhanced sense of professional competence and their enhanced belief that they were significantly intervening for the better in the lives of some very troubled juveniles.

For the juveniles themselves, intrinsic motivation followed primarily from their growing sense that the skills they were learning were, in fact, relevant and functional in their every day lives in the facility, on the street, at school, and at home. We promoted such skill relevance and function by regular use of "negotiating the curriculum." Rather than, for example, beginning each skill-streaming session with a staff member modeling a skill, which they had selected, staff members were asked to engage the juveniles in a brief discussion of their current life events and concerns, and from that discussion the skill to be taught was mutually selected. Thus, a juvenile recently fired from his job in a fast food outlet for telling his boss to "shove it" may profitably choose to learn, and be taught the skill "Standing Up for Your Rights." The shy juvenile, wanting to reach out to an opposite sex peer but afraid to do so, will become more motivated to remain in the group and learn its lessons if he or she is taught "Starting a Conversation" and uses it effectively with that peer.

... for both staff trainers and juvenile delinquent trainees, "catching them being good" was our most consistently effective motivation maintainer.

Finally, as both folklore and several hundred studies of the consequences of positive reinforcement make clear, for both staff trainers and juvenile delinquent trainees, "catching them being good" was our most consistently effective motivation maintainer. For staff, such praise following competent implementation of Aggression Replacement Training procedures and, for juveniles, such approval following competent skill use (or role playing, homework completion, dilemma discussion, etc.) regularly appeared to promote the desire for them to continue their involvement in program activities.

As project managers, we had overall management responsibility for both agency staff and participating juveniles. But agency staff also had management obligations, in their case "hands on," "front line," or "direct care" obligations, including the motivation of trainee attendance and participation. In one of our program's investigations, it was instructive to observe that the two agencies which participated employed contrasting motivational tactics. One, following the lead we sought to operationalize in our own management style, was managed mostly by using the "carrots" of the "carrots and stick" approach—i.e., praise, material reinforcers, communication of both positive expectations for change and staff availability (and eagerness) to assist in such change. The second agency relied much more heavily on the "sticks" for its motivational effort, primarily by reiteration of the judge's threat of more time in or a return to detention for failure to attend Aggression Replacement Training sessions. This latter agency had many times more attendance and management problems over the course of its project participation than did the former.

Coordination of Functions and Resources

As noted at the outset, a number of organizations and agencies were "interested parties" over the life of this research and evaluation program—a university; a state-agency funding source; two private agencies and a state agency providing implementation sites; media representatives; and a number of state and local political figures. Their interests, with rare exceptions, intersected and were not a source of management difficulty. Yet, they were repeatedly sources requiring management activity. Grant proposals, quarterly project reports, meeting and implementation schedules, budgets, evaluation measures and other reports, forms, memos, and accountings each had to be prepared in an accurate and timely manner. Meetings had to be regularly (and sometimes irregularly) prepared for, scheduled, and conducted, with an eye to both team building and the project's ultimate evaluation goals. The several interested parties—their sheer number and dispersed locations—also meant many planned and unplanned telephone conversations. In some of these conversations the content mattered a great deal. For some, the act of calling was primarily to solidify the relationship-maintaining goal.

Adding to the picture of diverse and numerous management requirements was the fact that the mass media developed considerable interest in Aggression Replacement Training, especially as we implemented it with juvenile gangs. Newspaper and television reporters, both local and national, became a presence, first to appreciate and then, to contend with, over the course of the evaluation sequence. They, too, have their own legitimate needs and demands, but on more than a few occasions their presence functioned as an intrusive detriment to appropriate intervention implementation. Tactful, but firm, management intervention proved necessary here.

Data Collection and Analysis

In operational terms, evaluating the efficacy of Aggression Replacement Training was a multistage process. While reflecting the primary goal of standardization across conditions and studies, we also had to be responsive to the realities of the participating agencies and institutions. Even given realities, such as staff schedules, other juvenile programs in operation, security needs, and confidentiality needs, data collection proceeded in a generally "as planned" manner in all four program studies.

The specific management requirements constituting this aspect of the program included the following:

- the developing and selecting of appropriate evaluation measures
- duplicating and disseminating them to study sites
- instructing site staff in measurement administration
- preparing a measurement schedule
- administering tests to participating juveniles and staff as scheduled and in a standardized manner
- scoring and recording of the measures thus administered
- conducting appropriate data analyses

Although we had our share of missing answers, participants who did not show up, last-minute scheduling changes, and similar events, the procedures and contents of the measurement effort remained intact.

Management Principles

We recommend that administrators or research managers consider following a more general, strategic set of valuable management principles we tried to implement during the life of this project.

1. **Give respect to get respect.** The biblical teaching urging you to do unto others as you would have them do unto you is an especially valuable management principle for successful program implementation. Ideally, the project manager will—with consistency and initiative—seek to overtly demonstrate respect for each participating staff member's job knowledge and skill performance. The program-implementing staff members, in turn, should be urged to display similarly respectful attitudes and behaviors, when appropriate, toward participating juveniles' opinions, choices, and overt behaviors. When staff members perceive themselves and their work to be respected, on-line performance of project responsibilities may be enhanced, feedback may more freely be given and received, and staff self-esteem may be favorably affected. Similarly beneficial consequences can also emerge as participating trainees experience respect from staff and one another.

2. **Employ and encourage open and honest communication**. Underpinning the effort to promote mutual respect is open and honest communication between and among management, staff, and juveniles. Not only staff, but especially participating juveniles, know when half-truths are being told or information is being withheld. Such departures from open and "straight up" communication can seriously sabotage important aspects of program procedure. We urge, on both ethical and pragmatic grounds, that "telling it like it is" be adopted as a management principle. Even when the message is more work for the person to whom one is speaking, or disappointing, open and honest communication must be sought.

3. **Define roles and responsibilities clearly**. Early and open communication is especially necessary, in regard to who is to do what, when, and how, as well as who "reports" to whom, about what, and when. Such clear definition of roles and responsibilities is the backbone of successful program management. It must be made explicit to study participants as early as the initial invitation. If offered early and explicitly, discussed openly, and concretized fully so that cross-cutting lines of authority and obligation are minimized, subsequent role/responsibility confusion or conflict is less likely to occur.

4. **Share project planning, process, and product**. In a number of ways, a research program will benefit greatly when decision making about its substance and implementation, as well as the fruits it yields, are not owned exclusively by its management but, instead, are genuinely shared. In addition to "up front" matters such as program planning and process, the sense of ownership and participatory sharing also should fully characterize project products. The "products" of the present program were most importantly the intangible sense of accomplishment as juveniles changed, became less aggressive and more prosocially skilled, dropped out of gangs, stayed out of juvenile detention, got jobs, or went back to school. These were big victories, with credit to all participants openly offered. Such a spirit of shared ownership should and did characterize tangible products of the program. This included invitation to professional meetings, workshops, or other agencies to describe the program and its results; joint authorship of descriptive articles, chapters, and monographs; and financial remuneration for one's project time and effort. Clearly, the shared ownership of project planning, process, and product meant a better project in all three regards.

The management strategies we have described and the management tactics we have sought to implement form an ethically responsible and pragmatically functional means for planning and conducting a long-term research program, as well as for disseminating its outcomes. Used conscientiously, such strategies and tactics can yield utilitarian research outcomes fully reflecting the rigor-relevance balance sought by rigorous clinicians.

References

Arbuthnot, J., and D. A. Gordon. 1983. Moral reasoning development in correctional intervention. *Journal of Correctional Education* 34(2): 133-38.

Coleman, M., S. Pfeiffer, and T. Oakland. 1991. Aggression replacement training with behavior disordered adolescents. Unpublished manuscript,University of Texas.

Curulla, V. L. 1990. Aggression replacement training in the community for adult learning disabled offenders. Unpublished manuscript,University of Washington.

Feindler, E. L., S. A. Marriott, and M. Iwata. 1984. Group anger control training for junior high school delinquents. *Cognitive Therapy and Research* 8(4):299-311.

Goldstein, A. P., and B. Glick. 1987. *Aggression replacement training.* Champaign, Ill.:Research Press, (1987).

——. 1989. *Reducing delinquency: Intervention in the community.* New York: Pergamon Press.

——. 1994. *The prosocial gang: Implementing aggression replacement training.* Thousand Oaks, Calif.:Sage Publications.

Goldstein, A. P., et al. 1980. *Skill streaming the adolescent.* Champaign, Ill.: Research Press.

Jones, Y. 1990. Aggression replacement training in a high school setting. Unpublished manuscript. Center for Learning and Adjustment Difficulties, Brisbane, Australia.

Kohlberg, L. 1969. Stage and sequence: The cognitive-developmental approach to socialization. In *Handbook of Socialization Theory and Research.* ed. D.A. Goslin. Chicago: Rand McNally.

Kohlberg, L. (ed.) 1973. *Collected papers on moral development and moral education.* Cambridge, Mass.: Harvard University, Center for Moral Education.

Leeman, L. W., et al. 1991. Evaluation of multi-component treatment program for juvenile delinquents. Unpublished manuscript. Ohio State University.

Lindsley, O. R. 1964. *Personal communication.* Syracuse, N.Y.

Maltz, D. 1984. *Recidivism.* New York: Academic Press.

Meichenbaum, D. 1977. *Cognitive behavior modification: An integrative approach.* New York: Plenum.

McGinnis, E., and A. P. Goldstein. 1984. *Skill streaming the elementary school child.* Champaign, Ill.: Research Press.

——. 1990. *Skill streaming in early childhood.* Champaign, Ill.: Research Press.

Novaco, R. W. 1975. *Anger control: The development and evaluation of an experimental treatment.* Lexington, Mass.: Lexington Books.

Zimmerman, D. 1983. Moral education. In *Prevention and Control of Aggression,* ed. Center for Research on Aggression. New York: Pergamon Press.

Part V

Managing System Issues

13 Cultural Sensitivity in Delinquency Prevention and Intervention Programs*

Fernando I. Soriano, Ph.D. and Leticia Lleva

All societies, whether large or small, have been concerned with deviance—behavior going beyond society's standards of conduct. Religious institutions of all social groups often oversee or are directly involved in determining guidelines for what is considered "good" (appropriate behavior) or "bad" (inappropriate behavior). More than any other subject of study, delinquency has historically been laden with value judgments highlighting particular groups for their proneness to delinquency. For example, early sociological studies on delinquency suggested that particular ethnic groups, such as Latinos and African Americans, were more likely to be linked to crime and delinquency compared to Anglo Saxons (Staples and Mirande 1980).

Mirande (1987) and Soriano (in press) refer to these early studies as subjective and pejorative in their views towards minority groups. (In this chapter, the term, "minority groups," which has traditionally referred to numerical presence, is used. However, in many regions of the United States, those we call ethnic minorities will soon become majorities due to their numerical increases, concomitant with decreases in the Anglo-Saxon population.) The cultural values of Latinos, for example, were considered responsible for an early socialization leading to a life of crime and delinquency. "Machismo," in particular, was considered a barrier for Latino families instilling in their children a sense of respect for others and the law (Romano 1973). There still remains a lack of understanding about the role of culture in delinquent behavior.

Because ethnic and racial minorities are disproportionately associated with crime and delinquency (Trojanowicz and Morash 1987; Hindelang, Hirschi, and Weis 1991), it is important that delinquency and intervention

---

Dr. Fernando I. Soriano is a professor and researcher at the University of Missouri in Kansas City in the Department of Behavioral Science; Leticia Lleva has conducted research with Dr. Soriano at Stanford University, where she is pursuing her Ph.D.

*Portions of this chapter were adapted from "Cultural Sensitivity and Gang Intervention," by Dr. Soriano (1993) in **The Gang Intervention Handbook,** eds. A.P. Goldstein and C.R. Huff. Champaign, Ill.: Research Press.*

programs be culturally sensitive. Program evaluations of juvenile prevention and intervention programs suggest six characteristics of effective programs:

- involve juveniles after school
- provide outreach to home and family
- coordinate with community agencies, particularly the police
- target juveniles about to become involved in, or already involved in, gang (or delinquent, antisocial) activities
- provide support and remedial strategies for juveniles failing in school
- exhibit a strong, structured supervised approach (Sweet 1992)

A major component missing from this list is the need for programs to be culturally sensitive or culturally relevant. The purpose of this chapter is not to examine cultural causes or correlates of delinquency or to refute a link, but to point out general guiding principles around which to develop juvenile delinquency prevention or intervention programs that are culturally sensitive or relevant.

Cultural Sensitivity Defined

According to Soriano (1993), cultural sensitivity refers to:

> a person's or a program's objective understanding, appraisal, appreciation, and knowledge of a particular cultural group that is used equitably in behavioral dispositions towards members of the cultural group. Cultural sensitivity is developed through self-awareness, the elimination of stereotypes and unfounded views, and through gaining objective knowledge and actual interaction with members of a particular cultural group.

This definition encompasses many of the characteristics commonly used as indicators of cultural sensitivity, such as language capability, ethnic background, social science training, cultural training, and background experience of program staff members. Community prevention and intervention programs for ethnic minorities have often relied on any one of these characteristics singly or in combination to develop cultural sensitivity.

Linguistic and Behavioral Communication

Like all community-based programs, juvenile delinquency intervention efforts require clear and effective communication with juvenile delinquents. Communication is accomplished both verbally (through language) and behaviorally (through gestures and body movements). Verbal and behavioral methods of communication are extremely important in conveying clear program expectations and in developing trust and rapport with clients.

Verbal communication is an obvious, yet often overlooked barrier to developing culturally sensitive intervention programs. Understanding the targeted group's language is essential to developing the types of interpersonal relationships necessary for effective juvenile delinquency intervention efforts. This has led many social scientists to agree with Grove (1976) that "... language barriers may be the most easily surmounted of the many impediments blocking communications across cultures."

The benefits of effective communication are clear. In a recent study on communication and on common understanding between physicians and monolingual Spanish-speaking elderly patients, Seijo, Gomez, and Friedenberg (1991) found that Hispanic patients maintained better recall of patient information and asked more questions of physicians when their doctor was bilingual compared to those with monolingual English-speaking doctors. Similarly, using staff without appropriate language capability, juvenile delinquency intervention projects unwittingly, but systematically, exclude from meaningful participation such minority subgroups as monolingual nonEnglish-speaking Asians, Caribbeans, and Hispanics. African Americans also are affected by communication problems (e.g., "Black English" [Blake 1987]).

It is important to note, however, that a program staff's capability to speak a targeted group's language or a juvenile delinquent's ability to speak English does not necessarily preclude the emergence of communication problems, which can lead to misunderstandings and distrust. Effective communication involves more than just sharing the same language. It involves applying the same meaning to behavior verbally and nonverbally.

For example, two Hispanics fluent in Spanish can misunderstand each other if they attach different meanings to the same words or actions. A comical, but daunting, incident illustrates this problem. A man from Puerto Rico once asked his Cuban girlfriend for her "pepita" in a crowded bus full of the girlfriend's relatives. A physical attack of the man was averted by a knowledgeable and understanding rider who was quick to explain to the angry crowd that a "pepita" to Puerto Ricans refers to a fruit seed and not to the woman's vagina, as Cubans commonly understand it! The Puerto Rican man simply wanted to help his girlfriend discard her litter.

Grove (1976) has reported that speech is responsible for only about 35 percent of all communication in all face-to-face interactions. This percent is reduced even further when considering communication across cultures, and particularly, when considering communication with juvenile delinquents who often use specific slang. Juvenile delinquents develop their own language called "Spanglish" or "Calo" when referring to Hispanic members, and "Black English" when referring to African Americans (Blake 1987). These variants of mainstream languages, such as English and Spanish, are often compared to a particular middle-class English standard, which quickly leads to misunderstandings and mistrust.

D. W. Sue and S. Sue (1977) have called attention to problems arising from human service providers, such as counselors, expecting the use of standard English by lower-income groups. The use of and expectation of the use of standard English in human service programs can discriminate against ethnic minorities and lead to an improper impression that "... minorities are inferior, lack awareness, or lack conceptual thinking powers" (Sue and Sue 1977). There are key language differences between the standard English of the middle class and the English spoken by major ethnic groups. Standard English is more centered on verbal expressions of feelings, emotions, and behaviors, while communication by lower-class minorities tends to center more on nonverbal communication.

The combination of verbal and nonverbal communication will result in effective interpersonal communication that conveys respect, confidence, and trust.

According to Sue and Sue (1977), the lower-class African American tends to use black street language, which places greater importance on nonverbal communication involving "... a great deal of implicitness in communication, such as shorter sentences and less grammatical elaboration." Similarly, lower-class Chicanos and Hispanics tend to be less verbal and involve the use of Spanish. Like Hispanics, Asians tend to use silence as a form of respect and deference and also make use of their native language. For Hispanics and Asians, there is a preference for one-way communication from authority figures to other persons. Many Native Americans share these same characteristics, but also tend to be creative, experiential, intuitive, and nonverbal (Sue and Sue 1977).

Linguistic considerations require juvenile delinquency intervention workers and researchers to understand the linguistic dominance, preference, and nuances of particular cultural subgroups, as well as to pay particular attention to nonverbal behavior and cues. Because most communication is nonverbal, juvenile delinquency workers need to learn the appropriateness of nonverbal communication, such as making eye-contact and maintaining physical distance. The combination of verbal and nonverbal communication will result in effective interpersonal communication that conveys respect, confidence, and trust.

Ethnic Background of Program Staff

Community programs are frequently believed to be culturally relevant and sensitive if they maintain program personnel who are of the same cultural background, ethnicity, or race as those being targeted. Unfortunately, this tenuous assumption is perhaps one of the least challenged. This assumption of ethnic homogeneity incorrectly assumes *all* members of an ethnic group are homogeneous and have the same background and hold common experiences, attitudes, values, norms, beliefs, and expectations.

This is not to deny that there is a somewhat higher probability of holding common cultural values and norms among those of similar ethnic backgrounds. Nor does this deny the probable tendency for many members of an ethnic group to be more sensitive and understanding of experiences of being discriminated against, feeling helpless, and feeling frustrated. At one level, common ethnicity or race does facilitate quicker rapport (Gim, Atkinson, and Kim 1991). However, the initial gain in rapport due to common background can quickly lead to mistrust if the program worker lacks the sensitivity and understanding that come with knowledge and experience. The mere presence of minority members within intervention programs does not, in and of itself, lead to a program that is culturally sensitive.

There are other reasons why the presence of cultural group members does not ensure that a program is culturally sensitive. First, assuming that a program has ethnic members who are culturally sensitive, this does not mean that the intervention program and its objectives and materials are culturally sensitive or relevant. Even if culturally sensitive, workers from minority groups may not have decision-making power to help direct the program's efforts in a culturally sensitive and relevant direction.

Assuming that both ethnic minority and nonminority members are culturally sensitive, the question still remains: Does it matter that program staff are of the same ethnicity or race as members of the targeted group? The accumulating research on psychotherapeutic outcomes based on culture pairing suggests that there are negligible differences based on whether the therapist is white or of the same ethnicity as the client *(see* Sue [1988] for a comprehensive review of this literature).

Instead, the research suggests that it is the therapist's communication (all aspects of communication—linguistic and otherwise), sensitivity, and understanding of the client's values, lifestyle and background that determines treatment success (Sue et al. 1976; Trimble and LaFromboise 1985; Leong 1986; Jenkins 1985; Casas 1985; Sue 1988). Furthermore, a recent study by Wade and Bernstein (1991) suggests that even ethnic minorities, such as African Americans, can benefit from cultural sensitivity training. In this study it was found that cultural sensitivity training of experienced African-American counselors led to increased credibility, follow-up sessions, and greater satisfaction when compared with comparably experienced African-American counselors not participating in the cultural sensitivity training.

According to Miller (1990), the emphasis on the cultural background of community workers who interact with juvenile delinquents limits access to an existing pool of culturally sensitive nonethnic minorities, who can be just as effective as minorities. This view has much empirical support. However, the critical caveats are *if* they posses the right communication and linguistic skills, are knowledgeable about the culture, are experienced, and have developed the skills in working with members of the ethnic group in question.

Although nonminorities can be as successful as minorities in working with ethnic juvenile delinquents, the physical characteristics of ethnic minorities give them the initial advantage over nonminorities of leading ethnic juvenile delinquents to assume greater commonality in background than is often the case. This initial advantage can lead to more rapidly established rapport. Furthermore, minorities are more likely to have the past experiences and background, such as exposure to poverty and discrimination, that would facilitate understanding.

Although ethnic background may not be essential to develop cultural sensitivity, cultural training *is* important. Perceptions of appropriate cultural sensitivity training varies greatly and range from general training in the social sciences to more specialized training. It is necessary to examine the range of cultural training, including common assumptions and implications.

Social Science Training

Many community-based programs try to satisfy the cultural sensitivity requirement by hiring staff with training in the social sciences. This is based on the assumption that training in the social sciences prepares a person to work with the full range of social and cultural diversity found in society. This is similar to the common misconception among lay persons that all psychologists are trained in therapy and psychopathology.

Most social scientists agree that traditional social science training does not automatically lead to cultural understanding or sensitivity. In fact, it is the admitted lack of potential sensitivity that has led many professional social science journals to submit "blind" manuscripts, which keep the names of the writers confidential, for peer review. This tactic reduces the likelihood of biased or disparate reviews based on the ethnicity or gender of names or other potential areas of bias.

There is a growing recognition in the social sciences that the traditional training in higher education is deficient in training its students to understand, study, and work with culturally diverse populations (Leong and Kim 1991; Ponterotto and Casas 1987; Rogler 1989; Parker, Valley, and Geary 1986). There is an obvious need for social science training programs to increase student awareness and knowledge regarding ethnic groups.

Human service professionals will need to increase their knowledge and understanding of ethnic minority groups in response to the numerical growth and presence of minorities in the United States. However, it is unclear what constitutes appropriate cultural sensitivity training for human service workers interacting with ethnic minority communities. What type of information leads to adequate knowledge of ethnic minorities? Is cultural knowledge sufficient to instill cultural sensitivity?

Cultural Knowledge

Many community programs have considered the question of whether imparting cultural knowledge is the answer to becoming culturally sensitive. A common question is whether a person automatically becomes culturally sensitive to a particular ethnic group once he or she has gained a significant amount of knowledge of the cultural group. Many cultural sensitivity training programs have, in fact, traditionally emphasized cultural knowledge within cultural sensitivity training programs.

Social psychology research on attitude formation and change clearly suggests that simply introducing information to someone does not automatically lead to that person adopting or incorporating the new information into his or her belief system (McGuire 1985). Resistance to the incorporation of new information is likely to fail to be adopted by someone if it is inconsistent with prior well-established information that is part of an existing belief system, such as when new favorable information about an ethnic group confronts a strong prejudicial belief system (McGuire 1960).

A study of fifty-one desegregated high schools found that the use of multiethnic texts, which acquainted the readers with values, norms, and perceptions of African Americans and other cultural groups, did not lower whites' or African-Americans' prejudice levels (Slavin and Madden 1979). Other studies reported by Stephen (1985) that suggest that informational interventions have no effect included one by Greenberg, Pierson, and Sherman (1957). They found that single lectures, debates, and discussions designed to reduce prejudice did not do so. Best and others (1975) similarly found that a twelve-hour, race-related curriculum for white elementary children had no effect on racial attitudes. Lessing and Clarke (1976) found that even a comprehensive eight-week curriculum for junior high school students during which students read and prepared reports about different ethnic groups and received supplementary materials did not have any effect on prejudice.

Even with these negligible results found by some researchers, many cultural sensitivity training programs, including college textbooks, continue to emphasize the importance of cultural knowledge in developing cultural sensitivity (Leong and Kim 1991; Rogler et al. 1987; Atkinson, Morten, and Sue 1989; Sue 1981). In their literature review on effective cultural sensitivity training programs, Parker, Valley, and Geary (1986) concluded that cultural knowledge has been one of the most emphasized factors in cultural sensitivity training programs.

Merely providing knowledge does not necessarily lead to cultural sensitivity. Instead, research suggests that various social psychological conditions bearing on the learner or trainee determine whether the knowledge or information provided about a culture results in improved sensitivity or not. There is research evidence in social psychology suggesting that ethnic and racial attitudes can and do change with the introduction of new information, particularly if the new information capitalizes on preexisting information that is compatible with the new information (McGuire 1985).

After reviewing the literature on the effectiveness of interethnic training on changing ethnic attitudes, Stephen (1985) concluded:

> The most remarkable aspect of these studies of changes in intergroup cognitions and behavior is the relative ease with which changes can be brought about. A variety of [cognitive-or cultural-knowledge-based] approaches to reducing prejudice, stereotyping, and discrimination have been reviewed, and most have been shown to be effective.

Research on attitude change suggests that information provided in training is most likely to be adopted when it is compatible with preexisting and extant knowledge (McGuire 1985; Cialdini, Petty, and Cacioppo 1981). Applied to cultural concerns, the knowledge conveyed through cultural sensitivity training is most likely to be adopted and used by those trainees who have preexisting attitudes towards the cultural group that are compatible with the information provided in training. After reviewing extant empirical studies on intergroup relations, Stephen (1985) concluded: "Considered in the aggregate, these [attitude change] studies indicate that [preexisting] evaluative inferences about ethnic group members increasingly override factual information across time."

Applied to juvenile delinquency intervention and cultural sensitivity, research on intergroup relations suggests that the goal of sensitizing delinquency program personnel is more easily accomplished through knowledge-based programs provided that the previous attitudes of those attending the training are at least neutral, if not positive, towards the ethnic group in question (even if the positive appraisal lacks a firm knowledge basis). Pedersen's (1991) broader understanding of culture allows the consideration of ethnic juvenile groups, such as gangs, to be considered as living in their own unique culture.

Hence, cultural sensitivity training offered to professionals and paraprofessionals working with juvenile groups, like gangs, should include a focus on the positive aspects of these groups, such as the role they play in the protection and socialization of juveniles (Miller 1990). When learning about the positive and functional roles of juvenile groups, it is not only important to develop a sensitivity toward juvenile delinquents, but also toward their broader ethnic cultures. Otherwise, the cultural knowledge given in sensitivity training, while holding preexisting negative attitudes, will more than likely be soon forgotten or dismissed (Higgins and King 1981; Stephen 1985).

It is for this reason that Pedersen (1988) suggests that prior to conveying cultural-knowledge training, the audience's existing attitudes should be assessed. Those with preexisting negative views toward a cultural group would particularly benefit from participating in awareness (preknowledge) training that is designed to help increase self-awareness of beliefs and attitudes toward cultural groups, as well as reveal the basis for them (Pedersen 1988). Accordingly, only by first dealing with pejorative cultural attitudes can a person benefit from knowledge about a cultural group's unique values, beliefs, and norms that give meaning to its behavior and motivations.

In general, cultural information or knowledge is critical for developing cultural sensitivity. Cultural knowledge cannot be assumed due to educational training or due to ethnic group membership. Cultural knowledge is also not static, but rather is dynamic and susceptible to changing. Open-mindedness and receptivity to learning different modes of thinking and behaving is a critical part of developing cultural sensitivity (Casas 1986).

Juvenile delinquency interventions will become increasingly culturally sensitive as projects are designed and are staffed by personnel who are sensitive to the cultural values and norms and the broader cultural context of ethnic minorities.

From the preceding discussion, it is clear that cultural knowledge, although essential, is not enough to develop cultural sensitivity. Other important and related considerations are the appreciation and acceptance of the juvenile delinquent's subculture and ethnic culture. Yet another characteristic that has been frequently considered a viable indicator of cultural sensitivity is whether past experience with the ethnic group leads to sensitivity.

Role of Background Experience

A common misconception in community programs is that ethnic group membership automatically leads to cultural sensitivity. A related question arises whether experience in interacting with a targeted ethnic group leads to cultural sensitivity toward it. More specific in the work with juvenile delinquents, is the question—is it important or helpful in facilitating cultural sensitivity to include former juvenile delinquent members in intervention programs?

Former Gang Members and Cultural Sensitivity

Former delinquents are often used in juvenile-focused intervention and prevention programs and have served as outreach workers or as researchers (Moore 1978; Vigil 1988; Jankowski 1991). Should individuals who share common past experiences with these group members be preferred due to their background and experience? Does this facilitate meeting a community intervention program's objective of becoming culturally sensitive?

According to Spergel (1966) the selection of street gang workers is critical due to the complexity and demands of intervention efforts. The specific background characteristics of the worker can facilitate the acceptance of workers by gangs. Spergel suggested that it is not one single characteristic of the street worker that is optimal, but a combination of attributes of which ethnicity is but one. Other desirable background attributes include having lower-class origin, having similar interests, being well trained, and possessing relevant skills and experience (Spergel 1966). The same argument can be made in the realm of juvenile delinquency.

What is important when working effectively with juvenile delinquents is an understanding of, appreciation for, and genuine interest in establishing rapport with them.

Also relevant in his ethnographic study of thirty-five gangs, Jankowski (1991) indicated that gaining access to the various white, black, and Hispanic gangs required displaying several personal attributes, which included demonstrating confidentiality, respect, and a lack of fear. Jankowski noted that his own Hispanic background facilitated gaining access to Hispanic and African-American gangs, but proved to be a barrier to gaining access to white gangs. However, he was eventually able to gain access to white gangs. Jankowski noted that his own background of growing up in Chicago among various cultural gangs sensitized him to gangs in general and to ethnic gangs, in particular. Jankowski's experience suggests that ethnicity and background experience of interacting with gangs facilitate working with gangs.

Both Spergel (1966) and Jankowski (1991) pointed to the importance of individual and background characteristics that improve gang-intervention efforts. Moore's (1978) own experience in working with gangs similarly suggested the need to enhance shared values among community workers and gang members and to emphasize those common objectives held by gang members and workers or researchers (e.g., a reduction in the threat of potential death or injury due to gang violence).

Spergel (1966) emphasized the importance of the worker's background to a gang project. Although Spergel and others have focused on street workers and researchers, community program administrators similarly need to develop cultural knowledge and sensitivity. Unlike street workers, administrative staff are required to develop the program, set policy and guidelines, as well as implement and operate the program. Critical decisions, such as hiring personnel, are made by program administrators. This level of responsibility requires a special sensitivity and knowledge of the targeted population.

Former juvenile delinquents involved in intervention programs can help programs establish rapport with delinquents. Former delinquents' intimate understanding of juvenile delinquents also can help to ensure cultural sensitivity of the program, because former juvenile delinquents can potentially serve to train other program staff to better understand and appreciate delinquent members. However, nondelinquents can be just as effective as former juvenile delinquents in intervention programs. What is important when working effectively with juvenile delinquents is an understanding of, appreciation for, and genuine interest in establishing rapport with them.

Past Experience with Ethnic Groups

Social psychologists have wondered whether contact or experience in interacting with ethnic groups itself reduces prejudice or negative attitudes towards ethnic groups. Are those with previous experience and contact with ethnic minority groups and with juvenile delinquents more culturally sensitive and therefore more effective in working in community intervention programs? As was the case with ethnic group appreciation and cultural knowledge, past contact and experience with ethnic groups or juvenile delinquents does not necessarily lead to cultural sensitivity.

Research on intergroup relations (Sherif and Sherif 1953; Allport 1954; Williams 1947) suggests that intergroup or interethnic contact is not sufficient to develop or improve cultural sensitivity. More recent studies, such as those by Aronson and his colleagues (Aronson and Osherow 1980; Aronson et al. 1978; Blaney et al. 1977), have shown that the interdependence among members of small interethnic groups, where group objectives can be achieved only through cooperative efforts, significantly increases interethnic liking and appreciation. The following are adapted from Stephen's list of conditions that are conducive to the improvement of interethnic relations or to the development of cultural sensitivity. They are based on existing research on intergroup relations, but they are particularly applicable to programs seeking to enhance intercultural cooperation and sensitivity. In accordance with Stephen's (1985) list, the research suggests that cultural sensitivity is enhanced when the relationship between cultural groups is characterized by the following:

- maximized cooperation and minimized competition between groups
- equal social status between groups
- increased similarity of groups on nonstatus dimensions (beliefs, values)
- avoidance of pointing out differences in competence between groups
- positive intergroup outcomes
- strong normative and institutional support for intergroup contact
- increased potential for intergroup contact going beyond the immediate situation
- promotion of individualization of group members
- nonsuperficial contact (e.g., a mutual disclosure of information)
- voluntary contact (noncompulsory)
- correlation of positive effects with the duration of the contact
- contact in a variety of contexts with a variety of minority and nonminority members—alternatively, gang and nongang members
- equal number of group members

Several implications for juvenile delinquent intervention programs can be derived from this list. First, intercultural contact, in and of itself, is not sufficient for promoting cultural sensitivity. This means that both street workers and administrative personnel can have extensive contact with culturally different gang members and still be culturally insensitive.

Second, past contact with delinquents should have included conveying respect, appreciation, and equal social status to gang members.

Third, the list points to important interpersonal conditions that are conducive to the development of sensitivity to specific cultural groups, which has implications for the development of effective cultural sensitivity training programs, such as making a commitment to ongoing contact and treating group members as individuals rather than as groups. Finally, the list can serve to assess the cultural sensitivity of candidates for administrative and staff positions in terms of their background, experience, and training.

Cultural sensitivity may best be reached through applying a tridimensional perspective that emphasizes the importance of self-awareness, cultural knowledge, and interpersonal skill in working effectively with culturally diverse populations.

A Tridimensional Perspective Toward Cultural Sensitivity

The common indicators of cultural knowledge reviewed in this chapter contribute to cultural sensitivity. For example, understanding the verbal and nonverbal forms of juvenile delinquent communication, being sensitive to universal human needs and concepts taught in social science training, gaining cultural knowledge through specialized training, and acquiring experience in interacting with gang members all contribute to developing cultural sensitivity. A tridimensional perspective attempts to synthesize and encompass each of the individual contributors of cultural sensitivity within three general and sequential factors or dimensions: self-awareness, cultural knowledge, and skill.

This is in keeping with Pedersen's (1988) view of multicultural training, which proceeds in a three-stage process moving from awareness, to knowledge, and finally to skill. According to Pedersen, awareness refers to an initial assessment of a person's current attitudes, opinions, and assumptions regarding a particular culture. It reveals or points out assumptions of cultural differences, similarities of behavior, attitudes, and values different from one's own. According to Sue and Sue (1982), awareness training involves acquiring several of the following competencies:

- developing an understanding of one's own cultural values and biases
- becoming aware of how one's cultural values and biases affect ethnic minority clients
- becoming comfortable with cultural differences between one's own values and norms and those of culturally different persons
- knowing your own limitations in working with culturally different persons either because of your own personal biases towards particular ethnic groups or individuals, or because others would rather work with those of the culture; developing a sensitivity and understanding for situations when working with a culturally different person is not advisable due to personal biases, preferences due to ethnic identity, or other reasons.

Knowledge is considered the beginning of true cultural understanding. It consists of facts about a culture's history, social position, and the culture's values, norms, and beliefs. According to Sue and Sue (1982), cultural knowledge training for counselors should offer several competencies that are geared specifically for working with multicultural persons. They suggest the following four things:

1. Cultural knowledge training should offer a good understanding of the sociopolitical system in the United States and of its past and present treatment of ethnic minorities.

2. Knowledge training should include specific information about the culture itself—about its salient cultural values, beliefs, practices, and norms. This information should also describe the heterogeneity found in cultural groups, including describing the role of assimilation and acculturation in altering cultural characteristics.

3. Knowledge training should develop an acute understanding of those intervention strategies being considered for implementation and their

appropriateness in light of knowledge of the culture, including the role of language.

4. Cultural knowledge training should include information about institutional barriers to accessing services and intervention efforts. Common institutional barriers include: language, geographic access, a perceived lack of confidentiality, and mistrust due to cultural ignorance.

Being skilled refers to the stage at which one is able to use what one learns about oneself and about a particular cultural group and being able to apply this knowledge to have effective interpersonal contact with members of the ethnic group. Sue and Sue (1982) provide guidance to develop the following three relevant skill competencies:

1. Cultural knowledge previously gained needs to be used to develop a broad range of verbal and nonverbal responses that are acceptable, appropriate, and sensitive to the values and norms of ethnic minorities.

2. Cultural skill requires being able to receive from culturally different groups both verbal and nonverbal communication appropriately and to interpret it accurately.

3. Skill development requires implementing intervention efforts in a respectful way that is mindful of the cultural context.

An additional requirement to intercultural skill development is having actual interaction and meaningful contact with minority group members. It is the actual contact with culturally different groups that puts cultural awareness and knowledge to the test. Interaction allows behavioral and verbal repertoires that are respectful of cultural beliefs, norms, and values to emerge.

Taken altogether, the tridimensional components of cultural awareness, knowledge, and skill are comprehensive and dynamic. They are dynamic because competencies in each change as the culture changes. According to Pedersen (1988), many cultural sensitivity training programs traditionally emphasize one component over another. For example, knowledge about a cultural group, by itself, does not mean a counselor or community worker knows how to apply this knowledge to a work setting. Similarly, overemphasis on awareness can lead to guilt and self-consciousness due to awareness of false assumptions and stereotypes regarding a cultural group. At the same time, a premature emphasis on skill development, without the necessary awareness or knowledge of a particular cultural group, can lead to the blind or inappropriate development of verbal and nonverbal behavioral patterns.

Within the tridimensional perspective, knowledge—whether gained through self-awareness, from attending training programs, or from interpersonal interaction with cultural members—is a central part of developing cultural sensitivity. With ethnic juvenile delinquents, the worker needs to integrate this universal knowledge, but also to combine it with the unique social and cultural, experiences of juvenile delinquents.

The Sociocultural Context of Delinquents

Being sensitive to ethnic delinquents requires recognizing that universal human needs apply to juvenile delinquents as well as to nondelinquents—whether they are physical, psychological, or social needs. Unfortunately, the current law enforcement approach in dealing with delinquency and violence emphasizes an elimination of delinquent groups altogether, such as gangs (California State Task Force Report included in Goldstein 1991). Delinquents are viewed as enemies not fit for a civilized society. This view hides the fact that delinquent groups often have a benign role in the socialization of juvenile delinquents (Miller 1990) and can form part of a member's social support system.

Sensitivity to ethnic delinquents requires adopting a more complex view of juvenile delinquents. They live in social realms that require them to adopt multiple social roles, including the role as a delinquent. But juvenile delinquents assume other roles as well, such as son/daughter, father/mother, employee, and member of a cultural group. These multiple roles promote the development of multiple identities. Delinquency intervention workers need to be sensitive to the multiple identities and subcultures that juvenile delinquents have and belong to—not just the juvenile's identity as a delinquent.

To understand multicultural identities, it may be helpful to examine identities at three general levels: the international level, the ethnic level, and the social role level (Pedersen 1988). At the international level, delinquents and nondelinquents can identify with being an "American" or with being some other nationality (e.g., Jamaican citizen or Mexican citizen). At the ethnic level, juvenile delinquents, like others, may strongly identify with a particular ethnic group, such as Chicano/Mexican, African American, Jamaican, Puerto Rican, Vietnamese, Mong (Cambodian), Chinese, Irish, Italian, or even a combination of two or more. At the social role level, a juvenile delinquent often has a strong identity with being a delinquent. However, the social role level can also include strong identities that are associated with one's gender, occupation, or role within the family.

Not only do juvenile delinquents have multiple identities, but the importance of each varies from individual to individual. The importance of these identities may be related to the centrality and organizational position held within the delinquency subculture. Those working with delinquents need to be attuned to the individual differences inherent in juvenile delinquents, which would reveal the importance of different roles and identities. The awareness of one's assumptions and stereotypes regarding delinquents needs to be constantly checked and monitored, as do those regarding the cultural group.

Finally, intervention programs need to be tied closely to those identities held by delinquents that are associated with class-bound values (Sue 1989) and with multiple oppressions (a combination of being poor, a member of an ethnic-minority group, and being a delinquent) (Reynolds and Pope 1991). The combined influences of these characteristics is believed to form an individual's self-concept and influence the individual's behavior and those of others toward the individual.

Goldstein and Glick (1987) proposed a "prescriptive" approach to juvenile delinquency prevention and intervention efforts at the individual, group, community, and state levels. The prescriptive approach "... recognizes that different juveniles will be responsive to different change methods." This approach asks which types of juveniles meeting with which types of change agents for which types of interventions will yield optimal outcomes (Goldstein and Glick 1987).

The prescriptive approach recognizes the social, psychological, and cultural diversity of gang members. Recognizing the important role of culture in juvenile delinquent social groups, especially in gang participation, Goldstein (1991) states:

> [Gang members] bring to their gang participation diverse and often culture-specific motivations, perceptions, behaviors, and beliefs. The meaning of aggression; the perception of gang as family; the gang as an arena for acquiring status, honor or "rep"; the gang's duration, cohesiveness, and typical and atypical legal and illegal pursuits; its place in the community—these features and many more are substantially shaped by cultural traditions and mores.

A multidimensional approach to ensure cultural sensitivity in juvenile delinquency intervention efforts needs to adopt a prescriptive approach, which recognizes the multiple identities of delinquent members and the salience of culture within them. Table 1 points to the main developmental stages for intervention programs and to those groups involved in each of them.

It is suggested that cultural sensitivity should not be relegated to simply a concern of street workers, but the need for cultural sensitivity should be recognized at all program levels. It is equally important for street workers to be culturally sensitive as it is for program sponsors, program administrators, and evaluators. The major program stakeholders need to develop a minimal level of awareness of their own assumptions, knowledge of cultural groups, and skill at relating to cultural groups—whether they interact with gang members directly or not.

Table 1
Gang Intervention Program Stages and Stakeholders

Program Stages	Stakeholders
Program Objectives	Sponsoring Organization Administrative Staff
Program Design	Sponsoring Organization Administrative Staff
Program Implementation	Administrative Staff Street Workers Support Staff
Program Evaluation	Administrative Staff Evaluators

Achieving cultural sensitivity at each organizational stage would assist program sponsors to promote more culturally responsive programs. Administrators would also be able to appreciate and understand the role of culture in delinquent juveniles' motivation and behavior and thus be more in tune with those who work directly with juvenile delinquents. Finally, cultural sensitivity training for those working directly with juvenile delinquents (e.g., street workers) will help them place delinquent and antisocial activities within a sociocultural context. They will understand that delinquent activity, disruptive as it may be at times, forms part of only one level of involvement for juvenile delinquents, which is tied to a single social identity and role.

Developing culturally sensitive gang intervention programs requires both a program commitment and an individual commitment to gain cultural understanding and intercultural skills. The tridimensional perspective points to the three main components that lead to cultural sensitivity (self-awareness, cultural knowledge, and intercultural skills) and to their sequence of development. Developing cultural sensitivity requires a better understanding and appreciation of the many sociocultural and individual characteristics associated with ethnic juvenile delinquents and their environment. Within this framework, delinquents cannot be seen as solely responsible for the increased violence and delinquency in communities. A broader *and* deeper understanding of the unmet, but basic physical, social, and psychological needs of ethnic communities is needed, which may better point to true etiological factors responsible for the increase in participation in juvenile delinquency and violence throughout the United States.

Conclusion

Clearly, cultural minorities are disproportionately being affected by delinquency, both as victims and delinquents. Although knowledge is growing on the characteristics associated with successful delinquency intervention and prevention programs (Clements 1988), very few address the role of culture in program development and implementation. Cultural sensitivity has been discussed in social science literature, but has not been well defined. A review of commonly used indicators or characteristics of cultural sensitivity (e.g., language and cultural knowledge) reveals short-comings inherent in using each as a single indicator of cultural sensitivity.

A tridimensional perspective of cultural sensitivity (Pedersen 1988) views self-awareness, cultural knowledge, and interpersonal skill development as critical in developing cultural sensitivity within community-based intervention programs. It is important that cultural sensitivity not be considered relevant to only outreach or street workers, but that it also be considered important at all organizational levels, including program sponsors, administrators, and outreach workers.

Promoting, developing, or maintaining cultural sensitivity in the current conservative ethnocentric zeitgeist is a formidable challenge for intervention programs to achieve. However, the success of any prevention or intervention program requires an acute understanding and appreciation of delinquency groups—of their functional roles for individual members and even for communities, because delinquency can serve to signal symptoms of the depressed social and economic conditions that exist within mostly ethnic communities. Therefore, a culturally sensitive view of ethnic minority juvenile delinquents requires that members not be viewed apart from a basic psychological and sociocultural perspective that acknowledges the basic physical, psychological, and social needs common to all humans—including juvenile delinquents.

Being culturally sensitive to one ethnic group does not necessarily mean being culturally sensitive or knowledgeable about any other ethnic group. Although there may be some similarities across some cultural groups, clearly there are many differences that need to be understood (Atkinson, Morten, and Sue 1989; Sue 1981; Pedersen 1988). Failing to understand the unique meaning of languages, gestures, and behavior as exhibited by a particular group can easily lead to miscommunications and misunderstandings. For example, to an African-American counselor, an Asian-American client's quiet and shy behavior may be interpreted as being part of his or her personality, while it may actually be an exercise of a culturally appropriate form of deference to authority (Sue 1989).

It is hoped that the views presented in this chapter will spur interest, debate, and research on this very critical topic, which will lead to an even better understanding of cultural sensitivity and its effect on ethnic members targeted by community programs. However, even apart from cultural considerations, research clearly points to the importance of early prevention and intervention efforts to address delinquency. Clements (1988) suggests that the junior-high or middle-school age adolescent is one of the most important age groups to target for delinquency prevention and intervention programs. These programs, like programs for younger and older juveniles, need to seriously consider the extent to which they are culturally relevant and sensitive to the juveniles targeted.

References

Allport, G. W. 1954. *The nature of prejudice.* Cambridge, Mass.: Addison-Wesley.

Aronson, E., and N. Osherow. 1980. Cooperation, prosocial behavior, and academic performance: Experiments in the desegregated classroom. In *Applied Social Psychology Annual,* ed. L. Bickman. Beverly Hills, Calif.: Sage.

Aronson, E., et al. 1978. *The jigsaw classroom.* Beverly Hills, Calif.: Sage.

Atkinson, D. R., G. Morten, and D. W. Sue. 1989 *Counseling American minorities: A cross cultural perspective* (3d ed). Dubuque, Iowa: Wm. C. Brown Publishers.

Best, D. L., et al. 1975. The modification of racial bias in preschool children. *Journal of Experimental Child Psychology,* 20:193-205.

Blake, T. A. 1987. The meaning of culturally appropriate treatment for the Hispanic adolescent. In *Alcohol Use and Abuse among Hispanic Adolescents,* ed. M. Singer, L. Davidson and F. Yalin. Hartford, Conn.: Hispanic Health Council.

Blaney, N., et al. 1977. Interdependence in the classroom: A field study. *Journal of Educational Psychology* 69:121-28.

Casas, J. M. 1985. The status of racial- and ethnic-minority counseling: A training perspective. In *Handbook of Cross-cultural Counseling and Therapy,* ed. P. Pedersen. (267-74). Westport, Conn.: Greenwood.

——. 1986. Making effective use of research to impact the training of culturally sensitive mental health workers. In *Mental Health Research and Practice in Minority Communities: Development of Culturally Sensitive Training Programs,* ed. M. R. Miranda and H. H. L. Kitano. Rockville, Md.: National Institute of Mental Health.

Cialdini, R. B., R. E. Petty, and J. T. Cacioppo. 1981. Attitude and attitude change. *Annual Review of Psychology* 32:357-404.

Clements, C. 1988. Delinquency prevention and treatment: A community-centered perspective. *Criminal Justice and Behavior* 15:286-305.

Dillard, J. M. 1982. *Multicultural counseling: Toward ethnic and cultural relevance in human encounters.* Chicago: Nelson-Hall.

Flores, J. L. 1978. The utilization of a community mental health service by Mexican-Americans. *International Journal of Social Psychiatry* 24:271-75.

Genelin, M., and B. Coplen. 1989. *Los Angeles street gangs.* Report and Recommendations of the Countywide Criminal Justice Coordination Committee Interagency Gang Task Force, Los Angeles.

Gim, R. H., D. R. Atkinson, and S. J. Kim. 1991. Asian-American acculturation, counselor ethnicity and cultural sensitivity, and ratings of counselors. *Journal of Counseling Psychology* 38(1): 57-62.

Glick, R., and J. Moore. 1990. *Drugs in Hispanic communities.* New Brunswick, N.J.: Rutgers University Press.

Goldstein, A. P. 1991. *Delinquent gangs: A psychological perspective.* Champaign, Ill.: Research Press.

Goldstein, A. P., and B. Glick. 1987. *Aggression replacement training: A comprehensive intervention for aggressive youth.* Champaign, Ill.: Research Press.

Greenberg, H., J. Pierson, and S. Sherman. 1957. The effects of single-session education techniques on prejudiced attitudes. *Journal of Educational Sociology* 31:82-86.

Grove, C. L. 1976. *Communications across cultures.* Washington, D.C.: National Education Association.

Higgins, E. T., and G. King. 1981. Accessibility of social constructs: Information processing consequences of individual and contextual variability. In *Personality, Cognition and Social Interaction,* ed. N. Cantor and J. F. Kihlstrom. Hillsdale, N.J.: Erlbaum.

Hindelang, M. J., T. Hirschi, and J. Weis. 1991. Correlates of delinquency: The illusion of discrepancy between self-report and official measures. In *Juvenile Delinquency: Classic and Contemporary Readings,* ed. W. E. Thompson and J. E. Bynum. Boston: Allyn and Bacon.

Huff, C. R. 1990. Introduction: Two generations of gang research. In *Gangs in America,* ed. C. R. Huff. Newbury Park, Calif.: Sage Publications.

Jankowski, M. S. 1991. *Islands in the street: Gangs and American urban society.* Berkeley, Calif.: University of California Press.

Jenkins, A. H. 1985. Attending to self-activity in the Afro-American client. *Psychotherapy* 22:335-41.

Leong, F. T. L., and H. H. W. Kim. 1991. Going beyond cultural sensitivity on the road to multiculturalism: Using the intercultural sensitizer as a counselor training tool. *Journal of Counseling and Development* 70(1): 112-18.

Leong, F. T. 1986. Counseling and psychotherapy with Asian-Americans: Review of the literature. *Journal of Counseling Psychology* 33:196-206.

Lessing, E. E., and C. C. Clarke. 1976. An attempt to reduce ethnic prejudice and assess its correlates in a junior high school sample. *Educational Research Quarterly* 1:3-16.

McGuire, W. J. 1960. Direct and indirect persuasive effects of dissonance-producing messages. *Journal of Abnormal Social Psychology* 60:354-58.

——. 1985. Attitudes and attitude change. In *Handbook of Social Psychology* 2d ed. G. Lindsey and E. Aronson. New York: Random House.

Miller, W. B. 1974. American youth gangs: Past and present. In *Current Perspectives on Criminal Behavior,* ed. A. Blumberg. New York: Knopf.

——. 1990. Why the United States has failed to solve its youth gang problem. In *Gangs in America,* ed. C. R. Huff. Newbury Park, Calif.: Sage Publications.

Mirande, A. 1987 *Gringo justice.* Notre Dame, Ind.: University of Notre Dame Press.

Moore, J. 1978. Homeboys: *Gangs, drugs and prison in the barrios of Los Angeles.* Philadelphia: Temple University Press.

Needle, J. A., and W. V. Stapleton. 1982. Police handling of youth gangs. Washington, D.C.: National Juvenile Justice Assessment Center.

Nyamathi, A., and D. M. Shin. 1990. Designing a culturally sensitive AIDS educational program for Black and Hispanic women of childbearing age. NACOGS Clinical Issue in Prenatal Women's Health Nursing.

Parker, W. M., N. M. Valley, and C. A. Geary. 1986. Acquiring cultural knowledge for counselors in training: A multifaceted approach. *Counselor Education Supervision* 26(1): 61-71.

Pedersen, P. 1988. *A handbook for developing multicultural awareness.* Alexandria, Va.: American Association for Counseling and Development.

——. 1991. Multiculturalism as a generic approach to counseling. *Journal of Counseling and Development* 70(1): 6-12.

Pomales, J., C. D. Clairborn, and T. D. LaFromboise. 1986. Effects of black students' racial identity on perceptions of white counselors varying in cultural sensitivity. *Journal of Counseling Psychology* 33(1): 57-61.

Ponterotto, J. G., and J. M. Casas. 1987. In search of multicultural competence within counselor education programs. *Journal of Counseling and Development* 65(8): 430-34.

Reynolds, A. L., and Pope, R. L. 1991. The complexities of diversity: exploring multiple oppressions. *Journal of Counseling and Development* 70:174-180.

Rogler, L. H. 1989 The meaning of culturally sensitive research in mental health. *American Journal of Psychiatry* 146(3): 296-303.

Rogler, L. H., et al. 1987. What do culturally sensitive mental health services mean? The case of Hispanics. *American Psychologist* 42(6): 565-70.

Romano, D. 1973. The anthropology and sociology of the Mexican Americans: The distortion of Mexican-American history. In *Voices: Readings from El Grito, A Journal of Contemporary Mexican-American Thought*, ed. D. Romano. Berkeley, Calif.: Quinto Sol Publications.

Seijo, R., H. Gomez, and J. Freidenberg. 1991. Language as a communication barrier in medical care for Hispanic patients. *Hispanic Journal of Behavioral Science* 13(4): 363-76.

Sherif, M., and C. W. Sherif. 1953. *Groups in harmony and tension.* New York: Harper and Row.

Slavin, R., and N. A. Madden. 1979. School practices that improve race relations. *American Educational Research Journal* 16(2): 169-80.

Soriano, F. I. 1993. Cultural sensitivity and gang intervention. In *The Gang Intervention Handbook*, eds. A. P. Goldstein and C. R. Huff. Champaign, Ill.: Research Press.

——. In press. The Latino perspective: A sociocultural portrait. In *Managing multiculturalism in substance abuse services,* ed. J. V. Gordon. Newbury Park, Calif.: Sage Publications.

Soriano, F. I., and M. R. De La Rosa. 1990. Cocaine use and criminal activities among Hispanic juvenile delinquents in Florida. In *Drugs in His-*

panic communities, ed. R. Glick and J. Moore. New Brunswick, N.J.: Rutgers University Press.

Speight, S. L., et al. 1991. A redefinition of multicultural counseling. *Journal of Counseling and Development* 70(1): 29-36.

Spergel, I. 1966. *Street gang work: Theory and practice.* Reading, Mass.: Addison-Wesley Publishing Company, Inc.

Spergel, I. A., et al. 1989. *Survey of youth gang problems and programs in 45 cities and 6 states.* Washington, D.C.: Office of Juvenile Justice and Delinquency Prevention.

———. 1990. *Youth gangs: Problem and response; Stage 1: Assessment.* Washington, D.C.: Office of Juvenile Justice and Delinquency Prevention.

Staples and A. Mirande. 1980. Racial and cultural variations among American families: A decennial review of the literature on minority families. *Journal of Marriage and the Family* 40(4): 157-73.

Stephen, W. G. 1985. Intergroup relations. In *Handbook of Social Psychology* (Volume II), ed. G. Lindzey and E. Aronson. New York: Random House.

Sue, D. W. 1981. Counseling the culturally different: Theory and practice. New York: Wiley Press.

———. 1989. Ethnic identity: The impact of two cultures on the psychological development of Asians in America. In *Counseling American Minorities: A Cross Cultural Perspective,* ed. D. R. Atkinson, G. Morten, and D. W. Sue. Dubuque, Iowa: Wm. C. Brown Publishers.

Sue, D. W., and S. Sue. 1977. Barriers to effective cross-cultural counseling. *Journal of Counseling Psychology* 24(5): 420-29.

———. 1982. Cross-cultural counseling competencies. *The Counseling Psychologist* 19(2): 45-52.

———. 1985. Asian-Americans and Pacific Islanders. In *Handbook of Cross-cultural Counseling and Therapy,* ed. P. Pedersen. Westport, Conn.: Greenwood.

Sue, S. 1988. Psychotherapeutic services for ethnic minorities: Two decades of research findings. *American Psychologist* 43(4): 301-08.

Sue, S., et al. 1976. Conceptions of mental illness among Asian and Caucasian American students. *Psychological Reports* 38: 703-08.

Thrasher, F. M. 1963. *The gang: A study of 13 gangs in Chicago.* Chicago: The University of Chicago Press.

Trimble, J. E., and T. LaFromboise. 1985. American Indian and the counseling process: Culture, adaptation, and style. In *Handbook of Cross-cultural Counseling and Therapy,* ed. P. Pedersen. Westport, Conn.: Greenwood.

Trojanowicz, R. C., and M. Morash. 1987. *Juvenile delinquency: Concepts and control.* Englewood Cliffs, N.J.: Prentice-Hall, Inc.

Vigil, J. D. 1988. *Barrio gangs: Street life and identity in southern California.* Austin: University of Texas Press.

Wade, P., and B. L. Bernstein. 1991. Culture sensitivity training and counselor's race: Effects on black female clients' perceptions and attrition. *Journal of Counseling Psychology* 38(1): 9-15.

Williams, R. M. 1947. The reduction of intergroup tensions: A survey of research on problems of ethnic, racial and religious group relations. New York: Social Science Research Council, Bulletin 57.2

14

Understanding the Public-Private Partnership: The Administrator's Role

Kevin C. Walsh

As the juvenile justice system has evolved and changed its philosophical approach to the development of services and programs, so have the nonprofit organizations that provide the treatment programs. The Berkshire Farm Center and Services for Youth in Canaan, New York, is one example of a nonprofit organization that has adapted to the changing requirements of government juvenile justice agencies.

Prior to the 1960s, Berkshire Farm was a long-term residential program where juveniles received individual counseling in a supportive, nurturing environment. It was designed to teach appropriate behavior. This experience helped juveniles learn to function positively when they returned to their communities. Until recently, however, work with families in the community and other noninstitutional services were practically nonexistent.

As the identified needs of the juvenile system began to change, the organization recognized it would need to expand its services and change its focus. For example, work with families in community settings was recognized as a needed service, and was, therefore, developed.

Along with this recognition came a change in the development of the role of nonprofit organizations. Beginning in 1964, Berkshire Farm Center initiated an extensive Community Services Program. This program served not only boys returning to their communities from the residential center, but it also provided counseling services to each boy's family throughout the period the boy was at the program. Since this initial effort, Berkshire Farm has opened group and foster homes in the 1970s, prevention and nonsecure detention programs in the 1980s, and home-based intense supervision programs and independent living programs in the 1990s.

Historically, nonprofit organizations have been engaged in direct service activities that provide a network of program interventions for juvenile delinquents, and they have had an active relationship with federal, state, and local governments.

Kevin C. Walsh is associate director of Cottage Services at Berkshire Farm Center and Services for Youth in Canaan, New York.

Over time, as the demand for new services emerged, governments began to depend on nonprofit, private organizations to deliver services for several reasons. Primarily, the government did not have the same level of expertise and skill (as nonprofit organizations) to implement and support the new treatment approaches and services. According to Kramer (1979), nonprofit organizations have more expertise and better trained staff, more up-to-date facilities, and the ability to adapt to new demands. These nonprofit organizations also were not plagued by the difficulties associated with large bureaucracies.

Administrators of government-run juvenile justice agencies need to understand the system within which nonprofit organizations operate. Administrators of nonprofit organizations must identify where and how the organization interacts with the larger environment and develop a strategy to establish a relationship with these identified areas.

Administrator's Role: An Overview

Administrators must develop and sustain the organization's ability to receive appropriate referrals (clients), recruit and train competent staff to implement services, and generate a consistent level of revenue. This latter task is predominantly accomplished through contracts with government agencies. Some revenue is obtained through individual grants and private fundraising; however, these are often inconsistent and incapable of sustaining program operations. Grants and private fundraising can be used for specific tasks or projects, and initiating activities that eventually will be supported by government contracts.

Administrators must be able to identify, acknowledge, and deal with the community's demands, while at the same time remain committed to the program's treatment goals and objectives.

Administrators also have a public relations role. Juvenile-treatment organizations often encounter difficulties with the local community as a result of the juveniles in their care. It is not uncommon for juveniles to periodically run away from an institution and become involved in criminal activity, such as breaking and entering into homes, stealing cars, or committing vandalism. Obviously, members of the community, especially those who have been victimized, are upset and angry.

Often the community will demand restitution, blame the organization for the problem, and insist that the program become more secure to prevent further escapes. This type of community interaction creates considerable stress on an organization.

Administrators must be able to identify, acknowledge, and deal with the community's demands, while at the same time remain committed to the program's treatment goals and objectives. This delicate balance requires a patient, skillful interaction that demonstrates an appropriate level of empathy, yet does not, in an eagerness to resolve the concerns, support inappropriate and emotional reactions. Administrators must understand the community's concerns and work collaboratively to achieve a mutually acceptable resolution. Through this process the administrator affects the needed goal of returning the organization to a state of equilibrium.

Most nonprofit organizations rely on professional staff to implement their programs. However, professional staff usually value their autonomy and relate most comfortably with colleagues within their own discipline. In addition, staff often are worried that their discipline's authority is diminished when they are required to work collaboratively with other treatment areas.

That was one reason why, for example, Berkshire Farm's program development effort, which was designed to meet its juveniles' growing substance abuse treatment needs, was resisted. Although each department and professional discipline overtly acknowledged the importance of the new service, boundary issues and different priorities impeded the program's implementation. Clinical staff felt their individual and group therapy was the most important intervention, education staff viewed the academic needs of the delinquent as predominant, and the recreation staff saw their activities as the most effective in helping the delinquents to become more self-directed. The program's administrator had to get all these disparate parts together into a collaborative process. As an organization that values professionalism, Berkshire Farm wanted to support each discipline's desire for autonomy, while at the same time it wanted to recognize the need to integrate all of the efforts to maximize the treatment program.

Making It Work

Domestic policies formulated to meet identified needs are the result of a political process influenced by personal values and beliefs. Nonetheless, the public expects that this eventual operating policy will "solve" a problem and address ongoing concerns in the community. Emerging philosophies of juvenile delinquency treatment, the anger and fear generated by juvenile delinquents, and the public's demands for a "quick fix" to a complex problem all add to the challenges administrators face.

The Administrator's Role: Developing and Monitoring

Administrators of nonprofit organizations must develop and monitor their organizations. To be successful, administrators must continuously develop certain qualities, such as:

- being comfortable delegating authority and allowing staff to make decisions
- being focused when a problem has no clear or immediate solution
- employing flexibility in the problem-solving process

Administrators must be flexible enough to adapt to the variety of values and philosophies that shape the government's approach to problem solving. In the case of juvenile delinquency, these influences are almost always in flux. Recently, this aspect of the administrator's role has become more important for two reasons. First, juveniles are clearly more violent and becoming involved in more serious, aggressive activities. Second, emphasis on prevention and diversion designed to treat juveniles in the community has increased the opportunities for interaction between delinquent juveniles and community members. Juvenile delinquents are no longer treated exclusively in isolated settings. One of the most important challenges administrators face is to remain knowledgeable about these influences and how they affect juvenile justice.

Keeping Informed

One necessary task for the administrator is to remain informed about the latest theories of delinquency and state-of-the-art techniques and interventions. For example, historically, treatment plans for juvenile delinquents were designed as a rehabilitative process that evolved from a diagnostic assessment by clinical personnel. Treatment programs sought to remediate identified problems and work through underlying emotional conflicts affecting the delinquent's functioning.

Unfortunately, even when some of these underlying conditions were assuaged, the juveniles continued to experience problems. Over time it became clear that even when this intervention was successful, delinquents still needed skills and problem-solving abilities to function successfully in the community.

Consequently, an additional "habilitative" component was added to treatment plans to enhance the juvenile delinquent's prognosis and achieve the desired goal. Therefore, group counseling programs focusing on social skills, moral reasoning, problem solving, and anger control training were added to the services.

Understanding the Workplace

Administrators also need to understand the conditions within the organization, the larger environment within which it operates, and any influences impinging upon its goals. They must be able to respond to changing public perceptions, which also affect the activities of their organization. For example, as a result of the changing belief regarding the effectiveness of placing juvenile delinquents in institutional settings and growing support to keep the juveniles in community settings, administrators have had to become more community based and examine how programs can prevent future problems from occurring. Because of a trend toward twelve-month placements, administrators must now develop treatment programs that fit within the more limited time frames.

Qualities of the Administrator

Some of the key qualities required in a successful administrator is being able to take risks, to integrate services, to adapt leadership styles to various situations, and to be self-aware.

Taking Risks

Successful administrators should have the confidence and competence to take risks when developing programs. Administrators must demonstrate that they are in control, yet still able to explore innovative and creative options. Administrators should know how to identify the needs of juvenile delinquents, and how to organize programs and direct staff to create effective programs and services. This is accomplished by committing to responsible planning and following agency standards. Administrators should never take risks on the basis of personal goals, needs, or any other self-serving interests. Ideas or fads that sound good but have no realistic basis on which to evaluate potential merit must be avoided.

On the other hand, administrators cannot be so cautious that the only method to respond to a concern or a need to change is to follow the "way it's always been done." In a changing world, such a strategy inevitably brings the organization's downfall.

Despite the difficulties associated with risk taking, it is required of the administrator. Risks associated with any new venture and program planning for juvenile delinquents are intense. Administrators also must be comfortable dealing with ambiguities. The issues encountered when working with juveniles often have many potential solutions, all of which seem to have some right part of the solution. Bringing together these variables is an ongoing challenge for administrators, who must integrate many factors and build consensus when developing and implementing new services.

Integrating Services

Recent research about the causes of juvenile delinquency highlight the fact that juveniles are the products of a complex interrelationship of emotional, social, and psychological variables. Their personality profiles and level of functioning are characterized by social and academic deficiencies, emotional conflicts, and psychological development evolving from a history of abuse and neglect. The accumulative effect of these variables, combined with a lack of social skills to deal with their stress, leaves delinquents with no viable method to sustain positive functioning in the community.

In addition, most juvenile delinquents compound their problems by using drugs and alcohol. Effective intervention requires the coordination and integration of different services to deal with these complex problems. To accomplish this level of integration, administrators of nonprofit agencies must address issues on two levels: internal concerns within the organization itself and external concerns associated with regulatory bodies interacting with the agency.

Adapting Leadership Styles

Administrators assume responsibility for the collaboration and integration of their programs, services, and resources. Administrators often encounter resistance from individual services when they attempt to manage interdisciplinary team approaches. One of the skills administrators need to build consensus and facilitate team building is to adapt their leadership styles to the situation.

At times, administrators must be flexible and nondirective; while at other times they may need to be authoritative. For example, when developing policies and procedures for a program service, an administrator might solicit ideas from staff, discuss all recommendations, and then incorporate the suggestions into a final product. Providing staff the opportunity to participate in the process gives staff members a sense of ownership and usually makes them more supportive and comfortable with the new policies and procedures.

Sometimes, however, an administrator's role might be completely different. In a situation where a particular contractual arrangement with a regulatory body requires paperwork responsibilities, the administrator might need to be more directive and authoritative. For example, if some staff feel that these requirements are ridiculous and resist this obligation, an administrator might have to take a more direct, authoritative role.

Being Self-aware

Administrators must be self-aware. This is important so that personal beliefs and values, either overtly or covertly, do not unduly influence the coordination of the team effort in the integration process. Administrators must remember that they are directing a total team approach. For example, an administrator with a social work background must not feel that coordinating and integrating services means focusing on casework intervention and structuring other services as supports.

In an integrated approach, all disciplines work together. There is no hierarchical status assigned to any particular intervention. These are the types of boundary issues that are important for administrators to recognize and resolve in their role as integrators. If an administrator is unable to achieve this level of functioning, existing services and any additional needed new services will continue to be administered departmentally.

External Obstacles to Service Integration

In addition to internal obstacles, administrators also must address external obstacles. Often there are bureaucratic regulations and guidelines that can impede the process. It is not uncommon to encounter political influences, bureaucratic inertia, and regulatory inconsistencies when working with government bureaucracies.

For example, in an effort to develop a needed service, Berkshire Farm planned to operate an outpatient substance abuse program for its juveniles. Research and evaluation documented this need, so it was seen as an important service to be integrated into existing programming. Having identified the program need, the administrator then contracted with a funding source, coordinated the organization's resources, developed the program structure, and reached an agreement regarding needed licensing and certification with the appropriate state agencies. The New York State Office of Alcohol and Substance Abuse Service, the state regulatory agency, supported the concept, agreed to provide needed funding, and collaboratively worked out all required contractual arrangements with the organization.

Just as the state agency was about to issue a final certificate, a decision by the federal government almost ended the whole process. For an unrelated reason, the federal agency, Health Care Financing Administration, decided to reclassify all substance abuse programs using medical funds to Institutions for Mental Diseases. Their rationale was that since chemical dependency has a DSM-III diagnosis, the programs dealing with it should be classified with other mental diseases. While this seemed logical, with this reclassification, any one particular program could only receive one medicaid rate. Berkshire Farm already received a small medicaid rate based on the daily routine medical services it provided its clients, and this rate could not support the funding required for the new program. The clinical rate which had been negotiated did provide sufficient funding; however, because it was a second medicaid rate for the program, the new classification would not be allowed. With this one bureaucratic change, the program was jeopardized. To respond to this new development, the administrator initiated a problem-solving process with both the state and federal agencies. It was necessary to address the classification change and its implications on the program. Through negotiation, the administrator resolved the problem and ultimately received the needed support to open the new program.

Administrators must not lose vision or lack fortitude when dealing with inevitable obstructions and delays.

Unfortunately, this type of problem is not uncommon. It is important to be aware that the public sector bureaucracy presents these difficulties, and the administrator must be ready to respond accordingly. An administrator must be aware of this reality and not be overwhelmed or incapacitated when it arises. Problems, seen as challenges, can be resolved with administrative skills and a commitment to advocacy. These qualities are extremely important for all private sector administrators to acquire. In addition, there is a need to be persistent and patient, and not see concerns and challenges as so overwhelming that no solutions may be found. Administrators must not lose vision or lack fortitude when dealing with inevitable obstructions and delays. Persistence and commitment are required when meeting the need to integrate services and address complex problems.

Berkshire Farm Case Study

The following case study describes the activities implemented by an administrator of a program developed at Berkshire Farm Center. The case illustrates the many steps that the administrator had to follow and highlights skills and tasks required to successfully negotiate the private-public partnership.

Creating the Vision

As the theoretical analysis of the problems, causes, and solutions of juvenile delinquency evolved, studies indicated that an important aspect of a treatment program should include hands-on activities. Experiential learning postulates that juveniles learn more efficiently and incorporate more effectively into their personality structure values and skills taught in an experiential, interactive process. One way to incorporate this learning theory while teaching functional skills needed by the delinquent is to develop a work component in a treatment program.

Such a work program would provide job opportunities, as well as an opportunity to learn needed values and attitudes to maintain a job. Through participation in this work experience, the delinquent would develop feelings of responsibility, enhance self-esteem, learn important life skills, and have an opportunity to work with positive role models. Research has demonstrated that most delinquents have not been exposed to positive role models. Therefore, actually seeing an adult constructively handle everyday responsibilities, negotiate problems, and fulfill obligations, provides an important intervention in the overall treatment process.

The administrator developed a strategy to put this concept into operation. In this process, the administrator ensured the organization would maintain a basic level of revenue and referrals. The administrator posited that if the organization were able to provide a work program based on an experiential learning process, it would be able to continue to receive referrals for this service and generate fees that would ensure a continued source of revenue.

Implementing the Plan

Having identified the need, the next challenge was to implement the plan. This consisted of developing work sites and getting needed support and collaboration from the business community. Although it is easy to find a spirit of cooperation when discussing the benefits of such programs and soliciting resources, actually developing and sustaining these needed resources is often more difficult.

Juvenile delinquents are generally not good employees. Rarely do they possess the responsibility, motivation, or commitment needed to function appropriately in a job. They often resort to impulsive or antagonistic behavior when confronted with problems. It is not unusual for juvenile delinquents to quit their jobs when angry, or fight with coworkers if they feel they have not been treated respectfully.

In addition, depending on the nature of the work site, job placements often present opportunities to steal either money or goods. Given the lack of appropriate values, juvenile delinquents present a high risk. These potential problems, however, do not diminish the need to develop the services.

Administrators, therefore, should identify work sites in the community that would be suitable to meet the needs of the program and could be integrated into treatment planning. As a nonprofit organization, providing a service within a particular community, Berkshire Farm had a long history of maintaining good community relationships. The organization's management had been active in the local Rotary and other business associations. Out of this involvement, as well as through education and negotiation by the program administrator, the administrator obtained a commitment to provide the needed work opportunities in the community.

Restructuring the Organization

Once this step had been accomplished, the administrator made several structural changes within the organization. The administrator and staff developed a process to evaluate and select the most appropriate candidates for the program. They established clear protocols and procedures to frame this selection process. They defined policies to structure the program, and they trained staff to implement the service. However, training staff was not easy because many of the organization's own staff believed the new initiative "just created more problems." Staff also felt that providing this type of opportunity would be difficult, and it would diminish the organization's control of its juveniles.

Realizing that the success of the program depended on staff support, the administrator used leadership skills as a collaborator and consensus builder to effect needed changes. The administrator accomplished this by meeting with staff, identifying and discussing concerns, and providing training.

Monitoring

At the same time that the administrator was managing these functions within the organization, the administrator also had to communicate the program's needs to the community. Identifying and recruiting work sites and job opportunities was only the first step. Once the juveniles actually began working in their job placements, the administrator had to monitor the program. Staff from the organization and employees from the work site handled most of the daily operations.

However, the administrator incorporated ongoing monitoring and visibility—important intervention techniques—into the administrator's role. Understanding the importance of being in constant communication with work sites, work supervisors, and the juveniles involved in the program, the administrator provided an active presence. He understood that once the program had been developed and implemented, his role had not ended.

Due to the risks associated with working with juvenile delinquents and the continual need for the program to adapt, administrators must be available and accessible through their monitoring role. For example, in this work program, the administrator helps work supervisors at job sites understand that the juvenile delinquent's involvement in the program has significant clinical importance. The supervisors learn that the job placement is part of a treatment plan with long-term implications. The job is more than just the activity delineated in a job description. In this case, work-site supervisors also serve as mentors. Mentors are more tolerant of negative behavior and are better able to put that behavior into a meaningful context.

This case study illustrates how an informed administrator strategically completed needed organizational tasks and functions that ensured the organization's well-being. The administrator remained aware of theoretical developments, identified current needs, recruited and trained staff, procured needed resources, developed and monitored a new initiative, and continued to intervene to ensure the program's survival.

As a result, this initiative, which actually began in 1987 and included two clients working part-time, has expanded to sixteen clients working in the community on a regular basis, and another fifteen participating in a work program on the campus of the residential center. Also related to this initiative is a fourteen-week independent living skills program that serves approximately 180 clients a year and a transitional living apartment program that provides services and opportunities to meet the juvenile's needs.

Internal Problems: Personnel Issues

Nonprofit organizations working with juvenile delinquents are service organizations that rely heavily on staff to implement programs and achieve goals. Personnel costs often comprise between 70 to 80 percent of the total budget of nonprofit organizations. As a result, administrators need to deal with concerns associated with this resource. After all, staff implement tasks and activities, conduct programs, deliver services, and help an organization respond to changes. The following issues are associated with personnel:

- recruitment and retention
- supervision
- staff development and training

The positive resolution of these issues helps maintain morale and motivation of the work force.

Recruitment and Retention

Human service delivery systems include some combination of government, private for-profit and nonprofit organizations. Therefore, when trying to recruit from a limited number of available, qualified candidates, these other organizations are potential competitors.

Effectively recruiting staff requires the ability to offer competitive salaries and benefits and/or offsetting nonmonetary advantages (Young 1987). Unfortunately, these two major variables—economic compensation and nonmonetary advantages—are not always readily available to administrators of nonprofit organizations. Funding and revenue often are inaccessible or limited, and the ability to offer the nonpecuniary advantages may make a major difference. These nonpecuniary advantages include:

- professional autonomy
- control and selectivity regarding clients served
- work environment where team processes and consensus building determine policy (not the top-down management style of large bureaucracies)
- a greater commitment to professional development and training

Since the ability to offer nonpecuniary advantages is limited, these organizations have difficulty competing with their competitors. Although competing for scarce resources is a constant challenge for nonprofit agencies, they are able to recruit and maintain a professional work force due to the following reasons:

- their ability to exercise independence from governmental regulation because of their private, nonprofit status
- their control over the client population they serve
- their creation of a pleasant work atmosphere

Although some of these conditions have diminished due to changes in statutes, regulations, and economic conditions, nonprofit agencies have fewer restrictions and more options than their government counterparts.

Staff Development and Training

Staff development plays a vital role in the ongoing maintenance and expansion of an organization. An efficiently planned staff development program is needed. It should include input from all staff. Staff development functions may be implemented by one full-time staff member, whose specific responsibilities are related to staff development, or by a committee of staff members whose job descriptions reflect duties related to this role. Given the economic realities of nonprofit organizations and the size and scope of their operations, it is more realistic to assume that the responsibility will be shared by many staff.

The real challenge for the administrator comes from the influence the external environment places on the mission of the organization. In training staff, this issue must be consistently addressed, so that the staff development process does not communicate a value which mitigates the ideals upon which the organization is structured. Nonprofit agency administrators also must define the needed competencies that the staff need to accomplish specific tasks and objectives. While standard expectations and tasks are not easy to identify, there are certain similar elements related to direct work with juvenile delinquents.

Staff Supervision

Effective staff supervision is critical for the successful operation of any nonprofit organization. Supervision is the process by which staff receive information about required tasks and responsibilities, support to implement their assigned tasks, and feedback to grow and develop in their position. It is a process of guiding staff in goal directed behavior to enhance their development and implement an organization's mission and purpose.

Supervision should be an ongoing process with the dual purpose of promoting a staff member's growth on the job and determining whether the staff member meets the agency's standards for performance. For the employee, supervision is a source of support and a vehicle for individualized training. Self-awareness and professional skills are enhanced by a positive exchange of knowledge and experiences.

Supervision has the following three primary outcomes:

- providing education

- communicating administrative direction
- offering clinical support for staff

When beginning a supervisory process, the structure must be clear to both the supervisor and the person supervised. Goals, frequency of contact, supervisor availability, and performance evaluation standards must be specified and mutually understood. Once this structure has been defined, specific learning goals must be established. To define these learning goals, the supervisor must assess an individual's skills related to direct service tasks, knowledge of juvenile delinquency, and the person's developmental level as a human services worker.

Once goals and structure are established, it is important to identify which interventions will be used in the process itself. These can include: self-reporting, using audio and video tapes, modeling, role playing, observing and supervising, or employing other interventions, such as case note and treatment plan writing that develop cognitive and conceptual counseling skills. The choice of interventions must be determined by the level of the employee.

As individuals gain experience, confidence, and competence, they begin to view the supervisor as a resource person. There is a sharing of ideas in a collegial atmosphere. The focus is more on skill building related to service responsibilities. Staff want to discuss theory and practice concepts. Role playing, observing, and treatment plan writing assist at this level. Eventually, as staff begin to develop their own professional style and identity as service providers, supervision becomes increasingly consultative. The individual takes more responsibility for the focus of supervision, and the process becomes more peer-like rather than the hierarchical relationship of the initial stage. Self-reporting, modeling, and other process-type interventions often become a significant part of supervision at this level.

When functioning in this overall supervisory process, there are several areas of concern which administrators must resolve. In most nonprofit organizations, administrators implementing a supervisory role are involved both clinically and administratively with their employees. Playing this dual role can potentially put a supervisor in a conflicting situation. It is important that the administrative role does not restrict the clinical supervision role related to staff growth and development. A goal of clinical supervision is to help the employee develop professional skills and ability as a direct service provider. To accomplish this, the employee must be provided a degree of autonomy and given the opportunity to try new skills and techniques. As an agent of the organization, the administrator is responsible for ensuring that agency policies and procedures are implemented and that there is appropriate compliance with regulations and guidelines.

It also is important that administrators recognize their own professional influence in the supervisory process. They must ensure that the content of supervision does not only reflect their own theories and beliefs. It is necessary to support and respect the theoretical position of employees, so that they have an opportunity to develop their own identity and grow in their role. This is particularly important for nonprofit organizations, which must be sensitive to the nonpecuniary benefits for their professional staff. Supporting professional identity and autonomy are nonpecuniary benefits important to the process of recruitment and retention. Therefore, providing the opportunity to grow and develop in new directions is not only supportive of good supervision, but, on a practical basis, helps nonprofit organizations retain an important benefit for their staff.

In many nonprofit organizations, which do not characteristically have extensive career ladders, one method of supporting and recognizing staff achievement is promoting individuals to supervisory positions.

The supervisory process must be coherent, consistent, and efficient. These are necessary qualities to ensure its effective implementation. However, nonprofit organizations with diminishing resources, increasing administrative responsibilities, and large caseloads do not always have the opportunity to meet sound supervisory practices. Supervisory meetings often become a series of disconnected contacts which focus more on crisis management issues, rather than on staff growth and development. This is a condition that unfortunately characterizes many nonprofit organizations serving juvenile delinquents. Limited resources to support quality supervision, high caseloads, and paperwork responsibilities make it difficult to sustain this needed supervisory process.

Finally, the supervisory process must remain objective. This ensures that the collegial relationships which develop over time remain objective and that the evaluations and interactions between the supervisor and the employee support a planned developmental process. In many nonprofit organizations, which do not characteristically have extensive career ladders, one method of supporting and recognizing staff achievement is promoting individuals to supervisory positions. Supervisors who are promoted from the ranks have the advantage of understanding the dynamics of an organization and the needed tasks and functions to be completed. However, these supervisors also have many formal and informal relationships with coworkers, which potentially interfere with the supervisory process. Feelings of collegiality that have developed over time can make it difficult for supervisors to objectively interact with their employees. Although they might be able to provide needed education and support in the process, they need to confront workers, hold them accountable, and ensure they remain focused upon tasks. Administrators must be sensitive to this issue, discuss it with those they supervise, and establish guidelines to ensure appropriate professional relationships are developed.

External Problems

Nonprofit organizations serving the juvenile justice field face a number of external problems that affect operations, including community protection, government regulations and contracts, paperwork requirements, and institutional abuse regulations.

Community Protection

The community is becoming increasingly alarmed about the nature and level of juvenile violence. Statistical data on violent crimes supports these feelings, although effective interventions have been developed to respond to these conditions. Despite some gains, there remains a considerable amount of problematic behavior, which creates both a real, as well as perceived, belief that juvenile delinquents present a serious threat to their communities. This belief pressures nonprofit organizations to respond to these fears and perceptions. It is expected that agencies will address these fears, solve the problem, and alleviate the concerns.

It is also important to recognize and acknowledge the community's need to feel safe, not only because this is an acceptable value and right, but also because the community significantly impacts the political process that regulates needed resources. Therefore, attention to community safety is vital.

Community safety is difficult for the nonprofit administrator to manage, because governmental regulations require placement in the least restrictive environments, while advocates want juveniles to spend less time incarcerated, and politicians continue to reduce fiscal supports.

Yet, nonprofit agencies may develop programs to ensure community safety and still manage external priorities. Choices include: supervised independent living programs, intensive home supervision, and staff devoted to community liaison activities.

Governmental Regulations and Contracts

Governmental regulations and agency contracts with external systems pose yet another challenge for nonprofit agencies. Because both control fiscal resources, administrators must manage within the confines of the regulations and contracts. Because external systems vacillate between treatment and punitive interventions, regulations and contract processes are tentative, at best. Yet these processes influence what nonprofit organizations do and the interventions that are used. Administrators must be willing to manage these conditions and remain flexible to the external influences upon which they depend.

Paperwork Requirements

Contractual processes require documentation, which generally consists of a recording system that describes treatment contacts, clinical assessments, and treatment plans. The recording system is designed to communicate information and record activities relative to mutually agreed on standards.

Implementing a system designed to ensure consistency and promote communications sometimes requires professional staff to follow time frames and adhere to recording formats that are burdensome and arbitrary. For example, New York State county departments of social services will put fiscal sanctions on a nonprofit organization if it falls behind in its paperwork responsibilities. The department will withhold payments for all of the cases being served until the agency comes into compliance. For small, nonprofit agencies, this can present a significant cash flow problem. Consequently, required documentation becomes a primary focus of the service providers within the organization, and client needs are relegated to a lower priority.

One way to manage this problem is for administrators to be competent in computer skills and develop appropriate management information systems. In addition to the use of this management information system, it also is important for administrators to make use of available clerical staff. Clerical staff can help collect data and document and organize information related to government regulations and contracts.

Abuse Regulations

New York has joined many other states in protecting juveniles placed in nonprofit institutions and other custodial care. In 1987, New York passed the Child Abuse Prevention Act, which included sections relating to nonprofit organizations serving juvenile delinquents. Essentially, legislation applied the same definitions and policies that are used with familial situations in the community to agencies that operate institutions for juvenile delinquents. The problem in using the same standards when working with a delinquent population is that it creates unnecessary work and anxiety for staff in the nonprofit childcare system. The law did not take into account the violent nature of aggressive juvenile delinquents.

Having regulations that require an investigation be initiated based on "some credible evidence" leaves open the possibility of manipulation and unwarranted investigations. Investigations use significant resources and raise workers' anxiety. Workers often feel vulnerable in these situations, and the emotional turmoil of undergoing a process in which workers themselves begin to feel as if they have been victimized, significantly affects staff morale and how staff interact when implementing their responsibilities.

As such, it is important for administrators to ensure that these staff members are treated fairly and that they feel comfortable and secure when working with these potentially stressful situations. Administrators must interpret and evaluate what has transpired between the juvenile and the worker, often based on second-hand information. At the same time, it is important for administrators to ensure that a secure environment is maintained for both the juvenile delinquent and the organization's staff so that an effective treatment program continues. To address this issue, the administrator should do the following:

- design, develop, and implement in-service training that addresses appropriate physical restraint procedures and the prevention of restraint situations
- develop agency policies, procedures, and guidelines detailing what staff should do when faced with a child abuse investigation
- ensure medical services are available to evaluate alleged injuries
- provide administrative and supervisory support in an objective, nonthreatening manner

New Approaches, New Strategies

Given the evolving nature of theories regarding the causes and solutions of juvenile delinquency, new approaches, strategies and interventions are continuously emerging, particularly in the last twenty-five years.

A major problem many administrators face is identifying one type of approach or strategy from the other. Obviously, administrators strive to support new program initiatives, which would develop and expand an organization, while at the same time mitigate potential negative influences from more questionable approaches. How the new approach is interpreted determines the issues administrators must resolve. New approaches based on sound intellectual analysis and research present one type of challenge, while less developed and thought out approaches present another.

Although new strategies often are supported by research data and sound clinical analysis, it does not mean they will be easily integrated into a nonprofit organization. Because nonprofit organizations rely on professional staff to deliver their services, administrators might encounter resistance from professional staff when new ideas are introduced, even if the intervention has the potential to make a positive contribution. Staff have a tendency to retain familiar approaches because change inherently raises some anxiety. To work through this resistance, administrators must develop a working plan which includes the following strategic steps:

1. Develop a specific written program plan as a blueprint for action and outline the strategies needed to implement the program. The plan includes an administrative frame that identifies the goals and objectives of the new program, start up tasks, and a time frame to ensure that it is completed efficiently.

2. Disseminate and market the concept. The administrator should gather literature describing the theory, research, and program prototypes involving the new idea and share this with all staff. This process should demonstrate how the new program would help the organization in its work with juvenile delinquents. This is a major opportunity for the administrator to advocate for and sell the program.

3. Facilitate program implementation. The administrator must conduct discussions on program implementation, its impact on existing organizational structure, and how the new initiative will enhance services. The administrator also must be sensitive to staff concerns and process these both conceptually and experientially.

4. Build consensus. Assuming a collegial leadership style, the administrator must organize agencywide planning meetings to develop a specific framework to initiate and implement the program. Including staff in the planning and implementation stages provides them with empowerment and ownership of the program. The administrator uses this consensus building process to define timelines, assign staff to specific tasks, discuss and resolve concerns about program implementation, and settle any other problem which may be identified.

Conclusion

Nonprofit organizations play a significant role in delivering services in the field of juvenile delinquency. Their unique structure has grown, developed, and adapted to the changing values, programs, and approaches that have characterized this evolving field. The administrator, who is responsible for implementing necessary programs faces continual challenges and complex problems. This requires specific skills combined with flexibility and a commitment to deal with these problems.

References

Austin, M. J., D. Brannon, and P. J. Pecora. 1984. *Managing staff development programs in human services agencies*. Chicago: Nelson Hall Publishers.

Goldstein, A. P., B. Glick, S. Reiner, D. Zimmerman, and T. M. Coultry. 1987. *Aggression replacement training*. Champaign, Illinois: Research Press.

Kramer, R. M. 1979. Public fiscal policy and voluntary agencies in welfare state. *Social Services Review* 53(1):1-14.

Young, D. R. 1985. *Casebook of management for nonprofit organizations.* New York: The Haworth Press.

15 Budgets and Financing Juvenile Programs: What Every Program Manager Needs To Know About Budget and Finance

William J. Bradley

Budget and finance is as attractive to most juvenile program administrators as mathematics is to some elementary school students. Often, the budgetary process fails to attract the attention it deserves from professional human service administrators. It is important, however, that program administrators understand their role in the budget and finance process. This will enable them to provide leadership and control while working with the technocrats who are best qualified to implement budget and finance functions.

The budget process is the heart and soul of program administration. As program administrator, your primary function is to maximize the productivity of the workforce toward achieving the program's goals. To do this, you must get funding. Control over funding is a powerful tool of coordination and can dictate program philosophy and method of implementation.

The Budget Process

Once a year all top executives address the fundamental problem of dividing revenues among services whose legitimate demands exceed available revenue. During this period, you will receive opportunities to communicate the problems, needs, and goals of juvenile populations and programs. In short, it is the time of the year to sell, sell, sell. It is a time for you to rethink the problems with which you are faced and try to develop more cost-effective approaches to these basic problems. You must be able to communicate needs in a form that will encourage acceptance. The aim of a good budget presentation is to relate the problem, strategy, and numbers in a manner easily understood by decision makers.

William J. Bradley is a management consultant in Oviedo, Florida, specializing in assisting programs with management and fiscal control problems.

Understanding What A Budget Is

The budget is used to secure funding for a period of time, usually one year. The budget could simply be a statement of purpose and a total amount of money requested, or it could be a detailed listing of positions with salaries, a listing of "other than personal service" (OTPS), and anticipated expenditures. Varying degrees of detailed justification may be required, from full justification of every position and every item of OTPS expenditures to a justification of only new or increased expenditures from the prior year's budget.

Putting the Budget Together

As program administrator, your goal is to prepare a budget with the least amount of time taken away from program responsibilities. The first step is to find the budget analyst—the person in the organization who handled the program's budget last year and probably will be working with it again this year—and develop a professional relationship with that person.

Satisfying the Budget

A budget has a narrative—the justification or plan of action—and "numbers"—the actual funding request.

The narrative describes the problem, how you propose to solve it, and your authority to spend funding to address the problem. Thus, it is important to understand the problem, solution, and authority issues before beginning the budget preparation process because this forms the core of a budget presentation.

Defining the Problem

For example, if you are a program administrator assigned the task of establishing a nonresidential program for fifty juvenile delinquents, you justify the need by determining the program's annual capacity, which will relate to the projected stay. If the plan calls for a six-month stay, the annual capacity is one hundred; for a four-month length of stay, the annual capacity is 150. As in this example, it is important to relate the problem in quantitative terms to the size of the program proposed.

Next, you need to identify the source of the projected clientele. In a large city this might not be an issue, but in most situations analysts will want to know if there is a need for these placements. Will the placement source be the family court or other sources? Will this program replace existing programs? If this is a replacement program, can it be funded by cuts from the program it will replace? Will this program save money in any other part of the system? The agency you work for probably has ample data to justify this program and should have supplied the data to you for your budget justification. Unfortunately, program administrators sometimes have difficulty finding the information. Usually it is a matter of knowing who to ask—valuable sources include the person to whom you report, agency budget analysts, other program administrators, and research staff.

Taking the Next Step

Now that you have defined the problem, the next logical step is to outline a solution. It is important to first define the philosophy influencing the solution. Follow this up with a narrative description of the program's implementation that describes the program in action. This section should answer the following questions:

- In what part of the fiscal year will you recruit and train new staff?
- When is the planned opening of the center?
- How will the juveniles be recruited and from where?
- What are the clinical goals and objectives of the center?
- How do these clinical goals and objectives relate to program activities?
- Will the program begin with a full house on the first day of the new budget year or will the program gradually phase in juveniles, staff, and other costs?

New programs are frequently phased in over the fiscal year with juveniles and staff coming on board based on a predetermined schedule that should be included in the budget justification. Since the new program will require only part-year funding, you must lay the groundwork for the following year by showing the full, annual cost and projected juvenile participation.

The Lump Sum Budget

If the program is seen as a pressing political need, you may want to present a lump sum budget—one figure to cover start-up and operating costs for the coming year. This approach saves time and allows flexibility. It avoids commitments based on unrealistic estimates, and works well if the details of your project are not complete. A lump sum budget requires far less justification than a line item budget. The "numbers" part of your lump sum budget will consist of a single dollar amount. Your justification will center on the purpose and need for this initiative.

The Line Item Personal Service Budget

If your program is ongoing, or if a lump sum budget is not acceptable, it will be necessary to prepare a line item budget. You will justify the personal services (staffing) and "other than personal service" (things you must provide to operate). In residential programs, community-based programs, or nonresidential programs, 80 to 85 percent of the budget covers personnel services, such as professional and nonprofessional staff and consultants. The bulk of the balance will represent costs (over which you have relatively little control), such as rent, utilities, and food.

The Personal Services Budget

As program administrator, you should be prepared to commit significant amounts of time to the budget process to lay the foundation for a successful program. This is the point in the process to develop advocates for your program among the technocrats within the system and to establish your leadership and control.

Include human resources and finance staff, as well as budget analysts and legislative analysts in your staff meetings and take them on field trips—do everything you can to help them understand your program.

The success or failure of any program depends on staff, who represent more than 80 percent of the budget. Determining staffing patterns, position titles, qualifications, salary levels, recruiting methods, and the selection of staff are probably the most important decisions a program administrator will make. Often, these decisions are made by budget analysts or human resources staff who are unfamiliar with the juveniles or the difficulties in implementing the philosophical approach that is planned. It is important to develop a mutually respectful professional relationship with the budget and human resources staff. Invest time in orienting them in all aspects of the proposed program, including the program's environment, the problems of incoming juveniles, and the program's goals. Include human resources and finance staff, as well as budget analysts and legislative analysts in your staff meetings and take them on field trips—do everything you can to help them understand your program. As a result, you will probably cause them to become advocates for your program. This probably will be the most productive time you have ever spent.

Working with the agency personnel and budget staff will result in agreement on staff titles, salaries, and staffing patterns. This includes whether a position is to be full or part time, and at what point in the budget year each position will be filled. This process will give you the information necessary to present a staffing justification and the numbers needed for the line item personal services budget to be submitted in the coming year. You also have your budget execution blueprint, barring any changes made by higher authorities during the process.

The Line Item Personal Service Budget for Existing Programs

Justifying a personal service budget can be time consuming or simple. The determining factor is found in the guidelines used by your parent organization for the budget preparation process during the coming fiscal year. Once you have the guidelines, gather past budget justifications and determine whether existing material can be reused or modified. Budget preparation instructions for personal services may vary widely from year to year.

Do not be surprised if you are asked for a full justification of every position, including a detailed description of your staffing pattern one year, but only justification of requested new positions the next. Once you understand the instructions, provide the information that is requested. When describing position duties, emphasize what the position produces. Cost savings and workload information also is useful. Justify the need for and usefulness of each position in your program. After each position justification, ask yourself whether you would fund that position based on what you just read. It is not necessary to write a separate justification for every position when a single title covers numerous positions performing similar tasks.

What Will This Program Produce?

You have presented the problem and proposed solutions and costs. Now you need to determine what you can expect to get for your money. Are your goals and objectives clearly stated? Are they stated in measurable objectives? If not, a section of your budget justification should address this topic. Using the earlier example, we will examine the problems you need to deal with in presenting your measurable objectives. Examples of new and ongoing community-based and residential programs are illustrated below.

New Programs: Community-based or Residential

We will use our earlier example of a fifty-slot, nonresidential program for juvenile delinquents with an average stay of four months. If the total budget is $500,000, divided by fifty slots, the cost per unit is $10,000. The cost per juvenile is $3,333, based on projections of 150 juveniles served per year.

These figures are calculated on capacity. What about reality? Can a new program open its doors with a full population? Can the program maintain a maximum population once it is up and running? Should a program spend a full budget on fewer juveniles than it has contracted to serve? Obviously, a new program is going to be in a start-up phase during the first year. It will neither serve the numbers of juveniles it projects as its capacity, nor should it expect to be fully funded for the full budget year. Planning should include the addition of staff as populations increase. The objective is to allow for the training of new staff while keeping costs as low as possible in relation to juveniles served.

All new programs experience start-up costs. These costs need to be minimized. Assistance from staff members who have helped open new programs can be of immense value. Because personal services represent more than 80 percent of the budget, coordinating the addition of staff with juvenile admissions is the key to expenditure control for new programs.

Ongoing Residential Programs

The ongoing residential program presents a less difficult budgetary problem. Using the example of a fifty-bed capacity with semiannual turnover and a budget of $1.5 million, we could project a cost per juvenile of $15,000 or a per bed cost of $30,000. These are both based on 100 percent use of resources. Determine whether this is feasible. Can juveniles be admitted to keep all beds filled at all times? In most cases the answer to that key question is "no."

Next, determine whether you can develop an approach that will allow you to maintain an average of fifty juveniles or whether you should project a lower figure based on the realities of intake and turnover. To maintain an average capacity of fifty, you must operate above capacity to offset the times you are below capacity. If you do not believe you can maintain capacity, you should acknowledge that in your budget presentation and introduce the explanation with the projected costs.

For example, if the projected use is 90 percent, that is an average of forty-five beds filled and an average of ninety juveniles served at a cost of $1.5 million. The projected cost per bed rises from $30,000 to $33,333 ($1.5 million divided by forty-five beds), and the cost per juvenile changes from $15,000 to $16,666 ($1.5 million divided by ninety juveniles). A 10 percent loss of productivity causes more than a 10 percent increase in cost. It is impossible to make up this difference by reducing your expenditures because such a high percentage of your budget is in personal service. Instead, you should consider trying to accommodate as many extra juveniles as needed to offset the vacancies you expect.

It is better to operate a fully funded, fully staffed program with extra juveniles than to be forced to operate an almost full program with staff vacancies and budget cutbacks. However, if you are restricted in filling your positions and can project savings sufficient to offset the lower juvenile population, you may wish to operate with lower capacities in an effort to leverage the budget. Operating above capacity is especially important in very low capacity programs. In the operation of a group home with a budgeted capacity of seven, vacancies resulting in an average of six will increase your cost per juvenile by more than 14 percent.

Ongoing Community-based Programs

Budgeting for community-based programs is more difficult than budgeting for residential programs. You will operate in an environment in which you have less structure and control. For example, a community-based, nonresidential program with a capacity of fifty, a four-month turnover rate, and a budget of $500,000 has a projected cost per program slot of $10,000, ($500,000 divided by fifty beds) with a cost per juvenile of $3,333 ($500,000 divided by 150 juveniles). As in the residential example, determine whether you can keep these slots filled, and keep in mind the following questions:

- Will there be a waiting list?
- What will the dropout rate be?
- How quickly can you replace dropouts?
- Will you evaluate success or failure on the basis of program completion or on the number of days attended?
- How will you handle daily absence?
- To what extent will you be forced to deal with juveniles' problems outside the program's main objectives?
- How will that affect staff resources?

A program administrator is confronted with difficult budgeting and program planning decisions that need to be made early in the process so that the budget reflects those decisions. This becomes even more important for private agencies that are contracting to provide services funded by government agencies and whose contract evaluations will be based heavily, if not exclusively, on the budget presentation. Material from the budget justification is used to formulate the contract between funding agency and provider.

The wording of the following two budget presentations and an analysis of the commitment each program is making will help illustrate the importance of resolving important questions.

1. "Agency A *will provide the resources to train* forty eligible juveniles for sixteen weeks, five days per week, during three periods annually." Agency A is committed only to provide the resources and opportunity for as many as forty juveniles to be trained for five days per week for sixteen weeks, three times per year. Agency A has not taken any responsibility for filling the slots, maintaining attendance, or graduating any of the juveniles.

2. "Agency B *will train* forty eligible juveniles, five days per week for sixteen weeks, three times per year." Agency B is committed to train 120 juveniles who have each received sixteen weeks of training five days per week.

Neither presentation is acceptable. Agency A takes no responsibility for juvenile participation, involvement, or completion. Agency B has overlooked the problems of recruitment and retention and has made a commitment it cannot fulfill.

The budget narrative must reflect a plan of action that is doable, that can be measured quantitatively, and that can be delivered at the stated cost. The budget narrative needs to be a plan of action, summarized perhaps, but well thought out. The budget presentation asks for funding to produce a product at a given cost. You are competing against other needs, which will not be met if your proposal is funded. Your ability to deliver is on the line. Do not promise what you cannot accomplish. Do deliver what you promise—your professional credibility depends on it.

Dealing with the "Numbers"

As program administrator, you need to determine from where all these numbers are coming. After examining the sources of the numbers, you will see how simple it is to put together the numerical part of the budget document.

Personal Services

The personal service section covers the salaries of employees (full- or part-time), consultants, and other miscellaneous positions. For a new program, each position is listed and assigned a salary—usually the minimum of the salary range. Part-time positions are listed with the appropriate fraction of the annual salary for each position. Consultants and other positions are listed with the amount allocated for the year. Similar positions or titles are consolidated. For example, five typists with an annual wage of $10,000 each would be indicated by writing: Typist 5 @ $10,000, $50,000.

New programs generally will phase in positions showing some for a full year and others for a fraction of the year and a corresponding fraction of the annual salary. For example, a cook who would receive $10,000 for an annual salary would for six months of work receive half of that. This would be indicated by writing: Cook, 6 months, @$10,000 annually, request $5,000.

Existing programs usually show a comparison between the current year's budget and the new year's request. All existing, current year authorized positions, with actual salaries for filled positions and minimum or budgeted amounts for unfilled positions, are listed. In the next column, new year salaries will reflect increases for eligible staff members who occupy full- or part-time positions. Positions upgraded from phase-in status will be shown at the full annual rate. The positions of consultants and others will reflect any change in requested allocations from the current year.

	1992	**1993**	**Difference**
Typist, (5)	50,000	52,500	2,500
Cook	5,000	10,000	5,000

The five typists each were entitled to a $500 increase. The cook was added in the middle of 1992 but will work the full year in 1993, doubling the budget amount.

Computerization has made it common for personal service budgets to be prepared as a by-product of the payroll function. Before doing any work on your personal service budget, find out how your agency prepares that portion of the budget. You may only be responsible for the portion of newly requested positions.

New Position Requests

New positions are usually listed separately and require full justification. New positions may be requested for the full year or a part of it, and they may be full or part time. Usually, new positions are budgeted at the minimum of the pay grade. The program administrator justifies the personal service request, especially the portion devoted to new positions.

The personal services budget request is key to a successful program. As program administrator, you should provide leadership and direction to the budget analysts, who produce the "numbers" section of the budget. You should ask to review the numbers they submit to ensure the budget request is complete and reflects the staffing needed to carry out the program. Your task in this portion of the budget preparation is to know what is needed, communicate your needs, and check to make sure that your requests are included.

Other Than Personal Service (OTPS)

Other than personal service (OTPS) covers the purchases of objects or services such as food, utilities, rent, supplies, insurance, clothing, books, gasoline and car repairs, and office equipment, in other words, anything but salaries. The OTPS budget forms may look similar to the personal service budget format. There will be a column for categories of expenditure such as food and supplies, followed by a column for the current year's expenditures, a column for requested funding, and a column for the differences. Unlike personal service, OTPS incorporates many items grouped into categories.

Budget requests for the upcoming year are based on past years' expenditures and the justification for future program changes. Obviously, if you plan on using historical expenditure data, the closer to the start of the new budget year that the budget is prepared, the more useful the historical data, and the more accurately you and your budget analysts can predict future years' expenditures.

Private agencies may prepare their budgets a month or two before the actual execution date. Once the budget is prepared, it can be submitted to the board of directors for review and approval. Usually the board will act swiftly, and the new budget will be ready almost immediately. Unfortunately, most governmental organizations find it difficult to prepare their budgets as quickly. A residential facility operated by a state or county may be asked to prepare its budget six to nine months before it goes into effect.

How does this affect the use of historical data for budget preparation? A governmental agency may find the current year's expenditure data useless because it will be preparing next year's budget within the first three to six months of the current fiscal year. It will, therefore, be necessary to use expenditure data from the prior fiscal year, which means you and your budget analysts must adjust the prior year's expenditures to meet the needs of the future year's budget situation. Two years of projected inflation and other anticipated changes must be included. The current year's expenditures are estimates rather than actual expenditures. If the program reports current year estimated expenditures below the appropriated level, it is an invitation to reduce next year's appropriation.

If current year expenditures are reported in excess of the actual appropriation, there may be swift action to control and eliminate the deficit. Consequently, programs generally report total expenditures consistent with the appropriation. Individual categories can be reported accurately with the shortage transferred from a category where savings has accrued (frequently from personal service).

OTPS Budget Preparation for New Programs

Your first step is to enlist the aid of a budget analyst with experience in establishing new programs similar to the one you are planning. Then, review each budget category and explain what you plan to do that will cause expenditures in that category. Your plan, combined with the budget analyst's knowledge of expenditures for similar programs, should result in a reasonable estimate. You also may want to review budgets for similar programs and consult with program managers experienced in establishing new programs.

Categories of expenditure vary widely from jurisdiction to jurisdiction. For illustrative purposes budget categories are grouped under the following seven major headings:

- physical plant and utilities
- equipment
- communication
- food, clothing, and supplies
- transportation
- professional services
- fringe benefits

Physical Plant and Utilities

Physical space is needed to operate a program. However, sometimes the space will be provided free—which means that cost will not be included in the budget. The space may be in a public or private building that belongs to a government or nonprofit agency that budgets for the space separately.

If you need to construct one or more buildings, you will be required to prepare a capital construction budget request. These requests are usually handled separately from the agency's operational budget. To prepare a capital construction budget, the program administrator should contact the appropriate agency staff and develop a capital budget request. In most cases, building rehabilitation and/or renovations are handled in a separate capital budget request. Renting space involves a lease arrangement that will specify the monthly rentals and provide a basis for your budget request.

If space has not been found as of the date of budget preparation, it is not difficult to determine average rentals per square foot from knowledgeable real estate professionals. Determine the number of square feet required and the general location suitable to carry out the plan of action. Price per square foot is heavily influenced by location. You should understand the provisions of the lease. Will the landlord renovate the space; perform repairs; and provide utilities such as water and sewer, heat and air conditioning, and electricity?

After determining these issues, you must turn to the second component of your physical plant request. Utilities will either be provided by the landlord or be included in your operating budget. Experienced budget analysts can provide estimates based on current and prior experience with other programs.

Equipment

New programs usually require significant amounts of new equipment. Your equipment list may include items such as: vehicles; office equipment and furniture; residential furniture; computers; and medical, dental, and laboratory equipment. Discussing your list with an agency purchasing agent will enable you to determine which items should be purchased and which should be rented. This will enable you to assign estimated costs to each item.

Communication

At this point, consider again your computer needs, as well as telephone service, facsimile machines, postage and shipping, printing, and related program costs. New programs will need to consider initial installation charges as well as ongoing costs. Service providers and your budget analyst are good sources of information.

Food, Clothing, and Supplies

This category includes food purchased for juveniles and staff, including contracted food services. (Here, especially, estimates based on experience in similar programs will be helpful.) Clothing and uniforms for juveniles and staff are particularly important in residential programs. Your budget analyst should be able to provide data from other programs to help determine your needs in these areas. Other supplies that you will need include those in the category of household, office, computers, and medical, dental, and laboratory supplies.

Transportation

Vehicle and vehicle-related expenses such as gas, repairs, and insurance fall into this category. You will need to estimate travel expenses, including mileage, meals, lodging, and public transportation. Will you be transporting juveniles and staff, and, if so, to what extent?

Professional Services

Determine to what extent your program will require the services of the following categories of individuals:

- consultants
- accountants and auditors
- lawyers
- architects
- medical, dental, and laboratory technicians
- computer experts and technicians
- physical plant maintenance services

Fringe Benefits

Governmental agencies generally budget for all fringe benefits separately from the individual agency budget. However, private agency administrators must budget for all fringe benefits required and provided.

OTPS Budget Preparation for Existing Programs

Administrators of existing programs will have a much easier time with OTPS budgeting. The backbone of OTPS budgeting is based on historical data taken from financial records, adjustments for changing circumstances, inflationary impact, and new program components.

Historical data means actual and estimated expenditures from prior years. Adjustments for changing circumstances will reflect specific rate increases or decreases, such as in utility rates. Another example might be a rent increase or an increase in the amount of rental space leased. Adjustments for inflation, where appropriate, generally use the federal consumer price index (CPI) and are frequently provided by the central budget agency. New program components may mean the addition of an educational approach to a counseling program that creates a need for school supplies and books. A change in the age of the population served also might affect other budget categories.

As program administrator, it is your responsibility to point out the program changes that influence the budget. A program administrator who monitors expenditures during the year will be better prepared to identify the areas where more or less money is needed and to justify the changes. Otherwise, the budget will repeat itself with only the cost-of-living changes.

Budget Preparation Instructions

Most program administrators receive a prescribed format with detailed budget preparation instructions. It is important to follow these instructions precisely. The budget instructions will dictate the format of the "numbers" presentation on preprinted forms while the budget narrative will allow a flexible and creative presentation. You will save time if you understand what is expected and not rely on your memory, rumors, or copies of past submissions.

The Executive Summary

The executive summary is of utmost importance. It tells the story of your program and its budgetary request in one or two pages. Place the executive summary in front of your detailed budget request. You may find it helpful to write the executive summary first and revise it after you prepare your detailed budget. It will help you focus on the big picture before you get lost in the details of the actual budget forms.

The Budget Cycle

You have heard the term "budget cycle," but do you know what it means? The budget cycle consists of your budget's submission date, a period of internal review, a submission date to the executive budget agency, a review period and hearing schedule, submission to the legislature or your in-house governing body and their review process, and the actual legislative budget process prior to passage.

Selling Your Budget

Selling your budget in-house has to be your top priority. Do not assume that because the agency director approved your request that the agency budget staff is prepared to sell it to the executive budget office. Take whatever steps are necessary to convince all in-house staff involved in this process that your request has merit. Remember the agency budget staffer is your representative. Make sure he or she understands your program and its objectives. Prepare visual aids, charts, slide presentations, videos, and photo albums.

After you have garnered in-house administrators' support, selling your program at the legislative level is your next hurdle. This involves selling it to legislative staff and possibly the legislators themselves. At this level, the executive summary, charts, and visual aids become even more useful.

Make every effort to have the legislative analyst visit your program during the year and during the budget cycle. Try to ensure that legislative staff members have everything they need to communicate your program's importance.

Of course, nothing is as convincing as support from voters. You need support from groups and individuals who will lobby on your behalf. Use your executive summary (or a modified version of it), visual aids, and personal contacts to prepare your support groups for their lobbying efforts. This is the time to marshal your constituents, advisory groups, and juvenile advocacy groups who will let their legislators know there is grassroots interest in this program and that it affects the legislators' home community. Timing is absolutely essential during this phase. Constituent group lobbying just prior to budget decision making in the legislature is far more effective than scattered expressions of support throughout the year.

Comparing Costs of Similar Programs

The budget presentation and analysis process may result in cost comparisons between your proposed budget and other public or private programs. Therefore, it is important to understand the problems in comparing costs of similar programs. You will need to prepare a comparative analysis of the programs and a budget analysis to deal intelligently with these comparisons. It is important to anticipate questions and have answers prepared in advance.

Having answers to the following questions will be helpful in preparing a budgetary analysis:

1. Does the budget reflect the capital construction, rehabilitation, renovation, and debt service costs of the physical facility? Many government agencies do not include capital construction, rehabilitation and renovation, and related costs in their operating budget or in their "cost per juvenile" calculations.

2. Does the program use physical facilities for which it does not pay rent and/or utilities? Again, both public and private agencies frequently use buildings owned and maintained by the parent organization with no cost for space and sometimes no cost for utilities (or even telephone services) reflected in the programs' budget.

3. Is the agency self-insured? In other words, is it protected by a parent organization or insured by a parent organization with no cost reflected in the program budget? Government agencies are frequently self-insured. When insured for liability purposes, claims are usually paid outside the program budget. Auto insurance is frequently purchased for the government as a whole and budgeted outside the pro-

gram budget. In some jurisdictions, governments charge agencies for space, auto insurance, and other services provided by a general services division. In the private sector, parent organizations often provide "off budget" services (those not included in the agency's budget), as well.

Private agencies, however, are much more likely to budget for most, if not all costs, but may or may not include them in their "cost per juvenile" calculations.

4. Are the personal services fringe benefits included in the budget? Many government agencies budget fringe benefits separately and do not reflect these costs in the program budget or in the "cost per juvenile" calculations. Private agencies more frequently include fringe benefits in their program budgets.

5. Does the budget include expenses related to services provided by other agencies within the parent organization? Services provided by a state or county, such as civil services, budget functions, legal services, architectural and engineering services, central purchasing, accounting, and payroll, usually are not charged to individual agencies or program budgets. In the private sector, most, if not all, of these costs are reflected in the agency and program budget and, hence, in cost per juvenile calculations.

All too often, program administrators hire additional staff without considering the budgetary consequences ...

Budget Execution

The heart and soul of expenditure control is also the heart and soul of program implementation. Control of spending greatly influences program direction. For both program and budgetary reasons, it is important to control the selecting and the timing of hiring staff. Obviously, who is hired is related to program philosophy and implementation. The timing, although also related to program implementation, has a great effect on your budget. Because 80 to 85 percent of the budget is in personal service, control of personal service expenditures is crucial. All too often, program administrators hire additional staff without considering the budgetary consequences, because they have no way to illustrate the consequence of their action on the annual budget they are trying to administer. For this reason, the monthly expenditure report should be your primary budget execution tool.

The OTPS budget, representing the other 15 percent of your budget, is more complicated to control. Here, you need to balance time against control. In a small program, an administrator can approve every purchase. However, as programs get larger, this approach becomes impractical. In larger programs, it is appropriate to rely on your finance staff, who understand your program's philosophy. Using this approach, it is important to be accessible to your finance staff and constantly show them that you are appreciative when they point out questionable purchases.

In addition, program administrators should review all purchase orders, although not in detail. If you know what you are looking for, you can scan large numbers of purchase orders in minutes. Purchased items that are inappropriate for your program include those with a high unit cost: expensive items may flag questionable purchases.

For example, a director of a residential program developed a new approach to encouraging juveniles in his program to read outside the classroom. He placed paperbacks, both new and used, on racks in the dormitory, with no controls. If the juvenile took a book, read and returned it, fine; if the juvenile kept the book, that was also fine—the basic idea was to encourage reading. Paperbacks are very inexpensive items. When the program administrator, who had been briefed by the director, saw a purchase order from that facility for a complete, bound set of Shakespeare's works and a bookcase with lock, he realized this expensive purchase was clearly inappropriate for a director's purposes and consumed the total educational supply budget for the year. The facility director had neglected to review the purchase order, although he had signed it. The order had been placed by a new teacher, unfamiliar with the needs of the clientele, but who had a personal interest in the works of Shakespeare. This incident, of course, also raised the question of the appropriateness of the hire.

Monthly Expenditure Report

In addition to reviewing the purchase order, the monthly expenditure report is an excellent tool for managing the OTPS budget. Designing this expenditure report will take more care and time. It requires the budget analyst and the program administrator to work very closely so each understands the complexities of the report.

The basic concept underlining the expenditure report is a comparison of monthly allocations against actual expenditures and their resulting differences. This report is useful only if the program administrator agrees with the monthly allocations, and they do not exceed the total annual budget.

Monthly Expenditure Report: Personal Service

To allocate personal service monthly, you must first determine how many pay periods will be reflected in each month. If you have a monthly or semimonthly payroll, you have either one or two payrolls per month. Weekly or biweekly payrolls present more complicated allocation problems, but they are easily computed. The monthly report should indicate the number of pay periods included and the date of the last payroll included.

Example of a Monthly Expenditure Report
Personal Service (P.S.)—(12) Pay Periods in Fiscal Year
Fiscal Year January 1, through December 31, 199_
Pay Period 10 of 12
October 29, 199_

Categories	Allocated to Date	Expended to Date	Difference + or (-)	Annual Allocation	Projected Expenditure	Difference + or (-)
P.S. Reg.	500,000	450,000	+50,000	600,000	530,000	+70,000
P.S. Temp.	50,000	60,000	(10,000)	60,000	72,000	(12,000)
P.S. P/T	100,000	150,000	(50,000)	120,000	180,000	(60,000)
Consultant	10,000	10,000	0	12,000	12,000	0

If you allocate on the basis of a monthly payroll for an ongoing program, you would divide the total allocation by twelve and allocate one-twelfth each month on a cumulative basis. Comparing the Allocated to Date category with the Expended to Date category will provide a difference (plus or minus) the current status of that single category.

In the example, Personal Service Regular shows a $50,000 surplus after ten months and $70,000 after twelve months. Thus, it appears possible to hire additional staff up to $70,000 on a full annual basis. Looking beyond Personal Service Regular, the report indicates a need to transfer funds from Personal Service Regular to other categories in the budget.

Looking at the second and third categories in the example, you will notice a deficit in both. Unless you take immediate steps to reduce this spending, you will have even larger year-end deficits in both categories. In addition, the deficits in these two categories will exceed the surplus in Personal Services Regular at the end of the year.

What are the available options? First, if you had been using your expenditure reports each month, you could have taken corrective steps earlier in the fiscal year. At this point, you can reduce your spending in Personal Service Temporary, Personal Service Part-time, and Consultants, and transfer your surplus from Personal Service Regular to cover the deficits. The transfer, often called an interchange of funds, will eliminate your ability to use these funds for additional hiring.

Now, you should step back and ask, "What has this monthly expenditure report done for me as a program manager?" It has raised a red flag. It tells you to meet with your budget analyst to explore your options before making decisions that will increase your expenditures.

If you did not have this report, you probably would see vacancies and hire in the Personal Services Regular category, finish the year with a deficit, and begin the following year with a payroll you could not support. This is irresponsible and could cause you to lose your job or your authority to fill positions or spend money without prior approval of a budget control authority. If you were administering a grant or a private agency budget, you would not have the money to make the year-end payroll.

Monthly Expenditure Report: OTPS

In your personal service section, you allocated budgeted funding based on the number on pay periods in each month. In OTPS, you will need to allocate each category individually.

Example of an OTPS Monthly Expenditure Report
January 1, through December 31, 199_
As of October 31, 199_

Categories	Allocated to Date	Expended to Date	Difference + or (-)	Annual Allocation	Projected Expenditure	Difference + or (-)
Rent*	10,000	10,000	0	12,000	12,000	0
Electric**	11,000	10,600	+400	12,000	12,000	0
Clothing***	6,000	5,500	+500	6,000	6,000	0

Assumption: Rental of equipment and building space are contracted for the full fiscal year, and the monthly payments are equal; hence a 1/12th allocation can be used.

**Assumption: Electrical use is higher in summer months when air conditioning is used; hence, monthly allocations are scheduled based on the prior year's expenditure patterns. The budget request will consider utility company rate adjustments.*

***Assumption: Clothing for the residential program is purchased by contract and is ordered at the beginning of each fiscal year. A small amount is reserved for miscellaneous items purchased during the year. The full annual allocation is assigned at the beginning of the year. Unexpended balances reflect the amounts available for the balance of the year.*

The OTPS expenditure report will use categories dictated by the financial system of the parent organization. It is important that program management and financial staff understand the definitions of each category. The finance staff can be very helpful in assisting with the assumptions used in the various categories; however, it is your role to point out planned activities that may affect the timing of expenditures. For example, if 50 percent of the travel allowance is to be reserved for a trip in the last month of the year, you do not want to allocate funds based on the one-twelfth per month formula. If you do, you may find you have only one-twelfth of your travel allowance instead of having one-half left for your planned year-end trip.

The importance of fully understanding the assumptions used for each category, as well as understanding how the expenditure report is prepared are vital. For example, does your report represent actual payments made for goods and services or the encumbrance of funds to cover future payment for items ordered or purchase orders written? Actual payments may lag significantly, leaving your monthly report showing little expenditure and a large surplus, while the truth may be that the full allocation has been committed. To deal with the lag, it may be necessary to allocate funds covering a thirteen- or fourteen-month period to allow for payment of unpaid commitments at the end of the fiscal year. Working with your budget analyst to design your monthly expenditure report will ensure that you end up with meaningful reports. By carefully analyzing each month's report, the budget analyst should help you discover ways to modify your reports to more accurately reflect your true fiscal position. All assumptions used to allocate budgeted funds should be presented with each monthly report. In addition, basic financial information, which most financial staff take for granted, should be included with each report.

Purpose of the Monthly Expenditure Report

The monthly expenditure report is the primary tool that a program administrator uses to achieve the dual objectives of program implementation within the confines of a budget.

Because the budget is split into many parts, you should understand the amount of flexibility you have to move money from one category to another. Maximum flexibility allows total interchangeability of funds. In other words, actual control relates only to the bottom line or total budget figure. Many systems do not allow interchangeability between categories without approvals either within the parent organization or from a central budgeting authority. It is important to know in advance the restrictions placed on your authority to expend funds within the budget allocation.

The "Short Budget"

In a short budget, funds are withheld and the allocations do not represent a fully funded budget. For example, a pay raise of 3 percent is instituted for all staff members, but no additional funds are added to the individual budgets. At the end of the fiscal year, programs that are overspent are given the additional funding to cover their deficits. Programs that stayed within their budgets do not need the additional funds. This may be implemented by a central budget agency when the appropriation is not sufficient to allocate the full 3 percent to all programs.

As a program administrator, you need to determine whether your program is meeting its obligations quantitatively. If it is, determine whether absorbing this pay raise will affect the quality of programming for the juveniles in your program. If it will, you may want to add the 3 percent to your monthly report and assume it will be added at the end of the fiscal year.

Other examples of the short budget include the holding back of part of the total budget to cover payments due after the end of the fiscal year. This may be a legitimate procedure; however, the amount held back should appear in your monthly expenditure report as an unallocated amount, with the understanding that these funds are available to cover end-of-year payments. This is a good example of the importance of communications and trust within the organization.

The holding back of part of a program's budget allocation is a fairly common occurrence. Program administrators should be quick to investigate the reasons and deal with this problem appropriately.

Living Within the Budget

As program administrator, you need to know the budgetary milieu in which you must operate. In some organizations, it is unheard of to exceed the budget, while in other organizations it is a routine event. The budgetary facts of life in many organizations are that future appropriations are related to past expenditures. This translates into "the one who spends the most, gets the most." Naturally, if through good management, you save the organization money this fiscal year and your reward is to see your budget cut the next year, you will change your behavior. Instead of trying to save money, you will make sure you spend your full budget in the future. Auditors frequently find stockpiles of equipment and supplies as a result of this situation.

In a well-run organization, budgetary and financial management is a joint responsibility shared by program and fiscal staff. Finance and budgetary staff, after all, should be in a support role, trying their best to empower the program staff to fulfill the agency's mission. Program administrators make it clear they intend to operate their programs within the authorized budget. They seek the help of every staff member to get the most for the budgeted dollar for their juveniles. Achievement of this goal is frequently pursued by the establishment of "cost centers" within the total budget. These may be separate programs or even components of a program.

Efficiently managed organizations allocate funds accurately, report expenditures in a timely manner, and place authority in the hands of their program administrators and fiscal and budgetary oversight in the hands of fiscal staff. These organizations heavily emphasize trust and communication among all staff members.

Summary

Most of this chapter discussed the preparation of an operating budget, consisting of personal services and nonpersonal services. In addition, distinctions were made between a lump sum and a line item budget and between budget preparation for a new versus an existing program. Various categories of expenditure were addressed, examples were provided, and the author indicated that there were variations among jurisdictions. The necessity to prepare a separate capital budget for construction projects was covered briefly. Other specialty budgets may be required, depending on your situation.

Before you begin budget preparation, research the guidelines used by your parent organization for the budget preparation process during the coming fiscal year. Do not assume the guidelines are the same each year. Once you understand the instructions, provide only the information requested; this will save you substantial time and demonstrate that you are a team player.

Prepare an executive summary—it tells the story of your program and its budgetary request in one or two pages. You may find it helpful to write the executive summary first and revise it after you prepare your detailed budget. This will help you focus on the big picture before you get lost in the detail of the actual budget forms.

Be prepared to participate in the full "budget cycle," defined as the budget submission, internal review, submission to the executive budget agency for its review and hearing, and the legislative budget process. An effective program manager needs funding, which necessitates selling the budget. The agency budget staff person is your representative—make sure he or she understands your program and its objectives and is armed with the tools to sell your program. Make every effort to have your agency representative, the executive budget analyst, and the legislative analyst visit your program during the year. Make sure that these staff persons have everything they need to communicate your program's importance. Arm them with your executive summary, visual aids, charts, slide presentations, videos, and photo albums. Use these tools to marshal your constituents, advisory groups, and juvenile advocacy groups, who will tell their legislators about the grassroots interest in this program and how it affects the legislator's home community.

Funding is followed by program and budget execution. The heart and soul of expenditure control is also the heart and soul of program implementation. Control of spending greatly influences program direction. For both programmatic and budgetary reasons, it is important for the program manager to control the selecting and timing of hiring staff. Obviously, who is hired is related to program philosophy and implementation. Also, the timing of this hiring has a major impact on the budget. Maintaining budgetary control is enhanced by the use of a monthly expenditure report and a close working relationship with agency finance and budget staff.

Program administrators must understand their role in the budget and finance process if they are to provide leadership and control of their program. The program administrator's primary function is to maximize the productivity of the work force toward achieving the program's goals. The ability to attract funding and to control its expenditure is a powerful tool of coordination and a prerequisite to dictating program philosophy and the method of implementation.

The purpose of this chapter is to emphasize to you, the program administrator, how important the budget process is to your success as a juvenile delinquency program manager.

It is hoped that this review of the budget process will motivate you to meet the challenges of your status as an administrator. The budget process is not only numbers and justifications—it is a dynamic interaction with people who have the power to help you help your clients. It requires strategy, community organization, negotiation, persuasion, and patience. It also requires you to work with people other than your staff and clients—for many, this is a difficult transition. Accept the challenge and enjoy the rewards of a successful adventure.

16

The Changing Role of Professional Associations

James A. Gondles, Jr.

While resources are dwindling, public demand for successful strategies to manage delinquency among youth remains a high priority. This imbalance creates the need for professional associations to step in to foster the development of effective solutions.

Because of divergent interests and views concerning the causes and cures for juvenile delinquency, there are many agendas. The questions then become: Whose needs or agendas are most important? Where should our energies and resources be committed? As a result of varying opinions, professional associations have been able to play a crucial role in sorting through the verbosity and leading the way toward discovering promising solutions.

Solutions will not come simply from expecting governmental institutions to unravel the missing links concerning juvenile crime and violence. Instead, answers will be found by asking the community, including professional associations, to shoulder some of the burden and to promote activities that represent an investment in youths. Greater citizen and association involvement means less overall dependence on government. Since the turn of the century, professional organizations have taken on more pivotal and challenging roles in managing some of society's most pervasive problems, including delinquency.

Professional organizations can arise from grassroots campaigns that start with a basic idea about a particular cause. It is easy to see how the National Football League Players Association came into existence when there was a need to create a fund in support of retired players and to reduce health risks and exploitation of active players. More notably, the National Association of Blacks in Criminal Justice, an affiliate of the American Correctional Association, was initiated to provide minority members with an opportunity to have a better forum for their views and to focus on those issues in corrections that are unique to them.

Some people view the haphazard efforts aimed at solving the problem of juvenile delinquency as tantamount to cultivating the next crop of adult of-

James A. Gondles, Jr., is executive director of the American Correctional Association in Laurel, Maryland, and a former sheriff of Arlington County, Virginia.

fenders. To go beyond rhetoric and make a substantive difference in the lives of juveniles, decision makers need to understand that gaps in programs create problems. Counterproductive strategies include attempts to solve problems without special programs or by ignoring the mental health needs of juveniles in overcrowded facilities. Professional associations, such as the American Correctional Association and others, are seeking to get this view out to the public and to those legislators and administrators who are in positions to decide the shape of policies and programs.

Managing delinquency is about encouraging lifestyle changes to help youth stay out of juvenile facilities ...

Associations that are in the forefront of discussing problems and finding solutions to issues of managing delinquency have discovered that solutions require more than simply countering chemical dependency with a myriad of treatment modalities and drug testing. Managing delinquency is about encouraging lifestyle changes to help youth stay out of juvenile facilities, but if they do get involved they need to be properly classified and treated with appropriate programs and trained staff, and given adequate support in their aftercare.

Many professional associations, including the American Correctional Association, are advocating for community recreational programs and mentoring programs to give youth positive role models so that they can be prevented from even entering the juvenile justice system. However, if they do enter it, these organizations are examining a range of alternatives including intermediate sanctions rather than simply locking up the youth. Once the youth have been released from the system, these associations are also advocating that there be a strong system of aftercare that includes working with the families of the youth so that the structure that was built in custodial care is kept on their return to the environment that originally caused them the problems. This aftercare includes: mentoring, education, and recreation, as well as close coordination with churches, other religious bodies, and the schools.

Shaping and Influencing Change

By their unique nature, professional associations can shape and influence change within society. For example, the National Juvenile Detention Association is active in lobbying to keep juveniles out of being housed in adult facilities. They are joined in this effort by the National Association of Juvenile Correctional Agencies, the American Jail Association, as well as the American Correctional Association. These associations are challenging conflicting state and federal laws and the reality of budget constraints that counties face in dealing with the growing numbers of juveniles who are part of the juvenile justice system.

Many professional associations provide a fresh perspective to those of governmental agencies by focusing on issues of public interest. They may often substitute for government by developing and applying standards and certification in areas where some form of regulatory control is necessary to improve conditions, such as within correctional systems. Or, they may conduct research that can become the basis for new laws or regulations. The compliance standards of the American Correctional Association, for example, are used in juvenile facilities nationally.

Complex goals are being accomplished through the work of consortiums of kindred associations such as the National Association of Juvenile Correctional Agencies, the National Juvenile Detention Association, and the American Correctional Association. These associations have taken leadership roles in managing juvenile delinquency. By working together they help ensure that public policy concerning managing delinquency is viewed on a continuum—from prevention strategies for at-risk youth to improved aftercare during juveniles' transition back to the community. In addition to their research, these associations are promoting the idea of alternatives to adolescents "just hanging out."

Several organizations working together can focus on problem areas and have a greater impact than one association alone. Such a situation occurs with the National Coalition for the Mentally Ill in the Criminal Justice System, an umbrella group whose activities are sometimes sponsored by the American Correctional Association and other organizations. This coalition sponsored congressional briefings and is in the forefront of helping to develop an effective public policy on how to manage juveniles with mental health problems who are in the juvenile justice system. Their report, *Responding to Mental Health Needs of Youth in the Juvenile Justice System* (Cocozza (ed.) 1992), describes some of the issues that can be the basis for legislative or administrative action.

Associations that work with foundations such as The Edna McConnell Clark Foundation, a philanthropic group that supports a range of juvenile correctional programs, could exert considerable influence by promoting legislation and contributing money for research and other innovative activities aligned with their causes.

On other occasions, associations may donate resources or lend the name of their organization to support the efforts of various worthwhile programs, such as supporting the rights of juvenile victims.

Similarly, working under a grant from the National Institute of Justice, the American Correctional Association has supported the less-than-lethal weapons research technology in correctional settings because of its potential to provide greater safety for both staff and offenders in many situations.

Standards

The American Correctional Association has developed standards for the treatment of juveniles in corrections. The association states that juvenile corrections officials and agencies should, among other things, "provide a range of community and residential programs and services to meet individual needs, including educational, vocational training, recreation, religious opportunities, facility, aftercare medical, dental, mental health, and specialized programs and services such as substance abuse treatment" (American Correctional Association 1991).

Professional associations testify on crime bills to provide legislators with a variety of perspectives and expert advice. In 1994, the American Correctional Association testified about the need for models and established community activities to provide a greater array of intervention activities, as well as urged legislators to examine alternatives to youthful incarceration, including boot camps, and mentoring for youth reentering the community.

As professional organizations expand their role in finding ways to manage juvenile delinquency, they must continually reappraise their efforts to "serve the greater good." A recent CNN/Gallup Poll indicated that violent crime among juvenile male offenders has increased significantly; as a result, more people are seeking to treat juveniles the same as adult offenders with regards to punishment (Meddis 1993).

If there is a trend toward greater intolerance by voters about "youthful transgressions" and if the public's faith in the juvenile justice system is diminishing, this is also reflected in the shifting paradigms concerning how professional organizations and associations will be expected to contribute to solving these problems. Associations educate the public and leaders through national forums and publications. Several professional associations, including the American Correctional Association and the National Association of Counties, work to help the public and the media understand the complexities of the issues surrounding youth and delinquency. When the public has this level of comprehension, they can understand that the government is not the total answer; locally appropriate and unique solutions can be found, as well.

The Mission and Purpose

In professional associations, the mission and purpose evolve over time. Sometimes the original purposes of the association may not endure, so an association may need to alter its mission to remain relevant. The position an organization adopts on any issue, including juvenile delinquency, may reflect changes in laws or new laws, research, technology, or a reappraisal of the situation by its membership and governing board.

In addition, for professional organizations to survive, they must adapt to external influences. If economic or social forces impinge on their growth or acceptance, they must determine which actions are necessary to sustain the commitment and involvement of their members, as well as their capacity to influence government or other organizations.

Internal and External Goals

Through membership in professional associations, individuals can band together to insure that the issues they support gain publicity and support. The primary purpose of most professional organizations and associations is to amplify the individual members' voices in ways that they could not do alone. Membership allows individuals to increase their knowledge, understanding, and influence over circumstances or situations typically beyond their control. At its 1994 Winter Conference, the American Correctional Association passed two resolutions on juvenile detention and juvenile justice that concerned conditions of confinement.

Similarly, the groundwork for a professional organization's effectiveness lies in its ability to influence its own members (Galbraith 1983). By enlisting members to its goals and causes, professional organizations increase their power to be the catalysts for change in society. However, the first step for most professional organizations is to build a consensus among its members regarding the directions, positions, and actions it desires to take. Without this consensus, an effective external position that will influence change is improbable. Often this requires substantial changes in positions or a shift in view for some members, particularly on controversial issues, such as whether juveniles should be treated under the same system as adults.

Education as the Tool of Influence

The process of gaining internal agreement among members and reducing the chance that members will oppose the professional organization's official position is a delicate one. Education is the principal method to influence and to encourage support for new ideas and change. An effective educational campaign creates persuasive ties, promotes cohesion, and reduces confusion among individual members. Educational opportunities occur through a variety of methods, including: working on committees; attending meetings, training sessions, and conferences; and reading publications.

Through publications and training courses associations provide their members with education that fills gaps in their professional development and advances the state of the profession. In the areas such as preventing and managing juvenile delinquency, for example, the American Correctional Association offers videos on *Juvenile Justice in the United States*, *Suicide in Juvenile Justice Facilities*, *Admission in Juvenile Justice Detention*, and *Dealing with Anger: A Violence Prevention Program for African-American Youth*.

Most professional organizations use education not only as a key means of influencing its members, but also as a primary source for generating revenues to achieve its goals. By keeping its members informed about the latest discoveries, technological advances, or developments occurring within their profession, organizations prepare members for new trends and paradigm shifts so that they can maximize limited resources and effectively respond to change.

Shared Leadership: Charting the Course for Change

Most professional organizations have a democratic process for creating internal agreement, representing their membership and their interests, reaching decisions, and maintaining order. Formal rules and statements regarding governance and voting procedures, as well as individual or group authority, are usually identified in the organization's constitution and bylaws.

To share leadership challenges, many professional associations value the need for diversity. This may mean continually seeking greater understanding and more involvement from all members on governing bodies, committees and task forces, as well as in chapters and with affiliates.

Conducting elections and infusing a broad variety of members into an association's governing structures is a way to insure that the ideas and interests belonging to different segments of the organization can be heard. By carefully balancing the makeup of the governing body of the association and ensuring diversity in other sensitive political areas, the concerns of those representing the interests of the juvenile community may be heard and not be drowned out by other competing needs.

Committees and task forces often play a fundamental role in creating opportunities for more individuals to participate in leadership roles and to help form the organization's opinion on various issues. Committees are central to building alliances and coalitions, both within and outside of the professional associations. By using committees and task forces, professional organizations create trust and openness among their members. Such activities build partnerships among members and other constituencies, but particularly among the local and state chapters or its affiliates.

Committees may also conduct research that they share throughout the organization. Their findings may serve as the catalyst for the development of new positions. One of the newly formed working groups at the American Correctional Association is the task force on children, youth, and families. It is charged with studying the problems of at-risk youth and reporting its findings concerning prevention strategies for this population to the membership.

Managing Its Resources

The principal means for accomplishing the daily work of professional organizations is through their staff. In most instances, a chief executive director is hired to administer all operations and staff, as well as to act as a central conduit for issues that arise when the volunteer leadership is not in session. The staff must be trained and educated on issues of importance to the association so that they too can guide the organization and its members.

Professional associations have evolved into one of the greatest mechanisms for transforming and challenging the way society prioritizes and develops strategies for resolving the conflicts of a troubled world.

To be responsive to their members some associations provide their staff with subject matter training. At the American Correctional Association the staff receive training on correctional issues, including juvenile issues. Staff are encouraged to take relevant courses. Staff are also trained to be computer literate so that they can give the most accurate information available to members. The idea that employees are an organization's most valuable resource has to be accepted if maximum performance is to be obtained and quality services rendered. Therefore, whatever steps that are taken to commit to the employee are certain to nurture member needs.

Managing the resources of professional organizations in the twenty-first century will take keen vision and skills to use new technologies to bring relevant products and services to benefit the members and the profession.

What issues are key to the role of professional organizations in addressing the needs of the juvenile justice system? The answers remain in their ability to influence their members and become partners with other organizations and agencies. To do these things, the organization must make an appropriate commitment of resources to the issue.

Professional associations have evolved into one of the greatest mechanisms for transforming and challenging the way society prioritizes and develops strategies for resolving the conflicts of a troubled world. They are challenging the way society has traditionally viewed juvenile delinquency. As this metamorphosis has taken place, associations employ eight distinct roles to accomplish their mission and goals. They function as:

- advocates
- lobbyists
- public policy reformers
- researchers
- educators
- regulators
- fund raisers

Advocates

By advocating various reforms at all levels of government, professional organizations define and shape public opinion on critical areas involving delinquency and its management. For example, many professional organizations and associations, such as the American Correctional Association, the National Sheriff's Association, the Association of State Correctional Administrators, and the Correctional Education Association, participated in developing and defining specific areas where the National and Community Service Trust Act of 1993 could provide citizens with valuable experience and an opportunity to fulfill unmet human needs in our society. Organizations or associations also can lend credibility to issues of peripheral interest that might otherwise be overlooked, such as literacy, health care, life skills training, and the mental health of juvenile offenders.

Lobbyists

Some professional organizations operating under a special tax status may not be allowed to engage in direct lobbying but can engage in educational efforts. Federal laws and regulations dictate how much direct involvement in legislative activities professional associations may have. The changing laws governing the lobbying activities of nonprofit entities are now a source of concern for many organizations and associations. However, this has not stopped them from contributing to finding solutions to the problems involved in managing juvenile delinquency. Professional organizations and associations have strengthened their reputation by lobbying for or against certain legislation. Most often, the decision to get involved by supporting, opposing, or maintaining a stance of neutrality usually depends on whether the association has a stake in the outcome of the legislation. Further, any action taken is at the discretion of the governing bodies of the organization and its membership.

To get more involved in the legislative arena some associations employ staff to track legislative issues of concern to those in the corrections field. With regard to juvenile delinquency issues, some issues present organizations with the opportunity to influence legislative initiatives. These include:

- lowering the age under which capital punishment may be applied in sentencing for juvenile offenders
- determining whether violent juvenile offenders will be treated as adults in the criminal justice system
- ensuring juveniles are not placed in detention facilities in cases where mental health problems are the sole reason for such placement

Public Policy Reformers

Professional organizations have helped develop public policy on issues vital to their interests. There are two driving forces behind these efforts for many organizations. The first is to bring public attention to their mission. The second is to ensure that practitioners, who are usually affected by changing laws and judicial decisions, have a stated position which may be considered in the formulation of national public policies.

Perhaps the single most important event that has affected the issue of managing delinquency has been the development of national standards and the accreditation process. Accreditation in corrections, which began in 1975, currently involves more than 80 percent of all correctional agencies and youth services on the federal, state, and local levels. It demonstrates that an association, like the American Correctional Association in partnership with diverse member organizations comprising the Commission on Accreditation for Corrections, can be an effective substitute for government.

Some guidelines are often necessary to assist policy administrators with step-by-step instructions for translating standards into effective policies and procedures. American Correctional Association publications that do this include: *Policies and Procedures for Juvenile Detention Facilities, Policies and Procedures: Juvenile Community Residential Facilities*, and *Policies and Procedures: Juvenile Training Schools*. Publications also include *Standards for Small Juvenile Detention Facilities, Standards for Juvenile Day Treatment Programs, Standards for Juvenile Community Residential Facilities, Standards for Juvenile Detention Facilities*, and *Standards for Juvenile Probation and Aftercare Services*.

Professional organizations, such as the National Juvenile Detention Association, the National Association of Juvenile Correctional Agencies, the Juvenile Justice Trainers Association, and the American Correctional Association, have used their collective influence in a variety of ways (including the development of standards) to help practitioners in managing delinquency. For example, the American Correctional Association has promulgated a public correctional policy on juvenile corrections. It states that "juvenile corrections must provide a continuum of programs, services, and facilities ...." It emphasizes that "service and care for the individual youth must be of primary concern" (American Correctional Association 1991).

American Correctional Association members and affiliates have worked together to advance other public policies on delinquency prevention and intervention strategies. The objective of the American Correctional Association's *Handbook for Juvenile Justice Advisory Boards* is to help administrators and managers of juvenile justice programs create and effectively manage community advisory boards.

However, organizations concerned with public policy reform must themselves be realistic about the scope and substance of the areas in which they are calling for action. In attempting to develop the framework for public policies, professional associations would be wise to put these concepts to the "acid test" by using a thorough public policy analysis. Conducted properly, this analysis will provide the costs or benefits of implementing policies, programs, and activities. It evaluates the success of programs and tells what benefits will be derived from them and at what total cost. It is a practical analysis that decision makers need to have. Otherwise, the final product of a particular national policy may have an unintended impact on other systems.

Researchers

Professional organizations often conduct research to support efforts on such topics as managing juvenile delinquency. Through collaborative partnerships with governmental and nongovernmental agencies, professional associations conduct surveys, monitor pilot programs, and collect data in connection with other studies. These organizations make valuable contributions that lead to an understanding of what can and will work, and where future resources are necessary. An example of this is *Recommendations for Juvenile Corrections and Detention In Response to Conditions of Confinement Report*, a government project that included the work of the American Correctional Association (Office of Juvenile Justice and Delinquency Prevention 1993). One result of this effort was an awareness of the need to consider the feasibility and applicability of performance-based standards within juvenile detention facilities and programs.

Professional associations also can help create new resources and products. They support research that advances technologies for the continual development of professional standards, which in turn fosters accountability and improvements in various business or social systems. The American Correctional Association's diversity curriculum, written under a grant from the Office of Juvenile Justice and Delinquency Prevention, is an example of a practical product that came from the research done by an association.

Educators

The single most valuable responsibility professional organizations must accept is to communicate information that will educate members, the profession they represent, and the public about its vision, values, and beliefs. Through their publications, associations often report research results.

In this capacity, associations can help with managing delinquency by sharing information on studies, selecting facilities to serve as model programs, providing technical assistance and training, and preparing updates on current trends and important issues. Offering professional development and training for correctional workers with such correspondence courses such as *The Juvenile Careworker Correspondence Course* is one example of what the American Correctional Association is doing to help manage juvenile delinquency.

Associations concerned with juvenile justice and delinquency prevention, such as the National Juvenile Detention Association and the American Correctional Association, hold conferences and forums where information is shared among juvenile justice practitioners. Through these meetings, juvenile justice practitioners can determine how to interpret the effects of the national agenda on their areas of interest.

Regulators

Many professional organizations have been cast in quasi-regulatory roles as a result of the need for accountability in the ways that training academies, detention centers, and juvenile justice agencies are managed.

With the help of committees and task forces composed of representatives from various associations, such as: the Association of State Correctional Administrators, the American Institute of Architects, the American Bar Association, the American Medical Association, the National Association of Counties, and the American Correctional Food Services Association, the American Correctional Association consistently develops national standards for the operation of juvenile and adult correctional facilities and programs that have redefined the profession.

Fund Raisers

Professional organizations often seek to raise funds to help support their role in juvenile corrections. Because there are so many areas to be served and extraordinary circumstances affect these needs, they are able to place financial resources in areas that have been neglected. As fund raising and the business activities converge, government and philanthropic groups seek help from professional associations to manage delinquency.

Conclusion

Increasingly, professional organizations are part of the strategic planning necessary for the management of juvenile delinquency. Their role should be expanded to include oversight of more resources to bring together professionals from a variety of disciplines who will set the tone and future agendas on this issue. It is not enough for these diverse entities to relegate themselves to minor roles when the attitude and public concern about delinquency has created a climate of doubt about whether any effective solutions can be found. Professional associations must continue to offer sound and cost-effective solutions.

There also is a need to pay more attention to the expanding area of juvenile community corrections and to provide more support for targeting at-risk families with delinquent youth and for developing and researching a greater range of technologies for use in managing delinquency. In particular, more sophisticated and less intrusive drug testing or electronic monitoring systems open up a wider use of intermediate sanctions for appropriate juvenile offenders. As our nation continues to search for answers, professional associations represent a source of hope and promise to a public that demands that delinquency be managed rationally and responsibly.

References

[Note: Items marked with an asterisk may be ordered directly from the American Correctional Association, 8025 Laurel Lakes Court, Laurel, MD 20707-5075]

*American Correctional Association. *The Critical Hour: Admission in Juvenile Justice Detention.* 41 minutes. Laurel, Maryland: American Correctional Association. 1988. Video.

*American Correctional Association. *Dealing with Anger: A Violence Prevention Program for African American Youth.* 52 minutes. Laurel, Maryland: American Correctional Association. 1991. Video.

*American Correctional Association. 1991. *A Handbook for Decision Makers: Public Policy for Corrections*, 2d ed., Laurel, Maryland: American Correctional Association.

*American Correctional Association. *Juvenile Justice in the United States: A Video History.* 24 minutes. Laurel, Maryland: American Correctional Association. 1992. Video.

*American Correctional Association. 1992. *Policies and Procedures for Juvenile Detention Facilities.* Laurel, Maryland: American Correctional Association.

*American Correctional Association. 1990. *Policies and Precedures: Juvenile Community Residential Facilities.* Laurel, Maryland: American Correctional Association.

*American Correctional Association. 1987. *Policies and Procedures: Juvenile Training Schools.* Laurel, Maryland: American Correctional Association.

*American Correctional Association.1994. *Standards for Juvenile Community Residential Facilities.* Laurel, Maryland: American Correctional Association.

*American Correctional Association. 1994. *Standards for Juvenile Day Treatment Programs.* Laurel, Maryland: American Correctional Association.

*American Correctional Association. 1991. *Standards for Juvenile Detention Facilities.* Laurel, Maryland: American Correctional Association.

*American Correctional Association. 1983. *Standards for Juvenile Probation and Aftercare Services.* Laurel, Maryland: American Correctional Association.

*American Correctional Association. 1991. *Standards for Small Juvenile Detention Facilities.* Laurel, Maryland: American Correctional Association.

*American Correctional Association. *Suicide in Juvenile Justice Facilities: The Preventable Tragedy.* 32 minutes. Laurel, Maryland: American Correctional Association. 1990. Video.

Cocozza, ed. 1992. *Responding to Mental Health Needs of Youth in the Juvenile Justice System.*

de Tocqueville, A. 1945. *Democracy in America,* (Vol. 2). New York: Random House.

Dunlop, J. J. 1989. *Leading the association: Striking the right balance between staff and volunteers.* Washington, D.C.: The Foundation of the American Society of Association Executives and James J. Dunlop.

Galbraith, J. K. 1983. *The anatomy of power.* Boston: Houghton Mifflin Co.

Meddis, S. V. 1993, October 29. Poll: Treat juveniles the same as adult offenders. *USA Today* 6A, 12A.

Office of Juvenile Justice and Delinquency Prevention. 1993. *Recommendations for juvenile corrections and detention in response to conditions of confinement: A study to evaluate the conditions in juvenile detention and correctional facilities.* Washington, D.C.: Office of Juvenile Justice and Delinquency Prevention.

Robert, H. M. 1990. *Robert's Rules of Order.* Glenview, Ill.: Scott, Foresman and Company.

Index

Index of Authorities Cited